CONCEPTS OF PROGRAMMING LANGUAGES

The Benjamin/Cummings Series in Computer Science

Booch, *Software Engineering with Ada, Second Edition*

Booch, *Software Components with Ada: Structures, Tools, and Subsystems*

Brookshear, *Computer Science, An Overview, Second Edition*

Etter, *Problem Solving with Structured FORTRAN 77*

Etter, *Structured FORTRAN 77 for Engineers and Scientists, Second Edition*

Etter, *Problem Solving in Pascal for Engineers and Scientists*

Etter, *WATFIV: Structured Programming and Problem Solving*

Fischer/LeBlanc, *Crafting a Compiler*

Helman/Veroff, *Intermediate Problem Solving and Data Structures: Walls and Mirrors*

Helman/Veroff, *Walls and Mirrors: Intermediate Problem Solving and Data Structures—Modula II Edition*

Kelley/Pohl, *A Book on C: An Introduction to Programming in C*

Kelley/Pohl, *C by Dissection: The Essentials of C Programming*

Kelley/Pohl, *The Essentials of C Programming*

Lamb, *Pascal: Structure and Style*

Savitch, *Pascal: An Introduction to the Art and Science of Programming, Second Edition*

Savitch, *TURBO Pascal: An Introduction to the Art and Science of Programming, Second Edition*

Savitch, *TURBO Pascal 4.0: An Introduction to the Art and Science of Programming, Second Edition*

Sobell, *A Practical Guide to the UNIX System, Second Edition*

Sobell, *A Practical Guide to UNIX System V*

Touretzky, *LISP: A Gentle Introduction to Symbolic Computation* (forthcoming in 1990)

CONCEPTS OF PROGRAMMING LANGUAGES

ROBERT W. SEBESTA
UNIVERSITY OF COLORADO AT COLORADO SPRINGS

THE BENJAMIN/CUMMINGS PUBLISHING COMPANY, INC.
Redwood City, California • Fort Collins, Colorado • Menlo Park, California • Reading,
Massachusetts • New York • Don Mills, Ontario • Wokingham, U.K. • Amsterdam • Bonn •
Sydney • Singapore • Tokyo • Madrid • San Juan

Sponsoring Editor: Alan R. Apt

Production Supervisor: Mary B. Shields

Production: George Calmenson, The Book Company

Text and Cover Design: Wendy Calmenson, The Book Company

Copy Editor: Carole Dondrea

Composition: Graphic Typesetting Service

Cover Painting: Morris Louis, *Alpha-Pi.* Courtesy The Metropolitan Museum of Art, Arthur H. Hearn Fund, 1967

The basic text of this book was designed using the Modular Design System, as developed by Wendy Earl and Design Office Bruce Kortebein.

To Jake and Darcie

Chapter epigraphs:

Chapter 2: Knuth, D.E., and Luis Trabb Pardo. (1977) "Early Development of Programming Languages." In *Encyclopedia of Computer Science and Technology*, Vol. 7. Dekker, New York, pp. 419–493.

Chapter 12: Goodenough, J.B. (1975) "Exception Handling: Issues and Proposed Notation." *Commun. ACM*, Vol. 18, No. 12, pp. 683–696.

Chapter 13: Darlington, J. (1984) "Functional Programming:" In *Distributed Computing*, ed. R.B. Chambers, D.A. Duce, and G.P. Jones. Academic Press, London.

Chapter 14: Hogger, C.J. (1984) *Introduction to Logic Programming*, Academic Press, London.

Chapter 15: Kaehler, T. and D. Patterson (1986) *A Taste of Smalltalk*, W.W. Norton, New York.

Library of Congress Cataloging-in-Publication Data

Sebesta Robert W.
    Concepts of programming languages

    Bibliography: p.
    Includes index.
    1. Programming languages (Electronic computers)
I. Title.
QA76.7.S43   1989   005.13   88-7393
ISBN 0-8053-7011-0

BCDEFGHIJ-HA-89

The Benjamin/Cummings Publishing Company, Inc.
390 Bridge Parkway
Redwood City, California 94065

PREFACE

The central goal of this book is to provide readers with the necessary tools for critically evaluating existing and future languages and language constructs. An additional goal is to prepare the reader for a study of the design and construction of compilers.

There are two ways in which a book on the concepts of programming languages can be organized: a horizontal approach and a vertical approach. In the horizontal approach, languages are selected, and each is presented in some depth. With the vertical approach, the general concepts and constructs of programming languages are described using some particular sequence. For each concept, examples from a variety of languages are presented. Both methods have merit. In order to accurately describe individual language concepts, it is important to concentrate on the concepts and define their impact on programming and the evolution of languages. However, a chronological analysis of language developments necessitates the study of specific languages and their origins and development. Furthermore, the design of a specific facility of a particular language is often influenced by other characteristics of the language. Because of these considerations, this book combines the best aspects of both horizontal and vertical approaches.

In this book, I describe the fundamental concepts of programming languages by defining the design issues of the various language constructs, examining the design choices for these constructs in some of the most common languages, and critically comparing the design alternatives.

Doing this effectively requires studying a collection of closely related topics. To discuss languages and language constructs, descriptive tools are vital. Therefore, I discuss in detail the most effective and widely used methods of syntax description. I also introduce the most common methods for describing the semantics of programming languages. To understand some of the reasons why the particular design choices for existing languages were made, I describe the historical context and environmental needs that spawned them. In addition, ease of implementation is always a significant influence on language design. Therefore, discussions of implementation methods and issues are integrated throughout the book.

Chapter 1 begins with a rationale for studying programming languages. It then discusses the criteria for evaluating programming languages. I recognize that defining these criteria is risky; however, evaluation principles are essential to any serious study of the design of programming languages. The primary influences on language design and the basic approaches to implementation are also examined in Chapter 1.

Chapter 2 uses the horizontal approach to chart the chronological evolution of the major imperative languages. Although no language is described completely, the origins, purposes, and contributions of each are discussed. This historical overview is valuable because it provides the background necessary to understand the practical and theoretical basis for contemporary language design. It also motivates the further study of language design and evaluation. However, since none of the remainder of the book depends on Chapter 2, it can be skipped in its entirety.

Chapter 3 describes the primary formal methods for describing the syntax of programming languages: EBNF and syntax graphs. The difficult task of semantic description is then explored, including brief introductions to three of the most common methods: operational, axiomatic, and denotational semantics. A description of attribute grammars is included, reflecting the prominent role they have attained in recent years in compiler design.

In Chapters 4–12, I use the vertical approach to describe in detail the design issues and design choices for example languages. I also evaluate the major constructs of the imperative languages. Specifically, primitive data types and variables are covered in Chapter 4; expressions and assignments statements in Chapter 5; control statements in Chapter 6; data types in Chapter 7; subprograms and their implementation in Chapters 8 and 9; data abstraction facilities in Chapter 10; concurrent program units in Chapter 11; and exception handling in Chapter 12. I use the vertical approach here because it is inappropriate to describe and evaluate the details of a particular facility in several different parts of the book, which is what the horizontal approach requires. Discussing in a single chapter the various methods for providing concurrency, for example, allows for a concise comparison and evaluation of those methods.

Languages such as Ada, Modula-2, and C are frequently used to exemplify the concepts and constructs of the imperative languages.

The last three chapters briefly describe three of the most important alternative programming paradigms: functional programming, logic programming, and object-oriented programming. Each is discussed as a programming methodology, and then exemplified through a brief introduction of a specific language. The chosen languages are LISP, PROLOG, and Smalltalk. In these three chapters, the horizontal approach is used again, because these languages have few basic concepts in common. Each of the three chapters includes the historical development for its respective language.

This book does not teach any complete programming language. We do not even introduce any particular imperative language. However, the three chapters on nonimperative languages do introduce the fundamentals of programming in LISP, PROLOG, and Smalltalk, and the reader will be able to write simple programs in these languages based on the contents of these chapters.

Use of the Book

This book is intended to fulfill the goals of CS 8 in the ACM 1978 Curriculum Recommendations. We assume that the reader is a competent programmer in some contemporary imperative language.

The manuscript of this book evolved from use in six semesters of a junior-level course in concepts of programming languages.

We typically cover Chapters 1 and 3 in detail. Our experience is that Chapter 2 requires little lecture time, because of its lack of hard technical content. Students, however, find it interesting and beneficial reading. Because no material in subsequent chapters depends on Chapter 2, it can, as noted earlier, be skipped entirely.

Chapters 4–8 and 10 should be relatively easy for students with extensive programming experience in Pascal, Modula-2, or Ada. Chapters 9, 11, and 12 are more challenging and require careful and detailed lectures.

Chapters 13–15 are entirely new to most students at the junior level. Ideally, language processors for LISP and PROLOG should be available for Chapters 13 and 14. Sufficient material is included in these chapters to allow students to dabble with some simple programs. Use of Smalltalk (Chapter 15) requires an introduction to its user interface, which is not included here.

Undergraduate courses will probably not be able to cover all of the last three chapters in detail. Graduate courses, however, by skipping over parts of the early chapters on imperative languages will be able to discuss completely the nonimperative languages.

Acknowledgments

The students of CS 316 (Concepts of Programming Languages) at the University of Colorado at Colorado Springs deserve credit, both for tolerating the many versions of this book and also for their corrections and suggestions for improvement. Credit is also due the reviewers of the manuscript. In particular, the lengthy and enormously detailed suggestions of Andrew Oldroyd were highly influential. His painstaking efforts resulted in extensive improvements in the book. Also helpful were the reviews of Henry Bauer, Mary Louise Soffa, and Jon Mauney.

Alan Apt and his staff at Benjamin/Cummings in Ft. Collins deserve thanks for their encouragement and efforts to ensure that the book would be completed, as well as for their insistence on high standards of quality by everyone involved.

Finally, I thank my wife, Joanne, and our children, Jake and Darcie, for their patience in enduring my absence from them throughout the endless hours I invested in the development of this book.

CONTENTS

Key Concepts

- Readability
- Simplicity
- Orthogonality
- Writability
- Reliability
- Language cost
- Machine architecture
- Program design methodologies
- Compilation
- Pure interpretation
- Impure interpretation

1

PRELIMINARIES

The intent of this book is to provide the reader with a detailed critique of the designs of the major programming languages of the past 30 years. The insight to be gained from the book will allow the reader to critically evaluate languages and language features, both old and new, from several important viewpoints.

Before we begin our exposition of the concepts of programming languages, we need to consider a few preliminaries. First, we discuss some reasons why computer science students and computer professionals should study general language design concepts. This discussion is valuable for those who believe that a working knowledge of one or two programming languages is sufficient for computer scientists. Next, because the book evaluates language features, we present a list of criteria by which judgments can be made. The major influences on language design, machine architecture, and program design methodologies are then discussed.

Because this book is also about the implementation of programming languages, this chapter also includes a brief outline of the most common approaches to implementation.

1.1 Reasons for Studying Concepts of Programming Languages

It is reasonable for students to wonder how they will benefit from the study of programming language concepts. After all, there is an abundance of other topics in computer science that are worthy of serious study. The following is what we believe to be a compelling list of benefits of studying language concepts.

1. *Increased capacity to express ideas.* It is widely believed that our thinking is restricted by the expressive power of the language in which we communicate our thoughts. Those with a limited grasp of natural language are limited in the complexity of their thoughts, particularly in depth of abstraction. In other words, it is difficult for people to conceptualize in ways they cannot verbalize. Programmers in the process of developing software are similarly constrained. The language in which they develop software places limits on the kinds of control structures, data structures, and abstractions they can use, and thus the forms of algorithms they can construct.

   Awareness of a wider variety of programming language features can reduce such limitations in software development. Programmers can increase the range of their software development thought processes by learning new language constructs.

   It could be argued that learning the capabilities of other languages does not help a programmer who is forced to use a language that lacks those capabilities. That argument does not hold up, however, because there are often ways in which language facilities can be simulated in other languages that do not support those features.

For example, having learned of the string manipulation functions of FORTRAN (ANSI, 1978a), a Modula-2 (Wirth, 1983) programmer would naturally be led to building process abstractions for those operations, in the form of subprograms. The same is true for many of the other, more complex constructs that are discussed in depth in this book.

2. *Improved background for choosing appropriate languages.* Many professional programmers have had little formal education in computer science and were trained on the job or through in-house training programs. Such programs often teach one or two languages that are directly relevant to the current work of the organization. Many other programmers received their formal training in the early days of computer science education, when few languages were taught and many features now available in programming languages were not widely known or used. The result of this narrow background is that many programmers, when given a choice of languages for a new project, continue to use the language with which they are most familiar, even if it is poorly suited to the new project. If these programmers were familiar with the other languages available, and especially the particular features available, they would be in a better position to make informed language choices.

3. *Increased ability to learn new languages.* The process of learning a new programming language can be lengthy and difficult, especially for someone who is comfortable with only one or two languages and has never examined programming language concepts in general. Once a thorough understanding of the fundamental concepts of languages is acquired, it becomes far easier to see how these concepts are incorporated into the design of the language one is trying to learn.

For example, programmers who understand the concept of data abstraction will have a much easier time learning how to construct abstract data types in the Ada language (Goos and Hartmanis, 1983) than those who are not at all familiar with data abstraction.

4. *Better understanding of the significance of implementation.* In learning the concepts of programming languages, it is necessary to touch on the implementation issues that affect those concepts. In some cases, an understanding of implementation issues leads to an understanding of why languages are designed the way they are. This, in turn, leads to the ability to use a language more intelligently, as the tool it was designed to be. The better a programmer understands the tool, the better he or she will be able to use it.

5. *Increased ability to design new languages.* To a student, the possibility of someday having to design a new programming language may seem remote. However, most professional programmers frequently do design

languages of one sort or another. For example, most software systems require the user to interact in some way, even if only to enter data and commands. In all such cases, the form of that input is designed by the system designer, and the criteria for judging it is similar to criteria used to judge the design of a programming language. A critical examination of programming languages, therefore, will help in such designs.

6. *Overall advancement of computing.* Finally, there is a global view of the use of computers that can justify the study of programming language concepts. Although it is usually possible to determine why a particular programming language became popular, it is not always clear, at least in retrospect, that the most popular languages are the best available. In some cases, we might conclude, a language became widely used, at least in part, because those in positions to choose languages were not sufficiently well informed in the area of programming language concepts.

For example, many believe that it would have been better if ALGOL 60 (Backus et al.,1962) had displaced FORTRAN in the early 1960s. That it did not is due partly to the programmers and software development managers of that time, many of whom did not clearly understand the conceptual design of ALGOL 60. They found its description difficult to read (which it was), and even more so to understand. They did not appreciate the benefits of block structure, recursion, and well-structured control statements, and thus they failed to see the benefits of ALGOL 60 over FORTRAN.

Of course, many other factors, such as lack of support by IBM and the cost of change, contributed to the failure to accept ALGOL 60. However, the fact that computer users were generally unaware of the benefits of the language played a significant role.

In general, if those who choose languages are better informed, better languages will more quickly squeeze out poorer ones.

1.2   Language Evaluation Criteria

As noted previously, the purpose of this book is to examine carefully the underlying concepts of the various constructs and capabilities of programming languages. We will also evaluate these features, especially their impact on computer design and software development methodologies. To accomplish this, we must use some set of evaluation criteria. However, a list of such criteria is necessarily controversial, since it is virtually impossible to get even two computer scientists to agree on the value of a given language characteristic relative to others. In spite of these differences, though, most would agree that the criteria discussed in the following subsections are important.

1.2.1   Readability

One of the most important criteria for judging a programming language is the ease with which programs can be read and understood. Before 1970 software development was largely thought of in terms of writing code. In the 1970s, however, the software life cycle concept was developed; coding was relegated to play a much smaller role, and maintenance was recognized as a large part of the cycle, particularly in terms of cost. Because ease of maintenance is determined in large part by the readability of programs, readability became an important measure of the goodness of a programming language.

The following subsections describe a number of characteristics of programming languages that contribute to their readability.

1.2.1.1   Overall Simplicity

The overall simplicity of a programming language strongly affects its readability. A language that has a large number of elementary components is usually more difficult to learn than one with a small number of elementary components. Programmers who must use a large language have a tendency to learn a subset of the language and then ignore its other features. This learning pattern is sometimes used to justify the large number of language components, but the argument is not solid: Readability problems will occur if the program's author has learned a different subset from the person who is attempting to read the program.

Having too many features is not the only detriment to language simplicity. Another problem is feature multiplicity—that is, having more than one way to accomplish a particular operation. For example, in the language C (Kernighan and Ritchie, 1978) a user can increment a simple integer variable in four different ways:

```
count = count + 1
count++
++count
count += 1
```

These variations are discussed in Chapter 5.

A third problem is operator overloading, in which a single operator symbol has more than one meaning. Although this can be a useful feature, it can also lead to reduced readability if users are allowed to create their own overloading. For example, it is clearly acceptable to overload + by using it for both integer and floating-point addition. In fact, this overloading simplifies the language by reducing the number of operators. However, suppose the programmer defined + between single-dimensioned arrays to mean the sum of all elements of both arrays. Because the usual meaning of vector addition is quite different from this, it would make the program more confusing for both the author and all readers. An even more extreme exam-

ple of program confusion would be a user defining + between two vectors
to mean the difference between their respective first elements. Operator
overloading is discussed again in Chapter 5.

Language statements can also be simplified too much. For example, the
syntax and meaning of most assembly language statements are models of
simplicity. This very simplicity, however, is what makes assembly language
programs less readable: They lack the more complex control statements and
they are larger in size.

1.2.1.2   Orthogonality

Orthogonality in a programming language means that there is a relatively
small set of primitive constructs that can be combined in a relatively small
number of ways to build the control and data structures of the language.
Furthermore, every possible combination is legal and meaningful. Thus,
orthogonality follows from a symmetry of relationships among primitives.

The use of orthogonality as a design concept can be illustrated by comparing one aspect of the assembly languages of the IBM mainframe computers and the VAX series of superminicomputers. We consider only a
single simple situation, that of adding two 32-bit integer values that reside
either in memory or registers, and replacing one of the two values with the
sum. The IBM mainframes have two instructions for this purpose, which
have the forms

    A   Reg, memory_cell
    AR   Reg1, Reg2

where Reg, Reg1, and Reg2 represent registers. The semantics of these are

    Reg ← contents(Reg) + contents(memory_cell)
    Reg1 ← contents(Reg1) + contents(Reg2)

The VAX add instruction for 32-bit integer values is

    ADDL   operand_1, operand_2

whose semantics is

    operand_2 ← contents(operand_1) + contents(operand_2)

In this case, either operand can be a register or a memory cell.

The VAX instruction design is orthogonal in that there is a single instruction that can use either registers or memory cells as the operands. There
are two ways to specify operands, which can be combined in any conceiv-
able way. The IBM design is not orthogonal. Only two operand combinations are legal out of four possibilities, and the two require different instructions, A and AR. The IBM design is more restricted and therefore less
writable. For example, you cannot add the value in a register to the value
in a memory location. Furthermore, the IBM design is more difficult to
learn because of the restrictions and the additional instruction.

Orthogonality is closely related to simplicity: The more orthogonal the design of a language, the fewer exceptions the language rules will require. Fewer exceptions means a higher degree of regularity in the design, which makes the language easier to learn, read, and understand. All of us who have learned a significant part of the English language can testify to the difficulty of learning its multitude of rule exceptions (for example, i before e except after c).

Although Pascal (Ledgard, 1984) is a relatively modern language, its design has a large number of inconsistent type rules that must be followed. Procedures can have both "var" and "value" type parameters, unless the procedure is passed itself as a parameter. Functions can return only unstructured types. Formal parameter types must be named; they cannot be complete type descriptions. Files cannot be passed by value. And on and on. In other words, the type rules of Pascal are not orthogonal.

Too much orthogonality can also cause problems. Perhaps the most orthogonal programming language is ALGOL 68. Every language construct in ALGOL 68 has a type, and there are no restrictions on those types. In addition, most constructs produce values. This combinational freedom allows extremely complex constructs. For example, conditionals can appear as the left sides of assignments, along with declarations and other assorted statements, as long as the result is a location. This extreme form of orthogonality leads to unnecessary complexity.

Simplicity in a language, therefore, results from a combination of a relatively small number of primitive constructs and limited use of the concept of orthogonality.

Functional languages offer an optimal combination of simplicity and orthogonality. A functional language is one in which computations are made primarily by applying functions to given parameters. In contrast, in the imperative languages such as FORTRAN, BASIC, and Pascal, computations are made primarily by variables, expressions, and assignment statements. LISP (McCarthy, 1965) is currently the most widely used functional language. Functional languages offer potentially the greatest overall simplicity because they can accomplish everything with a single construct, the function call, which can be combined with other function calls in simple ways. This simple elegance is the reason why many language researchers are attracted to functional languages as the primary alternative to complex nonfunctional languages such as PL/I (ANSI, 1976) and Ada.

1.2.1.3 Control Statements

The structured programming revolution of the 1970s was a reaction to the poor readability caused by the limited control structures of some of the languages of the 1950s and 1960s. In particular, it became widely recognized that indiscriminate use of goto statements severely reduces program readability. Programs that can be read from top to bottom are much easier to understand than programs that require the reader to jump from one statement to another, nonadjacent statement in order to follow the execution order. However, in certain languages goto's that branch upward are sometimes required; for example, they are required in order to construct WHILE loops in FORTRAN 77. Nevertheless, restricting goto's so that (1) they precede their targets except when used to form loops, (2) their targets are never too distant, and (3) their numbers are limited can make programs far more readable.

The versions of BASIC (Mather and Waite, 1971) and FORTRAN that were available in the early 1970s all lacked the control statements that allow strong restrictions on the use of goto's, so writing highly readable programs in those languages was difficult. Most programming languages designed since the late 1960s, however, have included sufficient control statements that the need for the goto statement has been nearly eliminated.

Thus, the control statement design of a language can be an important factor in the readability of programs written in that language.

1.2.1.4   Data Structures

The presence of adequate facilities for defining data types and data structures in a language is another significant aid to readability. For example, suppose a numeric type is used for on-off flags because there are no Boolean types in the language. In such a language, we might have an assignment such as

        flag = 1

which is ambiguous, whereas in a language that includes Boolean types, we would have

        flag = **true**

which is not. Similarly, a record data type provides a more readable way to represent employee records than a parallel array scheme, which must be used in a language without records.

1.2.1.5   Syntax Considerations

The syntax, or form, of the elements of a language also has a significant effect on the readability of programs. Following are three examples of syntactic design choices that affect readability:

1. *Identifier forms.* Restricting identifiers to very short forms detracts from readability. If identifiers can have only up to six characters, as in FORTRAN 77, it is often not possible to use connotative names for variables. A more extreme example is the original American National Standards Institute (ANSI) BASIC (ANSI, 1978b), in which an identifier could consist only of a single letter or a single letter followed by a single digit.

The availability of connector characters, such as the underscore, in identifiers is a great aid to readability. SUM_OF_SQUARES is certainly clearer than SUMOFSQUARES.

Identifier forms are discussed further in Chapter 4.

2. *Special words.* Program appearance, and thus program readability, is strongly influenced by the form of a language's special words (for example, **begin**, **end**, and **for**). Especially important is the method of forming compound statements, or statement groups, primarily in control constructs. Several languages use matching pairs of special words or symbols to form groups. Pascal requires **begin-end** pairs to form groups for all control constructs except the **repeat** statement, where they can be omitted (another example of Pascal's lack of orthogonality). C uses braces for the same purpose. Both of these languages suffer because groups are always terminated in the same way, which makes it difficult to determine which group is being ended when an **end** or } is found. FORTRAN 77 and Ada make this clearer by using a distinct closing syntax for each type of statement group. For example, Ada uses **end if** to terminate a selection construct, and **end loop** to terminate a loop construct. This is an example of the conflict between the simplicity of Pascal and the greater readability of Ada.

Also important is whether the special words of a language can be used as names for program variables. If so, the resulting programs can be very confusing. For example, in FORTRAN 77, special words such as DO and END are legal variable names, so the appearance of these words in a program may or may not connote something special.

3. *Form and meaning.* Designing statements so that their appearance at least partially indicates their action is an obvious aid to readability. Semantics, or meaning, should follow directly from syntax, or appearance. In some cases, this principle is violated by two language constructs that are similar in appearance but have different meanings. In FORTRAN 77, for example, there are two statements, the assigned GOTO and the computed GOTO, whose appearances are very similar but whose meanings are different, although both are multiple-way branches. For example, the statements

```
GO TO (10, 20, 30), I
GO TO I, (10, 20, 30)
```

are used quite differently. In the first, the variable I is used to store a numeric value. In the second, it stores a label value. The semantics of these two statements are described in Chapter 6.

One of the primary complaints about the shell commands of UNIX (Kernighan and Pike, 1984) is that their appearance does not indicate their function. For example, the UNIX command grep can be deciphered only through prior knowledge, or perhaps cleverness and familiarity with the UNIX editor, ed. Its appearance connotes nothing to UNIX beginners. (grep searches a specified file for a specified string pattern.)

1.2.2 Writability

Writability is a measure of the ease with which a language can be used to create programs for a chosen problem area. Most of the language characteristics that affect readability also affect writability. This follows directly from the fact that the process of writing a program requires the programmer frequently to reread portions of the existing program.

Writability must be considered in the context of the target problem domain of a language, as it is not reasonable to compare the writability of two languages in the realm of a particular application when one was designed for that application and the other was not. For example, the writabilities of COBOL (ANSI, 1974) and APL (Gilman and Rose, 1976) are dramatically different for creating a program to deal with two-dimensional data structures, for which APL is ideal. Their writabilities are also quite different for producing reports with complex formats, for which COBOL was designed.

The following subsections describe the most important factors influencing the writability of a language.

1.2.2.1 Simplicity and Orthogonality

If a language has a large number of different constructs, programmers may not be completely familiar with all of them. This can lead to a misuse of some features and a disuse of others that may be either more elegant or more efficient, or both, than those that are used. It may even be possible, as noted by Hoare (1973), for unknown features to be used accidentally, with bizarre results. Therefore, a smaller number of primitive constructs and a consistent set of rules for combining them (orthogonality) is much better than simply having a large number of primitives. A programmer can achieve the complexity required for a problem solution after learning only a simple set of primitive constructs.

In the same vein, too much orthogonality can be a detriment to writability. Errors in writing programs can go undetected when nearly any combination of primitives is legal. This can lead to absurdities in code that cannot be discovered by the compiler.

1.2.2.2 Support for Abstraction

Briefly, abstraction means that complicated structures or operations can be stated in simple ways by ignoring many of the details. Abstraction is a key concept in contemporary programming language design. This is a reflection of the central role that abstraction plays in modern program design methodologies. The degree of abstraction allowed by a programming language and the naturalness of its expression are therefore very important to its writability. As the reader will discover exploring this book, a good deal of time and effort are spent discussing abstraction.

A simple example of process abstraction is the use of a subprogram to implement a sort algorithm that is required several times in a program. Without the subprogram, the sort code would have to be replicated in all places where it was needed, which would make the program much longer and more tedious to write.

As an example of data abstraction, consider a binary tree that stores integer data in its nodes. Such a binary tree is often implemented in FOR-TRAN as three parallel integer arrays, where two of the integers are used as subscripts to specify offspring nodes. In Pascal, these trees can be implemented by using an abstraction of a tree node in the form of a simple record unit with two pointers and an integer. The naturalness of the latter representation makes it much easier to write in Pascal a program that uses a binary tree than to write one in FORTRAN. It is a simple matter of the problem solution domain of the language being closer to the problem domain.

The overall support for abstraction is clearly an important factor in the writability of a language.

1.2.3 Reliability

A program is reliable if it performs to its specifications under all conditions. Although a desirable goal of programming language design is to allow and encourage reliable programs, it is not completely clear how this characteristic can be measured and compared among languages.

The following subsections describe several language features that have a significant effect on the reliability of programs in a given language.

1.2.3.1 Type Checking

Type checking is testing for type compatibility between two variables or a variable and a constant that are somehow involved with one another. Two of the most common forms of such involvement are as the operands of an arithmetic operator and as the left and right sides of an assignment statement. Type checking is an important factor in language reliability. Because run-time type checking is expensive, compile-time checking is more desirable. One of the most recently designed languages, Ada, checks the types of nearly all variables at compile time, except when the user explicitly states that type checking is to be suspended. Types and type checking are discussed in depth in Chapter 7.

One example of lack of type checking, at either compile time or run time, that has led to countless program errors is parameter correspondence in FORTRAN 77 subprograms. Parameter correspondence refers to the way in which parameters in a subprogram call statement are related to the formal parameters in the subprogram definition. In FORTRAN 77, an INTEGER type variable can be used as an actual parameter in a call to a subroutine that expects a REAL type as its formal parameter, and neither the compiler nor the run-time system can detect the inconsistency. This naturally leads to problems, the source of which is often difficult to determine. Subprograms and parameter-passing methods are discussed in Chapter 8.

In Pascal, the subscript range of an array variable is part of the variable's type. Therefore, subscript range checking is part of type checking, although it must be done at run time. Because most types are checked in Pascal, subscript ranges are also checked. Such checking is extremely important to program reliability, because out-of-range subscripts usually cause errors that appear after the range violations, making the errors difficult to diagnose.

1.2.3.2   Exception Handling

The ability of programs to intercept run-time errors and other unusual conditions, take corrective measures, and continue is also a great aid to reliability. This facility is called **exception handling.** The Ada language includes extensive capabilities for exception handling, but such facilities are practically nonexistent in many widely used languages, such as Pascal, Modula-2, and FORTRAN. Exception handling is discussed in Chapter 12.

1.2.3.3   Aliasing

Aliasing is, loosely, having two distinct referencing methods, or names, for the same memory cell. It is now widely accepted that aliasing, without restrictions, is too dangerous to justify its advantages. Most programming languages allow some kind of aliasing—for example, equivalenced variables in FORTRAN and pointers in Pascal. In both cases, two different program variables can refer to the same memory cell.

In some languages aliasing is used to overcome deficiencies in the language's data abstraction facilities. Other languages attain higher reliability by greatly restricting aliasing. Aliasing is examined more thoroughly in Chapter 4.

1.2.3.4   Readability and Writability

Both readability and writability influence reliability. A program written in a language that does not support natural ways to express the required algorithms will necessarily use unnatural methods. Unnatural methods will be less likely to be correct for all possible situations. The easier a program is to write, the more likely it is to be correct.

Readability affects reliability in both the writing and maintenance phases of the life cycle. Programs that are difficult to read are difficult both to write and to modify.

1.2.4 Cost

The ultimate total cost of a programming language is a function of many of its characteristics.

First, there is the cost of training programmers to use the language. This is a function of the language's simplicity and orthogonality, its closeness in purpose to the particular application, and the experience of the programmers. More powerful languages need not be harder to learn, though they often are.

Second is the cost of writing programs in the language. This is a function of the expressiveness, or writability, of the language. The original efforts to design and implement high-level languages were driven by the desire to lower the costs of creating software.

Third is the cost of compiling programs in the language. A major impediment to the early use of Ada was the prohibitively high cost of running the first-generation Ada compilers. This problem is becoming less severe as compilers become better.

Fourth, the cost of executing programs written in a language is greatly influenced by that language's design. A language that requires many run-time type checks, such as PL/I, will prohibit fast code execution, regardless of the quality of the compiler.

A simple trade-off can be made between compilation cost and execution speed of the compiled code. Optimization is the name given to the collection of methods that compilers may use to decrease the size and/or increase the execution speed of the code they produce. If little or no optimization is done, compilation can be done much faster than if a significant effort is made to produce optimized code. The extra compilation effort results in much faster code execution. The choice between the two alternatives is determined by the environment in which the compiler will be used. In a laboratory for first-year computer science majors, who use a great deal of compiling time but little code execution time (their programs are small and they must execute correctly only once), little or no optimization should be done. In a production environment, where completed programs are executed many times, it is better to pay the extra cost to optimize the code.

Finally, there is the cost of maintaining programs, which includes both repairs and modifications to add new capabilities. The cost of software maintenance depends on a number of language characteristics, but primarily readability. Because maintenance is often done by people other than the original author of the software, poor readability can make the task extremely difficult.

Of all these contributions to language costs, two are most important: program development and maintenance. Because these are functions of writability and readability, these two evaluation criteria are, in turn, the most important.

A final note on evaluation criteria: Most criteria, particularly readability and writability, are neither measurable nor scientifically defined. They are useful concepts, however, and they provide valuable insight into the design and evaluation of programming languages.

1.3   Influences on Language Design

Several fundamental factors influence the basic design of programming languages. The most important of these are computer architecture and program design methodologies.

1.3.1   Computer Architecture

The basic architecture of computers has a large effect on language design. The most popular languages have all been designed around the prevalent architecture, called the von Neumann architecture after John von Neumann, one of its originators. In a computer that has the von Neumann architecture, both data and programs are stored in the same memory. The processor is a unit separate from the memory. Therefore, instructions and data must be piped, or transmitted, from memory to the processor. Results of operations in the processor must be moved back to memory. Nearly all digital computers built since the 1940s have been based on the von Neumann architecture.

The von Neumann architecture causes the central features of the imperative languages to be variables, which model the memory cells; assignment statements, which are based on the piping operation; and the iterative form of repetition, which is the most efficient method on this architecture, as explained below. Operands in expressions are piped from memory to the processor, and the result of evaluating the expression is piped back to the memory cell represented by the left side of the assignment. Repetition in imperative languages is done by iteration because the instructions in a von Neumann computer are stored in adjacent cells of memory, making iteration very efficient. However, it discourages the use of recursion for repetition, although recursion is often more natural.

The von Neumann architecture spawned the imperative languages, and the universal use of this architecture has meant that nearly all widely used languages are imperative.

As stated earlier, a functional, or applicative, language is one in which the primary means of making computations is by applying functions to given parameters. Programming can be done in a functional language without variables, assignment statements, and iteration. Although many computer scientists have expounded on the myriad benefits of functional languages such as LISP, until a non–von Neumann computer is designed that will allow efficient execution of programs in functional languages, it is unlikely that they will displace the imperative languages. Among those bemoaning this fact, John Backus, the principal designer of the original version of FORTRAN, has been the most eloquent (Backus, 1978).

The close connection between the von Neumann architecture and the design of the imperative languages demonstrates that architecture is among the most important factors in programming language design.

1.3.2 Programming Methodologies

The 1970s brought an intense analysis, begun in large part by the structured programming movement, of both the programming process and programming language design. The results of these efforts have been consolidated under the heading "software engineering."

An important reason for the research in software engineering was the shift in the major cost of computing from hardware to software, as hardware costs decreased and programmer costs increased. In addition, progressively larger and more complex problems were being solved by computers. Rather than simply solving sets of equations to track satellites, programs were being written to control large, complex petroleum refining facilities.

The primary programming language deficiencies that were discovered in the 1970s were incompleteness of type checking, inadequacy of control statements (requiring the extensive use of goto's), and lack of facilities for exception handling.

In the area of program design methodologies, object-oriented design has had an important impact on language design. The concept of object-oriented design revolves around the use of data abstraction, which is briefly and informally described in Section 1.2.2. Simply put, object-oriented design emphasizes data design, concentrating on the use of logical, or abstract, data types to solve problems.

For data abstraction to be used effectively in software system design, it should be supported by the languages used to write the system. The first language to provide even limited support for data abstraction was SIMULA 67 (Birtwistle et al., 1973), although that language certainly was not propelled to vast popularity because of it. The benefits of data abstraction were not widely recognized until the early 1970s. More recently, Mesa (Mitchell et al., 1979), CLU (Liskov et al., 1978), Modula-2, and Ada all support some degree of data abstraction. Even FORTRAN 77 provides a clumsy way to build partial data abstractions (through subprograms, functions, and globally accessible data). It is likely that any general-purpose language designed over the next decade will provide support for this important idea. Data abstraction is discussed in detail in Chapter 10.

The evolving method of process-oriented design and the extensive efforts in the area of concurrency that are taking place in the 1980s are bringing with them the need for complete language facilities for creating and controlling concurrent program units. The Ada language includes such capabilities. So programming evolution is again requiring new language capabilities. Concurrency is discussed in detail in Chapter 11.

1.4   Implementation Methods

A computer has a number of components, but its internal mechanism consists of only two major parts: memory and processor. The internal memory is used to store programs and data. It is usually supported by at least one other level of memory that is external to the processor–memory combination. Most computers now use a rotating magnetic disk for this external memory. The processor is a collection of circuits that provides a realization of a set of primitive operations, such as those for arithmetic, logic, and data moving. In many cases, some of this circuitry is actually in the form of an even lower-level set of instructions called microinstructions, but because these are irrelevant to our discussion, we will assume that the processor is built from actual circuits. We will consider a processor to be an implementation of a low-level language called a machine language.

In the absence of other supporting software, its own machine language is the only language that most hardware computers "understand." A few computers have been designed and built with a particular high-level language as their machine language, but such computers are very complex and expensive. Furthermore, they are highly inflexible, because it is difficult (though not impossible) to then use them with other high-level languages. A more practical machine design choice is to implement in the hardware a very low-level language that provides the most commonly needed primitive operations and requires system software to create an interface to programs in other languages.

The software that provides the high-level language interface to a computer can take several different forms—compilers, interpreters, and pure interpreters—as discussed below. This software depends not only on the computer's machine language, but also on a large collection of programs called the operating system that supplies higher-level primitives than those of the machine language. These primitives provide system resource management, input and output operations, a file management system, text and/ or program editors, and a variety of other commonly needed operations. Because high-level language implementations need many of the operating system facilities, they interface to the operating system rather than to the machine language.

The operating system and language implementations are layered over the machine language interface of a bare computer. These layers can be thought of as virtual computers, providing interfaces to the user at higher

Figure 1.1
The layered inter-
faces, or virtual com-
puters, provided by a
typical computer
system

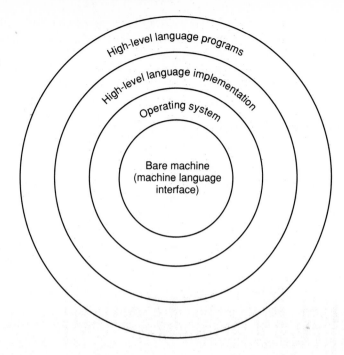

levels. For example, an operating system and a Pascal compiler provide a
virtual Pascal computer.

The layered view of a computer is shown in Figure 1.1.

The software implementations of the first high-level programming languages, constructed in the late 1950s, were among the most complex software systems of that time. In the 1960s widespread research efforts were
made to understand and formalize the process of constructing these high-
level language implementations. The success of those efforts was mainly
in the area of syntax analysis, primarily because that part of the implementation process is an application of parts of automata theory and formal
language theory that were then very well understood.

1.4.1 Compilation

Programming languages can be implemented by any of three general methods. At one extreme, programs can be translated to machine code, which
can then be executed directly on the computer. We call this a compiler
implementation. This method has the advantage of very fast program execution, once the translation process is complete. Most production implementations of languages such as FORTRAN, COBOL, and Ada are by compilers.

The language that a compiler translates is called the source language. The process of compilation involves several phases, the most important of which are shown in Figure 1.2.

The intermediate program forms shown in Figure 1.2, lexical units and parse trees, are described in Chapter 3.

The machine code generated by a compiler is rarely able to run directly on the hardware by itself. Instead, most user programs also require programs from the operating system. Among the most common of these are programs for input and output. The compiler builds calls to required system programs when they are needed by the user code. Before the machine language programs from a compiler can be executed, the required programs from the operating system must be found and "linked" to the user program. The linking operation connects the user code to the system programs by placing the addresses of the entry points of the system programs in the calls to them in the user code. The user and system code together are sometimes called a load module, or executable image. The process of collecting system programs and linking them to user programs is called linking and loading, or sometimes just linking. It is accomplished by a program in the operating system called the linker.

The execution of a machine code program on a von Neumann architecture computer occurs in a process called the fetch–execute cycle. As stated in Section 1.3.1, programs reside in memory but are executed in the processor. Each instruction to be executed must be moved from memory to the processor. The fetch–execute cycle can be simply described by the following:

```
repeat forever
    fetch the next instruction
    decode the instruction
    execute the instruction
```

This process terminates when a stop instruction is executed, although on an actual computer a stop instruction is rarely executed. Rather, control simply transfers from the operating system to a user program for its execution, and then back to the operating system when the user program execution is completed. In a computer system in which more than one user program may be in memory at a given time, this process is far more complex.

The speed of the connection between a computer's memory and its processor usually determines the speed of the computer, because instructions often can be executed faster than they can be moved to the processor for execution. This connection is called the von Neumann bottleneck; it is the primary limiting factor in the speed of von Neumann architecture computers.

1.4.2   Pure Interpretation

At the opposite extreme of implementation methods, programs can be interpreted by another program called an interpreter, with no translation whatever. The interpreter program acts as a software simulation of a machine

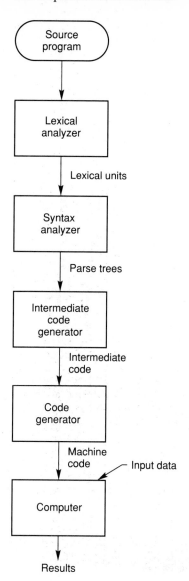

Figure 1.2
The compilation
process

whose fetch–execute cycle deals with high-level language program statements, rather than machine instructions. Such a software simulation obviously
provides a virtual machine for the language.

   This technique, called **pure interpretation,** or simply interpretation, has
the advantage of allowing easy implementation of many source-level
debugging operations, because all run-time error messages can refer to
source-level units. For example, if an array index is found to be out of range,
the error message can easily indicate the source line and the name of the

Figure 1.3
Pure interpretation

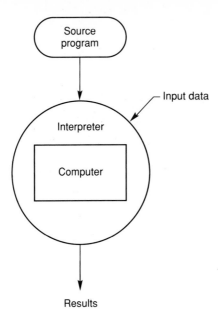

array. On the other hand, this method has the serious disadvantage that execution is often ten times slower than in compiled systems. The primary source of this slowness is the decoding of the high-level language statements, which are far more complex than machine language instructions. Therefore, statement decoding, rather than the connection between the processor and memory, is the bottleneck of a pure interpreter.

Interpretation is a difficult process on programs written in a complicated language, because the meaning of each expression and statement must be determined directly from the source program at run time. Languages with simpler structure lend themselves to pure interpretation. For example, APL, SNOBOL (Griswold et al., 1971), and LISP are sometimes implemented as pure interpretive systems. Conversely, more complex languages such as FORTRAN and Ada rarely are.

The process of pure interpretation is shown in Figure 1.3.

1.4.3 Impure Interpretation

Some language implementation systems are a compromise between compilers and pure interpreters; they translate high-level language programs to an intermediate language designed to allow easy interpretation. This method is faster than pure interpretation because the source language statements are decoded only once. The UCSD Pascal P-system is one of the most popular impure interpretive systems.

Figure 1.4
Impure interpretation

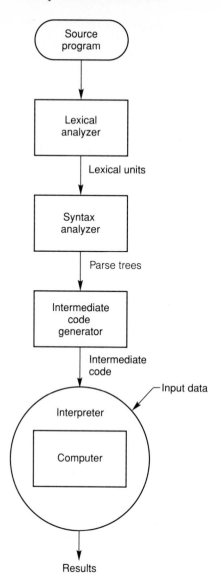

The process of **impure interpretation** is shown in Figure 1.4. Note that this process is a hybrid of the two methods. Instead of translating intermediate language code to machine code, it simply interprets the intermediate code.

As stated previously, some languages are implemented more naturally by one method than another. For example, FORTRAN's complexity, static nature, and emphasis on efficiency lead naturally to compiler implementations. The simplicity and dynamic nature of LISP, on the other hand, has historically led to pure interpretive implementations. However, there have been some impure interpretive implementations of FORTRAN. In addition, the FORMAT statements of FORTRAN are always interpreted, even if the remainder of the language is compiled, which leads to a different concept of impure interpretation. Further, there has been an increased emphasis on efficiency in LISP programs, and thus many contemporary implementations of LISP use the compiler method.

Sometimes, an implementor may provide both compiled and interpreted implementations for a language. In these cases, the interpreter is used to develop and debug programs. Then, after a bug-free state is reached, the programs are compiled to increase their execution speed.

One other gap in our seemingly clean trichotomy of implementation methods is the lack of universal acceptance of our definitions of the method names. Although the UCSD Pascal systems are, strictly speaking, impure interpreters, they are commonly called compilers because the intermediate language that is used is at the level of an assembly language. On the other side of the coin, most SNOBOL implementations are called interpretive even though they translate source programs into an intermediate language, because the intermediate language is at a much higher level than an assembly language.

We describe implementation models for several different language constructs as we discuss those constructs throughout the book.

SUMMARY

The study of programming languages is valuable for a number of solid reasons. It increases one's capacity to use different constructs in writing programs, enables one to choose languages more intelligently for projects, and makes learning new languages easier.

Among the most important criteria for evaluating languages are readability, writability, reliability, and overall cost. These will be the basis on which we examine and judge the various language features discussed in the remainder of the book.

The major influences on language design have been machine architecture and software design methodologies.

The major methods of implementing programming languages are compilation, pure interpretation, and impure interpretation.

BIBLIOGRAPHY

ANSI. (1974) *American National Standard Programming Language COBOL.* ANSI X3.23-1974, American National Standards Institute, New York.

ANSI. (1976) *American National Standard Programming Language PL/I.* ANSI X3.53-1976, American National Standards Institute, New York.

ANSI. (1978a) *American National Standard Programming Language FORTRAN.* ANSI X3.9-1978. American National Standards Institute, New York.

ANSI. (1978b) *American National Standard Programming Language Minimal BASIC.* ANSI X3.60-1978. American National Standards Institute, New York.

Backus, J. (1978) "Can Programming Be Liberated from the von Neumann Style? A Functional Style and Its Algebra of Programs." *Commun. ACM*, Vol. 21, No. 8, pp. 613–641.

Backus, J., F.L. Bauer, J. Green, C. Katz, J. McCarthy, P. Naur, A.J. Perlis, H. Rutishauser, K. Samelson, B. Vauquois, J.H. Wegstein, A. van Wijngaarden, and M. Woodger. (1962) "Revised Report on the Algorithmic Language ALGOL 60." *Commun. ACM*, Vol. 6, No. 1, pp. 1–17.

Birtwistle, G.M., O-J. Dahl, B. Myhrhaug, and K. Nygaard. (1973) *Simula BEGIN.* Van Nostrand Reinhold, New York.

Gilman, L., and A.J. Rose. (1976) *APL: An Interactive Approach.* 2d ed. J. Wiley, New York.

Goos, G., and J. Hartmanis (eds.) (1983) *The Programming Language Ada Reference Manual.* Lecture Notes in Computer Science 155. Springer-Verlag, New York.

Griswold, R.E., J.F. Poage, and I.P. Polonsky. (1971) *The Snobol 4 Programming Language.* 2d ed. Prentice-Hall, Englewood Cliffs, NJ.

Hoare, C.A.R. (1973) "Hints on Programming Language Design." *Proceedings ACM SIGACT/SIGPLAN Conference on Principles of Programming Languages.* Also published as Technical Report STAN-CS-73-403, Stanford University Computer Science Department.

Kernighan, B.W., and R. Pike. (1984) *The UNIX Programming Environment.* Prentice-Hall, Englewood Cliffs, NJ.

Kernighan, B.W., and D.M. Ritchie. (1978) *The C Programming Language.* Prentice-Hall, Englewood Cliffs, NJ.

Ledgard, H. (1984) *The American Pascal Standard.* Springer-Verlag, New York.

Liskov, B., E. Moss, C. Schaffert, R. Scheiffer, and A. Snyder. (1978) "CLU Reference Manual." In *Computation Structures Group Memo 161.* MIT Laboratory for Computer Science, Cambridge, MA.

Mather, D.G., and S.V. Waite (eds.) (1971) *BASIC.* 6th ed. University Press of New England, Hanover, NH.

McCarthy, J. (1965) *LISP 1.5 Programmer's Manual.* 2d ed. MIT Press, Cambridge, MA.

Mitchell, J.G., W. Maybury, and R. Sweet. (1979) *Mesa Language Manual, Version 5.0,* CSL-79-3. Xerox Research Center, Palo Alto, CA.

Wirth, N. (1983) *Programming in Modula-2.* 2d ed. Springer-Verlag, New York.

PROBLEM SET

1. Do you believe our thinking capabilities are shaped by our language? Support your opinion.

2. What are some features of programming languages you know whose rationale is a mystery to you?

3. Name and explain another criterion by which languages can be judged (in addition to those in this chapter).

4. What common programming language statement, in your opinion, is most detrimental to readability?

5. Modula-2 uses END to mark the end of all compound statements. What are the arguments for and against this design?

6. Some languages, notably C and Modula-2, distinguish between uppercase and lowercase in identifiers. What are the pros and cons of this design decision?

7. Explain the different aspects of the cost of a programming language.

8. What are the arguments for writing efficient programs even though hardware is relatively inexpensive?

9. What major features would a perfect programming language include, in your opinion?

10. Was the first high-level programming language you learned implemented with a pure interpreter, an impure interpreter, or a compiler? (You would not necessarily know this without research.)

11. What arguments can you make for and against the inclusion of the const declarative statement in Pascal?

12. How do type declaration statements for simple variables affect the readability of a language, considering that some languages do not require them?

13. Write an outline for the design of a pure interpreter for a subset of Pascal in which there are no subprograms, no **char**, **file**, or **boolean** types, no user-defined types, no **case** statements, and no input and output.

It is interesting and instructive to study the history of a subject not only because it helps us to understand how the important ideas were born— and to see how the "human element" entered into each development—but also because it helps us to appreciate the amount of progress that has been made.

DONALD E. KNUTH AND LUIS TRABB PARDO

Key Concepts

- Programming language evolution
- Language design environments
- Programming problems with machine code
- Interpretive pseudocodes
- Compiled high-level languages
- Universal scientific languages
- Interactive languages
- Universal application languages
- Requirements specifications for a language

2

EVOLUTION OF THE MAJOR IMPERATIVE PROGRAMMING LANGUAGES

This chapter follows chronologically the development of a collection of programming languages, with emphasis on the environment in which each was designed. In each case we emphasize the contribution of the language and the motivation for its development. Overall language descriptions are not included; rather, we focus on the new features introduced by each language. Of particular interest are the features that most influenced subsequent languages or the fields of computing and computer science.

This chapter does not include an in-depth discussion of any language feature or concept; that is left for the later chapters. Brief informal explanations of features will suffice for our trek through the development of these languages.

The choice as to which languages to discuss here was subjective, and many readers will unhappily note the absence of one or more of their favorites. However, to keep this historical coverage to a reasonable size, it was necessary to leave out several languages that some regard highly. The choices were based on our estimate of the language's importance to language development and the computing world as a whole.

Histories of the development of three nonimperative languages—LISP, PROLOG, and Smalltalk—are included in Chapters 13, 14, and 15, respectively.

Figure 2.1 is a chart of the geneology of the languages discussed in this chapter.

2.1 Zuse's Plankalkül

The first programming language discussed in this chapter is highly unusual in several respects. For one thing, it was never implemented, for a variety of reasons. Furthermore, although developed in 1945, its description was not published until 1972. As a result of the general ignorance of the language, some of its capabilities did not appear in other languages until 15 years after Plankalkül's development (1960).

2.1.1 Historical Background

Between 1936 and 1945 the German scientist Konrad Zuse constructed from electromechanical relays a series of complex and sophisticated computers. By 1945, the war had destroyed all but one of his latest models, a Z4, so he moved to a remote Bavarian village, Hinterstein, and his research group members went their separate ways.

Working alone, Zuse embarked on an effort to develop a language for expressing computations, a project he had begun in 1943 as a proposal for his Ph.D. thesis. He named this language Plankalkül, which means program calculus. In a lengthy manuscript dated 1945 but not published until

Figure 2.1
Genealogy of the
imperative languages

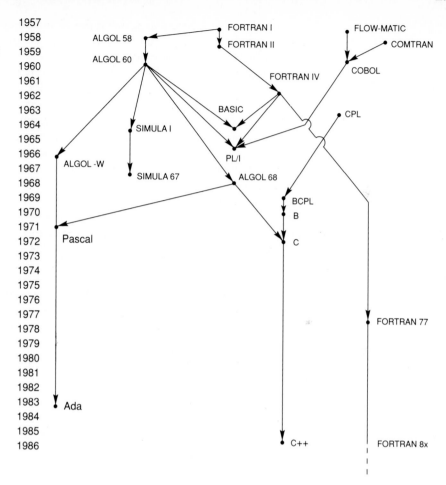

1972 (Zuse, 1972), Zuse defined Plankalkül and wrote algorithms in the
language for a wide variety of problems.

2.1.2 Language Overview

Plankalkül was remarkably complete, with some of its most advanced features in the area of data structures. The simplest type in Plankalkül was
the single bit. From the bit type were built types for integer and floating-
point numeric types. The floating-point type used two's-complement notation and the "hidden bit" scheme currently used to avoid storing the most
significant bit of the normalized fraction part of a value. Special representations were used for "infinite," "very small," and "undefined" quantities.

In addition to these usual scalar types, Plankalkül allowed arrays and record structures. Further, the record structures could use recursion to include other records as elements.

Although the language had no explicit goto, it did include an iterative structure similar to the Pascal **for**. It also had a command "Fin" with a superscript, which indicated a jump out of a specified number of iteration loop nestings or to the beginning of a new iteration cycle. Plankalkül also had a conditional, but it did not allow an else clause.

One of the most interesting features of Zuse's programs was his inclusion of mathematical expressions showing the relationships between program variables. These expressions stated what would be true during execution at the points in the code where they appeared. These are very similar to the invariants used today in axiomatic semantics to prove the correctness of programs. Axiomatic semantics is discussed in Chapter 3.

Zuse's manuscript contained programs of far greater complexity than any written prior to 1945. Included were programs to sort given lists of numbers; test the connectivity of a given graph; carry out integer and floating-point operations, including square root; and perform syntax analysis on logic formulas that had parentheses and operators in six different levels of precedence. Perhaps most remarkable were his 49 pages of algorithms for playing chess, a game in which he was not an expert.

If a computer scientist had found Zuse's description of Plankalkül in the early 1950s, the single aspect of the language that would have hindered its implementation as defined would have been the notation. Each statement consisted of two or three lines of code. The first line was most like the statements of contemporary languages. The second line contained the subscripts of the array references in the first line. It is interesting to note that the same method of indicating subscripts was used by Charles Babbage in programs for his Analytical Engine in the middle nineteenth century. The last line of each Plankalkül statement contained the type names for the variables mentioned in the first line. This notation is quite intimidating when first seen.

The following example assignment statement, which assigns the value of the expression $A(4) + 1$ to $A(5)$, demonstrates this notation. The row labeled V is for subscripts and the row labeled S is for the data types. In this example, $1.n$ means an integer of n bits:

```
  | A   +   1  => A
V | 4              5
S | 1.n            1.n
```

One can only speculate on the speed and direction that programming language design and computer development might have taken if Zuse's work had been widely known in 1945 or even 1950. It is also interesting to consider how his work might have been different had he done it in a peaceful environment surrounded by other scientists, rather than in Germany in 1945 in virtual isolation.

Minimal Hardware
2.2 Programming: Pseudocodes

The computers that became available in the late 1940s and early 1950s were far less usable than those of today. In addition to being slow, unreliable, and expensive, and having extremely small memories, the machines of that time were difficult to program due to the lack of supporting software.

There were no high-level programming languages or even assembly languages, so programming was done in machine code, which is both tedious and error-prone. Among its problems is the use of numeric codes for specifying instructions. For example, an ADD instruction may be specified by the code 14 rather than a connotative textual name, even if only a single letter. This makes programs extremely difficult to read. A more serious problem is absolute addressing, which makes programs extremely difficult to modify. For example, suppose we have a machine language program that is stored in memory. Many of the instructions in such a program refer to other locations within the program, usually to reference data or the targets of branch instructions. Inserting an instruction at any position in the program other than at the end destroys the correctness of all instructions that refer to addresses beyond the insertion point, because those addresses must be increased to make room for the new instruction. To make the addition correctly, we must find and modify all those instructions that refer to addresses that follow the addition. A similar problem occurs with deletion of an instruction. In this case, however, machine languages often include a "no operation" instruction that can replace deleted instructions, thereby avoiding the difficulty.

These are standard problems with all machine languages and were the primary motivations for inventing assemblers and assembly languages. In addition, most programming problems of that time were numerical, and required floating-point arithmetic operations and indexing of some sort to allow the convenient use of arrays. Neither of these capabilities, however, was included in the architecture of the computers of the late 1940s and early 1950s. These deficiencies naturally led to the development of somewhat higher-level languages that did include them.

2.2.1 Short Code

The first of these new languages, named Short Code, was developed by John Mauchly in 1949 for the BINAC computer. Short Code was later transferred to a UNIVAC I computer, and for a number of years was one of the primary means of programming those machines. Although little is known of the original Short Code, because its complete description was never published, a programming manual for the UNIVAC version did survive

(Remington-Rand, 1952). It is safe to assume that the two versions were very similar.

The UNIVAC had words that consisted of 72 bits, grouped as twelve 6-bit bytes. Short Code consisted of coded versions of mathematical equations that were to be evaluated. The codes were byte-pair values, and most equations fit into a word. Some of the codes were:

01	-	06	abs value	1n	(n+2)nd power
02	)	07	+	2n	(n+2)nd root
03	=	08	pause	4n	if <= to n
04	/	09	(	58	print and tab

Variables, or memory locations, were named with byte-pair codes, as were locations to be used as constants. For example, X0 and Y0 could be variables. The statement:

```
X0 = SQRT (ABS (Y0))
```

would be coded in a word as 00 X0 03 20 06 Y0. The initial 00 was used as padding to fill the word. Interestingly, there was no multiplication code; multiplication was indicated by simple juxtaposition of the operands, as in algebra.

Short Code was not translated to machine code; rather, it was interpreted directly. Using the UNIVAC with Short Code was thus a purely interpretive operation. This process was called automatic programming at the time. It clearly simplified the programming process, but at the expense of execution time. Short Code interpretation was approximately 50 times slower than machine code.

2.2.2 Speedcoding

In other places, interpretive systems were being developed that extended machine languages to include floating-point operations. The Speedcoding system developed by John Backus for the IBM 701 is an example of such a system (Backus, 1954). The Speedcoding interpreter effectively converted the 701 to a virtual three-address floating-point calculator. The system included pseudoinstructions for the four arithmetic operations on floating-point data, as well as operations such as square root, sine, arc tangent, exponential, and logarithm. Conditional and unconditional branches and input/output conversions were also part of the virtual architecture. To get an idea of the limitations of such systems, consider that the remaining usable memory after loading the interpreter was only 700 words, and that the add instruction took 4.2 milliseconds to execute. On the other hand, Speedcoding included the novel facility of automatically incrementing address registers, which only later reappeared in the hardware of the PDP-11 in 1970. Because of such features, matrix multiplication could be done in 12 Speedcoding instructions. Backus claimed that problems that could take 2 weeks to program in machine code could be programmed in a few hours using Speedcoding.

2.2.3 The UNIVAC "Compiling System"

Between 1951 and 1953, a team led by Grace Hopper at UNIVAC developed a series of "compiling" systems named A-0, A-1, and A-2 that expanded a pseudocode into machine code in the same way as macros are expanded into assembly language. The pseudocode source for these "compilers" was still quite primitive, although even this was a great improvement over machine code because it made source programs much shorter. Wilkes (1952) independently suggested a similar process.

2.2.4 Related Work

Other means of easing the task of programming were being developed at about the same time. At Cambridge University, David J. Wheeler developed a method of using blocks of relocatable addresses to partially solve the problem of absolute addressing (Wheeler, 1950), and later Maurice V. Wilkes (also at Cambridge) extended the idea to design an assembly program that could combine chosen subroutines and allocate storage (Wilkes et al., 1951, 1957). This was indeed an important and fundamental advance.

We should also mention that assembly languages, which are quite different from the pseudocodes mentioned, evolved during the early 1950s. With rare exceptions, however, they had little impact on the design of high-level languages.

2.3 The IBM 704 and FORTRAN

A great leap forward in computing came with the introduction of the IBM 704, in large measure because its capabilities prompted the development of FORTRAN. One could argue that if it had not been IBM with the 704 and FORTRAN, it would soon thereafter have been some other organization with a similar computer and related high-level language. However, IBM was the first with the foresight and resources to undertake these developments.

2.3.1 Historical Background

One of the primary reasons why interpretive systems were tolerated through the late 1940s to the middle 1950s was the lack of floating-point hardware in the available computers. All floating-point operations had to be simulated in software, a very time-consuming process. Because so much time was spent in software floating-point processing, the overhead of the interpretation process and the simulation of indexing were considered insignificant. As long as floating-point had to be done by software, interpretation was an acceptable expense. However, many programmers of that time never used interpretive systems, preferring the additional efficiency of hand-coded machine language. The announcement of the IBM 704 system in 1954, with both indexing and floating-point instructions in hardware, heralded the end of the interpretive era, at least for scientific computation.

Although FORTRAN is often credited with being the first compiled high-level language, the question of who deserves credit for implementing the first such language is somewhat open. Knuth and Pardo (1977) give the credit to Alick E. Glennie for his Autocode compiler for the Manchester Mark I computer. Glennie developed the compiler at Fort Halstead, Royal Armaments Research Establishment, in England. The compiler was operational by September 1952. According to John Backus (Wexelblat, 1981, p. 26), however, Glennie's Autocode was so low level and machine-oriented that it should not be considered a compiled system. Backus gives the credit to Laning and Zierler at Massachusetts Institute of Technology.

The Laning and Zierler system (Laning and Zierler, 1954) was the first algebraic translation system to be implemented. By algebraic, we mean that it translated arithmetic expressions, used function calls for mathematical functions, and included subscripted variable references. The system was implemented on the MIT Whirlwind computer, in prototype experimental form, in the summer of 1952, and in a more usable form by May 1953. The translator generated a subroutine call to code each formula, or expression, in the program. The source language was easy to read and the only actual machine instructions included were for branching. Although this work preceded the work on FORTRAN, it never escaped MIT.

In spite of these earlier works, the first widely accepted compiled high-level language was FORTRAN. The following subsections chronicle this important development.

2.3.2   Design Process

Even before the 704 system was announced in May 1954, plans were begun for FORTRAN. By November 1954, John Backus and his group at IBM had produced the report entitled "The IBM Mathematical FORmula TRANslating System: FORTRAN" (IBM, 1954). This document described the first version of FORTRAN, which we refer to as FORTRAN 0, prior to its implementation and also boldly stated that FORTRAN would provide the efficiency of hand-coded programs and the ease of programming of the interpretive pseudocode systems. In another burst of optimism, the document stated that FORTRAN would eliminate coding errors and the debugging process. Based on this premise, the first FORTRAN compiler included little syntax error checking.

The environment in which FORTRAN was developed was as follows: (1) Computers were still small, slow, and relatively unreliable. (2) The primary use of computers was scientific computations. (3) There were no existing acceptable ways to program computers. (4) Because of the high cost of computers compared to the cost of programmers, speed of the generated object code was the primary goal of the first real compilers. The characteristics of the early versions of FORTRAN follow directly from this environment.

2.3.3   FORTRAN I Overview

FORTRAN 0 was modified during the implementation period, which began in January 1955 and continued until the release of the compiler in April 1957. The implemented language, which we will call FORTRAN I, is described in the first FORTRAN *Programmer's Reference Manual,* published in October 1956 (IBM, 1956). The changes from FORTRAN 0 included the following: input/output formatting was added; the maximum length of variable names was increased from two to six characters; and user-defined subroutines were added, although they could not be separately compiled. FORTRAN 0 included a logical IF statement whose Boolean expression used relational operators in their algebraic form—for example, $>$. Because the 704 character set did not include $>$, but the machine had a three-way branch instruction based on the comparison of a value in storage with the value in a register, the original logical IF was replaced with the arithmetic selection, which has the form

    IF (arithmetic expression) N1, N2, N3

where N1, N2, and N3 are statement labels. If the value of the expression is negative, the branch is to N1; if zero, it is to N2; if greater than zero, to N3. This statement is still part of FORTRAN.

The form of the FORTRAN I iterative statement was

    DO   N1 variable = first, last

where N1 was the label of the last statement of the loop, and the statement on the line following the DO was the first.

The FORTRAN I DO loop was posttest, which means that the test for completion was at the bottom, rather than the top, of the loop. The disadvantage of posttest loops is that they always execute their loop statements once. For example,

    DO 10 K = 5, 1

causes the statements between the DO and the statement labeled 10 to be executed once, in spite of the fact that last is greater than first.

As with the IF statement, the 704 had a single instruction to implement the DO. Because the instruction was designed for posttest loops, FORTRAN's DO was designed in that way. A pretest loop could have been implemented in FORTRAN, but that would have required one additional machine instruction, and since efficiency was the overriding concern in the design of FORTRAN, it was not done.

All of FORTRAN I's control statements were based on 704 instructions. It is not clear whether the 704 designers dictated the control statement design of FORTRAN, or whether the designers of FORTRAN suggested these instructions to the 704 designers.

There were no data-typing statements in the FORTRAN I language: Variables whose names began with I, J, K, L, M, and N were implicitly integer type, and all others were implicitly floating-point. The choice of the letters for this convention was based on the fact that at that time integers were used primarily as subscripts, and scientists usually used i, j, and k for subscripts. To be generous, they threw in the three additional letters.

The most outrageous claim made by the FORTRAN development group during the gestation period of the language was that the machine code produced by the compiler would be about as efficient as what could be produced by hand. This, more than anything else, made skeptics of potential users and prevented a great deal of interest in FORTRAN before its actual release. To almost everyone's surprise, however, the FORTRAN development group nearly achieved its goal in efficiency. The largest part of the 18 worker-years of effort used to construct the first compiler had been spent on optimization, and the results were remarkably effective.

2.3.4 FORTRAN II Overview

FORTRAN II was distributed in the spring of 1958. It fixed many of the bugs in the FORTRAN I compilation system and added some significant features, the most important being the independent compilation of subroutines. Without independent compilation, any change in a program requires that the entire program be recompiled. FORTRAN I's lack of an independent compilation capability, coupled with the poor reliability of the 704, placed a practical restriction on the length of programs to about 300–400 lines (Wexelblat, 1981, p. 68). Longer programs had a poor chance of being compiled completely before a machine failure occurred. The capability of including precompiled binary versions of subprograms shortened the compilation process considerably. The first compilers were very slow, however, largely due to the slowness of the computers.

The early success of FORTRAN is shown by the results of a survey made in April 1958. At that time, roughly half of the code being written for 704s was being done in FORTRAN—this in spite of the extreme skepticism of most of the programming world only a year earlier.

2.3.5 FORTRAN IV, FORTRAN 77, and FORTRAN 8x

There was a FORTRAN III, although it was never widely distributed. FORTRAN IV, however, became one of the most widely used programming languages.

It evolved over the 1960–1962 period and was the standard version until 1978, when the FORTRAN 77 report (ANSI, 1978a) was released. FORTRAN IV was an improvement over FORTRAN II in many ways. Among its most important additions were type declarations, a logical IF construct, and the capability of passing subprograms as parameters to other subprograms.

FORTRAN 77 retains most of the features of FORTRAN IV and adds character string handling, logical loop control statements, and an IF with an optional ELSE clause.

FORTRAN 8x is the name of the next version of FORTRAN (Metcalf and Reid, 1987), which is not yet an approved standard, although it is expected to become the standard FORTRAN of the 1990s. New features of FORTRAN 8x include dynamically allocated arrays, many array operations, user-defined data types, modules, and a CASE statement.

2.3.6 Evaluation

The original FORTRAN design team thought of the language design only as a necessary prelude to the critical task of designing the translator. Further, it never occurred to them that FORTRAN would be used on computers not manufactured by IBM. Indeed, they were forced to consider building FORTRAN compilers for other IBM equipment only by the fact that the successor to the 704, the 709, was announced before the 704 FORTRAN compiler was released. The effect that FORTRAN has had on the use of computers and the fact that all subsequent programming languages owe a debt to FORTRAN are indeed impressive in light of the modest goals of its designers.

One of the features of FORTRAN I, and all of its successors except 8x, that allows highly optimizing compilers is the fact that the types and storage for all variables are fixed before run time. No new variables or space can be allocated during run time. This is a sacrifice of flexibility to simplicity and efficiency. It eliminates the possibility of recursive subprograms and makes it difficult to implement data structures that grow or change shape dynamically. Of course, the kinds of programs that were being built at the time of the development of the early versions of FORTRAN were primarily numerical in nature and were simple in comparison with contemporary software projects. Therefore, the sacrifice was not a great one.

The overall success of FORTRAN is difficult to overstate: It dramatically changed, forever, the way computers are used. This is, of course, partially due to its being the first widely used high-level language. In comparison with concepts and languages developed later, early versions of FORTRAN suffer in a variety of ways, as should be expected. After all, Model T Fords are not to be compared across the board with Thunderbirds. Nevertheless, in spite of the inadequacies of FORTRAN, the momentum of the huge investment in FORTRAN software has kept it one of the most widely used of all high-level languages.

2.4   The First Step Toward Sophistication: ALGOL 60

ALGOL 60 has had a great influence on subsequent programming languages and is therefore of central importance in any historical review of languages.

2.4.1   Historical Background

ALGOL 60 came into being as a result of efforts to design a universal language. By late 1954 the Laning and Zierler algebraic system had been in operation for over a year and the first report on FORTRAN had been published. FORTRAN became a reality in 1957, and several other high-level languages were being developed. Most notable among them were IT, which was designed by Alan Perlis at Carnegie Tech, and the two languages MATH-MATIC and UNICODE for the UNIVAC computers. The proliferation of languages was making communication among users difficult. Furthermore, the new languages were all growing up around single architectures, some for UNIVAC computers and some for IBM 700 series machines. In response to this language proliferation, several major computer user groups in the United States, including SHARE (the IBM scientific user group) and USE (UNIVAC Scientific Exchange, the large-scale UNIVAC scientific user group), submitted a petition to the Association for Computing Machinery (ACM) on May 10, 1957, to form a committee to study and recommend action to create a universal programming language. Although FORTRAN might have been a candidate, it could not become a universal language because at the time it was solely owned by IBM.

Previously, in 1955, GAMM (a German acronym for Society for Applied Mathematics and Mechanics) had also formed a committee to design one universal, machine-independent, algorithmic language for use on all kinds of computers. The desire for this new language was in part due to the Europeans' fear of being dominated by IBM. By late 1957, however, the appearance of several high-level languages in the United States convinced the GAMM subcommittee that their effort had to be widened to include the Americans, and a letter of invitation was sent to ACM. In April 1958, after Fritz Bauer of GAMM presented the formal proposal to them, the two groups officially agreed to a joint language design project.

2.4.2   Early Design Process

GAMM and ACM decided that the joint design effort should be made at a meeting to which each group would send four members. The meeting was held in Zurich from May 27 to June 1, 1958.

The committee began with the following goals for the new language:

1. The language should be as close as possible to standard mathematical notation, and programs written in it should be readable with little further explanation.

2. It should be possible to use the language for the description of computing processes in publications.

3. Programs in the new language should be mechanically translatable into machine language.

The first goal indicates that the new language was to be used for scientific programming, which was the primary application area at that time. The second was something entirely new to the computing business. The last goal is an obvious necessity for any programming language.

Depending on how it is viewed, the Zurich meeting either produced momentous results or generated endless arguments. Actually, it did both. The meeting itself involved innumerable compromises, both among individuals and between sides of the Atlantic. In some cases, the compromises were difficult. The question of whether to use a comma (the European method) or a period (the American method) for a decimal point was not decided, at least not directly. From this small point grew the concept of having three separate language representations, which effectively side-stepped the problem.

The first of the three representations was the reference language, which made absolutely no assumptions about computers, character sets, or implementations. This was the only representation that was designed at the 1958 Zurich meeting. The second representation was the publication language, which was meant to be used in publishing algorithms. In this case, whatever characters were printable were allowed if they clarified programs; the character set was allowed to vary from country to country. The last representation was the hardware language, of which there would be one per implementation. The hardware language would use whatever character set was available on the machine, and each implementation was required to include a set of rules for transliterating from the reference language to the hardware language.

2.4.3 ALGOL 58 Overview

The language designed at the Zurich meeting was named the International Algorithmic Language (IAL). It was suggested during the design that the language be named ALGOL, but the name was rejected because it did not sufficiently reflect the international scope of the committee. During the following year, however, the name was changed to ALGOL, and the language subsequently became known as ALGOL 58.

In many ways ALGOL 58 was a descendant of FORTRAN, which is quite natural. It generalized many of FORTRAN's features and added several new constructs and concepts. Some of the generalizations had to do with the goal of not tying the language to any particular machine, and others were attempts to make the language more flexible. A rare combination of simplicity and elegance emerged from the effort.

ALGOL 58 formalized the concept of data type, although only variables that were not floating-point required explicit declaration. It added the idea of compound statements, which most subsequent languages incorporated. Some of the features of FORTRAN that were generalized were the following: Identifiers were allowed to have any length, as opposed to FORTRAN's restriction to six or fewer characters; any number of array dimensions was allowed, unlike FORTRAN's limitation to no more than three; the lower bound of arrays could be specified by the programmer, whereas in FORTRAN it was implicitly 1; nested **if** statements were allowed, which was not the case in FORTRAN; a **for** statement was included to do what FORTRAN's DO does, but then a **do** statement was added to allow a sort of subprogram process, complete with parameters.

ALGOL 58 procedures had the form

name(input parameters) =: (output parameters)

Because of this form it was and remains the only language to clearly separate the two kinds of parameters into different lists.

ALGOL 58 and all of its successors acquired the assignment operator in a rather unusual way. Zuse used the form

expression $\Rightarrow$ variable

in his Plankalkül for the assignment statement. Although Plankalkül had not yet been published, some of the European members of the ALGOL 58 committee were familiar with the language. The committee dabbled with the Plankalkül assignment form but, because of arguments about character limitations, the > was changed to :. Then, largely at the insistence of the Americans, the whole statement was turned around to the form

variable := expression

The Europeans preferred the opposite form (=:).

2.4.4 Reception of the ALGOL 58 Report

Publication of the ALGOL 58 report (Perlis and Samelson, 1958) in December 1958 was greeted with a good deal of enthusiasm. In the United States, the new language was viewed more as a collection of ideas for programming language design than as a universal standard language. Actually, the ALGOL 58 report was not meant to be a finished product, but rather a preliminary document for international discussion. Nevertheless, three major design and implementation efforts used the report as their basis. At the University of Michigan, the MAD language was born (Arden et al., 1961). The U.S. Naval Electronics Group produced the NELIAC language (Huskey et al., 1963). At System Development Corporation, JOVIAL was designed and implemented (Shaw, 1963). JOVIAL, an acronym for Jules' Own Version of the International Algebraic Language, represents the only widespread use of the original design of ALGOL 58 (Jules was Jules I. Schwartz, one of JOVIAL's designers). JOVIAL became the most widely used language based on ALGOL

58, for it was the official scientific language for the U.S. Air Force for a quarter of a century.

The rest of the U.S. computing community was not so kind to the new language. At first, both IBM and its major scientific user group, SHARE, seemed to embrace ALGOL 58. IBM began an implementation shortly after the report was published, and SHARE formed a subcommittee, SHARE IAL, to study the language. The subcommittee subsequently recommended that ACM standardize ALGOL 58 and that IBM implement it for all of the 700 series computers. The enthusiasm was short-lived, however. Both IBM and SHARE had had enough of the pain and expense of getting a new language started, both in terms of developing and using the first-generation compilers and in terms of training users in the new language and persuading them to use it. By the middle of 1959, both IBM and SHARE had developed such a vested interest in FORTRAN that they decided to retain it as *the* scientific language for the IBM 700 series machines.

2.4.5 ALGOL 60 Design Process

During 1959 ALGOL 58 was debated endlessly, in both Europe and the United States. Large numbers of suggested modifications and additions were published in the European *ALGOL Bulletin* and in *Communications of the ACM*. One of the most important events of 1959 was the presentation of the work of the Zurich committee to the International Conference on Information Processing, for it was there that Backus introduced his new notation for describing the syntax of programming languages, which later became known as BNF, for Backus–Naur form. BNF is described in detail in Chapter 3.

In January 1960 the second ALGOL meeting was held, this time in Paris. The work of this meeting was to debate the 80 suggestions that had been formally submitted for consideration. Peter Naur of Denmark had become heavily involved in the development of ALGOL, even though he had not been a member of the Zurich group. It was Naur who started and operated the *ALGOL Bulletin*. He spent a good deal of time studying Backus's paper that introduced BNF and decided that BNF should be used to describe formally the results of the 1960 meeting. After making a few relatively minor changes to BNF, he wrote a description of the new proposed language in BNF and handed it out to the members of the 1960 group at the beginning of the meeting.

2.4.6 ALGOL 60 Overview

Although the 1960 meeting lasted only six days, the modifications made to ALGOL 58 were dramatic. Among the most important new developments were the following:

1. The concept of block structure was introduced; this allowed the programmer to localize parts of programs by introducing new data envi-

ronments, or scopes. For example, consider the following code segment:

```
. . .
begin
  integer i, k;
  . . .
end;
  . . .
```

The **begin-end** pair delimits a block in which the variables i and k are local. They are not visible, nor do they have storage associated with them when control is outside the block.

2. Two different means of passing parameters to subprograms were allowed: pass by value and pass by name (they are referred to as call by value and call by name in the ALGOL documentation).

3. Procedures were allowed to be recursive. The ALGOL 58 description was unclear on this issue.

4. Semidynamic arrays were allowed. A semidynamic array is one for which the subscript range or ranges are specified by variables, so that the size of the array is set at the time storage is allocated to the array, which happens when the declaration is reached during execution. For example, consider the following ALGOL 60 procedure skeleton:

```
procedure insert (n, a);
  value n;
  integer n, a;
  begin
  integer array [1:n] list;
  . . .
  end insert;
```

In this procedure the array list is a local array of integer elements declared to have a subscript range of 1..n, where n is a parameter to the procedure. The size of list is not known until the procedure is called, so its storage cannot be allocated until then. Note that this is different from Pascal local array variables, which must have subscript ranges that are known at compile time.

Several features that might have had a dramatic impact on the success or failure of the language were proposed but rejected. Most important among these were input and output statements with formatting, which were omitted because they were thought to be too machine-dependent.

The ALGOL 60 report was published in May 1960 (Naur, 1960). A number of ambiguities still remained in the language description, and a third meeting was scheduled for April 1962 in Rome to address the problems. At this meeting the group dealt only with problems; no additions to the language were allowed. The results of this meeting were published under the title

"Revised Report on the Algorithmic Language ALGOL 60" (Backus et al., 1962).

2.4.7   ALGOL 60 Evaluation

In some ways ALGOL 60 was a wild success; in other ways it was a dismal failure. It succeeded in becoming, almost immediately, the only acceptable formal means of communicating algorithms, and it remained for over 20 years the sole language for publishing algorithms. Every imperative programming language designed since 1960 owes something to ALGOL 60. In fact, most are direct or indirect descendants; examples are PL/I, SIMULA 67, ALGOL 68, Pascal, ALGOL W, Modula-2, and Ada.

The ALGOL 58/ALGOL 60 design effort included a long list of firsts. It was the first time that an international group attempted to design a programming language. It was the first language that was designed to be machine-independent. It was also the first language whose syntax was formally described. This successful use of the BNF formalism initiated several important fields of computer science: formal languages, parsing theory, and compiler design. Finally, the structure of ALGOL 60 affected machine architecture. In the most striking example of this, an extension of the language was used as the systems language of a series of large-scale computers, the Burroughs B5000, B6000, and B7000 machines, which were designed with a hardware stack to efficiently implement the block structure and recursive procedures of the language.

On the other side of the coin, ALGOL 60 never achieved widespread or even significant use in the United States. Even in Europe it never became a dominant language. There are a number of reasons for its lack of acceptance. For one thing, some of the features of ALGOL 60 turned out to be too flexible; they made understanding difficult and implementation inefficient. The best example of this is the pass by name method of passing procedure parameters, which is explained in Chapter 8. The difficulties of implementing ALGOL 60 are evidenced by Rutishauser's statement in 1967 that few if any implementations included the full ALGOL 60 language (Rutishauser, 1967, p. 8).

The lack of input and output statements in the language was another major reason for its lack of acceptance. Implementation-dependent input/output made programs difficult to port to other implementations.

One of the most important contributions to computer science that is associated with ALGOL 60, BNF, was also a factor in its lack of acceptance. Although BNF is now considered a simple and elegant means of syntax description, to the world of 1960 it seemed strange and abstruse.

The character set of ALGOL 60 was also a problem, in spite of the option in the hardware versions of altering the implemented character set. Most problematic was the method of representing reserved words. The publication version of ALGOL 60 uses boldface for reserved words. Some compilers delimit reserved words with apostrophes, and others simply use normal characters. Unfortunately, these differences make programs difficult to port between implementations.

And finally, although there were many other problems, the entrenchment of FORTRAN among users and the lack of support by IBM were probably the most important factors in ALGOL 60's failure to gain widespread use.

The ALGOL 60 effort was never really complete, in the sense that ambiguities and obscurities were always a part of the language description (Knuth, 1967). It has been noted that the ALGOL 60 report was meant to be like the Bible: It was to be interpreted, not merely read. Those who studied the report carefully and interpreted it for the rest of the world became known as ALGOL theologians and ALGOL lawyers.

The ancestry of ALGOL 60 is shown in Figure 2.2.

2.5   Computerizing Business Records: COBOL

The story of COBOL is strange indeed. Although it has been used more than any other programming language, COBOL has had little effect on the design of subsequent languages, except for PL/I. It may still be the most widely used language, although it is very difficult to be sure one way or the other. Perhaps the most important reason why COBOL has had little influence is that few have attempted to design a new language for business applications since it appeared. That may be a tribute to how well COBOL's capabilities meet the needs of its application area.

2.5.1   Historical Background

The beginning of COBOL is somewhat similar to that of ALGOL 60, in the sense that the language was designed by a committee of people meeting for a relatively short period of time. The state of business computing at the time, which was 1959, was similar to the state of scientific computing several years earlier, when FORTRAN was being designed. One compiled language for business applications, FLOW-MATIC, had been implemented in 1957, but it belonged to one manufacturer, UNIVAC, and was designed for that company's computers. Another language, AIMACO, was being used by the U.S. Air Force, but it was only a minor variation of FLOW-MATIC. IBM had designed a programming language for business applications, COMTRAN (COMmercial TRANslator), but it had not yet been implemented. Several other language design projects were being planned.

2.5.2   FLOW-MATIC

The origins of FLOW-MATIC are worth at least a brief discussion, because it was the primary progenitor of COBOL. In December 1953 Grace Hopper at

Figure 2.2
Genealogy of ALGOL 60

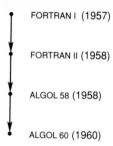

- FORTRAN I (1957)
- FORTRAN II (1958)
- ALGOL 58 (1958)
- ALGOL 60 (1960)

Remington-Rand UNIVAC produced a budget request that was indeed prophetic. It suggested that "mathematical programs should be written in mathematical notation, data processing programs should be written in English statements" (Wexelblat, 1981, p. 16). Unfortunately, it was impossible in 1953 to convince nonprogrammers that a computer could be made to understand English words. It was not until 1955 that a similar proposal had some hope of being funded by UNIVAC management, and even then it took a prototype system to do the final convincing. Part of this selling process involved compiling and running a small program, first using English keywords, then using French keywords, and then using German keywords. This demonstration was considered remarkable by UNIVAC management and was a prime factor in their acceptance of Hopper's proposal.

2.5.3 COBOL Design Process

The first formal meeting on the subject of a common language for business applications, which was sponsored by the Department of Defense, was held at the Pentagon on May 28–29, 1959 (exactly one year after the Zurich ALGOL meeting). The consensus of the group was that the language, then named CBL (for Common Business Language) should have the following general characteristics. Most agreed that it should use English to the extent possible, although a few argued for a more mathematical notation. The language must be easy to use, even at the expense of being less powerful, in order to broaden the base of those who could program computers. In addition to making the language easy to use, it was believed that the use of English would allow managers to read programs. Finally, the design should not be overly restricted by the problems of its implementation.

One of the overriding concerns at the meeting was that steps to create this universal language should be taken quickly, as a lot of work was already being done to create new business languages. In addition to the existing languages, RCA and Sylvania were working on their own business applications languages. If a universal language was not designed soon, its later acceptance would be more difficult. On this basis, it was decided that there should be a quick study of existing languages. For this task, the Short Range Committee was formed.

Initially, the goal of the Short Range Committee was not clearly understood: Was it only to evaluate existing languages or to design a new language? Whichever was intended, the committee chose the latter. The language design it initially produced, most of which is still part of COBOL, would probably have been significantly different had members known how long it would endure. Committee members operated under the assumption that they were designing an interim language for short-range use and that a different committee would have the time and resources to produce a high-quality language for the long term.

There were early decisions to separate the statements of the language into two categories—data description and executable operations—and to have statements in these two categories reside in different parts of programs. One of the great debates of the Short Range Committee was over the inclusion of subscripts. Many committee members argued that subscripts were too complex for the people in data processing, who were thought to be mathematically naive. Similar arguments evolved around whether arithmetic expressions should be included. The final report of the Short Range Committee was completed in December 1959.

The language specifications for COBOL 60, published by the Government Printing Office in April 1960 (Department of Defense, 1960), were described as "initial." Revised versions were published in 1961 and 1962 (Department of Defense, 1961, 1962). The language was standardized by the American National Standards (ANS) group in 1968. The next revision was standardized by ANS in 1974. The language continues to evolve today.

2.5.4 Evaluation

The COBOL language originated a number of novel concepts, some of which eventually appeared in other languages. For example, the DEFINE verb of COBOL 60 was the first high-level language construct for macros. More important, hierarchical data structures, which first appeared in Plankalkül, were first implemented in COBOL. They have since been included in the structured types of PL/I and the record types of ALGOL 68, Pascal, C, Modula-2, and Ada. COBOL was also the first language that allowed names to be truly connotative, because it allowed both long names (up to 30 characters) and word connector characters (dashes).

Overall, the data division is the strong part of COBOL's design, whereas the procedure division is relatively weak. Every variable is defined in detail in the data division, including the number of decimal digits and the location of the implied decimal point. File records are also described with this level of detail, as are lines to be output to a printer, which makes COBOL ideal for printing accounting reports. Perhaps the most important weakness of the procedure division lies in its lack of functions and its lack of subprograms with parameters.

Figure 2.3
Genealogy of COBOL

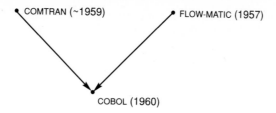

Our final comment on COBOL: It was the first programming language whose use was mandated by the Department of Defense. This mandate came after its initial development since COBOL was not designed specifically for DoD. In spite of its merits, COBOL probably would not have survived without that mandate. The poor performance of the early compilers simply made it far too expensive to use. Eventually, of course, people learned more about producing compilers and computers became much faster, larger, and cheaper. Together, these factors have made COBOL a great success, inside and outside DoD. Its appearance led to the electronic mechanization of accounting, an important revolution by any measure.

The ancestry of COBOL is shown in Figure 2.3.

2.6 The Beginnings of Timesharing: BASIC

BASIC (Mather and Waite, 1971) is another programming language that has enjoyed extremely widespread use but has gotten little respect. Like COBOL, it has been largely ignored by computer scientists. Once again like COBOL, it is inelegant and has not led to successor languages.

Nevertheless, BASIC has strongly influenced programmers, because for many of them it was their first language. This is due to its popularity on microcomputers, which follows directly from two of the main characteristics of BASIC: It is very easy for beginners to learn, especially those who are not science-oriented, and its smaller dialects can be implemented on computers with very small memories.

2.6.1 Design Process

BASIC was designed at Dartmouth College in New Hampshire by two mathematicians, John Kemeny and Thomas Kurtz, who were involved in the early 1960s in producing compilers for a variety of dialects of FORTRAN and ALGOL 60. Their science students had little trouble learning or using those languages in their work.

However, Dartmouth was primarily a liberal arts institution, where science and engineering students made up only about 25% of the student body. It was decided in the spring of 1963 to design a new language that would use terminals as the method of computer access. The goals of the system were:

1. It must be easy for nonscience students to learn and use.
2. It must be pleasant and friendly.
3. It must provide fast turnaround for homework.
4. It must allow free and private access.
5. It must consider user time more important than computer time.

The last goal was indeed a revolutionary concept. It was based at least partly on the belief that computers would become significantly cheaper as time went on.

The combination of goals 2, 3, and 4 led to the time-shared aspect of BASIC. Only with individual access through terminals by numerous simultaneous users could these goals be met in the early 1960s.

In the summer of 1963, Kemeny began work on the compiler for the first version of BASIC, using remote access to a GE 225 computer. Design and coding of the operating system for BASIC began in the fall of 1963. At 4 A.M. on May 1, 1964, the first program using the time-shared BASIC was typed in and run. In June the number of terminals on the system grew from 3 to 11, and by fall it had ballooned to 20.

2.6.2 Language Overview

The original version of BASIC was very small and, oddly, was not interactive: There was no means of getting input data from the terminal. Programs were typed in, compiled, and run, in a sort of batch-oriented way. The original BASIC had only 14 different statement types and a single data type, floating-point. Because it was believed that few of the targeted users would appreciate the difference between integer and floating-point types, the type was referred to as "numbers." Overall, it was a very limited language, though quite easy to learn.

2.6.3 Evaluation

The most important aspect of the original BASIC was that it was the first widely used method of remote terminal access to a computer. Terminals had just begun to be available at that time. Before then, most programs were entered into computers through either punched cards or paper tape.

Figure 2.4
Genealogy of BASIC

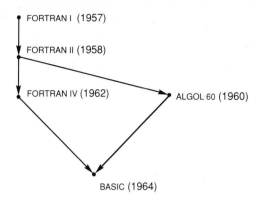

Much of the design of BASIC came from FORTRAN, with some minor influence from the syntax of ALGOL 60. Later it grew in a variety of ways, with little or no effort made to standardize it. The American National Standards Institute did issue a Minimal BASIC standard (ANSI, 1978b), but this represented only the minimum of essentials. In fact, the original BASIC was very similar to Minimal BASIC.

Although it may seem surprising, Digital Equipment Corporation used a rather elaborate version of BASIC named BASIC-PLUS to write significant portions of their largest operating system for the PDP-11 minicomputers, RSTS.

The most probable reasons for BASIC's success are the ease with which it can be learned and the ease with which it can be implemented, even on very small computers.

The ancestry of BASIC is shown in Figure 2.4.

2.7   Everything for Everybody: PL/I

PL/I represents the first large-scale attempt to design a language that could be used for a broad spectrum of application areas. All previous and most subsequent languages have focused on one particular application area, such as science, artificial intelligence, or business.

2.7.1   Historical Background

Like FORTRAN, PL/I was developed as an IBM product. By the early 1960s the users of computers in industry had settled into two separate and quite different camps. From the IBM point of view, scientific programmers could use either the large-scale 7090 or the small-scale 1620 IBM computers. This group used the floating-point data type and arrays extensively. FORTRAN was the primary language, although some assembly language was also used. They had their own user group, SHARE, and had little contact with people who worked on business applications.

Those in business applications used the large 7080 or the small 1401 IBM computers. They needed the decimal data type as well as elaborate and efficient input and output facilities. They used the COBOL language, although in early 1963, where our PL/I story begins, the conversion from assembly language to COBOL was only beginning. This category of users also had its own user group, GUIDE, and seldom had contact with scientific users.

In early 1963, IBM planners perceived the beginnings of a change in this situation. The two widely separated groups were moving toward each other in ways that were thought certain to create problems. Scientists began to gather large files of data to be processed, which required more sophisticated and more efficient input and output facilities. Business applications people began to do things such as regression analysis, which required floating-point data and arrays. It began to appear that computing facilities would soon require two separate computers, supporting two very different programming languages.

These perceptions quite naturally led to the concept of designing a single universal computer that would be capable of doing both floating-point and decimal arithmetic, and therefore both scientific and business applications. Thus was born the concept of the IBM System/360 line of computers. Along with this came the idea of a programming language that could be used just as easily for both business and scientific applications. For good measure, systems programming and list processing were thrown in as capabilities. Therefore, the new language was to replace FORTRAN, COBOL, LISP (the list-processing language for artificial intelligence; see Chapter 13), and systems applications in assembly language.

2.7.2 Design Process

The design effort began when IBM and SHARE formed the Advanced Language Development Committee of the SHARE FORTRAN Project in October 1963. This new committee quickly met and formed the "3 × 3" subcommittee, so named because it had three members from IBM and three from SHARE. The 3 × 3 Committee met for three or four days every other week to design the language.

As was the case with the Short Range Committee for COBOL, the initial design was scheduled for completion in a remarkably short time. Apparently, regardless of the scope of a language design effort, the prevailing belief was that it could be done in three months. The first version of PL/I, which was then named FORTRAN VI, was supposed to be completed by December, less than three months after the committee was formed. The committee actually pleaded successfully on two different occasions for extensions, moving the due date back to January and then to late February 1964.

The initial design concept was that the new language would be an extension of FORTRAN IV, maintaining compatibility, but that goal was dropped quickly along with the name FORTRAN VI. Until 1965, the language was known as NPL, an acronym for New Programming Language. The first published report on NPL was given at the SHARE meeting of March 1964. A more complete description followed in April, and the version that would actually be implemented was published in December 1964 (IBM, 1964) by the compiler group at the IBM Hursley Laboratory in England, whose members were chosen to do the implementation. In 1965 the name was changed to PL/I to avoid the confusion of the name NPL with the National Physical Laboratory in England. If the compiler had been developed outside the United Kingdom, the name might have remained NPL.

2.7.3 Language Overview

Perhaps the best single-sentence description of PL/I is that it included what were then considered the best parts of ALGOL 60 (recursion, block structure), FORTRAN IV (separate compilation with communication through global data), and COBOL 60 (data structures, input/output, and report-generating facilities), along with a few new constructs, all somehow blended together. We will not attempt, even in an abbreviated way, to discuss all the features of the language, or even its most controversial constructs. Instead we will mention briefly some of the language's contributions to the pool of knowledge of programming languages.

PL/I was the first programming language to have the following facilities:

1. Programs were allowed to create concurrently executing tasks. Although this was a good idea, it was poorly developed in PL/I. For example, no effective means were included for the synchronization of executing tasks.

2. It was possible to detect and handle 23 different types of exceptions, or run-time errors. Unfortunately, the design was too complex to be either understood by programmers or easily implemented.

3. Procedures were allowed to be used recursively, but the capability could be disabled, allowing more efficient code for nonrecursive procedures.

4. Pointers were included as a data type, although they were not as safe to use as those in later languages.

5. Cross sections of arrays could be referenced. For example, the third row of a matrix could be referenced as if it were a vector.

2.7.4 Evaluation

Any evaluation of PL/I must begin by recognizing the ambition of the design effort. In retrospect, it appears naive to think that so many constructs could have been combined successfully. However, that judgment must be tempered by acknowledging that there was little language design experience at the time. Overall, the design of PL/I was based on the premise that any construct that was useful and could be implemented should be included, with insufficient concern about how the many features would behave when thrown together. Edsgar Dijkstra, in his Turing Award Lecture (Dijkstra, 1972), made one of the strongest criticisms of the complexity of PL/I: "I absolutely fail to see how we can keep our growing programs firmly within our intellectual grip when by its sheer baroqueness the programming language—our basic tool, mind you!—already escapes our intellectual control."

In terms of usage, PL/I must be considered at least a partial success. It has seen significant use in both business and scientific applications. It has also been widely used as an instructional vehicle, primarily in several subset forms, such as PL/C (Cornell, 1977) and PL/CS (Conway and Constable, 1976).

The ancestry of PL/I is shown in Figure 2.5.

2.8 The Beginnings of Data Abstraction: SIMULA 67

Although SIMULA 67 never achieved widespread use and had little impact on the programmers and computing of its time, it is important for some of the concepts it introduced.

2.8.1 Design Process

Two Norwegians, Kristen Nygaard and Ole-Johan Dahl, developed the language SIMULA I during 1962–1964 at the Norwegian Computing Center (NCC). They were primarily interested in using computers for simulation and were also involved in operations research. SIMULA I was designed exclusively for system simulation and was first implemented by late 1964 on a UNIVAC 1107 computer.

As soon as the SIMULA I implementation was completed, Nygaard and Dahl began efforts to extend the language, by adding entirely new features and modifying some existing constructs in order to make the language useful for more general-purpose applications.

Figure 2.5
Genealogy of PL/I

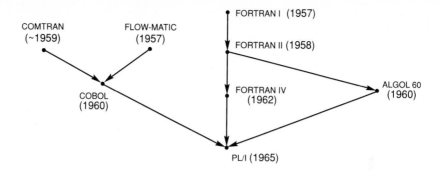

The result of this continued effort was SIMULA 67, whose design was first presented publicly in March 1967 (Dahl and Nygaard, 1967). We will discuss only SIMULA 67, although some of the features of interest in SIMULA 67 are also in SIMULA I.

2.8.2   Language Overview

SIMULA 67 is an extension of ALGOL 60, taking both block structure and the control statement structure from that language. The primary deficiency of ALGOL 60 (and other languages at that time) for simulation applications is the design of its subprograms. Simulation requires subprograms that are allowed to restart at the position where they previously stopped. Subprograms with this kind of control are known as coroutines because the caller and called subprograms have a somewhat equal relationship with each other, rather than the rigid hierarchical relationship they have in ALGOL 60 and FORTRAN.

2.8.2.1   Class Concept

To provide the coroutine concept in SIMULA 67, the class construct was developed. This was a very important development because our ideas of data abstraction began with it. The basic idea of a class is that a data structure and the routines that manipulate that data structure are packaged together. Furthermore, a class definition is distinct from a class instance, so a program can create and use any number of instances of a particular class. Class instances can contain local data that are static, or allocated at the time the instance is created. They can also include code that is executed at creation time, which can initialize some data structure of the class instance.

We present a more thorough discussion of classes and class instances in Chapter 10. It is interesting to note that the important concept of data

Figure 2.6
Genealogy of
SIMULA 67

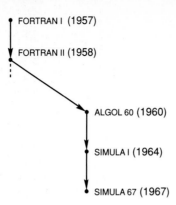

abstraction was not developed and attributed to the class construct until 1972, when Hoare (1972) recognized the connection.

The ancestry of SIMULA 67 is shown in Figure 2.6.

2.9 Orthogonal Design: ALGOL 68

ALGOL 68 was the source of several new ideas in language design, some of which were subsequently adopted by other languages. We include it here for that reason even though it never achieved widespread use in Europe or in the United States. Because we discuss some ALGOL 68 constructs in later chapters, in this chapter we will cover only a few of its most important contributions.

2.9.1 Design Process

The development of the ALGOL family did not end when the revised report (Backus et al., 1962) appeared in 1962, although it was six years until the next design iteration was published. The resulting language, ALGOL 68 (van Wijngaarden et al., 1969), was dramatically different from its predecessor.

One of the most interesting innovations of ALGOL 68 is one of its primary design criteria: orthogonality. Recall our discussion of orthogonality in Chapter 1. The use of orthogonality results in several innovative features of ALGOL 68.

2.9.2 Language Overview

The following three subsections describe three of the most significant innovations of ALGOL 68.

2.9.2.1   User-Defined Data Types

One important result of orthogonality in ALGOL 68 is its inclusion of user-defined data types. Earlier languages, such as FORTRAN, included only a few basic data structures. PL/I included a large number of data structures, which made it harder to learn and very difficult to implement; but it still could obviously not provide an appropriate data structure for every application.

The approach of ALGOL 68 to data structures was to provide a few primitive types and structures but to allow the user to combine those primitives into a large number of different structures. This provision for user-defined data types was carried over to some extent into all of the major imperative languages designed since then: Pascal, C, Modula-2, and Ada. User-defined data types are valuable because they allow the user to design data abstractions that fit particular problems very closely. All aspects of data typing are discussed in Chapter 7.

2.9.2.2   Reference Types

Another result of the orthogonality of design of ALGOL 68 is the type structure associated with pointers, which are completely generalized in the language. Furthermore, the problem of using the same syntax for both references and assignments to variables in assignment statements is now at least recognized. For example, consider the ALGOL 60 assignment statement:

```
SUM  : =  SUM  +  VALUE
```

The reference to the variable SUM on the left side of this statement refers to the address associated with SUM. The same syntax used on the right side of the statement, however, refers to the value associated with SUM.

In ALGOL 68, the same syntax is used. However, identifiers are all assumed to be references to variables, and the above statement requires that the reference to SUM in the right side be implicitly converted in order to cause its value to be used, not its address. This conversion is called dereferencing.

This recognition of the difference between the address and the value of a variable can be used explicitly, as we will demonstrate with an example. First, however, we must explain the confusing method used by ALGOL 68 to name types and the relationship of this method to declarations. A "normal" integer variable X is declared:

```
int X;
```

but is said to be of **ref int** type, because its normal use is as an address. When its value is needed, as when it appears in an expression, it must be dereferenced. A variable Y that is to be used as a pointer is declared:

```
ref int Y;
```

and is said to be of **ref ref int** type. Consider the following example:

```
int X;
ref int Y;
```

Now, the assignments

```
X := 5;
Y := X;
```

require no implicit conversion or dereferencing. In the first case, the constant is of **int** type. In the second, no conversions are required because the types of both identifiers are exactly what is required. The address of X, not its value (5), is moved to Y. A constant cannot be assigned to Y, because constants cannot be of **ref** type.

In the assignment:

```
X := Y
```

Y is dereferenced twice. The integer at the address pointed to by Y is moved to the address specified by X. For example, if the other two assignment statements above were executed, the 5 would be assigned to X by this statement.

Note that automatic dereferencing is not necessarily a positive language feature, as we discuss in Chapter 5.

Another interesting result of the orthogonality of ALGOL 68's type structure is that one can easily declare pointers to pointers. For example,

```
ref ref int ptr;
```

declares ptr to be a pointer to a pointer to an integer variable.

2.9.2.3   Dynamic Arrays

Also in the area of data types, ALGOL 68 introduced dynamic arrays. A dynamic array is one in which the declaration does not specify subscript bounds at all. Assignments to the dynamic array cause allocation of required storage. In ALGOL 68, dynamic arrays are called **flex** arrays. For example, the declaration

```
flex [1:0] int list
```

states that list is a dynamic array of integers with a single subscript whose lower bound is 1, but it allocates no storage. The aggregate assignment

```
list := (3, 5, 6, 2)
```

causes list to be allocated sufficient storage for four integers, effectively changing its bounds to [1:4].

2.9.3 Evaluation

ALGOL 68 is one of the most innovative of the imperative languages, including a significant number of features that had not been previously used. Its use of orthogonality, which some may argue was overdone, was nevertheless revolutionary. Many of the features that were introduced in ALGOL 68 became part of subsequent languages.

ALGOL 68 repeated one of the sins of ALGOL 60, however, and it was an important factor in its lack of widespread acceptance. The language was described using an elegant and concise but also unknown metalanguage. Before one could read the language-describing document (van Wijngaarden et al., 1969), he or she had to learn the new metalanguage, called van Wijngaarden grammars. To make matters worse, the designers invented a collection of words to explain the grammar and the language. For example, keywords are called indicants, substring extraction is called trimming, and the process of procedure execution is called a coercion of deproceduring, which might be meek, firm, or something else.

It is natural to contrast the design of PL/I with that of ALGOL 68. ALGOL 68 achieved complexity by the principle of orthogonality: a few primitive concepts and the unrestricted use of a few combining mechanisms. PL/I achieved complexity by simply including a large number of fixed constructs. ALGOL 68 extended the elegant simplicity of ALGOL 60, whereas PL/I simply added the features of several languages together to attain its goals. Of course, it must be kept in mind that the goal of PL/I was to provide a unified tool for a broad class of problems; ALGOL 68 was targeted to a single class: scientific problems.

PL/I achieved far wider use than ALGOL 68, due largely to IBM's promotional efforts and the problems of understanding and implementing ALGOL 68. Implementation was a difficult problem for both, but PL/I had the resources of IBM to apply to constructing a compiler. ALGOL 68 enjoyed no such benefactor.

The ancestry of ALGOL 68 is shown in Figure 2.7.

Figure 2.7
Genealogy of
ALGOL 68

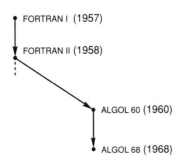

2.10 Two Important Descendants of the ALGOLs: Pascal and C

All imperative languages designed since 1960 owe some of their design to ALGOL 60 and/or ALGOL 68. The most widely used of these are Pascal and C. The Ada language, discussed in Section 2.11, is a second-generation descendant of ALGOL 60, being based on Pascal. Neither Pascal nor C added important new features to the collective constructs of previous languages, but both have enjoyed wide popularity and thus deserve some attention in this chapter.

2.10.1 Simplicity by Design: Pascal

2.10.1.1 Historical Background

Niklaus Wirth was a member of the International Federation of Information Processing (IFIP) Working Group 2.1, which was created to continue the development of ALGOL in the middle 1960s. As a contribution to that effort, Wirth and C.A.R. Hoare in August 1965 presented to the group a somewhat modest proposal for additions and modifications to ALGOL 60 (Wirth and Hoare, 1966). The majority of the group rejected the proposal as being too small an advance over ALGOL 60. Instead, a much more complex proposed revision was developed, which eventually became ALGOL 68. Wirth, along with a few other group members, did not believe that the ALGOL 68 report should have been released, based on the complexity of both the language and the metalanguage used to describe it. This position later proved to have some validity, because the ALGOL 68 documents, and therefore the language, were indeed found by the computer science community to be very difficult to understand.

The modified version of ALGOL 60 proposed by Wirth and Hoare was implemented at Stanford University and named ALGOL-W. It was used primarily as an instruction vehicle at a few universities. The primary contributions of ALGOL-W were the value-result method of passing parameters and the case statement for multiple selection. The value-result method is another technique for implementing the two-way communication provided by ALGOL 60's pass by name method. Both methods are discussed in Chapter 8.

Wirth's next major design effort, again based on ALGOL 60, was his most successful: Pascal. The original published definition of Pascal appeared in 1971 (Wirth, 1971). This version was modified somewhat in the implementation process and is described in Wirth (1973). The features that are often ascribed to Pascal in fact came from earlier languages. For example, user-defined data types were introduced in ALGOL 68, the case statement in ALGOL-W, and Pascal's records are like the structured variables of COBOL.

2.10.1.2 Evaluation

The largest impact of Pascal has been on the teaching of programming. In 1970, most students of computer science, engineering, and science were introduced to programming with FORTRAN, although some universities used PL/I, languages based on PL/I, and ALGOL-W. By the middle 1970s, Pascal had become the most widely used language for this purpose. This was quite natural, although perhaps not completely predictable, because Pascal had, in fact, been designed specifically for teaching programming.

Pascal's popularity, for both teaching programming and other applications, is based primarily on its remarkable combination of simplicity and expressive power. Although there are some insecurities in Pascal, as we discuss in later chapters, it is still a relatively safe language, particularly when compared with FORTRAN or PL/I.

The ancestry of Pascal is shown in Figure 2.8.

2.10.2 A Portable Systems Language: C

Like Pascal, C has contributed little to our knowledge of language design, but it has been very successful in terms of use. Although originally designed for systems programming, C is actually well suited for a wide variety of applications. (Systems programming is the generation of software systems that manage a computer system and make it accessible to all users, such as the operating system kernel, file systems, editors, and compilers.)

2.10.2.1 Historical Background

C's ancestors include CPL, BCPL, B, and ALGOL 68. CPL was developed at Cambridge University in the early 1960s. BCPL is a simple systems language

Figure 2.8
Genealogy of Pascal

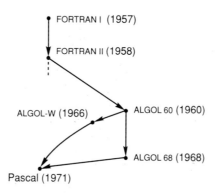

FORTRAN I (1957)

FORTRAN II (1958)

ALGOL-W (1966)   ALGOL 60 (1960)

ALGOL 68 (1968)

Pascal (1971)

developed by Martin Richards in 1967 (Richards, 1969). The first work on the UNIX operating system was done in the late 1960s by Ken Thompson at Bell Laboratories. The first high-level language implemented under UNIX was B, which was based on BCPL. B was designed and implemented by Thompson in 1970. It was semantically similar to BCPL but syntactically different. Its design was strongly influenced by the severe size limitations of the machine on which it was implemented, a PDP-7 with 4K 18-bit words.

Neither BCPL nor B is a typed language, which is an oddity among high-level languages, although both are much lower level than a language such as Pascal. Being untyped means that all data are considered machine words, which, although extremely simple, leads to many complications. For example, there is the problem of specifying floating-point rather than integer arithmetic in an expression. In one implementation of BCPL, the operands of a floating-point operation were preceded by periods. Operands not preceded by periods were considered to be integers. An alternative to this would have been to use different symbols for the floating-point operations.

This problem, along with several others, led to the development of a new language based on B. Originally called NB but later named C, it was designed and implemented by Dennis Ritchie at Bell Laboratories in 1972 (Kernighan and Ritchie, 1978). In some cases through BCPL, and in other cases directly, C was influenced by ALGOL 68. This is seen in the **for** and **switch** statements, in its assigning operators, and in its treatment of pointers.

A new version of C named C++ appeared in 1986 (Stroustrup, 1986). Like C, it was developed at Bell Laboratories. The primary advances of C++ over C are the class construct, modeled loosely on that of SIMULA 67; the checking of types of function parameters; and the ability to overload function names and operators. The class construct of C++ is designed to allow the language to be used for object-oriented programming, which is discussed in Chapter 15.

2.10.2.2   Evaluation

C has adequate control statements and data-structuring facilities to allow its use in many application areas. It also has a rich set of operators that allow a high degree of expressiveness.

One of the most important reasons why C is both liked and disliked is its lack of complete type checking. For example, a variable of any scalar type can appear in the same expression with a variable of any other scalar type. Those who like C appreciate the flexibility; those who do not like it find it too insecure. A major reason for its great popularity is that it is part of the widely used UNIX operating system. This inclusion in UNIX provides an inexpensive (often free with UNIX) and quite uniform compiler that is available to programmers on many different kinds of computers.

The ancestry of C is shown in Figure 2.9.

Figure 2.9
Genealogy of c

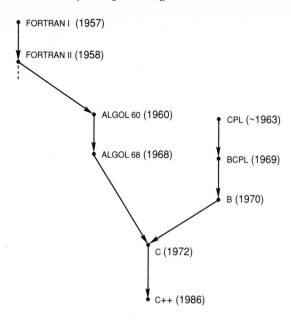

2.11　History's Largest Design Effort: Ada

The Ada language is the result of the most extensive and most expensive language design effort ever launched. It is the most recently designed imperative language that is likely to have a large impact on the language landscape. The Ada language was developed for the Department of Defense, so the state of the DoD computing environment was instrumental in determining its form.

2.11.1　Historical Background

By 1974, over half of the applications of computers in DoD were embedded systems. An embedded system is one in which the computer hardware is embedded in the device it controls or for which it provides services. Software costs were rising rapidly, primarily because of the increasing complexity of systems. More than 450 different programming languages were in use for DoD projects, and none of them was standardized by DoD. Literally every defense contractor could define a new and different language for every contract. Because of this language proliferation, application software was rarely reused. Furthermore, no software development tools were developed. A great many languages were in use, but none was actually suitable for embedded systems applications. For these reasons, the Army,

Navy, and Air Force each independently proposed in 1974 the development of a high-level language for embedded systems.

2.11.2 Design Process

Noting this widespread interest, Malcolm Currie, Director of Defense Research and Engineering, in January 1975 formed the High-Order Language Working Group (HOLWG), initially headed by Lt. Col. William Whitaker of the Air Force. The HOLWG had representatives from all of the military services and liaisons with England, France, and West Germany. Its initial charter was to:

1. Identify the requirements for a new DoD high-level language.
2. Evaluate existing languages to determine whether there was a viable candidate.
3. Recommend adoption or implementation of a minimal set of programming languages.

In April 1975, the HOLWG produced the Strawman requirements document for the new language (Department of Defense, 1975a). This was distributed to military branches, federal agencies, selected industrial and university representatives, and interested parties in Europe.

The Strawman document was followed by Woodenman (Department of Defense, 1975b) in August 1975 and Tinman (Department of Defense, 1976) in January 1976. The Tinman document was considered a complete set of requirements for a language with the desired characteristics. The principal author of these documents was David Fisher of the Institute for Defense Analysis. The group of participants in the effort was large, numbering over 200, with representatives from over 40 organizations outside DoD. In January 1977 the Tinman document was replaced by the Ironman requirements document (Department of Defense, 1977), which was nearly equivalent in content, but in a somewhat different format.

While the requirements documents were being developed, a parallel effort was under way to evaluate existing languages in terms of the requirements. The report on this work was released in January 1977 (Amoroso et al., 1977). It contained 2800 pages of comments on the 26 languages that had been studied. The conclusions of the report were that no existing language met the requirements but that a single language for all embedded systems applications was both possible and desirable. The report suggested that the new language be based on Pascal, ALGOL, or PL/I.

In April 1977, the Ironman document was used as the basis for an unrestricted request for proposals (RFP), which was then made public, thereby making Ada the first language to be designed by competitive contract. In July 1977 four of the proposing contractors, Softech, SRI International, Cii Honeywell/Bull, and Intermetrics, were chosen to produce, independently and in parallel, Phase 1 of the language design. All four of the resulting design proposals were based on Pascal.

When the 6-month Phase 1 was completed in February 1978, there was a 2-month evaluation by 400 volunteers in 80 review teams scattered around the world. The result of this evaluation was that two finalists—Intermetrics and Cii Honeywell/Bull—were chosen to go on to Phase 2 of the development.

In June 1978 the next iteration of the requirements document, Steelman, was released (Department of Defense, 1978).

At the end of Phase 2, another 2-month evaluation was done, and in May 1979 the Cii Honeywell/Bull language design was chosen as the winner. Interestingly, the winner was the only foreign competitor among the final four. The Cii Honeywell/Bull design team was led by Jean Ichbiah.

In the spring of 1979, Jack Cooper of the Navy Material Command recommended the name for the new language, Ada, which was then adopted. Augusta Ada Byron (1815–1851), Countess of Lovelace, mathematician and daughter of poet Lord Byron, is generally recognized as being the world's first programmer. She worked with Charles Babbage on his first mechanical computers, the Difference and Analytical Engines, writing programs for several numerical processes.

Phase 3 of the Ada design project began with the selection of the winning design. The design and the rationale for it were published by ACM in its *SIGPLAN Notices* (ACM, 1979) and distributed to a readership of over 10,000 people. A public test and evaluation conference was held in October 1979 in Boston, with representatives from over 100 organizations from the United States and Europe. By November more than 500 language reports had been received from 15 different countries. Most of the reports suggested small modifications rather than drastic changes and outright rejections. Based on the language reports, the next version of the requirements specification, the Stoneman document (Department of Defense, 1980), was released in February 1980.

A revised version of the language design was completed in July 1980 and was accepted as MIL-STD 1815, the standard *Ada Language Reference Manual*. The number 1815 was chosen because it was the year of the birth of Augusta Ada Lovelace. Another revised version of the *Ada Language Reference Manual* was released in July 1982. In 1983 the American National Standards Institute standardized Ada. This "final" official version is described in Goos and Hartmanis (1983). The Ada language design was then frozen for five years.

2.11.3 Language Overview

In this section we briefly describe four of the major features of the Ada language. Because we use the language as a major source throughout the remainder of the book other features will be described along the way.

Packages in the Ada language provide the means for encapsulating specifications for data types, data objects, and procedures. This, in turn, provides the support for the use of data abstraction in program design, as described in Chapter 10.

The Ada language includes excellent facilities for exception handling, which allows the programmer to gain control after a wide variety of exceptions, or run-time errors, have been detected. There is, thus, a good deal of flexibility in handling possible errors. Exception handling is discussed in Chapter 12.

Program units can be generic in Ada. For example, it is possible to write a sort procedure that uses an unspecified type for the data to be sorted. Such a generic procedure must be instantiated for a specified type before it can be used. This is done with a statement that causes the compiler to generate a version of the procedure with the given type. The availability of such generic units increases the scope of program units that might be reused, rather than duplicated, by programmers. Generics are discussed in Chapters 8 and 10.

The Ada language also provides for concurrent execution of program units named tasks, using the rendezvous mechanism. Rendezvous is the name of a method of intertask communication and synchronization. Concurrency is discussed in Chapter 11.

2.11.4 Evaluation

Perhaps the most important aspects of the Ada language to consider are the following:

1. Because the design was competitive, there was no limit on participation.

2. The Ada language embodies most of the contemporary concepts of software engineering and language design. Although one can argue with the actual methods used to include these features, and also with the wisdom of including such a large number of features in a language, most agree that the features are valuable.

3. Although many contractors did not initially realize it, the development of a compiler for the Ada language is an extremely difficult task. Only in 1985, after almost five years, did truly usable Ada compilers begin to appear. Not only is the sheer size of the language a burden on the compiler writer, but also such features as generic units and tasking pose problems that are not amenable to quick or easy solutions.

It is too early to assess the value or impact of the Ada language. It has certainly been controversial—and was so even before any compilers existed to provide a base of experience. The most serious criticism is that it is too large and too complex. In particular, Hoare has stated that it should not be

Figure 2.10
Genealogy of Ada

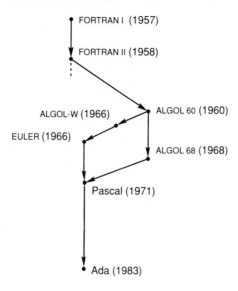

used for any application where reliability is critical (Hoare, 1981)—which is precisely the type of applications for which it was designed. On the other hand, others have praised it as the epitome of language design.

Largely because of the length of Ada's definition (331 pages) and its inherent complexity, a subculture of computer scientists has appeared whose chosen occupation is the interpretation of the Ada definition. These people, in the tradition of ALGOL 60, are called Ada lawyers.

The ancestry of Ada is shown in Figure 2.10.

SUMMARY

We have investigated the development and development environments of a number of the most important imperative programming languages. This chapter should have given the reader a good perspective on current issues in language design. We hope we have set the stage for an in-depth discussion of the important features of contemporary languages.

Chapters 13, 14, and 15 describe three different programming paradigms and three nonimperative languages that were designed for those paradigms. Histories of the development of these languages—LISP, PROLOG, and Smalltalk—are included in those chapters.

BIBLIOGRAPHIC NOTES

Perhaps the most important source of historical information about the development of programming languages is *History of Programming Languages*, edited by Richard Wexelblat (Wexelblat, 1981). It contains the developmental background and environment of each of 13 important programming languages, as told by the designers themselves.

The paper "Early Development of Programming Languages" (Knuth and Pardo, 1977), which is part of the *Encyclopedia of Computer Science and Technology*, is an excellent 85-page work that provides a large amount of detail about the development of languages up to and including FORTRAN, including example programs to demonstrate the features of many of those languages.

Another book of great historical interest is *Programming Languages: History and Fundamentals*, by Jean Sammet (Sammet, 1969). It is a 785-page work filled with details of 80 programming languages of the 1950s and 1960s. Sammet has also published several updates to her book, such as Sammet (1976).

BIBLIOGRAPHY

ACM. (1979) "Part A: Preliminary Ada Reference Manual" and "Part B: Rationale for the Design of the Ada Programming Language." *SIGPLAN Notices*, Vol. 14, No. 6.

Amoroso, S., P. Wegner, D. Morris, and D. White. (1977) "Language Evaluation Coordinating Committee Report to the High Order Language Working Group." January.

ANSI. (1978a) *American National Standard Programming Language FORTRAN.* ANSI X3.9-1978. American National Standards Institute, New York.

ANSI. (1978b) *American National Standard Programming Language Minimal BASIC.* ANSI X3.60-1978. American National Standards Institute, New York.

Arden, B.W., B.A. Galler, and R.M. Graham. (1961) "MAD at Michigan." *Datamation*, Vol. 7, No. 12, pp. 27–28.

Backus, J.W. (1954) "The IBM 701 Speedcoding System." *J. ACM*, Vol. 1, pp. 4–6.

Backus, J.W., F.L. Bauer, J. Green, C. Katz, J. McCarthy, P. Naur, A.J. Perlis, H. Rutishauser, K. Samelson, B. Vauquois, J.H. Wegstein, A. van Wijngaarder, and M. Woodger. (1962) "Revised Report on the Algorithmic Language ALGOL 60." *Commun. ACM*, Vol. 6, No. 1, pp. 1–17.

Conway, R., and R. Constable. (1976) "PL/CS—A Disciplined Subset of PL/I." Technical Report TR76-293, Department of Computer Science, Cornell University, Ithaca, NY.

Cornell University. (1977) *PL/C User's Guide, Release 7.6.* Department of Computer Science, Cornell University, Ithaca, NY.

Dahl, O.-J., and K. Nygaard. (1967) "SIMULA 67 Common Base Proposal." Norwegian Computing Center Document, Oslo.

Department of Defense. (1960) "COBOL, Initial Specifications for a Common Business Oriented Language."

Department of Defense. (1961) "COBOL—1961, Revised Specifications for a Common Business Oriented Language."

Department of Defense. (1962) "COBOL—1961 EXTENDED, Extended Specifications for a Common Business Oriented Language."

Department of Defense. (1975a) "Requirements for High Order Programming Languages, STRAWMAN," July.

Department of Defense. (1975b) "Requirements for High Order Programming Languages, WOODENMAN," August.

Department of Defense. (1976) "Requirements for High Order Programming Languages, TINMAN," June.

Department of Defense. (1977) "Requirements for High Order Programming Languages, IRONMAN," January.

Department of Defense. (1978) "Requirements for High Order Programming Languages, STEELMAN," June.

Department of Defense. (1980) "Requirements for High Order Programming Languages, STONEMAN," February.

Dijkstra, E.W. (1968) "Cooperating Sequential Processes." In *Programming Languages*, F. Genuys (ed.). Academic Press, New York, pp. 43–112.

Dijkstra, E.W. (1972) "The Humble Programmer." *Commun. ACM*, Vol. 15, No. 10, pp. 859–866.

Goos, G., and J. Hartmanis. (eds.) (1983) *The Programming Language Ada Reference Manual*. American National Standards Institute, ANSI/MIL-STD-1815A-1983, Lecture Notes in Computer Science 155. Springer-Verlag, New York.

Hoare, C.A.R. (1972) "Proof of Correctness of Data Representations." *Acta Informatica*, Vol. 1, pp. 271–281.

Hoare, C.A.R. (1981) "The Emperor's Old Clothes." *Commun. ACM*, Vol. 24, No. 2, pp. 75–83.

Huskey, H.K., R. Love, and N. Wirth. (1963) "A Syntactic Description of BC NELIAC." *Commun. ACM*, Vol. 6, No. 7, pp. 367–375.

IBM. (1954) "Preliminary Report, Specifications for the IBM Mathematical FORmula TRANslating System, FORTRAN." IBM Corp., New York.

IBM. (1956) "Programmer's Reference Manual, The FORTRAN Automatic Coding System for the IBM 704 EDPM." IBM Corp., New York.

IBM. (1964) "The New Programming Language." IBM UK Laboratories.

Kernighan, B.W., and D.M. Ritchie. (1978) *The C Programming Language*. Prentice-Hall, Englewood Cliffs, NJ.

Knuth, D.E. (1967) "The Remaining Trouble Spots in ALGOL 60." *Commun. ACM*, Vol. 10, No. 10, pp. 611–618.

Knuth, D.E., and Luis Trabb Pardo. (1977) "Early Development of Programming Languages." In *Encyclopedia of Computer Science and Technology*, Vol. 7. Dekker, New York, pp. 419–493.

Laning, J.H., Jr., and N. Zierler. (1954) "A Program for Translation of Mathematical Equations for Whirlwind I." Engineering memorandum E-364, Instrumentation Laboratory, Massachusetts Institute of Technology, Cambridge, MA.

Mather, D.G., and S.V. Waite. (eds.) (1971) *BASIC*. 6th ed. University Press of New England, Hanover, NH.

Metcalf, M., and J.K. Reid. (1987) *FORTRAN 8x Explained*. Oxford University Press, New York.

Naur, P. (ed.) (1960) "Report on the Algorithmic Language ALGOL 60." *Commun. ACM*, Vol. 3, No. 5, pp. 299–314.

Perlis, A., and K. Samelson. (1958) "Preliminary Report—International Algebraic Language." *Commun. ACM*, Vol. 1, No. 12, pp. 8–22.

Remington-Rand. (1952) "UNIVAC Short Code." unpublished collection of dittoed notes. Preface by A.B. Tonik, dated October 25, 1955 (1 p.); Preface by J.R. Logan, undated but apparently from 1952 (1 p.); Preliminary exposition, 1952? (22 pp., where pp. 20–22 appear to be a later replacement); Short code supplementary information, topic one (7 pp.); Addenda #1, 2, 3, 4 (9 pp.).

Richards, M. (1969) "BCPL: A Tool for Compiler Writing and Systems Programming." *Proc. AFIPS SJCC*, Vol. 34, pp. 557–566.

Rutishauser, H. (1967) *Description of ALGOL 60.* Springer-Verlag, New York.

Sammet, J.E. (1969) *Programming Languages: History and Fundamentals.* Prentice-Hall, Englewood Cliffs, NJ.

Sammet, J.E. (1976) "Roster of Programming Languages for 1974–75." *Commun. ACM*, Vol. 19, No. 12, pp. 655–669.

Shaw, C.J. (1963) "A Specification of JOVIAL." *Commun. ACM*, Vol. 6, No. 12, pp. 721–736.

Stroustrup, B. (1986) *The C++ Programming Language.* Addison-Wesley, Reading, MA.

van Wijngaarden, A., B.J. Mailloux, J.E.L. Peck, and C.H.A. Koster. (1969) "Report on the Algorithmic Language ALGOL 68." *Numerische Mathematik*, Vol. 14, No. 2, pp. 79–218.

Wexelblat, R.L. (ed.) (1981) *History of Programming Languages.* Academic Press, New York.

Wheeler, D.J. (1950) "Programme Organization and Initial Orders for the EDSAC." *Proc. R. Soc.* London, Ser. A, Vol. 202, pp. 573–589.

Wilkes, M.V. (1952) "Pure and Applied Programming." In *Proceedings of the ACM National Conference*, Vol. 2, Toronto, pp. 121–124.

Wilkes, M.V., D.J. Wheeler, and S. Gill. (1951) *The Preparation of Programs for an Electronic Digital Computer, with Special Reference to the EDSAC and the Use of a Library of Subroutines.* Addison-Wesley, Reading, MA.

Wilkes, M.V., D.J. Wheeler, and S. Gill (1957) *The Preparation of Programs for an Electronic Digital Computer.* 2d ed. Addison-Wesley, Reading, MA.

Wirth, N. (1971) "The Programming Language Pascal." *Acta Informatica*, Vol. 1, No. 1, pp. 35–63.

Wirth, N. (1973) *Systematic Programming: An Introduction.* Prentice-Hall, Englewood Cliffs, NJ.

Wirth, N., and C.A.R. Hoare. (1966) "A Contribution to the Development of ALGOL." *Commun. ACM*, Vol. 9, No. 6, pp. 413–431.

Zuse, K. (1972) "Der Plankalkül." Manuscript prepared in 1945, published in *Berichte der Gesellschaft fur Mathematik und Datenverarbeitung*, No. 63 (Bonn, 1972); Part 3, 285 pp. English translation of all but pp. 176–196 in No. 106 (Bonn, 1976), pp. 42–244.

PROBLEM SET

1. What features of Plankalkül do you think would have had the greatest influence on FORTRAN 0 if the FORTRAN designers had been familiar with Plankalkül?

2. Determine the capabilities of Backus's 701 Speedcoding system and compare them with those of a contemporary programmable hand calculator.

3. Write a short history of the A-0, A-1, and A-2 systems designed by Grace Hopper and her associates. (This will require some library research.)

4. Which class of languages found in every operating system is implemented as a pseudocode?

5. As a research project, compare the facilities of FORTRAN 0 with those of the Laning and Zierler system.

6. What argument would you make to support the removal from FORTRAN 0 of the DO statement form that allowed the loop body to be elsewhere?

7. Which of the three original goals of the ALGOL design committee, in your opinion, was most difficult at that time?

8. Choose one of the three languages MAD, NELIAC, and JOVIAL, and compare it feature by feature with ALGOL 58.

9. Describe in detail the three most important reasons, in your opinion, why ALGOL 60 did not become a very widely used language.

10. Why, in your opinion, did COBOL allow long identifiers when FORTRAN and ALGOL did not?

11. What is the primary reason you have heard why computer scientists seldom use BASIC?

12. Outline the major motivation of IBM in developing PL/I.

13. Was IBM's major motivation for developing PL/I correct, given the history of computers and language developments since 1964?

14. Describe, in your own words, the concept of orthogonality in programming language design.

15. What is the primary reason, in your opinion, why PL/I became more widely used than ALGOL 68?

16. Describe the connection between the development of ALGOL 68 and Pascal.

17. What are the arguments both for and against the idea of a typeless language?

18. What do the Ada and COBOL languages have in common?

19. What is your opinion of the argument that languages that are too complex are too dangerous to use and we should therefore keep all languages very small and simple?

20. Do you think language design by committee is a good idea? Support your opinion.

21. Languages continually evolve. What sort of restrictions do you think are appropriate for changes in programming languages?

22. Build a table identifying all of the major language developments, together with when they occurred, in what language they first appeared, and the identities of the developers.

Key Concepts

- Syntax versus semantics
- Recognition and generation devices
- Backus–Naur form
- Syntax abstractions
- Rules
- Derivations
- Parse trees
- Ambiguity
- Operator precedence and associativity
- Extended BNF
- Syntax graphs
- Operational semantics
- Axiomatic semantics
- Weakest preconditions
- Predicate transformers
- Denotational semantics
- Attribute grammars

3

DESCRIBING SYNTAX AND SEMANTICS

The study of programming languages, like the study of natural languages, can be divided into examinations of syntax and semantics. The primary formal methods of describing the syntax of programming languages are context-free grammars—a formalism that is also known as Backus–Naur form—and syntax graphs. For semantics specification the most common formal techniques are the operational, axiomatic, and denotational methods. Because of the inherent complexity of these semantics description methods and their lack of widespread acceptance, our discussion of them will be in the form of brief overviews.

The chapter also includes a section on attribute grammars, which can describe both the syntax and some aspects of the semantics—called the static semantics—of programming languages.

3.1   Introduction

The task of providing a concise yet understandable description of a programming language is difficult, but essential to the language's success. ALGOL 60 and ALGOL 68 were first presented using concise descriptions; in both cases, however, the descriptions were not readily understandable, partly because each used a new notation. The levels of acceptance of both languages suffered as a result.

One of the problems in describing a language is the diversity of the groups who must understand those descriptions. Most new programming languages are subjected to a period of public scrutiny before their designs are completed. The success of this feedback cycle depends heavily on the clarity of the description.

Programming language implementors obviously must be able to determine how the statements of a language are formed and what they mean. The difficulty of their job is in part determined by how much effort they must make to understand the language description.

Finally, language users must be able to decide how to encode software systems by referring to a language reference manual. Textbooks and courses enter into this process, but language manuals are usually the final printed information source about a language.

The **syntax** of a programming language is the form of its expressions, statements, and program units. Its **semantics** is the meaning of those expressions, statements, and program units. For example, the syntax of a Pascal goto statement is:

    goto label

The semantics of this statement is that the next statement in the execution sequence is the one with the specified label.

Although they are often separated for discussion purposes, syntax and semantics are clearly related. In a well-designed programming language, semantics should follow directly from syntax; that is, the form of a statement should strongly suggest what the statement is meant to accomplish.

Describing syntax is easier than describing semantics, partly because a concise and universally accepted notation is available for syntax description but none has yet been invented for semantics.

3.2 The General Problem of Describing Syntax

Languages, whether natural (such as English) or artificial (such as BASIC), are sets of strings of characters from some alphabet. The strings of a language are called sentences or statements. The syntax rules of a language specify which strings of characters from the language's alphabet are legal, and are thus in the language. English, for example, has a complex and lengthy collection of rules for specifying the syntax of its sentences. By comparison, even the largest programming languages are syntactically very simple.

Language syntax descriptions, for simplicity's sake, often do not include descriptions of the lowest-level language units. These small syntactic units are called **lexemes.** The description of lexemes can be given by a lexical specification, which can be separate from the syntactic description of the language. The lexemes of a programming language include its identifiers, constants, operators, and special words. One can think of language statements as strings of lexemes, rather than simply as characters.

A **token** of a language is a category of its lexemes. For example, identifier is a token in Pascal that can have lexemes, or instances such as sum and total. In some cases lexemes and tokens are the same. For example, the arithmetic operator symbols of a programming language are both lexemes and tokens.

The example language descriptions in this chapter are very simple, and most include lexeme descriptions.

3.2.1 Language Recognizers

Languages can be formally defined in two distinct ways: by **recognition** and by **generation.** Suppose we have a language L that uses the alphabet A of characters. To formally define L using the recognition method, we would need to construct a mechanism R capable of inputting strings of characters from the alphabet A. R would need to be designed so that it indicated that a given input string was or was not in L. In effect, R would either accept or reject the given string. Such devices are like filters, separating correct sentences from those that are incorrectly formed. If R, when fed all possible strings of characters from A, accepts exactly those that are in L, then R is a description of L. Because most useful languages are, for all practical purposes, infinite, this might seem like a lengthy process. Recognition devices, however, are not used to enumerate all the sentences of a language.

The syntax analysis portion of a compiler is a recognizer for the language the compiler translates. In this role, the recognizer need not describe the complete language; rather, it need only determine whether given programs are in the language. In other words, it must determine whether they are syntactically correct.

3.2.2   Language Generators

A language generator is a device that can be used to generate the sentences of a language. One can think of the generator as having a button that, when pushed, produces a sentence of the language. Because it is unclear which sentence will be generated by the generator when its button is pushed, the generator seems like a much less useful language descriptor. However, for people, certain forms of generators are better than recognizers, because they are more easily read and understood. By contrast, the syntax-checking portion of a compiler is not as useful a language description for a programmer, because it can only be used in trial-and-error mode.

There is a close connection between formal generation and recognition devices for the same language. This was one of the seminal discoveries in computer science, and it has led to much of what is now known about formal languages and compiler design theory. We return to the relationship of generators and recognizers in the next section.

3.3   Formal Methods of Describing Syntax

This section discusses the formal language generation methods that are commonly used to describe the syntax of programming languages.

3.3.1   Backus–Naur Form and Context-Free Grammars

In the middle to late 1950s, two apparently disconnected efforts resulted in a notation that has since become the most widely used method for formally describing programming language syntax.

3.3.1.1 Chomsky's Hierarchy

In the middle 1950s, Noam Chomsky, a noted linguist, described generative devices that define four classes of languages (Chomsky, 1956,1959). These four language classes are called recursively enumerable, context-sensitive, context-free, and regular. Regular is the smallest class, and each successively larger class completely contains the smaller ones. Because Chomsky was a linguist, his primary interest was the theoretical nature of natural languages.

3.3.1.2 Origins of Backus–Naur Form

Shortly after Chomsky's work on language classes, the ACM-GAMM group began designing ALGOL 58. A landmark paper describing ALGOL 58 was presented by John Backus at an international conference in 1959 (Backus, 1959). This paper introduced a new formal notation for specifying programming language syntax. The new notation was later modified slightly by Peter Naur for the description of ALGOL 60 (Naur, 1960). This revised method of syntax description became known as Backus–Naur form, or simply BNF.

Although the use of BNF in the ALGOL 60 report was not readily accepted by the untrained world, it soon became and still remains the most popular method of concisely describing programming language syntax. It is remarkable that BNF is nearly identical to Chomsky's generative devices for context-free languages, called context-free grammars. In the remainder of the chapter we refer to context-free grammars simply as grammars. Furthermore, we use the terms BNF and grammar interchangeably.

3.3.1.3 Fundamentals

A **metalanguage** is a language that is used to describe another language. BNF is a metalanguage for programming languages.

BNF uses abstractions for syntactic structures. A Pascal assignment statement, for example, might be represented by the abstraction <assign>. Pointed brackets are often used to delimit names of abstractions. The actual definition of <assign> may be given by:

<assign> → <var> : = <expression>

The symbol on the left side of the arrow, which is aptly called the left-hand side (LHS), is the abstraction being defined. The text to the right of the arrow is the definition of the LHS. It is called the right-hand side (RHS), and consists of tokens, lexemes, references to other abstractions, or some mixture of these. Altogether, the definition is called a **rule,** or production. In the example rule just given, the abstractions <var> and <expression> must be defined before the <assign> definition becomes useful.

This particular rule specifies that the abstraction <assign> is defined as the sequence of symbols: an instance of the abstraction <var>, followed by the lexeme : = , followed by an instance of the abstraction <expression>. One concrete example of the abstract syntactic structure described by the rule is:

```
total  : = sub1  +  sub2
```

The abstractions in a BNF description, or grammar, are often called **nonterminal symbols,** or simply **nonterminals,** and the lexemes and tokens of the rules are called **terminal symbols,** or simply **terminals.** A **grammar** is a collection of rules, where each nonterminal symbol represents a syntactic structure in the language.

Nonterminal symbols can have two or more distinct definitions, or forms, reflecting two or more possible syntactic forms in the language. Multiple definitions can be written as a single rule, with the different definitions separated by the symbol |, representing OR. For example, a Pascal **if** statement can be described as:

<if_stmt> → **if** >logic_expr> **then** <stmt>
<if_stmt> → **if** <logic_expr> **then** <stmt> **else** <stmt>

or as:

<if_stmt> → **if** <logic_expr> **then** <stmt>
| **if** <logic_expr> **then** <stmt> **else** <stmt>

3.3.1.4   Describing Lists

Variable-length lists in mathematics are often written using an ellipsis (. . .)— for example, 1, 2, ... BNF does not include an ellipsis, so an alternative method is required for describing lists of objects in programming languages. The most common technique used is recursion. A rule is **recursive** if its LHS appears in its RHS. For example, the list of identifiers on a variable declaration in Pascal can be described as follows:

<ident_list> → identifier
| identifier , <ident_list>

This defines <ident_list> as either a single token (identifier), or an identifier followed by a comma followed by another instance of <ident_list>.

3.3.1.5   Grammars and Derivations

BNF is a generative tool for defining languages. The sentences of the language are generated through repeated application of the rules, beginning with a special nonterminal of the grammar called the start symbol. Such a generation is called a **derivation.** In a grammar for a complete language, the start symbol represents a complete program, and is usually named <program>. The following simple grammar is used to illustrate derivations.

Example 3.1

A grammar for a small language.

<program> → **begin** <stmt_list> **end**
<stmt_list> → <stmt>
         | <stmt> ; <stmt_list>
<stmt> → <var> : = <expression>
<var> → A | B | C
<expression> → <var> + <var>
         | <var> - <var>
         | <var>   ∎

This language has only one statement form: assignment. A program consists of the special word **begin**, followed by a list of statements separated by semicolons, followed by the special word **end**. The expressions allow either a single variable, or two variables and either a + or - operator. The only allowable variable names are A, B, and C.

A derivation of a program in this language follows:

<program> ⇒ **begin** <stmt_list> **end**
      ⇒ **begin** <stmt> ; <stmt_list> **end**
      ⇒ **begin** <var> : = <var> + <var> ; <stmt_list> **end**
      ⇒ **begin** A : = <var> + <var> ; <stmt_list> **end**
      ⇒ **begin** A : = B + <var> ; <stmt_list> **end**
      ⇒ **begin** A : = B + C ; <stmt_list> **end**
      ⇒ **begin** A : = B + C ; <stmt> **end**
      ⇒ **begin** A : = B + C ; <var> : = <var> **end**
      ⇒ **begin** A : = B + C ; B : = <var> **end**
      ⇒ **begin** A : = B + C ; B : = C **end**

This derivation, like all derivations, begins with the start symbol, in this case <program>. The symbol ⇒ is read "derives." Each successive string in the sequence is derived from the previous string by replacing one of the nonterminals with one of its definitions. Each of the strings in the derivation, including <program>, is called a **sentential form.** In this derivation, the replaced nonterminal is always the leftmost nonterminal in the previous sentential form. Derivations that use this order of replacement are called leftmost derivations. The derivation continues until the sentential form contains no nonterminals. That sentential form, consisting of only terminals, or lexemes, is the generated sentence, which is in the language.

In addition to leftmost, a derivation may be rightmost or in an order that is neither leftmost nor rightmost. Derivation order in a generative system has no effect on the generated language.

By choosing alternative definitions, or alternative RHSs of rules, with which to replace nonterminals in the derivation, different sentences in the language can be generated. By exhaustively choosing all combinations of choices, the entire language can be generated. This language, like most others, is infinite, so one cannot actually generate *all* the sentences in the language in finite time.

The following is another example of a grammar for part of a typical programming language.

Example 3.2   **A grammar for simple assignment statements.**

$$
\begin{aligned}
&<assign> \rightarrow <id> := <expr> \\
&<id> \rightarrow A \mid B \mid C \\
&<expr> \rightarrow <id> + <expr> \\
&\qquad\qquad \mid <id> * <expr> \\
&\qquad\qquad \mid (<expr>) \\
&\qquad\qquad \mid <id>
\end{aligned}
$$

■

This grammar describes assignment statements whose right sides are arithmetic expressions with multiplication and addition operators and parentheses. For example, the statement:

    A := B * (A + C)

can be generated by the derivation:

$$
\begin{aligned}
<assign> &\Rightarrow <id> := <expr> \\
&\Rightarrow A := <expr> \\
&\Rightarrow A := <id> * <expr> \\
&\Rightarrow A := B * <expr> \\
&\Rightarrow A := B * (<expr>) \\
&\Rightarrow A := B * (<id> + <expr>) \\
&\Rightarrow A := B * (A + <expr>) \\
&\Rightarrow A := B * (A + <id>) \\
&\Rightarrow A := B * (A + C)
\end{aligned}
$$

3.3.1.6 Parse Trees

One of the most attractive features of grammars is that they naturally describe the hierarchical syntactic structure of the sentences of the languages they define. These hierarchical structures are called **parse trees.** For example, the tree in Figure 3.1 shows the structure of the assignment statement derived above.

Every internal node of a parse tree is labeled with a nonterminal symbol; every leaf is labeled with a terminal symbol. Every subtree of a parse tree describes one instance of an abstraction in the statement.

One of the primary tasks of the syntax analyzer portion of a compiler is to analyze programs that are input to the compiler to determine whether they are syntactically correct. This process often produces a parse tree for the program. The parse tree is sometimes used by subsequent parts of the compiler to perform the translation.

Figure 3.1
A parse tree for a
simple assignment
statement

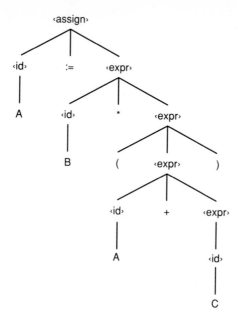

3.3.1.7 Grammars and Recognizers

It was suggested earlier in this chapter that there was a close relationship between generation and recognition devices for a given language. In fact, given a context-free grammar, a recognizer for the language generated by the grammar can be algorithmically constructed. A number of actual systems have been developed that perform this construction. Such systems allow the quick construction of the syntax analysis part of a compiler for a new language, and are therefore highly valued. One of the most widely used of these syntax analyzer generators is named yacc (yet another compiler-compiler) (Johnson, 1975).

3.3.1.8 Ambiguity

A grammar that generates a sentence for which there are two or more distinct parse trees is said to be **ambiguous**. Consider the following grammar, which is a minor variation of the grammar in Example 3.2.

Example 3.3   **An ambiguous grammar for simple assignment statements.**

<assign> → <id> : = <expr>
<id> → A | B | C
<expr> → <expr> + <expr>
        | <expr> * <expr>
        | (<expr>)
        | <id>

∎

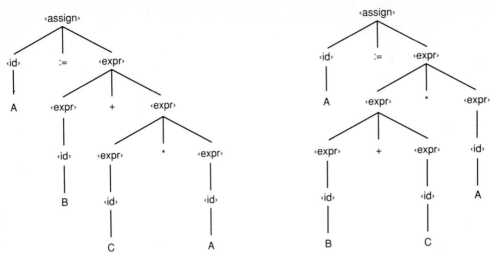

Figure 3.2
Two distinct parse trees for the same sentence

The grammar of Example 3.3 is ambiguous because the sentence:

```
A := B + C * A
```

has two distinct parse trees, as shown in Figure 3.2.

The ambiguity occurs because the grammar specifies slightly less syntactic structure than does the grammar of Example 3.2. Rather than allowing the parse tree of an expression to grow only on the right, this grammar allows growth on both the left and the right.

In general, ambiguity is a problem if part of the semantics of a language structure is based on its syntactic structure, which is frequently the case. If a language structure has more than one syntactic form, and syntax partially determines meaning, then the meaning of the construct cannot be determined. This problem is discussed in two specific examples in the following two sections.

3.3.1.9 Operator Precedence

As stated earlier, grammars can describe certain syntactic structures so that part of the meaning of the structure can follow from its parse tree. In particular, the fact that an operator in an arithmetic expression is generated lower in the parse tree (and therefore must be evaluated first) can be used to indicate that it has precedence over an operator produced higher up in the tree. In the first parse tree of Figure 3.2, for example, the multiplication operator is generated lower in the tree, which could be used to indicate that it has precedence over the addition operator in the expression. The second parse tree, however, indicates just the opposite. It appears, therefore, that the two parse trees indicate conflicting precedence information.

Notice that although the grammar of Example 3.2 is not ambiguous, the precedence order of its operators is not the usual one. Rather, in this grammar, a parse tree of a sentence with multiple operators has the rightmost operator at the lowest point, with the other operators in the tree moving progressively higher as one moves to the left in the expression.

A grammar can be written to separate the addition and multiplication operators so that they are consistently in a higher to lower ordering, respectively, in the parse tree. This ordering can be maintained regardless of the order in which the operators appear in an expression. It is done by using separate nonterminals and some new rules. The grammar of Example 3.4 is such a grammar.

Example 3.4   An unambiguous grammar for expressions.

<assign> → <id> : = <expr>
<id> → A | B | C
<expr> → <expr> + <term>
      | <term>
<term> → <term> * <factor>
      | <factor>
<factor> → (<expr>)
      | <id>

This grammar generates the same language as the grammars of Examples 3.2 and 3.3, but it indicates the proper precedence order of multiply and add operators. A derivation of the sentence A : = B + C * A follows:

<assign> ⇒ <id> : = <expr>
    ⇒ A : = <expr>
    ⇒ A : = <expr> + <term>
    ⇒ A : = <term> + <term>
    ⇒ A : = <factor> + <term>
    ⇒ A : = <id> + <term>
    ⇒ A : = B + <term>
    ⇒ A : = B + <term> * <factor>
    ⇒ A : = B + <factor> * <factor>
    ⇒ A : = B + <id> * <factor>
    ⇒ A : = B + C * <factor>
    ⇒ A : = B + C * <id>
    ⇒ A : = B + C * A

The unique parse tree for this sentence using the grammar of Example 3.4 is shown in Figure 3.3.

The connection between parse trees and derivations is very close: Either can be easily constructed from the other. Every derivation with an unambiguous grammar has a unique parse tree, although that tree can be

Figure 3.3
The unique parse tree
using an unambigu-
ous grammar

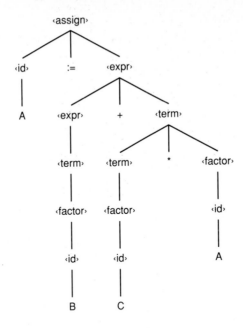

represented by different derivations. For example, the following derivation
of the sentence A : = B + C * A is different from the derivation of the same
sentence given previously. This is a rightmost derivation, whereas the previous one is leftmost. Both of these derivations, however, are represented
by the same parse tree.

$$\begin{aligned}
<assign> &\Rightarrow <id> : = <expr> \\
&\Rightarrow <id> : = <expr> + <term> \\
&\Rightarrow <id> : = <expr> + <term> * <factor> \\
&\Rightarrow <id> : = <expr> + <term> * <id> \\
&\Rightarrow <id> : = <expr> + <term> * A \\
&\Rightarrow <id> : = <expr> + <factor> * A \\
&\Rightarrow <id> : = <expr> + <id> * A \\
&\Rightarrow <id> : = <expr> + C * A \\
&\Rightarrow <id> : = <term> + C * A \\
&\Rightarrow <id> : = <factor> + C * A \\
&\Rightarrow <id> : = <id> + C * A \\
&\Rightarrow <id> : = B + C * A \\
&\Rightarrow A : = B + C * A
\end{aligned}$$

3.3.1.10 Associativity of Operators

Another interesting question concerning grammars for expressions is whether
associativity is also correctly described; that is, do the parse trees for expressions with more than one occurrence of a particular operator have those

Figure 3.4
A parse tree illustrating the associativity of addition

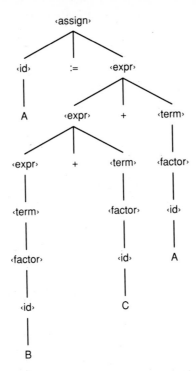

occurrences in proper hierarchical order? An example of an assignment statement with such an expression is:

```
A := B + C + A
```

The parse tree for this sentence, as defined with the grammar of Example 3.4, is shown in Figure 3.4. The parse tree of Figure 3.4 shows the left addition operator lower than the right addition operator. This is the correct order if addition is meant to be left associative, which is typical.

When a BNF rule has its LHS also appearing at the beginning of its RHS, the rule is said to be **left recursive.** The left recursion specifies left associativity. For example, the left recursion of the rules of the grammar of Example 3.4 cause it to make both addition and multiplication left associative.

The exponentiation operator in most languages that provide it is right associative. To describe right associativity, right recursion can be used. A grammar rule is **right recursive** if the LHS appears at the right end of the RHS. Rules such as:

$$\begin{aligned}
<\text{factor}> &\rightarrow <\text{exp}> ** <\text{factor}> \\
&\mid <\text{exp}> \\
<\text{exp}> &\rightarrow (\ <\text{expr}>\ ) \\
&\mid <\text{id}>
\end{aligned}$$

could be used to describe exponentiation as a right-associative operator.

3.3.2   Extended BNF

Because of a few minor inconveniences in BNF, the method has been extended in several ways. Most extended versions are called Extended BNF, or simply EBNF, even though they are not all exactly the same. Note that the extensions do not enhance the descriptive power of BNF; they are only conveniences.

Three extensions are usually included in EBNF. The first of these denotes an optional part of an RHS, and is delimited by brackets. For example, a Pascal **if** statement can be described as:

<if_stmt> → **if** <logic_expr> **then** <stmt> [**else** <stmt>]

The second extension is the use of braces in an RHS to indicate that the enclosed part can be repeated indefinitely, or left out altogether. This extension allows lists to be built with a single rule, instead of using recursion and two rules. For example, lists of identifiers can be described by the rule:

<ident_list> → <identifier> {, <identifier>}

This is a replacement of the recursion by a form of implied iteration; the part enclosed within braces can be iterated any number of times.

Some versions of EBNF allow a numeric superscript to be attached to the right brace to indicate an upper limit to the number of times the enclosed part can be repeated. Also, some versions use an asterisk (*) superscript to denote zero or more repetitions and a plus (+) superscript to indicate one or more repetitions.

Finally, when a single element must be chosen from a group, the options are sometimes stacked vertically in parentheses, as in:

$$<\text{for\_stmt}> \rightarrow \textbf{for} <\text{var}> := <\text{expr}> \begin{pmatrix} \textbf{to} \\ \textbf{downto} \end{pmatrix} <\text{expr}> \textbf{ do } <\text{stmt}>$$

Because of the difficulty of typing this form, the options are often placed in parentheses and separated by the OR operator, |. For example:

$$<\text{for\_stmt}> \rightarrow \textbf{for} <\text{var}> := <\text{expr}> (\textbf{to} \mid \textbf{downto}) <\text{expr}>$$
$$\textbf{do} <\text{stmt}>$$

Note that in all these cases the brackets, braces, and parentheses are metasymbols, which means they are notational tools and not terminal symbols in the syntactic entities they help describe.

3.3.3   Syntax Graphs

A **graph** is a collection of nodes, some of which are connected by lines called edges. A **directed graph** is one in which the edges are directional;

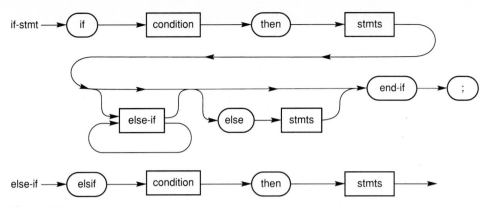

Figure 3.5
The syntax graph description of the Ada if statement

that is, they have arrowheads on one end to indicate a direction. A parse tree is a restricted form of directed graph.

The information in BNF rules can be represented in a directed graph. Such graphs are called syntax graphs, syntax diagrams, or syntax charts. A separate graph is used for each syntactic unit, in the same way a nonterminal symbol in a grammar represents such units.

There are two kinds of nodes in a syntax graph, which correspond to the terminal and nonterminal symbols of the right sides of a grammar's rules. A rectangle, which contains the name of a syntactic unit, or abstraction, represents a nonterminal. Circles or ellipses contain terminal symbols, which are lexemes in the language whose syntax is being described.

The Ada if statement syntax is described in EBNF below and with a syntax graph in Figure 3.5.

$$<\text{if\_stmt}> \rightarrow \textbf{if} <\text{condition}> \textbf{then} <\text{stmts}> \{<\text{else\_if}>\}$$
$$[\textbf{else} <\text{stmts}>] \textbf{end if};$$
$$<\text{else\_if}> \rightarrow \textbf{elsif} <\text{condition}> \textbf{then} <\text{stmts}>$$

Note that both the brackets and braces in the EBNF description are metasymbols, rather than terminal symbols in the Ada language.

Using graphics to describe syntax offers the same advantage as using graphics to describe anything: It makes information easier to understand by allowing us to visualize it.

Syntax graphs were developed at Burroughs for a compiler development project to use as a compact description of ALGOL 60 syntax (Taylor et al., 1961). They were later modified by A. Schai, director of the computer center at ETH in Zurich. This modified version first appeared in print in a book on ALGOL 60 by Rutishauser (1967).

3.4 Describing the Semantics of Programming Languages

We now turn to the difficult task of describing the semantics, or meaning, of statements in programming languages. Because of the power and naturalness of the available notation, describing syntax has become a relatively simple matter. On the other hand, no universally accepted notation has been invented for semantics. In this section we briefly describe several of the methods that have been proposed.

3.4.1 Operational Semantics

The idea behind operational semantics is to describe the meaning of a program by executing its statements on a machine, either real or simulated. The changes that occur in the machine's condition or state when it executes a given statement define the meaning of that statement. To further explain this concept, consider a machine language instruction. Let the state of a computer be the values of all its registers and memory locations, including condition codes and status registers. If one simply records the state of the computer, executes the instruction for which the meaning is desired, and then examines the machine's new state, the semantics of that instruction are clear: It is represented by the change in the computer's state caused by the execution of the instruction.

3.4.1.1 The Basic Process

Describing the operational semantics of high-level language statements requires the construction of either a real or a virtual computer. Recall from Chapter 1 that the hardware of a computer is a pure interpreter for its machine language. A pure interpreter for any programming language can be constructed in software, which becomes a virtual computer for the language. The operational semantics of a high-level language can be described using a pure interpreter for the language. There are two problems with this approach. First, the complexities and idiosyncrasies of the hardware computer and operating system that were used to run the pure interpreter would make the actions difficult to understand. Second, a semantic definition done this way would only be available to those with an identically configured computer.

These methodology problems can be avoided by replacing the real computer with a low-level virtual computer, implemented as a software simulation. The resulting system would be a hardware computer with its operating system, with a software simulated low-level idealized computer running on it. The registers, memory, status information, and execution process would all be simulated. The instruction set would be designed so that the semantics of each instruction was easy to describe and understand. In this way, the machine would be idealized and thus highly simplified, making its changes of state easy to understand.

To use operational semantics to describe the semantics of a programming language L requires the construction of two components. First, a translator is needed to convert statements in L to the chosen low-level language. The other component is the virtual machine for that low-level language. The state changes in the virtual machine brought about by executing the code that results from translating a given statement in the high-level language defines the meaning of that statement.

This basic process of operational semantics is not unusual. In fact, the concept is frequently used in programming textbooks and programming language reference manuals. For example, the semantics of the Pascal **for-to** construct can be described in terms of very simple instructions, as in:

```
PASCAL STATEMENT                OPERATIONAL SEMANTICS
for i := first to last do            i := first
   begin                  loop:   if i > last goto out
      .                              .
      .                              .
   end                            i := i + 1
                                  goto loop
                        out:   ...
```

The human reader of such a description is the virtual computer, and is assumed to be able to correctly "execute" the instructions in the definition and recognize the effects of the "execution."

A virtual machine for simple control statements like the **for** example just given could use the following instructions:

```
var := var
var := var + 1
var := var − 1
goto label
if var relop var goto label
```

> (where relop is one of the relational operators
> from the set {=, <>, >, <, >=, <= })

These are all simple and thus easy to understand and implement.

To expand this virtual machine instruction set to allow all the control statements in Pascal to be described, the only change required would be to allow general Boolean expressions in the conditional **goto**, rather than only relational expressions (those with only a single relational operator).

3.4.1.2 Evaluation

The first and most famous use of operational semantics was to describe the semantics of PL/I (Wegner, 1972). That particular abstract machine and the translation rules for PL/I were together named the Vienna Definition Language (VDL), after the city where it was devised by IBM.

Operational semantics provides an effective means of describing semantics for language users and language implementors, as long as the descriptions are kept as simple and informal as possible. The VDL description of PL/I, unfortunately, is so complex that it serves virtually no practical purpose.

3.4.2   Axiomatic Semantics

The structure of axiomatic semantics was defined with the primary goal of developing a method to prove the correctness of programs. To do this, mathematical rules of inference called axioms are defined for each syntactic category of the language. Given the constraints on the affected data before a statement is executed, these rules are used to deduce the data values after execution of the statement. This approach uses logical expressions that relate data values, rather than the entire state of an abstract machine, as with operational semantics.

Axiomatic semantics is based on mathematical logic. The logical expressions are called predicates, or **assertions.** An assertion immediately before a statement describes the constraints on the program variables. An assertion immediately following a statement describes the new constraints on those variables. These assertions are called the **precondition** and **postcondition,** respectively, of the statement. For example, if the postcondition {sum > 11} follows the statement:

```
sum := 2 * x + 1
```

in which sum and x are integer type variables, then one possible precondition is {x > 10}.

3.4.2.1   Weakest Preconditions

The **weakest precondition** is the least restrictive condition that will guarantee the validity of the associated postcondition. For example, in the above statement and postcondition, {x > 10}, {x > 50}, and {x > 1000} are all valid preconditions. The weakest of all preconditions in this case is {x > 5}.

If the weakest preconditions can be computed from given postconditions for every statement of a language, then correctness proofs can be constructed for programs in that language. The proof is begun by using as the overall postcondition the desired results of the program's execution and working backwards through the program, computing weakest preconditions for each statement, until the start of the program is reached. At that point, the first precondition states the conditions under which the program will compute correct results.

The process of computing weakest preconditions from given statements and postconditions is straightforward in some cases. A function to describe the process for a given statement form is called a **predicate transformer.** If P is the postcondition, W is the desired weakest precondition, and S is a statement form, the predicate transformer wp (for weakest precondition) is denoted by

$$wp(S, P) = W$$

3.4.2.2 Assignment Statements

In the case of assignment statements, the wp transformer function is especially simple:

$$wp(x := E, P) = P_{x \to E}$$

This specifies that if P is the postcondition for the assignment statement $x := E$, where E is some expression, then the weakest precondition, $P_{x \to E}$, can be computed by substituting E for every occurrence of x in the postcondition. For example, if we have the assignment statement:

```
a := b / 2 - 1
```

and the postcondition is {a < 10}, then the weakest precondition is computed by substituting b / 2 - 1 in the assertion {a < 10}, to get:

```
b / 2 - 1 < 10
    b / 2 < 10 + 1
        b < 22
```

Thus, the weakest precondition for the given assignment and postcondition is {b < 22}. Note that this predicate transformer is guaranteed to operate correctly only in the absence of function calls in the expression that have side effects. Functional side effects are changes made by the function to program variables that are not local to the function, but are either two-way parameters or globals.

The usual notation for axiomatic semantics for a given statement form is

$$\{P\} \ S \ \{Q\}$$

where P is the precondition, Q is the postcondition, and S is the statement form. In the case of the assignment statement, this is

$$\{P_{x \to E}\} \ x := E \ \{P\}$$

3.4.2.3 Sequences

Weakest preconditions for sequences of statements can be computed by the following method. If S1 and S2 are statements, and we have

$$\{P1\} \ S1 \ \{P2\}$$
$$\text{and} \ \{P2\} \ S2 \ \{P3\}$$

then $\{P1\}$ S1; S2 $\{P3\}$ describes the axiomatic semantics of the sequence S1; S2. If S1 and S2 are the assignment statements

$$x1 := E1$$
$$\text{and } x2 := E2$$

then we have

$$\{P3_{x2 \to E2}\} \; x2 := E2 \; \{P3\}$$
$$\{(P3_{x2 \to E2})_{x1 \to E1} \; x1 := E1 \; \{P3_{x2 \to E2}\}$$

so the weakest precondition for the sequence $x1 := E1$; $x2 := E2$ with postcondition P3 is $\{(P3_{x2 \to E2})_{x1 \to E1}\}$.

3.4.2.4 Logical Pretest Loops

Another essential construct of an imperative programming language is the logical pretest, or **while** loop. Computing the weakest precondition for a **while** loop is inherently more difficult than for a sequence because the number of iterations is not statically known. If it were, the loop could be treated as a sequence. In general, however, the number of iterations cannot be determined from the text of the statement.

The problem of computing the weakest precondition here is similar to the problem of proving a theorem about all positive integers. In the latter case induction is normally used, and the same inductive method can be used for **while** loops. The central step in induction is finding an inductive hypothesis. The corresponding step in the axiomatic semantics of a **while** loop is finding an assertion called a **loop invariant,** which is crucial to the finding of the weakest precondition.

The loop invariant must satisfy a number of constraints to be useful. First, the weakest precondition for the **while** must guarantee the truth of the loop invariant. In turn, the loop invariant must guarantee the truth of the postcondition upon loop termination. During execution of the loop, the truth of the loop invariant must be unaffected by the evaluation of the loop-controlling Boolean expression and the loop body statements.

Another complicating factor for **while** loops is the problem of loop termination. If Q is the postcondition that holds immediately after loop exit, then a precondition P for the loop is one that guarantees Q at loop exit and also guarantees that the loop terminates.

The axiomatic description of a **while** loop is written as

$\{P\}$ **while** B **do** S **end** $\{Q\}$

The complete description includes the following logic, in which $\Rightarrow$ means "implies" and I is the loop invariant:

$P \Rightarrow I$
$\{I\} \; B \; \{I\}$
$\{I \text{ and } B\} \; S \; \{I\}$
$(I \text{ and (not } B)) \Rightarrow Q$
the loop terminates

To compute a loop invariant, we use the method used for determining the inductive hypothesis in mathematical induction; that is, we compute the relationship for a few cases and hope that a pattern emerges that will apply to the general case. If the loop body contains a single assignment statement, we can use the predicate transformer for assignment statements to compute these cases. For the example:

while y <> x **do** y := y + 1   {y = x}

we proceed as follows:

For 0 iterations, the weakest precondition is simply {y = x}.

For 1 iteration, we have:

wp(y := y + 1, {y = x}) = {y + 1 = x}, or {y = x - 1}

For 2 iterations, we have:

wp(y := y + 1, {y = x - 1}) = {y + 1 = x - 1}, or {y = x - 2}

For 3 iterations, we have:

wp(y := y + 1, {y = x - 2}) = {y + 1 = x - 2}, or {y = x - 3}

Through these calculations, it is clear that {y < x} will suffice for cases of one or more iterations. Combining this with {y = x} for the zero iterations case, we get {y <= x}, which can be used for the loop invariant. Now, a precondition for the **while** statement can be determined from the loop invariant. The requirement is that the precondition, P, must imply the loop invariant, I, and that it must guarantee that the loop terminates. In our simple example, we could use P = I, because {y <= x} guarantees loop termination.

In more complex loops, finding a suitable loop invariant requires a good deal of ingenuity. Because computing the weakest precondition for a **while** loop depends on finding a suitable loop invariant, the use of axiomatic semantics for **while** loops is difficult.

3.4.2.5 Evaluation

To define the semantics of a complete programming language using the axiomatic method, a predicate transformer function is needed for each statement type in the language. Thus far, however, no general methods of creating predicate transformer functions have been found, except for very simple statement forms such as assignment.

Axiomatic semantics is a powerful tool for research into program correctness proofs, and it provides an excellent framework in which to reason about programs. Its usefulness in describing the meaning of programming languages to either language users or compiler writers is, however, more limited.

Research in axiomatic semantics was begun by Floyd (1967), and further developed by Hoare (1969). The semantics of a large part of Pascal was described by Hoare and Wirth (1973) using this method. The parts they did not complete involved functional side effects and goto statements. These were found to be the most difficult to describe.

3.4.3 Denotational Semantics

Denotational semantics is the most rigorous method of describing the meaning of programs. It is solidly based in logic and mathematics. A thorough discussion of the use of denotational semantics to describe the semantics of programming languages is long and complex. We must therefore restrict ourselves severely in our coverage of the topic.

The fundamental concept of denotational semantics is to define both a mathematical object for each language entity and a function that maps instances of that entity onto instances of the mathematical object. Because the objects are rigorously defined, they represent the exact meaning of their corresponding entities. The difficulty with this method lies in creating the objects and the mapping functions. The method is named denotational because the objects denote the meaning of the syntactic entities.

3.4.3.1 A Simple Example

We use a very simple language construct, binary numbers, to illustrate the method. The syntax of binary numbers can be described by the following grammar rules:

<bin_num> → 0
    | 1
    | <bin_num> 0
    | <bin_num> 1

A parse tree for an example binary number is shown in Figure 3.6.

To describe the meaning of binary numbers using denotational semantics and the grammar rules above, we associate the actual meaning with each rule that has a single terminal symbol as its RHS. The objects in this case are simple decimal numbers.

In our example, we must associate meaningful objects with the first two grammar rules. The other two grammar rules are, in a sense, computational rules because they combine a terminal symbol, to which a meaningful object can be associated, with a nonterminal, which can be expected to represent some construct. Presuming an evaluation that progresses upward in the parse tree, the nonterminal in the right side would already have its meaning attached. Then such a syntax rule would require a function that computed the meaning of the LHS, which must then represent the meaning of the complete RHS.

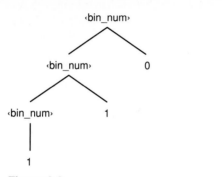

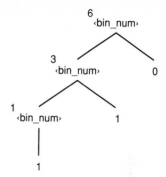

Figure 3.6
A parse tree of a
binary number

Figure 3.7
A parse tree with
denoted objects

We name the range of semantic values of the objects N, which is defined as {0, 1, 2, . . .}, the nonnegative decimal integer values we wish to associate with binary numbers. The semantic function, named N, maps the abstract syntax, as described in the grammar rules above, to the objects in N. The function N is defined as follows:

$N[[0]] = 0$
$N[[1]] = 1$
$N[[<bin\_num>0]] = 2 * N[[<bin\_num>]]$
$N[[<bin\_num>1]] = 2 * N[[<bin\_num>]] + 1$

The double square brackets are used to enclose the syntactic operands.

We can attach the meanings, or denoted objects (which in this case are decimal numbers) to the nodes of the parse tree above, yielding the tree in Figure 3.7.

This is, in a sense, syntax-directed semantics. We map abstract syntactic entities to mathematical objects with concrete meaning.

3.4.3.2 Evaluation

In a similar but more complex way objects and functions can be defined for the other syntactic entities of programming languages. When a complete system has been defined for a given language, it can be used to determine the meaning of complete programs. This provides a framework for thinking in a highly rigorous way about programming, as well as a method of proving the correctness of programs.

Denotational semantics can be used as an aid to language design. For example, statements for which the denotational semantic description is complex and difficult may indicate to the designer that such statements may also be difficult for language users to understand and that an alternative design may be in order.

A significant amount of work has been done on the possibility of using denotational language descriptions to automatically generate compilers (Jones, 1980; Milos et al., 1984; Bodwin et al., 1982). These efforts have shown that the method is feasible, but the work has not progressed to the point where it can be used to generate useful compilers.

Because of the complexity of denotational descriptions, they are of little use to language users.

Although the use of denotational semantics is normally attributed to Scott and Strachey (1971), the general denotational approach to language description can be traced back to the nineteenth century (Frege, 1892).

3.5   Attribute Grammars

Although context-free grammars have been indispensable tools for describing the syntax of programming languages and building compilers, they do not have sufficient descriptive power to enforce several essential syntactic rules of common programming languages. For example, they cannot state that program variables must be defined before they are used, or that the name on an Ada procedure **end** statement must match the name on the corresponding **procedure** statement. Both of these conditions require the use of context in the language description, which, of course, cannot be included in a context-free grammar. Because of this deficiency, a variety of more powerful mechanisms has been devised. One of these, attribute grammars, was designed to describe not only the syntax of programs but also their static semantics. The static semantics of a program is that part of its semantics that can be determined without executing its code. The static semantics of most contemporary languages include their type-checking rules. Attribute grammars can also describe those parts of language syntax that cannot be described by grammars, such as the rules described above. Attribute grammars were invented by Knuth (1968).

3.5.1   Basic Concepts

Attribute grammars are grammars with sets of attribute values associated with the grammar symbols. **Attributes** are similar to variables, and can have values assigned to them. **Attribute computation functions,** sometimes called semantic functions, are associated with grammar rules to specify how attribute values are computed. In addition, grammar rules may have associated **predicate functions** over the attribute values, which state some of the syntax and static semantic rules of the language.

These new concepts will become clearer after we formally define attribute grammars and provide an example.

3.5.2   Attribute Grammars Defined

An **attribute grammar** is a grammar with the following additions:

1. Associated with each grammar symbol X is a set of attributes A(X). The set A(X) consists of two disjoint sets S(X) and I(X), called synthesized and inherited attributes, respectively. **Synthesized attributes** are used to pass information up a parse tree, while **inherited attributes** pass information down a tree.

2. Associated with each grammar rule is a set of semantic functions and a possibly empty set of predicate functions over the attributes of the symbols in the grammar rule. For a rule X0 → X1...Xn, the synthesized attributes of X0 are computed with a semantic function of the form S(X0) = f(A(X1),...,A(Xn)), meaning that their values depend only on the attribute value of their children nodes. Inherited attributes of Xj, 1 <= j <= n, are computed with a semantic function of the form I(Xj) = f(A(X0)), meaning that their values depend only on the attribute values of their parent nodes. Predicate functions have the form of a Boolean expression on the attribute set {A(X0),...,A(Xn)}. The only derivations allowed are those in which the predicates associated with each nonterminal are all true. A false predicate function value indicates a violation of the syntax or static semantics rules of the language.

A parse tree of an attribute grammar is the parse tree based on its underlying BNF grammar, with a set of attribute values attached to each node. If all the attributes in a parse tree have values, the tree is said to be fully attributed. We think of attribute values as being computed after the complete unattributed parse tree has been constructed.

3.5.3   Intrinsic Attributes

Intrinsic attributes are synthesized attributes of leaf nodes, whose values are determined outside the parse tree. For example, the type of an instance of a variable in a program could come from a table—usually called a symbol table—used to store variable names and types. The contents of such a table are determined from earlier declaration statements. Initially, assuming that an unattributed parse tree has been constructed and that attribute values are desired, the only attributes with values are the intrinsic attributes of the leaf nodes. Given the intrinsic attribute values on a parse tree, the semantic functions can be used to compute the remaining attribute values.

3.5.4   An Example Attribute Grammar

We now present an example of a simple attribute grammar and show how it can be used to check the correctness of the static semantics of a simple assignment statement in a described language. The language consists entirely of simple assignment statements. The only variable names are A, B, and C. The right side of the assignments can either be a variable or an expression in the form of a variable added to another variable. The variables can be one of two types: int_type or real_type. The static semantic rules state that when there are two variables on the right side of an assignment, they need not be the same type. The type of the expression when the operand types are not the same is always real_type. When they are the same, the expression type is that of the operands. The type of the left side must match the type of the right side. So, the types of operands in the right side can be mixed, but the assignment is valid only if the LHS and the value resulting from evaluating the RHS have the same type. The attribute grammar specifies how these semantic rules can be checked for correctness.

The grammar portion of our example attribute grammar is:

<assign> → <var> : = <expr>
<expr> → <var> + <var>
        | <var>
<var> → A | B | C

The attributes are:

- **actual_type**   A synthesized attribute associated with the nonterminals <var> and <expr>. It is used to store the actual type, int_type or real_type in the example, of a variable or expression. In the case of a variable, the actual type is intrinsic. In the case of an expression, it is determined from the actual types of the child node or children nodes of the <expr> nonterminal.

- **expected_type**   An inherited attribute associated with the nonterminal <expr>. It is used to store the type, either int_type or real_type, that is expected for the expression, as determined by the type of the variable on the left side of the assignment statement.

- **lhs_type**   A synthesized attribute associated with <assign>. It is used to move the value of the synthesized actual_type of the LHS of an assignment statement to the inherited attribute expected_type for the <expr>.

- **env**   An inherited attribute associated with the nonterminals <assign>, <expr>, and <var>. It carries the reference to the correct symbol table entries to the instances of variables, where it is used for the lookup.

The environment attribute is inherited from above the root of the parse tree in this grammar. We assume that this grammar is embedded in a larger grammar that describes declarations, which could cause the generation of a symbol table. The value for the environment attribute would be a pointer to that symbol table.

The complete attribute grammar follows. Notice that when there is more than one occurrence of a nonterminal in a syntax rule, the nonterminals are subscripted with brackets to distinguish them. Neither the subscript nor the brackets are part of the described language.

Example 3.5   **An attribute grammar for simple assignment statements.**

1. Syntax rule: <assign> → <var> : = <expr>
   Semantic rules: <var>.env ← <assign>.env
                    <expr>.env ← <assign>.env
                    <assign>.lhs_type ← <var>.actual_type
                    <expr>.expected_type ← <assign>.lhs_type

2. Syntax rule: <expr> → <var>[2] + <var>[3]
   Semantic rules: <var>[2].env ← <expr>.env
                    <var>[3].env ← <expr>.env
                    <expr>.actual_type ←
                        if (<var>[2].actual_type = int_type)
                            and (<var>[3].actual_type = int_type)
                            then int_type
                            else real_type
                        end if
   Predicate: <expr>.actual_type = <expr>.expected_type

3. Syntax rule: <expr> → <var>
   Semantic rule: <expr>.actual_type ← <var>.actual_type
   Predicate: <expr>.actual_type = <expr>.expected_type

4. Syntax rule: <var> → A | B | C
   Semantic rule: <var>.actual_type ← look-up (RHS, <var>.env)   ■

The look-up function looks up a given variable name in a given table (or environment) and returns the variable's type.

An example of a parse tree of a sentence generated by this grammar is shown in Figure 3.8.

As in the grammar, bracketed numbers are added after the repeated node labels in the tree so they can be referenced unambiguously.

3.5.5 Computing Attribute Values

Now we will decorate the tree with attributes. This process could proceed in a completely top-down order, from the root to the leaves, if all attributes were inherited. Alternatively, it could proceed in a completely bottom-up order, from the leaves to the root, if all the attributes were synthesized. Because our grammar has both synthesized and inherited attributes, and

Figure 3.8
A parse tree for A: =
A + B

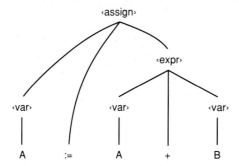

because of the interdependencies of the attributes, the evaluation process cannot be in any single direction. The following is an evaluation of the attributes, in an order in which those evaluations can be done. Each of the eight numbered steps in this evaluation depends on some attribute computation in a previous step. Note that determining attribute evaluation order for the general case of an attribute grammar is a complex problem, requiring the construction of a dependency graph in order to show all attribute dependencies.

1. <assign>.env ← inherited from the ancestor of <expr>
2. <var>[1].env ← <assign>.env (Rule 1)
   <expr>.env ← <assign>.env (Rule 1)
   <var> [2].env ← <var>[3].env ← <expr>.env (Rule 2)
3. <var>[1].actual_type ← look-up (A, <var>[1].env) (Rule 4)
4. <assign>.lhs_type ← <var>[1].actual_type (Rule 1)
5. <expr>.expected_type ← <assign>lhs_type (Rule 1)
6. <var>[2].actual_type ← look-up (A, <var>[2].env)
   <var>[3].actual_type ← look-up (B, <var>[3].env)
   (both from Rule 4)
7. <expr>.actual_type ← either int_type or real_type
   (Rule 2)
8. <expr>.expected_type = <expr>.actual_type is TRUE
   (Rule 2)

The tree in Figure 3.9 shows the flow of attribute values in this example. Solid lines are used for the parse tree; dashed lines show attribute flow in the tree.

The tree in Figure 3.10 shows the final attribute values on the nodes.

3.5.6 Evaluation

Attribute grammars have been used in a wide variety of applications. They have been used to provide complete descriptions of the syntax and static semantics of programming languages (Watt, 1979); they have been used as

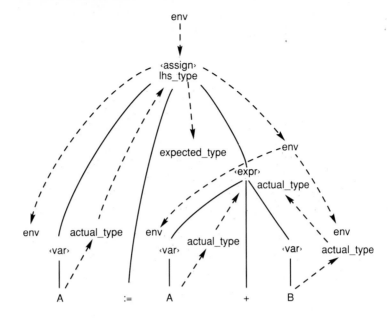

Figure 3.9
The flow of attributes in the tree

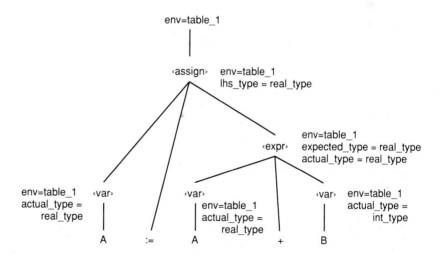

Figure 3.10
A fully attributed parse tree

the formal definition of a language that can be input to a compiler generation system (Farrow, 1982); and they have been used as the basis of several syntax-directed editing systems (Teitelbaum and Reps, 1981; Fischer et al., 1984).

One of the main difficulties in using an attribute grammar for a real language is its size and complexity. The large number of attributes and semantic rules required for a complete programming language make such grammars difficult to write and difficult to read. Furthermore, the attribute values on a large parse tree are costly to evaluate.

SUMMARY

Backus–Naur form and context-free grammars are equivalent metalanguages that are ideally suited for the task of describing the syntax of programming languages. Not only are they concise descriptive methods, but the parse trees that can be associated with their generative actions give graphical evidence of the underlying syntactic structures. Furthermore, they are naturally related to recognition devices for the languages they generate, which leads to the relatively easy construction of syntax analyzers for compilers for these languages.

Syntax graphs are simply graphical representations of grammars.

There are three primary methods of semantic description: operational, axiomatic, and denotational. Operational semantics is a method of describing the meaning of language constructs in terms of their effect on an ideal machine. Axiomatic semantics was devised as a tool for proving the correctness of programs. In denotational semantics mathematical objects are used to represent the meanings of language constructs.

An attribute grammar is a single formalism that can describe both the syntax and static semantics of a language.

In general, syntax description is a relatively easy task, whereas semantic description is very difficult. The only adequate formalisms of the latter are complex to learn and understand, which detracts mightily from their usefulness. If only static semantics is needed, attribute grammars offer some hope as a syntax/semantic descriptive tool. Thus far, however, no standard form of such a grammar has been universally adopted and they have not been widely used.

BIBLIOGRAPHIC NOTES

Syntax description using context-free grammars and BNF is thoroughly discussed in Cleaveland and Uzgalis (1976). Lengthy introductions to the three semantics description methods discussed in this chapter can be found in Marcotty et al., (1976). Another good reference for much of the material of this chapter is Pagan (1981).

BIBLIOGRAPHY

Backus, J. (1959) "The Syntax and Semantics of the Proposed International Algebraic Language of the Zurich ACM-GAMM Conference." *Proceedings International Conference on Information Processing*, UNESCO, Paris, pp. 125–132.

Bodwin, J.M., L. Bradley, K. Kanda, D. Litle, and U.F. Pleban. (1982) "Experience with an Experimental Compiler Generator Based on Denotational Semantics." *ACM SIGPLAN Notices*, Vol. 17, No. 6, pp. 216–229.

Chomsky, N. (1956) "Three Models for the Description of Language." *IRE Transactions on Information Theory*, Vol. 2, No. 3, pp. 113–124.

Chomsky, N. (1959) "On Certain Formal Properties of Grammars." *Information and Control*, Vol. 2, No. 2, pp. 137–167.

Cleaveland, J.C., and R.C. Uzgalis. (1976) *Grammars for Programming Languages: What Every Programmer Should Know about Grammar.* American Elsevier, New York.

Farrow, R. (1982) "LINGUIST 86: Yet Another Translator Writing System Based on Attribute Grammars." *ACM SIGPLAN Notices*, Vol. 17, No. 6, pp. 160–171.

Fischer, C.N., G.F. Johnson, J. Mauney, A. Pal, and D.L. Stock. (1984) "The Poe Language-Based Editor Project." *ACM SIGPLAN Notices*, Vol. 19, No. 5, pp. 21–29.

Floyd, R.W. (1967) "Assigning Meanings to Programs." *Proceedings Symposium Applied Mathematics*, in *Mathematical Aspects of Computer Science*, ed. J.T. Schwartz. American Mathematical Society, Providence, RI.

Frege, G. (1892) "Über Sinn und Bedeutung," *Zeitschrift für Philosophie und Philosophisches Kritik*, 100, pp. 25–50.

Hoare, C.A.R. (1969) "An Axiomatic Basis of Computer Programming." *Commun. ACM*, Vol. 12, No. 10, pp. 576–580.

Hoare, C.A.R., and N. Wirth. (1973) "An Axiomatic Definition of the Programming Language Pascal." *Acta Informatica*. Vol. 2, pp. 335–355.

Johnson, S.C. (1975) "Yacc—Yet Another Compiler Compiler." Computing Science Report 32, A.T.& T. Bell Laboratories, Murray Hill, NJ.

Jones, N.D. (ed.) (1980) *Semantic-Directed Compiler Generation.* Lecture Notes in Computer Science, Vol. 94. Springer-Verlag, Heidelberg, FRG.

Knuth, D.E. (1968) "Semantics of Context-Free Languages." *Mathematical Systems Theory*, Vol. 2, No. 2, pp. 127–146.

Liskov, B., and J. Guttag. (1986) *Abstraction and Specification in Program Development.* McGraw-Hill, New York.

Marcotty, M., H.F. Ledgard, and G.V. Bochmann. (1976) "A Sampler of Formal Definitions." *ACM Computing Surveys*, Vol. 8, No. 2, pp. 191–276.

Milos, D., U. Pleban, and G. Loegel. (1984) "Direct Implementation of Compiler Specifications." *ACM Principles of Programming Languages 1984*, pp. 196–202.

Naur, P. (ed.) (1960) "Report on the Algorithmic Language ALGOL 60." *Commun. ACM*, Vol. 3, No. 5, pp. 299–314.

Pagan, F.G. (1981) *Formal Specifications of Programming Languages.* Prentice-Hall, Englewood Cliffs, NJ.

Rutishauser, H. (1967) *Description of ALGOL 60.* Springer-Verlag, New York.

Scott, D.S., and C. Strachey. (1971) "Towards a Mathematical Semantics for Computer Language." *Proceedings Symposium on Computers and Automation*, ed. J. Fox. Polytechnic Institute of Brooklyn Press, New York, pp. 19–46.

Taylor, W., L. Turner, and R. Waychoff. (1961) "A Syntactic Chart of ALGOL 60." *Commun. ACM*, Vol. 4, p. 393.

Teitelbaum, T., and T. Reps. (1981) "The Cornell Program Synthesizer: A Syntax-Directed Programming Environment." *Commun. ACM*, Vol. 24, No. 9, pp. 563–573.

Watt, D.A. (1979) "An Extended Attribute Grammar for Pascal." *ACM SIGPLAN Notices*, Vol. 14, No. 2, pp. 60–74.

Wegner, P. (1972) "The Vienna Definition Language." *ACM Computing Surveys*, Vol. 4, No. 1, pp. 5–63.

PROBLEM SET

1. There are two different mathematical models of language description: generation and recognition. Describe how each can define the syntax of a programming language.

2. Write EBNF and syntax graph descriptions of the Pascal procedure header statement.

3. Write EBNF and syntax graph descriptions of the Pascal procedure call statement.

4. Using the grammar in Example 3.2, show a parse tree and a leftmost derivation for the statement:

   ```
   A := A * (B + (C * A))
   ```

5. Using the grammar in Example 3.4, show a parse tree and a leftmost derivation for the statement:

   ```
   A := (A + B) * C
   ```

6. A grammar is ambiguous if it generates a sentence that has two or more distinct parse trees. A grammar for a very small language that includes the Pascal form of the **if-then-else** construct is:

   ```
   <stmt>    → <assign> | <if_stmt>
   <assign>  → <id> := <expr>
   <if_stmt> → if <logic_expr> then <stmt>
             | if <logic_expr> then <stmt> else <stmt>
   ```

   (A complete grammar would need also to define <id>, <expr>, and <logic_expr>.)

      Prove that this grammar is ambiguous.

7. Write a grammar that describes the same language as the grammar of Problem 6, but which is not ambiguous.

8. Describe, in English, the language defined by the following grammar.

   ```
   S → A B C
   A → a A | a
   B → b B | b
   C → c C | c
   ```

9. Write a grammar for the language consisting of strings that have n copies of the letter a followed by the same number of copies of the letter b, where $n > 0$. For example, the strings ab, aaaabbbb, and aaaaaaaabbbbbbbb are in the language but a, abb, ba, and aaabb are not.

10. Write a grammar that describes the floating-point constants of your favorite programming language.

11. Draw parse trees for the sentences aabcc and aaabbbc, as derived from the grammar of Problem 8.

12. Using the virtual machine instructions of Section 3.4.1.1, give an operational semantic definition of:
    a. Pascal **repeat**
    b. Pascal **case**
    c. FORTRAN 77 DO of the form: DO N K = start, end, step

13. Compute the weakest precondition for the following assignment statement and postcondition:

    a := 2 * (b - 1) - 1   {a > 0}

14. Compute the weakest precondition for the following assignment statement and postcondition:

    x := 2 * y + x - 1   {x > 11}

15. Compute the weakest precondition for the following sequence of assignment statements and its postcondition:

    a := 2 * b + 1
    b := a - 3
    {b < 0}

Key Concepts

- Primitive data types
- Names
- Reserved words
- Keywords
- Variables
- Aliases
- Static versus dynamic binding
- Explicit versus implicit declarations
- Lifetime
- Strong typing
- Static versus dynamic scope
- Blocks
- Referencing environments
- Named constants
- Initialization

4

PRIMITIVE DATA TYPES AND VARIABLES

Imperative programming languages are, to varying degrees, abstractions of the underlying von Neumann computer architecture. The architecture's two primary modules are its memory, which stores both instructions and data, and its processor, which provides operations for modifying the contents of the memory. The abstractions in a language for the memory cells of the machine are variables. In some cases, the characteristics of the abstractions are very close to the characteristics of the cells; an example of this is integer variables, which are usually represented exactly as in individual hardware memory words. In other cases, the abstractions are far removed from the cells, as is the case with a three-dimensional array, which requires a software mapping function to provide the abstraction.

A variable can be characterized by a collection of properties, or attributes, the most important of which is type, a fundamental concept in programming languages. The design of the data types of a language requires that a variety of issues be considered. Among the most important of these are the scope and lifetime of variables. Related to these are the issues of type checking and initialization. A knowledge of all these concepts is requisite to understanding the imperative languages.

Variables of the simplest data types, along with these related concepts, are the topics of this chapter. In Chapter 7 we carry this discussion to the more complex data types.

4.1   Primitive Numeric Data Types

4.1.1   Integer

The most common primitive numeric data type is **integer.** An integer value is represented by a string of bits, with one of the bits representing the sign. Many computers now support several sizes of integers. The DEC VAX-11 superminicomputers, for example, support four different sizes: byte, word (2-byte), longword (4-byte), and quadword (8-byte). These capabilities are reflected in some programming languages. For example, Ada allows implementations to include several integer sizes, such as: SHORT INTEGER, INTEGER, and LONG INTEGER. DEC's VAX Ada also includes a fourth size, SHORT SHORT INTEGER. Some languages, for example C, include unsigned integer types, which are simply integer types to store integer values without signs.

4.1.2   Floating-Point

Floating-point data types model real numbers, but the representations are only approximations of most real values. For example, neither of the fundamental numbers, π or e (the base for the natural logarithms), can be correctly represented in floating-point notation. Of course, neither of these numbers can be accurately represented in any finite space, even this book.

On most computers, floating-point numbers are stored in binary, which exacerbates the problem. For example, even the value 0.1 in decimal cannot be represented by a finite number of binary digits.

Floating-point values are represented as fractions and exponents, with different implementations often choosing different formats. Floating-point data types are included in most languages, although many small computers do not have hardware support for such types. Languages that are designed to support scientific programming generally include two floating-point types, often called **real** and **double-precision,** after the original FORTRAN data type names. The real type is the standard size, and a value of real type is often stored in a single memory word. The double-precision type is provided for situations where larger fractional parts are needed. Double-precision variables usually occupy twice as much storage as real variables, and provide at least twice the accuracy.

Floating-point values have been stored in a variety of different formats, although all have the same basic components. These are the fractional part, sometimes called the mantissa; the sign of the fractional part; the exponent, sometimes called the characteristic; and the sign of the exponent. If implemented in hardware, the format of floating-point variables is that chosen by the hardware designer.

4.1.3 Decimal

All mainframe and large minicomputers that are designed to support business systems applications have hardware support for **decimal** data types. Decimal data types store a fixed number of decimal digits, with the decimal point at a fixed position in the value. These are the primary data types for business data processing, and are thus a fundamental in COBOL.

Decimal types have the advantage of being capable of precisely storing decimal values, at least those within a restricted range, which cannot be done in floating-point. The disadvantages of decimal types are that the range of values is restricted, because no exponents are allowed, and their representation in memory is wasteful.

Decimal types are stored very much like character strings. In some cases they are stored one digit per byte, but in others they are packed two digits per byte. Either way, they take more storage than binary representations. The operations on decimal values are done in hardware on machines that have such capabilities; otherwise, they are simulated in software.

4.2 Boolean Types

Boolean types are perhaps the simplest of all types. Their range of values has only two elements, one for true and one for false. They were introduced in ALGOL 60 and have been included in most general-purpose languages designed since 1960. One popular exception is C, in which all numeric type variables and constants can be referenced in Boolean expressions as if they were Boolean. In such expressions, all operands with nonzero values are considered true and the others are considered false.

A Boolean value could be represented by a single bit, but because a single bit of memory is difficult to access efficiently on many machines, they are usually stored in the smallest efficiently addressable cell of memory, typically a byte.

Boolean types are often used to represent switches or flags in programs. Although other types, such as integer, can be used for these purposes, the use of Boolean types is more readable. Recall our example in Chapter 1.

4.3   Names

Before we can begin our discussion of variables, we must cover a topic that has broader use than simply for variables of primitive types. Although the name of a variable is one of its fundamental attributes, names are also associated with labels, subprograms, and formal parameters, among other program entities.

4.3.1   Design Issues

The following are the primary design issues for names:

1. What is the maximum length of a name?
2. Can connector characters be used in names?
3. Are names case-sensitive?
4. Are special words reserved words or keywords?

These issues are discussed in the following two sections, which also include examples of several design choices.

4.3.2   Name Forms

A **name** is a string of characters used to identify some entity in a program. The earliest programming languages used single-character names. This was natural, because early programming was primarily mathematical, and mathematicians have long used single-character names for variables in their formal notations.

FORTRAN I broke with the tradition of the single-character name, allowing up to 6 characters in its names. COBOL names can have up to 30 characters; FORTRAN 77 restricts names to 6 characters; C allows them to have any length, but only the first 8 are significant; Ada names have no length limit and all are significant; FORTRAN 8x will limit names to 31 characters. Some languages do not specify a length limit on names, although implementors of those languages often do. They do this so the table where identifiers are stored during compilation need not be too large, and also to simplify the maintenance of that table.

The ideal name form is a string with a reasonably long length limit, if any, with some connector character such as the underscore (_) allowed to provide the capability of building multiple word names. The underscore serves the same purpose as a space in English text, but without terminating the name string in which it is placed. Pascal, Modula-2, and FORTRAN 77 do not allow connector characters in names; C, COBOL, and Ada do. FORTRAN 8x will allow the underscore as a connector in its names.

Some languages, notably C and Modula-2, recognize the difference between the cases of letters in names; that is, names in these languages are **case-sensitive.** For example, the following three names are distinct in both C and Modula-2: Sum, SUM, and sum. To some, this is a serious detriment to readability, because names that look highly similar in fact denote different entities. In that sense, case sensitivity violates the design principle that language constructs that look the same should have the same meaning.

Obviously, not everyone agrees that case sensitivity is bad for names, for if they did, C and Modula-2 would not have included the feature. In C the problems of case sensitivity can be avoided by exclusive use of lowercase for names. In Modula-2, however, the problem cannot be escaped, because many of the standard modules and functions have names that include both uppercase and lowercase letters. For example, the usual Modula-2 procedure for outputting an integer is WriteInt, and spellings such as WRITEINT are not recognized. This is a problem of writability rather than readability, because a need to remember odd spellings makes it more difficult to write correct programs. It is a form of intolerance on the part of the language designer that is enforced by the compiler.

In FORTRAN, only uppercase letters can be used in names, a needless restriction. Many FORTRAN implementations allow lowercase letters; they simply translate them to uppercase for internal use during compilation.

4.3.3 Special Words

Most programming languages have **special words** that are used to make programs more readable by naming actions to be performed. They are also used to separate the syntactic entities of programs. These words are either keywords or reserved words, depending on the language.

A **keyword** is a word of a programming language that is special only in certain contexts. FORTRAN is one of the languages whose special words are keywords. In FORTRAN, the word REAL, when found at the beginning of a statement and followed by a name, is considered a keyword indicating that the statement is a declarative statement. However, if the word REAL is followed by the assignment operator, it is considered a variable name. These two uses are illustrated in the following:

```
REAL APPLE
REAL = 3.4
```

FORTRAN compilers must recognize the difference between names and special words by context.

A **reserved word** is a special word of a programming language that cannot be used as a name. In COBOL, Pascal, and Ada the special words are reserved. As a language design choice, reserved words are better than keywords, because with keywords the ability to redefine special words can lead to readability problems. For example, in FORTRAN one could have

```
INTEGER REAL
REAL INTEGER
```

which declares the program variable REAL to be of INTEGER type and the variable INTEGER to be of REAL type. In addition to the strange appearance of these declaration statements, the appearance of REAL and INTEGER as variable names elsewhere in the program could be misleading to program readers.

ALGOL 60 took a different approach to the problem of recognizing the difference between names and special language words: Its definition specified that the reserved words be written with a different font. In computing literature, ALGOL 60 reserved words are usually printed in boldface, with the normal font being used for names. Computers of the time did not allow programmers to specify boldface, or italics, and often not even lowercase letters, so implementors had to invent alternatives. In some cases, the reserved words were delimited by apostrophes. Because the actual form of reserved words in programs was implementation-dependent, porting ALGOL 60 programs was difficult.

4.4   Variables

A program variable is nothing more than an abstraction of a computer memory cell, or collection of cells. Programmers often think of variables as names for memory locations. The great step from machine languages to assembly languages was largely one of replacing absolute numeric memory addresses with names, making programs far more readable, and thus easier to write and maintain. That step also provided an escape from the problem of absolute addressing, because the translator that converted the names to actual addresses also chose actual addresses, for both data operands and instructions.

A variable can be characterized as a sextuple of attributes: (name, address, value, type, lifetime, scope). Although this may seem too formal for such a simple concept, it provides the clearest way to explain the various aspects of variables.

Our discussion of variable attributes will lead to examinations of the important related concepts of aliases, binding times, declarations, type checking, strong typing, scoping rules, and referencing environments.

The name, address, type, and value attributes of variables are discussed in the following subsections. The lifetime and scope attributes are discussed in Sections 4.5.3 and 4.8, respectively.

4.4.1   Name

Variable names are the most common names in programs. They were discussed at length in Section 4.3 in the general context of entity names in programs. Most variables have names, although nameless variables do exist, as discussed in Section 4.5.3.3. Names are often referred to as identifiers.

4.4.2   Address

The address of a variable is the memory address with which it is associated. This association is not as simple as it may at first appear. In many languages it is possible for the same name to be associated with different addresses at different places in the program. For example, a Pascal program can have two procedures, P1 and P2, each of which defines a variable that uses the same name, say SUM. A reference to SUM in P1 is clearly unrelated to a reference to SUM in P2. Similarly, some languages allow the same name to be associated with different addresses at different times during program execution. A recursive Pascal procedure can have multiple versions of each locally declared identifier, one for each activation of the procedure. Finally, if a Pascal procedure, P1, has a local variable, X, and is called by two different procedures, X will likely be associated with a different address in each of the activations of P1. The process of associating variables with addresses is further discussed in Section 4.5.2. An implementation model for procedures and their activations for ALGOL-like languages is discussed in Chapter 9.

4.4.2.1   Aliases

It is possible to have multiple identifiers reference the same address. When more than one variable name can be used to access a single memory location, the names are called **aliases.** Aliasing is a hindrance to readability because it allows a variable to have its value changed by an assignment to a different variable. For example, if variables A and B are aliases, any change to A also changes B, and vice versa. A reader of the program must always remember that A and B are different names for the same memory cell. This is very difficult in practice. Aliasing also causes difficulty for program verification methods.

Aliases can be created in programs in a number of ways. Aliases can be created through procedure parameters in some languages. For example, suppose the Pascal procedure SUB is defined with two parameters of type INTEGER, X and Y, which are transmitted by address. Further, suppose SUB is called with SUB(A, A). During the resulting execution of SUB, X and Y are aliases, referring to the same location defined by A. This and several related kinds of aliasing associated with parameters are discussed in Chapter 8.

In FORTRAN, aliases can be explicitly created with the EQUIVALENCE statement. In fact, aliasing is the sole purpose of the EQUIVALENCE statement. Its general form is

    EQUIVALENCE equiv_list

where equiv_list consists of a list of elements of the form

    (name_1, name_2, . . . , name_n)

EQUIVALENCE means that within each list, every variable is an alias for all the others in the list. For example, in

    EQUIVALENCE (A, B(5), D(1))

the variable A, the fifth element of the B array, and the first element of the D array are all associated with the same memory address. When array elements are involved in EQUIVALENCE statements, all the other elements of the arrays are implicitly included. In the preceding example, the first element of the D array is aliased with the fifth element of the B array. Implicit in this is the aliasing of the sixth element of the B array with the second element of the D array, and so forth.

There are several reasons why language designers include aliasing in languages. The EQUIVALENCE statement of FORTRAN has several uses. When computer memories were small, it was frequently used to enable sharing of that scarce commodity. For example, if a program needed a large array of INTEGER type during part of its execution time and also needed a large array of REAL type during a different part of its execution, and the two uses were mutually exclusive in time, they could share the same block of memory by being made aliases with EQUIVALENCE.

Another use of EQUIVALENCE is to allow a program to refer to the same block of memory through two differently shaped structures. For example, consider the following declarations:

    INTEGER MAT(4,3), COL1(4), COL2(4), COL3(4)
    EQUIVALENCE (MAT(1,1), COL1(1)), (MAT(1,2), COL2(1))
    EQUIVALENCE (MAT(1,3), COL3(1))

The EQUIVALENCE statements here specify that the first element of MAT must coreside with the first element of COL1, and the (1,2) element of MAT must coreside with the first element of COL2, and so forth. Because of the ordering FORTRAN uses for multidimensional arrays, called column major order, COL1 has the same elements as the first column of MAT, COL2 has the same elements as the second column of MAT, and so forth.

The elements of the matrix MAT are accessible either as the single-dimensioned arrays COL1, COL2, and COL3, or through MAT. This would be convenient if one needed the average of each column of MAT and had a subprogram that computed the average of a single-dimensioned array. Such a subprogram could be sent the column arrays, one at a time.

Finally, a matrix can be EQUIVALENCEd to a single-dimensioned array for efficiency reasons. Accesses to the elements of a single-dimensioned array are faster than accesses to the elements of a matrix. So, in cases where elements of a matrix can be processed in column major order, an EQUIVALENCEd array can be used.

Aliases can be created using the variant record structures of Pascal and some of the languages related to Pascal. The aliases created by variant records are meant to save storage by allowing the same locations to be used by different type data. Variant records are discussed at length in Chapter 7.

In languages that have pointer variables, two pointer variables are aliases when they point to the same memory location. Aliasing with pointers is not meant to conserve storage, but rather is simply a side effect of the nature of pointers. This and other problems of pointers are discussed in Chapter 7.

When a language construct creates aliases for the purpose of reusing storage, it can be replaced by a dynamic storage management scheme, which will also allow reuse of storage but not necessarily create aliases.

The time when a variable becomes associated with an address is very important to an understanding of programming languages. This subject is discussed in Section 4.5.3.

4.4.3 Type

The **type** of a variable determines the range of values the variable can have and the set of operations that are defined for variables of the type. For example, the type INTEGER in some FORTRAN implementations specifies a value range of $-32,768$ to $32,767$, and arithmetic operations for addition, subtraction, multiplication, and division, along with some library functions for operations like absolute value.

Floating-point types have value ranges that are defined in terms of precision and range. Precision is the accuracy of the fractional part of a value. Range is a combination of the range of fractions, and, more important, the range of exponents.

As we stated in Section 4.1.2, floating-point types model the real numbers of mathematics. There are several problems with this modeling. In addition to the inability to accurately represent many real values, there is the problem of not including all the integer values in the same implementation, because on many systems integer values occupy the same amount of storage as floating-point values. Because integers do not have exponents, there is space for more digits. For this reason, in many implementations the fraction of floating-point variables stores only about seven decimal digits of accuracy whereas integers store about ten. Another problem with floating-point types is the loss of accuracy through arithmetic operations. For more information on the problems of floating-point notation, see Knuth (1981).

4.4.4 Value

The value of a variable is the contents of the memory cell or cells associated with the variable. It is convenient to think of computer memory in terms of *abstract* cells, rather than physical cells. A cell, or individually addressable part, of most contemporary computer memories is byte-sized, with a byte usually being eight bits in length. This size prevents cells from storing the value of most program variables. We define an abstract memory cell to have the size required by the variable with which it is associated. Although floating-point values may occupy four physical bytes in a particular implementation of a particular language, we think of floating-point values as occupying single abstract memory cells. We consider the value of each simple nonstructured type to occupy a single abstract cell. Henceforth, when we say memory cell, we mean abstract memory cell. We will sometimes use the term **object** to denote the combination of a memory cell and its contents.

The address of a variable is sometimes called its *l*-value, and the value is sometimes called its *r*-value. These names came about because the *l*-value of a variable is required when it is used on the left side of an assignment statement and the *r*-value is required when a variable is used on the right side. To access the *r*-value, the *l*-value must first be determined.

4.5 The Concept of Binding

In a general sense, a **binding** is an association, possibly between an attribute and an entity and possibly between an operation and a symbol. The time at which a binding takes place is called **binding time.** Bindings and binding times are very important concepts in the semantics of programming languages. Bindings can take place at language design time, language implementation time, compile time, load time, or at run time. For example, the asterisk symbol, *, is usually bound to the multiplication operation at language design time. A data type, such as INTEGER in FORTRAN, is bound to a range of possible values at language implementation time. At compile time, a variable in a Pascal program is bound to a particular data type. A variable may be bound to a storage cell when the program is loaded into memory. That same binding does not happen until run time in some cases, as with variables declared in Pascal procedures.

A complete understanding of binding time for the attributes of program entities is a prerequisite for understanding the semantics of a programming language. For example, to understand what a subprogram does, one must understand how the actual parameters in its call are bound to the formal parameters in its definition. To determine the current value of a variable, you may need to know when the variable was bound to storage.

4.5.1 Binding of Attributes to Variables

Because the focus of this chapter is primitive types and variables, the main concern here is the binding of attributes to variables.

A binding is **static** if it occurs before run time and remains unchanged throughout program execution. If it occurs during run time or can change in the course of program execution, it is called **dynamic.** Variables can be bound to attributes at a variety of times, such as compile time, load time, and run time. The physical binding of a variable to a storage cell in a virtual memory environment is complex because the page or segment of the address space in which the cell resides may be moved into memory many times during program execution. In a sense, such variables are bound and unbound, repeatedly. These bindings, however, are maintained by computer hardware, and the changes are invisible to the program and the user. Because they are not important to the discussion, we are not concerned with these hardware bindings. The essential point is to distinguish between static and dynamic bindings.

4.5.2 Type Bindings

Before a variable can be referenced or assigned in a program, it must be bound to a data type. The two important aspects of this binding are how the type is specified and when the binding takes place. Types can be specified statically through some form of explicit or implicit declaration.

4.5.2.1 Variable Declarations

An **explicit declaration** is a statement in a program that lists variable names and declares them to be of a particular type. An **implicit declaration** is a means of associating variables with types through default conventions, instead of declaration statements. In this case, the first appearance of a variable name in a program constitutes its implicit declaration. Both explicit and implicit declarations create static bindings to types.

Most programming languages designed since the middle 1960s require explicit declarations of all variables. Several earlier languages, notably FORTRAN, PL/I, and BASIC, have had some kind of implicit declarations. In FORTRAN, an identifier that appears in a program that is not explicitly declared is implicitly declared according to the following convention: If the identifier begins with one of the letters I, J, K, L, M, or N, it is implicitly declared to be INTEGER type; otherwise, it is implicitly declared to be REAL type. PL/I copied the implicit declaration convention of FORTRAN. BASIC assumes all undeclared variables are floating-point type. Subscripted variables that are undeclared are implicitly declared to be arrays of length 10.

The advantage of implicit declarations is programmer convenience. For example, FORTRAN programmers frequently use variables named I, J, and K for array subscripts and loop variables. Because they are always used as integers, it is considered by some a waste of programmer time to bother to declare them in every program.

On the other hand, implicit declarations can be detrimental to reliability, because they prevent the compilation process from detecting some programmer errors. Variables that are accidentally left undeclared by the programmer are given default types and unexpected attributes, which could cause subtle errors that are difficult to diagnose. For example, consider the following FORTRAN code segment:

```
    INTEGER COUNT
    REAL VALUE
    INSUM = 0
    DO 10 COUNT = 1, 10
      READ VALUE
      INSUM = INSUM + VALUE
 10 CONTINUE
    . . .
```

In this code, the variable INSUM is implicitly declared to be of INTEGER type, because it begins with I and was not explicitly declared. INSUM is meant to contain the sum of the input values. Each input value is read into the REAL type variable VALUE. It is then added to the current value of INSUM, and the sum of the two is truncated to an integer value (because the destination is INTEGER type). Finally, the truncated value is placed in INSUM. The problem is that the sum will be incorrect if the input values have fractional parts, because those fractional parts will be truncated away when the value of the expression INSUM + VALUE is placed in INSUM. Note that this problem is a result of two distinct design choices: implicit declarations and automatic type conversions. If the REAL variable VALUE were not allowed to appear as an operand of the addition operator with the integer operand INSUM, the error would be detected. Instead, the integer operand is automatically converted to floating-point. These mixed type expressions and automatic type conversions are discussed in Chapter 5.

FORTRAN 77 allows the programmer to change the default conventions, or rules, for implicit declarations. This is done with a declaration statement of the form

IMPLICIT type (default characters) {, type (default characters) }

This statement sets the default of all variables whose names begin with the listed letter(s) to the stated type. For example,

IMPLICIT INTEGER (A-K), REAL (L, M)

states that all variables whose names begin with A, B, . . . , K are implicitly declared to be INTEGER type, and all variables whose names begin with the letters L and M are implicitly declared to be REAL type.

4.5.2.2   Dynamic Type Binding

With dynamic type binding, the type is not specified by a declaration statement. Instead, the variable is bound to a type when it is assigned a value in an assignment statement. When the assignment statement is executed, the variable being assigned is bound to the type of the value, variable, or expression on the right side of the assignment.

Languages in which types are dynamically bound are dramatically different from those in which types are statically bound. The primary advantage of dynamic binding of variables to types is that it provides a great deal of programming flexibility. For example, a program to process a list of data in a language that uses dynamic type binding can be written as a generic program, meaning that it is capable of dealing with data of any type. Whatever type data is input will be acceptable, because the variables in which it is to be stored can be bound to the correct type when the data is assigned to the variables after input. By contrast, because of static binding of types, one cannot write a Pascal program to process a list of data without knowing the type of that data.

In APL (Polivka and Pakin, 1975), SNOBOL4 (Griswold and Griswold, 1973), and Smalltalk (Goldberg and Robson, 1983), the binding of a variable to a type is dynamic. For example, if an APL program contains the statement

LIST ← 10.2 5.1 0.0

regardless of the previous type of the variable named LIST, this assignment causes it to become a single-dimensioned array of length 3 of floating-point elements. If the statement

LIST ← 47

followed the assignment, LIST would then become a simple integer variable.

There are two disadvantages to dynamic type binding. First, the error detection capability of the compiler is diminished relative to a compiler for a language with static type bindings, because any two types can appear on opposite sides of the assignment operator. Incorrect types of right sides of assignments are not detected as errors; rather, the type of the left side is simply changed to the incorrect type. For example, suppose that in a particular program I and X are integer variables and Y is a floating-point variable. Further suppose that the program needs the assignment statement

    I : = X

but because of a keying error has

    I : = Y

In a language with dynamic type binding no error is detected by the compiler or run-time system. I is simply changed to floating-point type. But because Y was used instead of the correct variable X, the results are erroneous. In a language with static type binding (and in which it is illegal to assign a floating-point object to an integer variable, such as in Pascal) the compiler would detect the error and the program would not get to execution.

The other disadvantage of dynamic type binding is cost. The cost of implementing dynamic attribute binding is considerable, particularly in execution time. Type checking must be done at run time. Furthermore, every variable must have a descriptor associated with it to maintain the current type. The descriptors must also be of varying size, because more space is needed if the variable is a structured type than if it is a primitive type. Descriptors are discussed in Chapter 7.

Languages that have dynamic type binding for variables are often implemented using interpreters, rather than compilers. This is partially because it is difficult to dynamically change the types of variables in machine code. Furthermore, the time to do dynamic type binding is nicely hidden by the overall time of interpretation so that it seems less costly in that environment. On the other hand, languages with static type bindings are seldom implemented by interpretation, because programs in these languages can be easily translated to very efficient machine code versions.

4.5.3 Storage Bindings and Lifetime

The fundamental character of a programming language is in large part determined by the design of the storage bindings for its variables. It is therefore important to have a clear understanding of these bindings.

The memory cell to which a variable is bound must be somehow taken from a pool of available memory. This process is called **allocation. Deallocation** is the process of placing a memory cell that has been unbound from a variable back into the pool of available memory.

The **lifetime** of a program variable is the time during which the variable is bound to a specific memory location. So the lifetime of a variable begins when it is bound to a specific cell and ends when it is unbound from that cell. To investigate storage bindings of variables, it is convenient to separate variables into four categories, according to their lifetimes. We call these categories static, semidynamic, explicit dynamic, and implicit dynamic. In the following sections we discuss the meanings of these four categories, along with their purposes, advantages, and disadvantages.

4.5.3.1 Static Variables

Static variables are those that are bound to memory cells before execution begins and remain bound to those same memory cells until execution terminates. Variables that are statically bound to storage have several valuable applications to programming. Obviously, globally accessible variables are often used throughout the execution of a program, thus making it reasonable to have them bound to the same storage during that execution. Sometimes it is convenient to have variables that are declared in subprograms be history-sensitive; that is, have them retain values between separate executions of the subprogram. This is a characteristic of a variable that is statically bound to storage.

The greatest advantage of static variables is efficiency. All addressing of static variables can be direct; other kinds of variables often require indirect addressing, which is more costly. Furthermore, no run-time overhead is incurred for allocation and deallocation.

The disadvantage of static binding to storage is reduced flexibility; in particular, recursive subprograms are not allowed.

4.5.3.2 Semidynamic Variables

Semidynamic variables are those whose storage bindings are created when their declaration statements are elaborated, but whose types are statically bound. **Elaboration** of a declaration refers to the storage allocation and binding process indicated by the declaration, which takes place when execution reaches the code to which the declaration is attached. Therefore, elaboration occurs during run time. For example, a Pascal procedure consists of a declaration section and a code section. The declaration section is elaborated just before execution of the code section begins, which happens when the procedure is called. The storage for the variables in the declaration section is allocated at elaboration time and deallocated when the procedure returns control to its caller. The variables declared in a procedure are called **local** variables.

The design of ALGOL 60 and its successor languages allows recursive procedures. To be useful, at least in most cases, recursive procedures require some form of dynamic local storage, so that each active copy of the recursive procedure has its own version of the local variables. These needs are conveniently met by semidynamic variables. Even in the absence of recursion, having semidynamic local storage for procedures is a good idea, because all procedures share the same memory space for their locals. The disadvantages are the run-time overhead of allocation and deallocation, and the fact that locals cannot be history-sensitive.

In versions of FORTRAN prior to FORTRAN 77, all variables were static. The FORTRAN 77 standard (ANSI, 1978) allows implementors to use semidynamic variables for locals, but includes a statement

SAVE list

that allows the programmer to specify that some or all of the variables in the subprogram in which SAVE is placed are to be static. Most implementations of FORTRAN 77 simply make all variables static.

All attributes other than storage are statically bound to semidynamic variables of primitive types. That is not the case for some structured types, as we discuss in Chapter 7. Implementation of allocation/deallocation processes for semidynamic variables is discussed in Chapter 9.

4.5.3.3   Explicit Dynamic Variables

Explicit dynamic variables are nameless objects whose storage is allocated and deallocated by explicit run-time directives specified by the programmer. These variables can only be referenced through pointer variables.

An explicit dynamic variable is created by a call to a system procedure provided for that purpose. Such a procedure has a single parameter, which is a pointer variable. When called, an object, or explicit dynamic variable, of the type that the parameter can reference, is created and the parameter is set to reference it. Note that the type of the explicit dynamic variable can be determined at compile time. An explicit dynamic variable is bound to a type at compile time, but it is bound to storage at the time it is created, which is during run time. In addition to a procedure for creating explicit dynamic variables, some languages include a system procedure for destroying them.

As an example of explicit dynamic variables, consider the following Pascal code segment:

```
type intnode = ^integer;
var anode : intnode;
   . . .
new(anode);
   . . .
dispose(anode);
   . . .
```

In this example, an explicit dynamic variable of integer type is created by the call to the system procedure, new. This variable is then referenced through the pointer, anode. Later, the variable is destroyed by the call to the system procedure, dispose.

Explicit dynamic variables are often used for dynamic structures, such as linked lists and trees, which need to grow and shrink during execution. Such structures can be conveniently built using pointers and explicit dynamic variables.

The disadvantages of explicit dynamic variables are the difficulty of using them correctly and the cost of references, allocations, and deallocations. These considerations, pointer data types, and implementation methods for explicit dynamic variables are discussed at length in Chapter 7.

4.5.3.4   Implicit Dynamic Variables

Implicit dynamic variables are those that are bound to storage when they are assigned values. In fact, all of their attributes are bound every time they are assigned. In a sense, they are just names that adapt to whatever use they are asked to serve. The advantage of this is that such variables have the highest degree of flexibility. The disadvantage is the run-time overhead of maintaining all the dynamic attributes, which could include array subscript types and ranges, among others. Another disadvantage is the loss of some error detection by the compiler, as discussed in Section 4.5.2.2. Examples of implicit dynamic variables in APL also appear in Section 4.5.2.2.

4.6   Type Checking

Type checking is the activity of ensuring that two variables that are involved in some relationship are compatible. The two variables might be the two sides of an assignment, the two operands of an arithmetic operation, or an actual parameter and its corresponding formal subprogram parameter. Two variables are of compatible types if the two types are identical or if the language rules allow one of them to have its value automatically converted to the type of the other.

If all bindings of variables to types are static in a language, then type checking can be done statically. Dynamic type binding requires type checking at run time, which is called dynamic type checking. In some languages, other features of the language discourage static type checking. For example, the FORTRAN 77 definition does not require the actual parameters of a subprogram call to be type-checked with the formal parameters of the associated subprogram definition. This is because all subprograms can be separately compiled without the benefit of any information about any other program unit. Once a FORTRAN 77 subprogram has been compiled, the type information for its formal parameters is discarded. Note that separate compilation itself does not prevent parameter type checking; the FORTRAN 77 definition does not require parameter type checking, so, for efficiency reasons, implementations do not do it. Separate compilation is discussed in Chapter 8.

A different issue of type checking appears when a language allows a storage location to store, at different times, values of different types. This can be done with Pascal variant records and with FORTRAN EQUIVALENCE.

In these cases, type-checking problems of a new sort occur. If uses of variables involved in these constructs are to have their values type-checked, it must be done at run time. Such checking requires the run-time system to maintain the type of the current value of such variables.

The following definition takes into account both of the aspects of type checking that were just discussed. Type checking of two variables determines whether:

1. the types to which they are bound are compatible, and
2. the values to which they are currently bound are of compatible types.

In most cases, the types of the values need not be checked, because they cannot be different from the types of the variables.

Note that although we have discussed type checking in the context of two variables, it can also occur between a variable and a constant, between a variable and an expression value (as in an assignment statement), and even between two constants.

An aspect of type checking not addressed thus far is the checking of subscript ranges of references to array elements. For example, suppose list is an array declared to have a subscript range of 1..100 and there is a reference

```
list[sub]
```

where sub is a variable that can store values outside the range of 1..100. In languages such as Pascal and Ada, this reference is legal only if the current value of sub is in the range of 1..100. Because the subscript range of an array is part of its type, subscript range checking of references to array elements is a form of type checking. Although all of the attributes of an array may be statically bound, the subscript range of element references must be done at run time.

4.7 Strong Typing

One of the concepts of language design that became prominent in the so-called structured programming revolution of the 1970s is **strong typing.** Strong typing is widely acknowledged as being a good idea. Unfortunately, it is often loosely defined and sometimes used in computing literature without being defined at all.

One simple definition of a strongly typed language is: A strongly typed language is one in which each name in a program in the language has a single type associated with it and that type is known at compile time. The essence of this is that all types are statically bound. The weakness of this definition is that it ignores the possibility that a variable's type may be known, but its value may be, at different times, of different types. The following definition takes this problem into account. A programming language is **strongly typed** if:

1. Each variable is statically bound to a single type,
2. all instances of two variables (or a variable and a constant) combined in some operation require that the types of the two be statically checked for compatibility, and
3. when a variable is allowed to store values of more than one type, the type of its value can be checked either statically or dynamically.

The importance of strong typing lies in its ability to detect, at compile time, all programmer misuses of variables that result in type conflicts. A strongly typed language also allows the detection, at run time, of uses of the incorrect type values in variables that can store more than one type value.

FORTRAN 77 is not strongly typed because the relationship between actual and formal parameters, as stated previously, is not type-checked. Also, the use of EQUIVALENCE between variables of different types allows a variable of one type to refer to a value of a different type, without the system being able to check the type of the value when one of the EQUIVALENCEd variables is referenced or assigned. In fact, type checking of EQUIVALENCEd variables would eliminate most of their usefulness.

Pascal is nearly strongly typed, but fails in its design of variant records, because it allows omission of the tag that records the current type of a variable, which provides the means of checking for the correct value types. We discuss variant records and their potential problems in Chapter 7. Early versions of Pascal also fail in that the parameters of procedures and functions passed themselves as parameters cannot be statically type-checked. This problem is discussed in Chapter 8.

Modula-2 is not a strongly typed language, because its design of variant records is like that of Pascal. Furthermore, it has a type that intentionally avoids type checking, named WORD.

The Ada language is strongly typed. References to variables in variant records are dynamically checked for correct type values. This is much better than Pascal and Modula-2, where checking is not even possible, much less required. To breach the Ada type-checking rules, a programmer can specifically request that type checking be suspended for a particular type conversion. This temporary suspension of type checking can only be done using the library function UNCHECKED_CONVERSION. This function, of which there can be a version for every data type, takes a variable of its type as its parameter and returns the bit string that is the current value of that variable. No actual conversion takes place; it is merely a means of extracting the value of a variable of one type and using it as if it were of a different type. This can be useful for user-defined storage allocation and deallocation operations, in which addresses are manipulated as integers but must be used as pointers. Because no checking is done in UNCHECKED_CONVERSION, it is the programmer's responsibility to ensure that the use of a value gotten from it is meaningful.

Some languages, such as APL and SNOBOL4, because of their dynamic type binding, allow only dynamic type checking. It is much better to detect errors at compile time than at run time, because the earlier correction will always be less costly. The penalty for static checking is reduced programmer flexibility. Fewer shortcuts and tricks are possible. Such techniques, though, are now generally held in quite low esteem.

4.8   Scope

One of the most important factors having an effect on the understanding of variables is scope. The **scope** of a program variable is the range of statements over which the variable is visible.

A variable is **visible** in a statement if it can be referenced by its name in that statement. The scope rules of a language determine how a particular occurrence of a name is associated with a variable. In particular, scope rules determine how references to variables declared outside the currently executing procedure are associated with their declarations, and thus their attributes. A complete knowledge of these rules for a language is therefore essential to being able to write or read programs in that language.

As defined in Section 4.5.3.2, a variable is local in a program unit if it is declared there. The **nonlocal variables** of a program unit are those that are visible within the program unit but are not declared in the unit.

4.8.1   Static Scope

ALGOL 60 introduced a method of implicit access to nonlocal variables called **static scope,** which has been copied by most contemporary imperative languages. Static scope is thus named because the scope of a variable can be statically determined—that is, determined prior to execution.

Individual static scopes in most imperative languages are associated with program unit definitions. In some languages, however, collections of statements within program units can also create new scopes, as we explain later in this section. For now, however, we assume that all scopes are associated with program units. Furthermore, we assume that the program units are procedures. In this chapter we also assume that static scoping is the only method of accessing nonlocal variables in the languages under discussion. This is not true for all languages that use static scoping, but the assumption simplifies the discussion here. Additional methods used in languages that have static scoping are discussed in Chapter 8.

All procedures in a static scoped language are nested inside the main program, and procedures can also be nested inside other procedures. The main program and all procedures create their own scopes. This creates a hierarchy of scopes in a program.

When a reference to a variable is found by a compiler for a static scoped language, the attributes of the variable are determined by finding its declaration. This process can be thought of in the following way. Suppose a reference is made to a variable X in procedure A. The correct declaration is found by first searching the declarations of procedure A. If no declaration is found for the variable there, the search continues in the declarations of the procedure that declared procedure A, which is called its **static parent.** If a declaration of X is not found there, the search continues to the next larger enclosing unit (the unit that declared A's parent), and so forth, until a declaration for X is found, or the main program's declarations have been searched without success. In that case, an undeclared variable error has been detected. The static parent of procedure A, and its static parent, and so forth up to and including the main program, are called the **static ancestors** of A. Implementation techniques for static scoping, which are discussed in Chapter 9, are much more efficient than the process just described.

Consider the following Pascal procedure:

```
procedure BIG;
   var X : integer;
   procedure SUB1;
      var X : integer;
      begin
      SUB2
      end;
   procedure SUB2;
      begin
      ... X ...
      end;
   begin
   SUB1
   end;
```

Procedure BIG calls SUB1, which calls SUB2. Under static scoping, the reference to the variable X in SUB2 is to the X declared in the procedure BIG, because that X is the first found in (1) a search of the procedure in which the reference occurs, SUB2, and then (2) a search of the static ancestor units, in order of smallest first. In this example, the declarations of SUB2 are searched first. When no declaration for X is found there, the search moves to the static parent of SUB2, which is BIG, where a declaration for X is found.

The presence of predefined names complicates this process somewhat. For example, Pascal systems include a library of predefined subprograms for commonly needed functions, such as sin, cos, and writeln. In some languages, these are like keywords, and can be redefined by the user. In these cases, the library names are used only if the user program does not contain a redefinition. In other languages, the predefined names are reserved, which means the search for the meaning of a given name begins with the list of predefined names, even before the local scope declarations are checked.

In languages that use static scoping, some variable declarations can be hidden from some procedures. For example, consider the following skeletal Pascal program:

```
program MAIN;
  var X : integer;
  procedure SUB1;
    var X : integer;
    begin
    ..X..
    end;
  begin
  SUB1;
  end.
```

The reference to X in SUB1 is to SUB1's declared X. In some static scoped languages, such as Pascal, the X of the main program is hidden from the code of SUB1. In general, a declaration for a variable effectively hides any declaration of a variable with the same name in a larger enclosing scope.

In Ada, hidden variables from ancestor scopes can be accessed with selective references, which include the ancestor scope's name. For example, in the preceding program, the X declared in MAIN can be accessed in SUB1 by the reference MAIN.X.

4.8.2 Blocks

Some languages allow new static scopes to be defined in the midst of executable code. This powerful concept, introduced by ALGOL 60, allows a section of code to have its own variables, which are called local variables, that have their storage allocated when the section is entered and deallocated when the section is exited. For example, in the Ada language we could have the following:

```
...
declare TEMP : INTEGER;
  begin
  TEMP := FIRST;
  FIRST := SECOND;
  SECOND := TEMP;
  end;
...
```

This construct is called a **block.** It is the origin of the phrase **block-structured language.** Although Pascal and Modula-2 are called block-structured languages, they do not include these nonprocedure blocks.

In C, the scopes of subprograms cannot be nested because subprograms cannot be defined inside other subprograms. However, C allows any compound statement (a statement sequence surrounded by matched braces) to have declarations and thus define a new scope. Every compound statement in C can potentially be a block. This characteristic is inherited from ALGOL 60 and ALGOL 68. For example, if list were an integer array, we could have:

```
if (list[i] < list[j])
  { int temp;
    temp = list[i];
    list[i] = list[j];
    list[j] = temp;
  }
```

4.8.3 Evaluation

Static scoping provides a method of nonlocal access that works well in many situations. However, it is not without its problems. Consider the program whose skeletal structure is shown in Figure 4.1.

This program contains an overall scope for MAIN, with two procedures that define scopes inside MAIN, A and B. Inside A, there are scopes for the procedures C and D. Inside B is the scope of procedure E. We assume that the necessary data and procedure access determined the structure of this program. The procedure access is assumed to be MAIN calls A and B, A calls C and D, and B calls A and E.

It is convenient to view the structure of the program as a tree in which each node represents a procedure, and thus a scope. A tree representation of the program of Figure 4.1 is shown in Figure 4.2.

The structure of this program may appear to be a very natural program organization that clearly reflects the design needs. However, a graph of the

Figure 4.1
The structure of a program

Figure 4.2
The tree structure of
the program in Figure
4.1

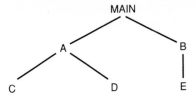

Figure 4.3
The potential call
graph of the program
in Figure 4.1

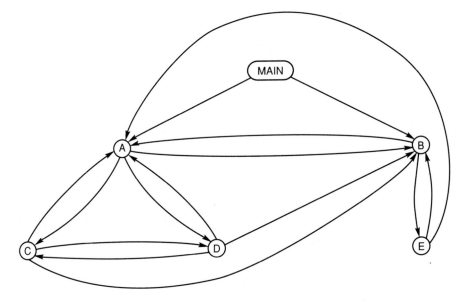

potential procedure calls of this system, as shown in Figure 4.3, shows that
a great deal of calling opportunity beyond that required is possible. (We
assume here that procedures need not textually precede calls to them.)

Figure 4.4 shows the desired calls of the example program. The difference between Figures 4.3 and 4.4 illustrates the number of possible calls
that are not desirable.

Too much data access is another problem with static scoping. For example, all variables declared in MAIN are visible to all of the procedures, whether
or not that is desired, and there is no way to avoid it.

To illustrate another kind of problem with static scoping, consider the
following scenario. Suppose that after the program has been developed and
tested, a modification of its specification is required. In particular, suppose
that procedure E must now gain access to some variables of the scope of D.
One way to provide that access is to move E inside the scope of D. But then
it can no longer access the scope of B, which it presumably needs (otherwise, why was it there). Another solution is to move the variables defined

Figure 4.4
The graph of the
desirable calls in the
program in Figure 4.1

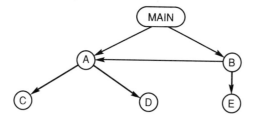

in D that are needed by E into MAIN. This would allow access by all the procedures, which would be more than is needed, and which thus creates the possibility of many incorrect accesses. For example, a misspelled identifier in a procedure can be taken as a reference to an identifier in some enclosing scope, instead of being detected as an error. Furthermore, suppose the variable that is moved to MAIN is named X. X is needed by D and E. But suppose that there is a variable named X declared in A. That would hide the correct X from its original owner, D. One final problem with moving the declaration of X to MAIN is that it is harmful to readability to have the declaration of variables so far from their uses.

A similar problem occurs because static scoping also determines procedure access. In the tree of Figure 4.2, suppose that due to some specification change, procedure E needed to call the procedure D. This could only be accomplished by moving D to nest directly in MAIN, assuming that it was also needed by either A or C. It would then also lose access to the variables defined in A. This solution, when used repeatedly, results in programs that begin with long lists of low-level utility procedures.

Thus, getting around the restrictions of static scoping can lead to program designs that bear little resemblance to the original. Designers are encouraged to use far more globals than are necessary. All procedures can end up being nested at the same level, in the main program, using globals instead of deeper levels of nesting. Moreover, the final design may be awkward, contrived, and not reflect the underlying conceptual design. These and other defects of static scoping are discussed in detail in Clarke, Wileden, and Wolf (1980). One solution to the problems of static scoping is the module concept used by Modula-2 and Ada, which is discussed in Chapter 8.

4.8.4 Dynamic Scope

The scope of variables in APL, SNOBOL4, and some dialects of LISP is dynamic. **Dynamic scoping** is based on the calling sequence of subprograms, not on their spatial relationship to each other. Thus, the scope is determined at run time.

Consider again the procedure BIG from Section 4.8.1, which is shown again here:

```
procedure BIG;
  var X : integer;
  procedure SUB1;
    var X : integer;
    begin
    SUB2
    end;
  procedure SUB2;
    begin
    ... X ...
    end;
  begin
  SUB1
  end;
```

Assume that dynamic scoping rules apply to nonlocal references. The meaning of the identifier X referenced in SUB2 is dynamic—it cannot be determined at compile time.

The following describes one way the correct meaning of X can be determined at run time. As in the static case, the search begins with the local declarations, but that is where the similarity ends. When the search of local declarations fails, the declarations of the dynamic parent, or calling procedure, are searched. The search continues until a declaration for X is found. If none is found, it is a run-time error. In our example, the search proceeds from the local procedure, SUB2, to its caller, SUB1, where a declaration for X is found. So the reference to X in SUB2, in this case, is to the X declared in SUB1. If SUB2 had been called from BIG, the reference would have been to the X declared in BIG.

4.8.5 Evaluation

The effect of dynamic scoping on programming is profound. The correct attributes of nonlocal variables visible to a program statement cannot be determined statically. Furthermore, such variables are not always the same. A statement in a subprogram that contains a reference to a nonlocal variable can refer to a different variable every time the statement is executed. Several kinds of programming problems follow directly from dynamic scoping.

First, during the time span beginning when a subprogram begins its execution and ending when that execution ends, the local variables of the subprogram are all visible to any other executing subprogram regardless of its textual proximity. There is no way to protect local variables from this accessibility. Subprograms are always executed in the immediate environment of the caller. Because of this, dynamic scoping results in less reliable programs than static scoping.

A second problem that results from dynamic scoping is the inability to statically type check references to nonlocals. This results from the inability to statically determine the declaration for a variable referenced as a non-local. Dynamic scoping also makes programs much more difficult to read, because the calling sequence of subprograms must be known in order to determine the meaning of references to nonlocal variables. This can be virtually impossible for a human reader.

On the other hand, dynamic scoping can be used to advantage in programming as well. For example, with dynamic scoping subprograms inherit the context of their callers; that is, any variable declared in the caller that is not also declared in the called subprogram is visible in the called subprogram. This can be a convenient method of communication between program units, although it is less safe than other methods.

Implementation methods for both static and dynamic scoping are discussed in Chapter 9.

4.9 Scope and Lifetime

Sometimes the scope and lifetime of a variable seem to be related. For example, consider a variable that is declared in a Pascal procedure that contains no procedure definitions. The scope of such a variable is from its declaration to the **end** reserved word of the procedure. The lifetime of that variable is the period of time beginning when the procedure is entered and ending when execution of the procedure reaches the **end**. Although the scope and lifetime of the variable are clearly not the same because static scope is a textual, or spatial, concept whereas lifetime is a temporal concept, they at least appear to be related in this case.

This apparent relationship between scope and lifetime is not present in other situations. In FORTRAN, for example, variables that are declared in subprograms are statically bound to the scopes of those subprograms, and usually are also statically bound to storage. So, their scope is static and local to the subprogram, but their lifetimes extend over the entire execution of the program.

Scope and lifetime are also unrelated when subprogram calls are involved. Consider the following Pascal-like program segment:

```
program EXAMPLE;
  procedure PRINTHEADER;

    . . .
    end;   {of PRINTHEADER}
  procedure COMPUTE;
    var SUM : integer;
    begin

    . . .

    PRINTHEADER;
    . . .

    end;   {of COMPUTE}
  begin

    . . .

  end;
```

The scope of the variable SUM is completely contained within the COMPUTE procedure. It does not extend to the body of the procedure PRINTHEADER, although PRINTHEADER executes in the midst of the execution of COMPUTE. The lifetime of SUM does extend over the time during which PRINTHEADER executes. Whatever storage location SUM is bound to before the call to PRINTHEADER, that binding will continue during and after the execution of PRINTHEADER.

4.10 Referencing Environments

The **referencing environment** of a program statement is the collection of all scopes that have declared variables that are visible in the statement. The referencing environment of a statement is needed while that statement is being compiled, so that code and data structures can be created to allow references to variables from other scopes during run time. Techniques for such references are discussed in Chapter 9.

The referencing environment of a statement in a statically scoped language is its local scope plus the collection of all of its ancestor scopes. In Pascal, where scopes are created only by procedure definitions, the referencing environment of a statement is the local procedure scope, plus all of the scopes of the procedures in which it is nested, plus the program scope. Each procedure definition creates a new scope, and thus a new environment. Consider the following Pascal skeletal program:

```
program EXAMPLE;
  . . .
  procedure SUB1;
    var X, Y : integer;
    . . .                    ←───────────────1
    end;   {of SUB1}
  procedure SUB2;
    var X : integer;
    . . .
    procedure SUB3;
      var X : integer;
      . . .                  ←───────────────2
      end;    {of SUB3}
    begin
    . . .                    ←───────────────3
    end;    {of SUB2}
  begin
    . . .                    ←───────────────4
  end.
```

The referencing environments of the indicated program points are:

POINT	REFERENCING ENVIRONMENT
1	SUB1 and EXAMPLE
2	SUB3, SUB2, and EXAMPLE
3	SUB2 and EXAMPLE
4	EXAMPLE

Now consider the variable declarations of this skeletal program. First note that although the scope of SUB1 is at a higher level (it is less deeply nested) than SUB3, the scope of SUB1 is not a static ancestor of SUB3, so SUB3 does not have access to the variables declared in SUB1. There is a good reason for this. The variables declared in SUB1 are semidynamic, so they are not bound to storage if SUB1 is not in execution. Because SUB3 can be in execution when SUB1 is not, it cannot be allowed to access variables in SUB1, which would not necessarily be bound to storage during the execution of SUB3.

A subprogram is **active** if its execution has begun but has not yet terminated. The referencing environment of a statement in a dynamically scoped language is the local scope plus the scopes of all other subprograms that are currently active. Once again, some variables in the referencing environment can be hidden. Recent subprogram activations can have declarations for variables that hide variables with the same names in previous subprogram activations.

4.11 Named Constants

A **named constant** is a variable that is bound to a value only at the time it is bound to storage; its value cannot be changed by assignment or by an input statement. Named constants are useful as aids to readability and to improve program reliability. Readability can be improved, for example, by using the name PI instead of the constant 3.14159.

Another advantageous use of named constants is in programs that process a fixed number of data values, say 100. Such programs usually use the constant 100 in a number of locations, for declaring array subscript ranges and for loop control limits. Consider the following skeletal Pascal program segment:

```
program EXAMPLE;
  type
    intarray = array [1..100] of integer;
    realarray = array [1..100] of real;
  . . .
  begin
  . . .
  for index := 1 to 100 do
    begin
    . . .
    end;
  . . .
  for index := 1 to 100 do
    begin
    . . .
    end;
  . . .
  end.
```

When this program must be modified to deal with a different number of data values, all occurrences of 100 must be found and changed. On a large program, this can be tedious and error-prone. An easier and more reliable method is to use a named constant, as in

```
program EXAMPLE;
  const LENGTH = 100;
  type
    intarray = array [1..LENGTH] of integer;
    realarray = array [1..LENGTH] of real;
  . . .
  begin
  . . .
  for index := 1 to LENGTH do
    begin
    . . .
    end;
  . . .
  for index := 1 to LENGTH do
    begin
    . . .
    end;
  . . .
  end.
```

Now, when the LENGTH must be changed, only one line must be changed, regardless of the number of times it is used in the program. This is another example of the benefits of abstraction. The name LENGTH is an abstraction for the number of elements in some arrays and the number of iterations in some loops. This illustrates how named constants can aid modifiability.

Pascal named constant declarations require simple values on the right side of the = operator. However, Modula-2 allows constant expressions to be used. These constant expressions can contain previously declared named constants, constant values, and operators. The reason for the restriction to constants and constant expressions in Pascal and Modula-2, respectively, is that both use static binding of values to named constants. Named constants in languages that use static binding of values are sometimes called **manifest** constants.

The Ada language allows dynamic binding of values to named constants. This allows expressions containing variables to be assigned to constants in the declarations. For example, the Ada statement

```
LENGTH : constant INTEGER := 2 * SIZE + 1
```

declares LENGTH to be an integer type named constant whose value is set to the value of the expression 2 * SIZE + 1, where the value of the variable SIZE must be visible when LENGTH is allocated and bound to its value. Ada also allows named constants of enumeration and structured types, which are discussed in Chapter 7.

4.12 Variable Initialization

The discussion of binding values to named constants naturally leads to the topic of initialization of variables, because binding a value to a named constant is the same process, except that it is permanent.

In many instances it is convenient for variables to have values before the code of the program or subprogram in which they are declared begins executing. The binding of a variable to a value at the time it is bound to storage is called **initialization.** If the variable is statically bound to storage, binding and initialization occur before run time. If the storage binding is dynamic, then initialization is also dynamic.

In FORTRAN, initial values of variables can be specified in a DATA statement, as in

```
INTEGER SUM
DATA SUM /0/
```

which initializes SUM to zero. The actual initialization takes place at compile time in this case. Once execution begins, SUM is like any other variable.

In Ada, initial values of variables can be specified in the declaration statement, as in

```
procedure EXAMPLE is
SUM : INTEGER := 0;
. . .
begin
. . .
end EXAMPLE;
```

In ALGOL 68, the only syntactic difference between the declaration of a variable that is initialized and that of a named constant is that the = is used for constants and the := is used for variables. The declarations

```
int first := 10;
int second = 10;
```

state that first is a variable with an initial value of 10, but second is a named constant with a fixed value of 10. This use of very similar symbols, = and :=, to specify two quite different meanings, is a violation of the design principle that constructs that look alike should have the same meanings.

In Ada, the only syntactic difference between a named constant declaration and a variable declaration with initialization is the reserved word **constant.** For example, consider:

```
LIMIT : constant INTEGER := OLD_LIMIT + 1;
COUNT : INTEGER := OLD_COUNT + 1;
```

In both cases, the variables used in the expressions can be either named constants or variables that are visible when the declarations are elaborated.

This use of the reserved word **constant** is a much better design than ALGOL 68's use of = because it is syntactically very different, and also connotative.

Neither Pascal nor Modula-2 provides a way to initialize variables, except at run time with assignment statements.

In general, initialization occurs only once for static variables, but it occurs with every allocation for dynamically allocated variables, such as the local variables in an Ada procedure.

SUMMARY

The primitive data types of most imperative languages include numeric and Boolean types, which are often directly supported by hardware.

The form of the names of a language can impact both the readability and writability of the language. The relationship of names to special words, which are either reserved words or keywords, is also a significant design decision.

Variables can be characterized by the sextuple of attributes: (name, address, value, type, lifetime, scope).

Aliases are two or more names bound to the same storage address. They are regarded as detrimental to reliability, but are difficult to eliminate entirely from a language.

Binding is the association of attributes with program entities. Knowledge of the binding times of attributes to entities is essential to understanding the semantics of programming languages. Binding can be static or dynamic. Declarations, either explicit or implicit, provide a means of specifying the static binding of variables to types. In general, dynamic bindings allow greater flexibility but at the expense of readability, efficiency, and reliability.

Variables can be separated into four categories by considering their lifetimes. These are static, semidynamic, explicit dynamic, and implicit dynamic.

Strong typing is, loosely, the concept of requiring variables to be of single and statically known types. The advantage of strong typing is increased reliability.

Static scoping has been a central feature of ALGOL 60 and all of its descendants. It provides an efficient method of allowing visibility of non-local variables and subprograms. The referencing environment of a statement is the collection of all of its static ancestor scopes. Dynamic scoping provides more flexibility, but again at the expense of readability, reliability, and efficiency.

Named constants are simply variables that are bound to values only when they are bound to storage. Initialization is the binding of a variable to a value at the time the variable is bound to storage.

BIBLIOGRAPHY

ANSI. (1978) *American National Standard Programming Language FORTRAN*. ANSI X3.9-1978, American National Standard Institute, New York.

Clarke, L.A., J.C. Wileden, and A.L. Wolf. (1980) "Nesting in Ada Is for the Birds." *ACM SIGPLAN Notices*, Vol. 15, No. 11, pp. 139–145.

Gehani, N. (1983) *Ada: An Advanced Introduction*. Prentice-Hall, Englewood Cliffs, NJ.

Goldberg, A., and D. Robson. (1983) *Smalltalk-80: The Language and Its Implementation*. Addison-Wesley, Reading, MA.

Griswold, R.E., and M.T. Griswold. (1973) *A SNOBOL4 Primer*. Prentice-Hall, Englewood Cliffs, NJ.

Knuth, D.E. (1981) *The Art of Computer Programming*, Vol. II. 2d ed. Addison-Wesley, Reading, MA.

Polivka, R.P., and S. Pakin. (1975) *APL: The Language and Its Usage*. Prentice-Hall, Englewood Cliffs, NJ.

PROBLEM SET

1. Decide which of the following identifier forms is most readable, and then support that decision:

   ```
   SumOfSales
   sum_of_sales
   ```

2. State the arguments for and against using reserved words instead of keywords in a programming language.

3. What are the arguments for and against representing Boolean values as single bits in memory?

4. Why does a decimal value waste memory space? (Consider the storage required to store five-digit decimal numbers as binary integers versus as decimal values.)

5. One common use of FORTRAN's EQUIVALENCE is the following: A large array of numeric values is made available to a subprogram as a parameter. The array contains many different unrelated variables, rather than a collection of repetitions of the same variable. It is represented as an array to reduce the number of names that need to be passed as parameters. Within the subprogram, a lengthy EQUIVALENCE statement is used to create connotative names as aliases to the various array elements, which increases the readability of the code of the subprogram. Is this a good idea, or not? What alternatives to aliasing are available?

6. Can FORTRAN's IMPLICIT statement be considered an aid to reliability? How?

7. Dynamic type binding is closely related to implicit dynamic variables. Explain this relationship.

8. Describe a situation in which a history-sensitive variable in a subprogram is useful.

9. Look up the definition of strongly typed as given in Gehani (1983) and compare it with the definition given in this chapter. How do they differ?

10. Consider the following Pascal skeletal program:

    ```
    program main;
      var x : integer;
      procedure sub1;
        var x : integer;
    ```

```
        procedure sub2;
            . . .
          end;   { sub2 }
      . . .
      end;   { sub1 }
  procedure sub3;
      var x : integer;
          . . .
      end;   { sub3 }
  . . .
  end.
```

Assume that the execution of this program is in the following unit order:

    main calls sub1
    sub1 calls sub3
    sub3 calls sub2

a. Assuming static scoping, which declaration of x is the correct one for a reference to x in:

    i. sub1   *x in sub1*   *x in sub1*

    ii. sub2   *x in sub1*   *x in sub3*

    iii. sub3   *x in sub3*   *x in sub3*

    iv. main   *x in main*   *x in main*

b. Repeat part a, but assume dynamic scoping.

11. Assume the following program was compiled and executed using static scoping rules. What value of X is printed in procedure A? Under dynamic scoping rules, what value of X is printed in procedure A? *(5)* *(10)*

```
program MAIN;
  var X : integer;
  procedure A;
    begin
    writeln('X =', X)
    end;
  procedure B;
    var X : integer;
    begin
    X := 10;
    A;
    end;   { of procedure B }
  begin   { of MAIN }
  X := 5;
  B
  end.
```

12. Consider the following program:

```
program MAIN;
  var x, y, z : integer;
  procedure SUB1;
    var a, y, z : integer;
    procedure SUB2;
      var a, b, z : integer;
```

SUB1
X, MAIN
a, y, z SUB1

SUB2
a b z SUB2
y SUB1
x MAIN
SUB3
a x w SUB3
y z MAIN

```
      begin
         . . .
      end;
      begin
         . . .
      end;
   procedure SUB3;
      var a, x, w : integer;
      begin
         . . .
      end;
   begin
      . . .
   end.
```

List all the variables, along with the program units where they are declared, that are visible in the bodies of SUB1, SUB2, and SUB3, assuming static scoping is used.

13. Consider the following program:

```
program MAIN;
   var x, y, z : integer;
   procedure SUB1;
      var a, y, z : integer;
      begin
         . . .
      end;
   procedure SUB2;
      var a, b, z : integer;
      begin
         . . .
      end;
   procedure SUB3;
      var a, x, w : integer;
      begin
         . . .
      end;
   begin
      . . .
   end.
```

Handwritten annotations:

VAR — where declared

a) a, x, w — SUB3
   b, z — SUB2
   y — SUB1

b) a x w — SUB3
   y, z — SUB1

Given the following calling sequences, and the fact that dynamic scoping is used, what variables are visible during execution of the last subprogram activated? Include with each visible variable the name of the unit where it is declared.

a. MAIN calls SUB1; SUB1 calls SUB2; SUB2 calls SUB3.
b. MAIN calls SUB1; SUB1 calls SUB3.
c. MAIN calls SUB2; SUB2 calls SUB3; SUB3 calls SUB1.
d. MAIN calls SUB3; SUB3 calls SUB1.
e. MAIN calls SUB1; SUB1 calls SUB3; SUB3 calls SUB2.
f. MAIN calls SUB3; SUB3 calls SUB2; SUB2 calls SUB1.

Key Concepts

- Operator evaluation order
- Operand evaluation order
- Functional side effects in expressions
- Operator overloading
- Mixed-mode expressions and coercion
- Relational and Boolean expressions
- Short-circuit evaluation
- Multiple targets of assignments
- Conditional parts of assignments
- Assigning operators
- Unary operator assignments
- Assignment statements as operands
- Mixed-mode assignment

5

EXPRESSIONS AND THE ASSIGNMENT STATEMENT

As we stated in Chapter 1, the essence of the imperative programming languages is the dominant role of variables, assignment statements, and iteration. We now embark on a discussion of the second of these three characteristics, assignment statements.

In the environment of von Neumann architecture, assignment is the most fundamental statement. It causes values to move from the memory to the processor, to be operated upon by the processor, and for the resulting value to be moved back to the memory.

To understand expression evaluation, it is necessary to be familiar with the orders of operator and operand evaluation. The operator evaluation order of expressions is governed by the associativity and precedence rules of the language. Although the value of an expression sometimes depends on it, the order of operand evaluation in expressions is often unstated by language designers, a situation which leads to programs that produce different results in different implementations. Other issues in expression design are type mismatches, coercions, and short-circuit evaluation.

Simple assignment statements specify an expression to be evaluated, the assignment operator, and a target location in which to place the result of the expression evaluation. As detailed in this chapter, there are a number of variations on this basic form.

5.1   Arithmetic Expressions

Automatic evaluation of arithmetic expressions was one of the primary goals of the first programming languages. Most of the characteristics of arithmetic expressions in programming languages were inherited from conventions that had evolved in mathematics. Arithmetic expressions are combinations of operators, operands, parentheses, and function calls. The operators can be **unary,** meaning they have a single operand, or **binary,** meaning they have two operands.

The purpose of an arithmetic expression is to specify an arithmetic computation. These computations involve evaluation of operand specifications and execution of arithmetic operations on those operands. In the following sections we investigate the common design details of arithmetic expressions in the imperative languages.

5.1.1   Operator Evaluation Order

The evaluation order of an arithmetic expression depends on the order in which the operators and operands are evaluated. First, we investigate the order of evaluation of operators.

5.1.1.1 Precedence

The value of an expression depends, at least in part, on the order of evaluation of the operators in the expression. Consider the following expression:

```
A + B * C
```

If we assume the variables A, B, and C have the values 3, 4, and 5, respectively, we can see how operator evaluation order affects the result. If evaluated left to right, the result is 35. If evaluated right to left, the result is 23.

Instead of simply evaluating the order from left to right or right to left, mathematics has evolved the concept of placing operators in a hierarchy of importance, and basing part of the evaluation order of expressions on this hierarchy. For example, multiplication is considered to be of higher priority than addition, so that in our example expression, the multiplication would be evaluated first.

The **operator precedence** rules for expression evaluation define the order in which adjacent operators of different precedence levels are evaluated. The operator precedence rules for expressions are based on the hierarchy of operator importance, as seen by the language designer. The operator precedence rules of most common imperative languages are similar. In FORTRAN, for example, the exponentiation operator has the highest precedence, followed by multiplication and division on the same level, followed by addition and subtraction on the same level.

Many languages also include unary versions of addition and subtraction. Unary addition is called the identity operator because it has no associated operation and thus has no effect on its operand. Unary minus, on the other hand, does have an effect on its operand: It changes the operand's sign. Unary addition and subtraction operators in the Ada language have a precedence level that is between binary addition and multiplication. In the Ada expression

```
- A + B * C ** 2
```

the evaluation order is: exponentiation first, followed by multiplication, followed by unary minus, followed by addition.

The identity and unary minus operators can appear in Ada expressions either at the beginning, or anywhere inside the expression as long as they are parenthesized to prevent them from being adjacent to another operator. For example,

```
A + (- B) * C
```

is legal, but

```
A + - B * C
```

is not.

APL is alone in that all of its operators are at the same level of precedence, as illustrated in the next section.

Precedence accounts for only some of the rules for the order of operator evaluation, as discussed in the following section.

5.1.1.2   Associativity

Consider the expression

```
A - B + C - D
```

If all the operators have the same level of precedence, the precedence rules say nothing about the order of evaluation of the operators in this expression.

When an expression contains two adjacent occurrences of operators with the same level of precedence, the question of which operator is evaluated first is answered by the **associativity** rules of the language. An operator can either have left or right associativity, meaning that the leftmost occurrence is evaluated first or the rightmost occurrence is evaluated first, respectively.

Most contemporary imperative programming languages use similar rules of associativity. Associativity is typically left to right, with the exception of the exponentiation operator in some of the languages that provide it. In the FORTRAN expression

```
A - B + C
```

the left operator is evaluated first. In the FORTRAN expression

```
A ** B ** C
```

the right operator is evaluated first.

As stated in Section 5.1.1.1, in APL all operators have the same level of precedence. Thus, the order of evaluation of operators in APL expressions is determined entirely by the associativity rule, which is right to left for all operators. For example, in the expression

```
A × B + C
```

the addition operator is evaluated first, followed by the multiplication (× is the APL multiplication operator.). If A = 3, B = 4, and C = 5, the value of this APL expression is 27.

Many compilers make use of the fact that most arithmetic operators are mathematically associative, meaning that the associativity rules have no impact on the value of an expression containing only those operators. For example, addition is mathematically associative, so the value of the expression

```
A + B + C
```

does not depend on the order of operator evaluation. In some situations, if the compiler is allowed to reorder the evaluation of operators, it may be able to produce slightly faster code for expression evaluation.

There are pathological situations in which floating-point addition on a computer is not associative. For example, suppose that 100,000 values are to be added together and that one of them is large, say 10,000,000, and all of the others are less than 1. Further suppose that the computer on which the computation is to be done stores seven significant digits in its floating-point types. If each of the small values is added to the large value, one at a time, they will not change its value at all, because none is as large as the least significant digit of the large number. However, if all of the small numbers are added together first, and then the result is added to the large value, a far more accurate sum will be computed.

Notice that this example would not be a problem for a compiler that can reorder operators in an expression, because the addition operations would be done in a loop, not in a single expression of 100,000 operations. However, less exaggerated examples are possible.

5.1.1.3 Parentheses

Programmers can alter the precedence and associativity rules by placing parentheses in expressions. A parenthesized part of an expression has precedence over its adjacent unparenthesized parts. For example, although multiplication has precedence over addition, in the expression

```
(A + B)  *  C
```

the addition will be evaluated first. Mathematically, this is perfectly natural. In this expression, the first operand of the multiplication operator is not available until the addition in the parenthesized subexpression is evaluated.

Languages that allow parentheses in arithmetic expressions could dispense with all precedence rules, and simply associate all operators left to right or right to left. The programmer would specify the desired order of evaluation with parentheses. This would be simple, because neither the author nor the readers of programs would need to remember any precedence or associativity rules. The down side of this scheme is that it makes writing expressions a more tedious process. Yet this was the choice made by Ken Iverson, the designer of APL.

5.1.2 Operand Evaluation Order

Another less commonly discussed design characteristic of the expressions of a language is the order of evaluation of operands. Variables in expressions are evaluated by fetching their values from memory. Constants are sometimes evaluated the same way. In other cases, a constant may actually be part of the machine language instruction, and therefore it requires no memory fetch. As we saw in the last section, if an operand is a parenthesized expression, then all operators it contains must be evaluated before its value can be used as an operand. The most interesting case of operand evaluation arises when the expression contains an operand that is a call to a function.

5.1.2.1 Side Effects

In most circumstances, the order of operand evaluation in an expression is irrelevant to the final expression value. However, if one operand in an expression (that has more than one operand) is a function call and functions are allowed to have side effects, then operand evaluation order can be important. A **side effect** in a function, called a **functional side effect,** occurs when the function changes one of its parameters, or changes some other variable that is declared outside the function but is accessible in the function.

Consider the expression

```
A + FUN(A)
```

If FUN does not have the side effect of changing A, then the order of evaluation of the two operands, A and FUN(A), has no effect on the value of the expression. But suppose that FUN changes its parameter to have the value 20. Then if A has the value 10 when execution reaches the expression and the first operand of the expression is evaluated first, the value of that first operand is 10. But if the second operand is evaluated first, then the value of the first operand is 20. So the expression value depends on the order of evaluation of the two operands.

The same problem can occur in a more subtle way. Consider the following Pascal code segment:

```
procedure sub1(...);
  var A : integer;
  function FUN(X: integer): integer;

    . . .
    A := 17;
    . . .
  end;  { FUN }
  procedure sub2(...);
    . . .
    A := A + FUN(B);
    . . .
  end;  { sub2 }
  . . .
end;  { sub1 }
```

Even though the actual parameter to FUN does not appear elsewhere in the expression A + FUN(B), the expression's value can still be affected by the order of operand evaluation. The change to the expression's value is caused by the side effect in FUN of changing the value of A, which is defined outside the definition of FUN.

There are two distinct solutions to this problem. First, the language designer could disallow function evaluation from affecting the value of expressions by simply disallowing functional side effects. The second method of avoiding the problem is to state in the language definition that operands in expressions are to be evaluated in a particular order and demand that implementors guarantee that order.

Disallowing functional side effects is difficult, and it eliminates some flexibility for the programmer. It takes one of the tricks away from his or her bag. The problem with having a strict evaluation order is that some code optimization techniques used by compilers involve reordering operand evaluations. A guaranteed order disallows those optimization methods when function calls are involved. There is, therefore, no perfect solution, as is borne out by actual language designs.

The designers of FORTRAN 77 envisioned a third solution. The FORTRAN 77 definition states that expressions that have function calls are legal only if the functions do not change the values of other operands in the expression. Unfortunately, it is not easy for the compiler to determine the exact effect a function can have on variables outside the function, especially in the presence of COMMON and the aliasing provided by EQUIVALENCE. This is a case where the language definition specifies the conditions under which a construct is legal, but leaves it to the programmer to ensure that such constructs are legally specified in programs.

Pascal allows most operands of binary operators to be evaluated in any order chosen by the implementor. Furthermore, Pascal functions can have side effects, so the problems illustrated above can occur in Pascal programs. Like Pascal, many other language definitions simply ignore the problem. The problems of functional side effects are further discussed in Chapter 8.

5.2   Overloaded Operators

Arithmetic operators are often used for more than one purpose. For example, + is frequently used for both integer and floating-point addition. In FORTRAN, it is used for INTEGER, REAL, COMPLEX, and DOUBLE PRECISION addition. Some languages, PL/I for example, also use it for string catenation. This multiple use of an operator is called **operator overloading,** and is generally thought to be acceptable in reasonable amounts. Some believe there is too much operator overloading in APL, where most operators are used for both unary and binary operations.

As an example of the possible dangers of overloading, consider the use of the ampersand, &, in C. As a binary operator it specifies a bitwise logical AND operation. As a unary operator, however, its meaning is totally different. When an ampersand precedes a variable as a unary operator, the expression value is the address of that variable. In this case the ampersand is called the address-of operator. For example, the execution of

    x = &y

causes the address of y to be placed in x. There are two problems with this multiple use of the ampersand. First, using the same symbol for two completely unrelated operations is detrimental to readability. Second, the simple keying error of leaving out the first operand for a bitwise AND operation can go undetected by the compiler because it is interpreted as an address-of operator. Such an error may be difficult to diagnose.

Virtually every programming language has some examples of a less serious, but similar, problem, which is often due to the overloading of the minus operator. In the case of the minus operator, the problem is only that the compiler cannot tell if the operator was meant to be binary or unary. So, once again, failure to include the first operand when the operator is meant to be binary cannot be detected as an error by the compiler. However, the meanings of the two operations, unary and binary, are at least closely related, so readability is not seriously affected.

Distinct operator symbols not only increase readability, they are some-times convenient to use for common operations, instead of using a single overloaded symbol, even for commonly overloaded operators. The division operator is an example. Consider the problem of finding the floating-point average of a list of integers. We normally compute the sum and number of those integers, as integers. Suppose we have done this in the variables SUM and COUNT, and want the floating-point average in AVG. In FORTRAN, as in several other languages, we would need to convert the values of SUM and COUNT to floating-point type, as in

```
AVG = FLOAT (SUM)  / FLOAT (COUNT)
```

If the explicit conversions are not included, an integer division operation takes place, in which the result is truncated to an integer. Then, in spite of the fact that the destination (AVG) is floating-point type, its value from this assignment can have no fractional part. The integer result of division is converted to floating-point for the assignment *after* the truncation from division.

When a distinct operator symbol for floating-point division is available (different from that for integer division), the situation is simplified. For example, in Pascal, where / means floating-point division, we can use

```
AVG  : = SUM  / COUNT
```

where AVG is floating-point type and SUM and COUNT are integer type, and be assured of getting the correct result. Both operands will be implicitly converted to floating-point, and a floating-point division operation takes place. This kind of implicit conversion operation is further discussed in the following section. Integer division in Pascal is specified by the **div** operator, which takes integer operands and produces an integer result.

The Ada language allows the programmer to overload operator symbols even more. For example, suppose a user wants to define the * operator between a scalar integer and an integer array to mean that each element of the array is to be multiplied by the scalar. This could be done by writing a function subprogram named * that performs this new operation. The Ada compiler will choose the correct meaning when an overloaded operator is specified, based on the types of the operands, as is the case with language-defined overloaded operators. In our example situation, the Ada compiler will use the new definition for * whenever the * operator appears with a simple integer as the left operand and an integer array as the right operand. Implementing user-defined overloaded operators is discussed in Chapter 8.

C++ also allows user-defined operator overloading, as does FOR-TRAN 8X.

5.3   Coercion in Expressions

One of the design decisions concerning arithmetic expressions is whether a single expression can contain operands of different types. Languages that do allow these expressions, which are called **mixed-mode,** must define conventions for implicit operand type conversions, because computers do not in general have operations that use operands of different types. These implicit conversions are commonly known as coercions. More precisely, a **coercion** is an implicit type conversion that is initiated by the compiler, interpreter, or run-time system. We refer to type conversions explicitly requested by the programmer as explicit conversions, not coercions.

Although some symbolic operators may be overloaded, we assume that a computer system, either in hardware or in some level of software simulation, has an operation for each operand type and operator in the language. For overloaded operators in a language that uses static type binding, the compiler chooses the correct type operation on the basis of the types of the operands. When the two operands of an operator are not of the same type and that is legal in the language, the compiler must choose one of them to be coerced, and supply the code for that coercion. In the following discussion, we examine the coercion design choices of several common languages.

FORTRAN has four numeric data types: INTEGER, REAL, DOUBLE PRECISION, and COMPLEX. For a binary operator in an arithmetic expression, the two operands can be any numeric types as long as DOUBLE PRECISION and COMPLEX are not both involved. The rules for the required coercions are given in the following table:

OPERANDS	COERCIONS
INTEGER, REAL	Convert INTEGER to REAL
INTEGER, DOUBLE PRECISION	Convert INTEGER to DOUBLE PRECISION
INTEGER, COMPLEX	Convert INTEGER to COMPLEX
REAL, DOUBLE PRECISION	Convert REAL to DOUBLE PRECISION
REAL, COMPLEX	Convert REAL to COMPLEX
COMPLEX, DOUBLE PRECISION	Illegal

The C language includes the numeric types int (integer), **short int** (short integer), **long int** (long integer), **float** (floating-point), and **double**

(double precision). The language definition dictates frequent coercions of operands. Although **float** and **short int** are legitimate data types, they are *always* coerced to **double** and **int**, respectively, when they appear in an expression or actual parameter list. For example, if x and y are **float** type variables in the expression x + y, regardless of where the expression occurs, both x and y are converted to **double** and a *double precision* addition takes place.

Most of the other imperative languages followed the lead of FORTRAN by allowing mixed-mode expressions. However, in recent years it has become widely believed that the frequent coercions required by such mixing are not good because they allow the programmer to make errors that are not detectable by the compiler, thus lowering reliability.

To illustrate the problem, consider the following: Suppose a FORTRAN 77 program contains a function named FUN that has a single INTEGER parameter. Further suppose that FUN is incorrectly used as follows:

```
INTEGER A, B, C
REAL D
. . .
C = FUN(A + D)
. . .
```

The actual parameter expression in the call to FUN contains references to the variables A and D. The programmer's mistake is that the D was supposed to be B. A is declared to be INTEGER type and D is declared to be REAL. As a result of the mistake and the consequent mixing of types, A is coerced to REAL type. The expression value is then REAL type. So FUN is sent a REAL value instead of the INTEGER type its expects. Because parameter types are not checked in user-written FORTRAN 77 subprograms, FUN detects no error, and carries out its operations on the parameter as if it were an INTEGER type. This cannot produce a sensible result.

This particular problem is the result of two design decisions: the lack of type checking of actual and formal parameters and the coercion of INTEGER to REAL in any expression that includes both types. In a language such as Ada that does not allow this kind of mixed-mode expression and does check the types of actual and formal parameters, this error is not possible. Although the problem in our example has two design sources, just allowing mixed-mode expressions can lead to similar though usually less subtle problems.

Because error detection is reduced when mixed-mode expressions are allowed, the two most recently designed imperative languages, Ada and Modula-2, allow very few mixed type operands in expressions. Neither allows mixing of integer and floating-point operands in an expression, with one exception: The exponentiation operator in the Ada language, ******, can take either a floating-point or integer type for the first operand, and an integer type second operand. Both languages allow a few other kinds of operand type mixing, usually related to subrange types, which are discussed in Chapter 7.

Both Modula-2 and Ada provide explicit conversion operations that have the syntax of function calls. For example, in Ada, we can have

```
AVG : = REAL(SUM)  /  REAL(COUNT)
```

where AVG is floating-point type and SUM and COUNT can be any numeric type. This assignment produces the same result as the FORTRAN version in the previous section, in addition to looking nearly the same.

As an example of the dangers and costs of too much coercion, consider PL/I's efforts to achieve flexibility in expressions. In PL/I, a character string variable can be combined with an integer in an expression. At run time, the string is scanned for a numeric value. If the value happens to contain a decimal point, it is assumed to be of floating-point type, the other operand is coerced to floating-point, and the resulting operation is floating-point. This coercion policy is very expensive because the type check and the decision to convert must be done at run time. It also eliminates the possibility of detecting programmer errors in expressions, because a binary operator can combine an operand of any type with an operand of virtually any other type.

5.4 Relational and Boolean Expressions

In addition to arithmetic expressions, programming languages include relational and Boolean, or logical, expressions.

5.4.1 Relational Expressions

A **relational operator** is an operator that compares the values of its two operands and returns some indication of whether the operator holds or does not hold. A relational operator holds if it states a true relationship between the operands.

A **relational expression** has two operands and one relational operator. The value of a relational expression is Boolean, except when Boolean is not a type in the language. The relational operators are usually overloaded for a variety of types. The operation to determine the truth or falseness of a relational expression depends on the operand types. It can be simple, as is the case for integer operands, or complex, as is the case for character string operands. Typically, the types of the operands that can be used for relational operators are numeric types, strings, and ordinal types. (Ordinal types are discussed in Chapter 7. The most common ordinal types are integer, character, Boolean, and user-defined enumerated types.)

- The syntax of the relational operators available in some common languages is as follows:

OPERATION	PASCAL	ADA	C	FORTRAN
equal	=	=	==	.EQ.
not equal	<>	/=	!=	.NE.
greater than	>	>	>	.GT.
less than	<	<	<	.LT.
greater than or equal	>=	>=	>=	.GE.
less than or equal	<=	<=	<=	.LE.

The FORTRAN I designers used English abbreviations because the symbols > and < were not on the card punches at the time of FORTRAN I's design. FORTRAN 8x allows both FORTRAN 77 relational operators and operators that are exactly like those of Pascal except that == is used for equality.

The relational operators always have lower precedence than the arithmetic operators, so that in expressions such as

```
a + 1 > 2 * b
```

the arithmetic expressions are evaluated first.

5.4.2   Boolean Expressions

Boolean expressions consist of Boolean variables, Boolean constants, relational expressions, and Boolean operators. The operators usually include those for the AND, OR, and NOT operations, and sometimes for exclusive OR and equivalence.

A variety of symbols have been used for the Boolean operators. FORTRAN 77 uses .AND., .OR., and .NOT. C uses && for AND, || for OR, and ! for NOT. C also has operators for bitwise logic operations, which can also appear in the operands of Boolean expressions.

In most languages, the Boolean operators, like the arithmetic operators, are evaluated in a hierarchical precedence order. Typically, the unary NOT has the highest precedence, followed by AND at a separate level, and OR at the lowest level. Because arithmetic expressions can be the operands of relational expressions, and relational expressions can be the operands of Boolean expressions, the three categories of operators must be placed in precedence levels relative to each other.

The precedence of all FORTRAN 77 operators is:

Highest: **
             *, /
             +, -
             // (string catenation)
             .EQ., .NE., .GT., .LT., .LE., .GE.
             .NOT.

```
            . AND.
            . OR.
Lowest:     . EQV. ,  . NEQV.  (equivalent and not equivalent)
```

In the FORTRAN expression

```
A + B .GT.  2 * C .AND. K .NE.  0
```

multiplication is evaluated first, followed by addition, greater than, not equal, and finally, AND.

The precedence of all Ada operators is

Highest: ******, **abs**, **not**
         *, **/**, **mod**, **rem**
         +, − (unary)
         +, −, & (binary)
         =, /=, <, >, <=, >=, **in**, **not in**
Lowest: **and**, **or**, **xor**, **and then**, **or else**

Notice that Ada's Boolean operators, with the exception of **not**, share the same precedence level. If more than one appears in an expression, the subexpressions of all must be parenthesized. For example,

```
A > B and A < C or K = 0
```

is illegal in Ada. This expression can be legally written as either

```
(A > B and A < C)  or K = 0
```

or

```
A > B and  (A < C or K = 0)
```

The Ada Boolean operators **and then** and **or else** are discussed in the next section. The **in** and **not in** operators are membership tests, which are discussed in Chapter 7.

Boolean operators usually take only Boolean operands and produce Boolean values. One notable exception occurs in C, in which there is no Boolean type, and thus no Boolean values. Instead, numeric values are used to represent Boolean values. In place of Boolean operands, numeric variables and constants are used, with zero considered false and all nonzero values considered true. The result of evaluating such an expression is an integer, with the value 0 if false and 1 if true.

One odd result of C's design is that the expression

```
a > b > c
```

is legal. The leftmost relational operator is evaluated first because the relational operators of C are left associative, producing either 0 or 1. Then this result is compared with the variable c. There is never a comparison between b and c.

Readability dictates that a language should include a Boolean type, as we stated in Chapter 4, rather than simply using numeric types in Boolean expressions.

5.5 Short-Circuit Evaluation

A **short-circuit evaluation** of an expression is one in which the result is determined without evaluating all of the operands and/or operators. Some expressions, both Boolean and arithmetic, can use the short-circuit evaluation method. For example, the arithmetic expression

```
A * B / C
```

has a value of 0 if A = 0 or B = 0, without evaluating C or performing the division. The Boolean expression

```
(A >= 0) and (B < 10)
```

has the value false if A is less than 0, without evaluating B, the constant 10, the second relational expression, or the **and** operation. Boolean expressions are more interesting than the arithmetic expressions, as is illustrated next.

Many Pascal programmers have encountered a problem when attempting to write a table look-up loop using the **while** statement. The Pascal code for such a look-up, assuming that LIST is the array to be searched for VALUE, and LIST has subscript range 1:LENGTH, is

```
INDEX := 1;
while (INDEX <= LENGTH) and (LIST[INDEX] <> VALUE) do
        INDEX := INDEX + 1
```

The problem with this is that most Pascal implementations do not do short-circuit evaluation, so both relational expressions in the Boolean expression of the **while** statement are usually evaluated, regardless of the value of the first. Thus, if VALUE is not in the array LIST, the program will terminate with a subscript out-of-range error. It will do this because the same iteration that has INDEX > LENGTH will reference LIST[LENGTH+1], which causes the indexing error because LIST is declared to have LENGTH as an upper-bound subscript value.

If a language allows short-circuit evaluation of Boolean expressions, this problem is alleviated. In the preceding example, a short-circuit evaluation scheme would evaluate the first operand of the AND operator, but then skip the second operand if the first operand is false.

The FORTRAN 77 definition simply states that the implementor may choose not to evaluate any more of an expression than is necessary to determine the result. The only caveat is that if the unevaluated part of the expression is a function reference that has the side effect of assigning a value to any variable that is declared outside the function definition, that variable must be undefined by the short-circuit evaluation. Once again, there is a problem in actually implementing the rule. For one thing, FORTRAN 77 provides no way of indicating an "undefined" value.

The Ada language allows the programmer to specify short-circuit evaluation of the Boolean operators AND and OR by using the two-word operators **and then** and **or else**. For example, again assuming that LIST is declared to have a subscript range of 1..LENGTH, the Ada code

```
INDEX := 1;
while (INDEX <= LENGTH) and then (LIST[INDEX] /= VALUE)
  loop
  INDEX := INDEX + 1;
  end loop;
```

will not cause an error because INDEX becomes too large.

The inclusion of both short-circuit and ordinary operators, as in the Ada design, is clearly the best design because it provides the programmer the flexibility of choosing short-circuit evaluation for any or all Boolean expressions.

In C and Modula-2, every evaluation of AND and OR expressions is short-circuit. In most cases this is acceptable. There are situations, however, where the correctness of a program may depend on the complete evaluation of Boolean expressions. In particular, if the right operand of a Boolean operator is a function call that has side effects, those side effects would be executed only on some executions. Furthermore, in the C language, assignment statements can be the operands of Boolean operators, so assignment operations can be lost by short-circuit evaluation. The use of assignment statements as operands in expression is discussed in Section 5.6.7.

5.6 The Assignment Statement

As we have previously stated, the assignment statement is the central construct in imperative languages. It provides the mechanism by which the user can dynamically bind values to variables. In the following section the simplest form of assignment is discussed. Subsequent sections describe a variety of alternatives.

5.6.1 The Simple Assignment

The general syntax of the simple assignment statement is

<target_variable> <assignment_operator> <expression>

FORTRAN, BASIC, PL/I, and C use the equal sign for the assignment operator. This can lead to confusion if the equal sign is also used as a relational operator. For example, the PL/I assignment

A = B = C

sets A to the Boolean value of the relational expression B = C, although it looks as though these variables are being set equal to each other. In the cases of FORTRAN and C, a different symbol is used for the relational operator for equality, which avoids the problem of overloading the assignment operator.

ALGOL 60 pioneered the use of : = as the assignment operator, and many later languages have followed that choice.

The design choices of how assignments are used in a language have varied widely. In some cases, such as in FORTRAN, Pascal, and Ada, it can only appear as a stand-alone statement and the destination is restricted to a single variable. There are, however, many alternatives.

5.6.2 Multiple Targets

One alternative to the simple assignment statement is to allow assignment of the expression value to more than one location. For example, in PL/I, the statement

```
SUM, TOTAL = 0
```

assigns the value zero to both SUM and TOTAL. Multiple target assignment statements are a convenience for programmers, but not a significant one.

5.6.3 Conditional Expressions

Sometimes **if-then-else** statements are used to perform a conditional expression assignment. For example, consider

```
if  (count = 0)
  then average  : = 0
  else average  : = sum / count
```

In C this can be done more conveniently with an assignment statement with a conditional expression. For example, the effect of the **if-then-else** here can be achieved with the conditional assignment:

```
average = (count == 0) ? 0 : sum / count
```

In effect, the question mark denotes the beginning of the **then** clause and the colon marks the beginning of the **else** clause.

5.6.4 Conditional Targets

ALGOL 68 allows conditional targets on assignment statements. For example, consider

```
(link = nil | next | link)  : = nil
```

This is equivalent to

```
if link = nil then next : = nil else link : = nil
```

Conditional target assignments are less useful and less readable than assignments with conditional right sides.

5.6.5 Assigning Operators

Assigning operators is a shorthand method of specifying commonly needed forms of assignments. The form of assignment that can be created with this technique has the destination variable also appearing as the first operand in the expression on the right side, as in

```
a = a + b
```

Assigning operators were introduced by ALGOL 68 and later adopted in a slightly different form by C. The syntax of C's assigning operators is the catenation of the desired binary operator to the = operator. For example,

```
sum += value
```

is equivalent to:

```
sum = sum + value
```

C has versions of the assigning operators for most of its binary operators.

5.6.6 Unary Operator Assignments

The C language includes two special unary arithmetic operators that are actually abbreviated assignments. They combine increment and decrement operations with assignment. The operators, ++ for increment and -- for decrement, can be used either in expressions, or to form stand-alone, single-operator assignment statements. They can appear as either prefix operators, meaning they precede the operands, or as suffix operators, meaning they follow their operands. In the assignment statement

```
sum = ++count
```

the value of count is incremented by 1 and then assigned to sum. This could also be stated as

```
count = count + 1
sum = count
```

If the same operator were used as a suffix operator, as in

```
sum = count++
```

the effect would be the same as the two statements

```
sum = count
count = count + 1
```

An example of the use of the unary increment operator to form a complete assignment statement is

```
count++
```

which simply increments count. It does not look like an assignment, but it certainly is one. It is precisely equivalent to the statement

```
count = count + 1
```

C's increment and decrement operators are frequently used to form array subscript expressions. In fact, their origin is in the autoincrement and autodecrement addressing modes of the PDP-11 computer, on which C was first implemented. These addressing modes are often used to implement arrays efficiently.

5.6.7   Assignment Statements as Operands

In C, the assignment statement produces a result, which is the value assigned to the target. It can therefore be used as an operand in expressions. This design treats the assignment operator much like any other binary operator. Although this may seem odd to those unfamiliar with C, it is a very convenient capability. For example, in C it is common to write statements such as:

```
while ((ch = getchar()) != EOF)
    { ... }
```

In this example, the next character from the standard input file, usually the terminal keyboard, is gotten with getchar and assigned to the variable ch. The result, or value assigned, is then compared with the constant EOF. If ch is not equal to EOF, the compound statement { ... } is executed. Note that the assignment must be parenthesized—in C the precedence of the assignment operator is lower than that of the relational operators. Without the parentheses, the new character would be compared with EOF first. Then the result of that comparison, which would be either 0 or 1, would be assigned to ch. The disadvantage of allowing assignment statements to be operands in expressions is that it can lead to expressions that are difficult to read and understand.

5.7   Mixed-Mode Assignment

We discussed mixed-mode expressions in Section 5.3. A similar situation frequently arises in assignment statements. The design question is whether the type of the expression must be the same as the type of the variable being assigned, or can coercion be used in some cases of type mismatch.

FORTRAN uses the same coercion rules for mixed type assignment that it uses for mixed type expressions; that is, many of the possible type mixes are legal, with coercion freely applied.

Pascal includes some assignment coercion; for example, integer expressions can be assigned to floating-point variables. Also allowed is some additional mixing involving subrange types. Ada and Modula-2 do not allow the coercion of integer to floating-point in their assignment, as Pascal does, but they do allow some type mixing in assignment, including subranges.

Assignments to structured data variables are discussed in Chapter 7. We also address the question of type compatibility in that chapter.

SUMMARY

Assignment statements include target variables, assignment operators, and expressions. Expressions consist of constants, variables, parentheses, function calls, and operators.

The associativity and precedence rules for operators in the expressions of a language determine the order of operator evaluation in those expressions. Operand evaluation order is important if functional side effects are possible. Coercion in expressions is common, although it eliminates some variable type checking, which in turn lowers reliability.

Assignment statements have appeared in a wide variety of forms, including conditional left sides, conditional right sides, and assigning operators.

PROBLEM SET

1. What is a situation in which you might want the compiler to ignore type differences in an expression?

2. State your own arguments for and against allowing mixed-mode arithmetic expressions.

3. Do you think the elimination of overloaded operators in Pascal would be beneficial? Why or why not?

4. Would it be a good idea to eliminate all operator precedence rules and require parentheses to show the desired precedence in expressions? Why or why not?

5. Should C's assigning operations (for example, +=) be included in other languages? Why or why not?

6. Should C's single-operand assignment forms (for example, ++count) be included in other languages? Why or why not?

7. Describe a situation in which the add operator in Pascal would not be commutative.

8. Describe a situation in which the add operator in Pascal would not be associative.

[handwritten margin notes:]

7. expression such as A + FUN(B) as on p. 146

given
8. A + B + C

A = 26,000
B = 25,000
C = - 20,000

machine has max int 32,767

if 1st Addition computed 1st, overflow.

if 2nd add done first, ok

9. Write a Pascal program segment, using a **while** construct to search an array of integers for a particular integer, that would work even if short-circuit evaluation Boolean expression were not done.

10. Assume the following rules of associativity and precedence:

Precedence: Highest: $*, /,$ **mod**
                      $+, -,$ &
                      $-$ (unary)
                      $=, /=, <, <=, >=, >$
                      or
        Lowest: **and, xor**
Associativity: left to right

Show the order of evaluation of the following expressions by parenthesizing all subexpressions and placing a superscript on the right parenthesis to indicate order. For example, for the expression

a + b * c + d

show

$((a + (b * c)^1)^2 + d)^3$

a. a * b - 1 + c
b. a * (b - 1) / c **mod** d
c. (a - b) / c & (d * e / a - 3)
d. - a **or** c = d **and** e
e. a > b **xor** c **or** d <= 17
f. - a + b

11. Show the order of evaluation of the expressions of Problem 10, assuming that there are no precedence rules and all operators associate right to left.

12. Write a BNF description of the language of Problem 10, assuming the only operands are the names a, b, c, d, and e.

13. Using the grammar of Problem 12, draw parse trees for the expressions of Problem 10.

14. Let the function FUN be defined as:

```
function FUN (var K : integer) : integer;
  begin
    K := K + 2;
    FUN := 2 * K
  end;
```

Suppose FUN is used in a program as follows:

```
. . .
I := 10;
SUM1 := I + 2 + FUN(I);
J := 10;
SUM2 := FUN(J) + 2 + J;
```

What are the values of SUM1 and SUM2?

Handwritten annotations:

c.
$(((a-b)^1 / c)^5$ &
$(((d*e)^2 /a)^3$
$- 3)^4)^6$

$((a*b)^1 - 1)^2 + c)^3$

$((a*(b-1)^1 / c)^2)^3$ **mod** d$)^4$

d.
$(((-a)^1$ **or** $(c=d)^2)^3$
and e$)^4$

e. $((a>b)^1$ **xor**
$(c$ **or** $(d<=17)^2)^3)^4$

f. $(- (a+b)^1)^2$

14.
left assoc
SUM1 = 24
SUM2 = 26

right assoc
SUM1 = 26
SUM2 = 24

15. What is your primary argument against (or for) the operator precedence rules of APL?

16. For some language of your choice, make up a list of operator symbols that could be used to eliminate all operator overloading.

17. Devise a situation in which mixed-mode expressions can lead to problems, such as that of Section 5.3, except without involving subprogram parameters.

18. Implement a simple version of the problem illustrated by the FORTRAN example of Section 5.3. Try the same program on a FORTRAN library function, such as MIN0.

12.   <expr> → <expr> and <e1> | <expr> xor <e1> | <e1>

<e1> → <e1> or <e2> | <e2>

<e2> → <e2> = <e3> | <e2> /= <e3> | <e2> < <e3>
| <e2> <= <e3> | <e2> > <e3> | <e2> >= <e3>
| <e3>

<e3> → − <e4> | <e4>

<e4> → <e4> + <e5> | <e4> − <e5> | <e4> & <e5>
| <e5>

<e5> → <e5> * <e6> | <e5> / <e6> | <e5> mod <e6>
| <e6>

<e6> → a | b | c | d | e | const | (<exp>)

17. if list of floats being added eg

```
for INDEX 1 = 1 to 100 do
    SUM := SUM + LIST [INDEX];
```

LIST real
but SUM int (in error)
SUM would be for from correct value

13 (b)

```
<expr>
  |
 <e1>
  |
 <e2>
  |
 <e3>
  |
 <e4>
  |
 <e5>
 /    \
<e5>   mod   <e6>
 /|\          |
<e5> / <e6>   d
/|\    |
<e5> * <e6>  c
 |
<e6>    etc
```

Key Concepts

- Control statements and control structures
- Single- and two-way selection
- Problems with nesting selectors
- Multiple selectors
- Repetitive constructs
- User location of control mechanisms
- Iterators
- Problems with unconditional branching
- Guarded commands

6

STATEMENT-LEVEL CONTROL STRUCTURES

Contents

The flow of control, or execution sequence, in a program can be examined at several levels. In Chapter 5 we discussed the flow of control within expressions, which is governed by operator associativity and precedence rules. At the highest level, there is the flow of control among program units, which is discussed in Chapters 8 and 11. Between these two extremes is the important issue of flow of control among program statements, which is the subject of this chapter.

Included are discussions of single and multiple selection statements, a large number of different iterative statements, and unconditional branching statements. We will describe the design issues and evaluate the alternatives in each of these categories.

6.1   Introduction

Computations in imperative language programs are accomplished by evaluating expressions and assigning the resulting values to variables. Programs that consist entirely of assignment statements do not, however, have wide application. At least two additional features are necessary to make programs flexible and powerful: some means of choosing among alternative paths of statements and some means of causing the repeated execution of certain collections of statements. Statements that provide these capabilities are called **control statements.**

The control statements of the first successful imperative language, FORTRAN, were, in effect, designed by the architects of the IBM 704. All were directly related to machine language instructions. Since then, much progress has been made.

A great deal of research has been devoted to control statements since the middle 1960s. One of the primary conclusions of these efforts was that only a minimal number of different control statements is needed in a language. In fact, it was proven that all algorithms that can be expressed by flowcharts can be coded in a programming language with only two control statements: one for choosing between two statement paths and one for logically controlled iterations (Bohm and Jacopini, 1966). An important result of this is the fact that unconditional branch statements are superfluous— possibly convenient, but not essential. This fact, combined with the problems of using the unconditional branches, or goto's, has led to a great deal of debate about the goto, which is discussed in Section 6.6.1.

A **control structure** is a control statement and the collection of statements whose execution it controls. The programming language research of the 1960s determined that control structures should have single entries and single exits. Multiple entries to iterative structures, in particular, make programs more difficult to read and understand.

Flowgraphs are useful methods of describing the actions of control statements. Figure 6.1 shows the flowgraph descriptions of the two fundamental

Figure 6.1
Flowgraph of a two-
way selector and a
logically controlled
loop

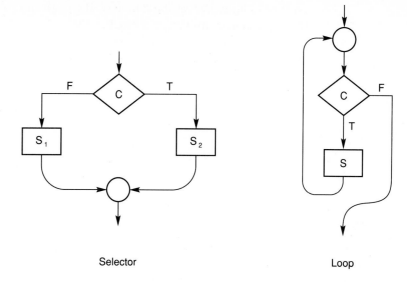

Selector   Loop

structures: two-way selection and one form of logically controlled iteration. Although only these two are necessary to express the control of all programs, language writability can be greatly enhanced by the presence of some other control statements.

The question of what is the best collection of control statements to provide the required capabilities and the desired writability has been furiously debated for the past quarter century. A corollary design question is how many additional control statements beyond the required constructs should be included in a language. This is essentially a question of how much should a language be expanded to increase its writability, at the expense of its simplicity and size.

6.2 Compound Statements

One of the auxiliary language features that help make control statement design easier is a method of forming statement collections. The primary reason for the inadequacies of the control statements of the early versions of FORTRAN was the lack of such a construct.

ALGOL 60 introduced the first statement collection structure, the **compound statement.** The form of the ALGOL 60 compound statement is:

```
begin
statement_1;
. . .
statement_n
end
```

Data declarations can be added to the beginning of a compound statement in ALGOL 60, making it a **block,** as in:

```
begin
integer i, j;
. . .
end
```

Pascal followed ALGOL 60's design for compound statements, but does not allow blocks. The C language uses braces to delimit both compound statements and blocks. Several recently designed languages have eliminated the need for specially delimited compound statements by integrating compound statements into their control structures. These are discussed in the following section.

6.3   Selection Statements

A **selection statement** provides the means of choosing between two execution paths in a program. Such statements are fundamental and essential parts of all programming languages.

6.3.1   Design Issues

The fundamental design issues for selection statements are the following:

1. What is the form and type of the expression that controls the selection?
2. Can a single statement, a sequence of statements, or a compound statement be selected?
3. Is it possible to select a single code segment, or must a choice be made between two segments? These two possibilities are called, respectively, **single-way** and **two-way selectors.** This design choice is illustrated in the flowgraphs of Figure 6.2.

6.3.2   Single-Way Selectors

FORTRAN 77 has a single-way selector called a logical IF, which has the form:

IF (Boolean expression) statement

where the selectable statement must be executable (not a declaration). The semantics of the single statement logical selector is that the selectable statement is executed only if the Boolean expression evaluates to true. The design choices for the logical IF are partially deducible from the general form: The selector control expression is Boolean type and only a single statement is

Figure 6.2
Single and two-way
selectors

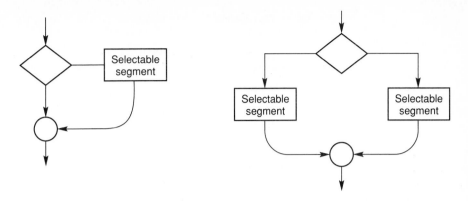

selectable, and it is a single-way selector. Nesting of logical IF statements is not allowed.

The logical IF is very simple and also highly inflexible. The fact that only a single statement can be selected promotes the use of goto statements, since usually more than one statement must be conditionally executed. The only reasonable way to conditionally execute a group of statements is to conditionally branch around the group. For example, suppose we wanted to conditionally initialize three variables to the values 1, 2, and 3. The typical way to do it in FORTRAN IV is:

```
        IF (.NOT. condition) GO TO 20
        I = 1
        J = 2
        K = 3
   20   CONTINUE
```

The negative logic required by this form is especially damaging to readability.

The compound statement provides, for the selection construct, a simple mechanism for conditionally executing groups of statements. This was one of the advances made by ALGOL 60 in selection constructs: It allowed either a single statement to be selected, as with FORTRAN's logical IF, or a compound statement to be selected, as in:

```
    if (Boolean expression) then
      begin
      statement_1;
      . . .
      statement_n
      end
```

Most of the languages that followed ALGOL 60, including FORTRAN 77, provide single-way selectors that can select a collection of statements.

6.3.3   Two-Way Selectors

Two-way selectors allow one of two statements or collections of statements to be selected. ALGOL 60 introduced the first two-way selector, with the general form:

> **if** (Boolean_expression)
>   **then** statement
>   **else** statement

where either or both selectable statements can be compound. The statement following the **then** reserved word is called the **then clause,** and the statement following the **else** reserved word is called the **else clause.**

The semantics of the ALGOL 60 selector is that the then clause is executed if the Boolean expression evaluates to true; otherwise, the else clause is executed. Under no circumstances are both clauses executed.

All of the important imperative languages designed since the middle 1960s have incorporated two-way selection statements, although the syntax has varied.

6.3.4   Nesting Selectors

An interesting problem arises when two-way selection constructs can be nested. Consider the following Pascal code:

```
if (sum = 0) then
   if (count = 0)
      then result := 0
      else result := 1
```

This construct can be interpreted in two different ways, depending on whether the else clause is matched with the first then clause or the second. Notice that the indentation seems to indicate that the else clause belongs to the last then clause, but indentation should not be considered a reliable method of disambiguation. Indentation has no meaning in most contemporary languages and is therefore ignored by their compilers.

The crux of the problem in this example is that the else clause closes two selection statements, and Pascal does not include any means of being more precise about mapping the then clause to the appropriate else clause.

The straightforward EBNF that appears in Chapter 3 to describe the Pascal two-way selection construct is also ambiguous, for the same reason. The syntax of the selector is not ambiguous, however. Our description simply does not state the rule as defined in Pascal's definition, which is that the else clause is always paired with the most recent unpaired then clause. It is possible with EBNF to describe it unambiguously.

The designers of ALGOL 60 recognized the ambiguity problem of nested selectors and solved it in the following way: An **if** statement is not allowed to be nested directly in a then clause. If an **if** must be nested in a then clause, it must be placed in a compound statement. This effectively removes the ambiguity. For example, if the selection construct above were to pair the else clause with the second then clause, in ALGOL 60 it would be written as:

```
if sum = 0 then
  begin
  if count = 0
    then result := 0
    else result := 1
  end
```

If the else clause were to be paired with the first then clause, it would be written as:

```
if sum = 0 then
  begin
  if count = sum then result := 0
  end
else result := 1
```

6.3.5 Special Words and Selection Closure

ALGOL 60 and Pascal then and else clauses can be either single statements or compound statements. If a clause is a single statement, the end of that statement closes it. If a clause is a compound statement, the **end** reserved word closes it. There is no general syntactic indication that the selector constructs of these languages have been closed. By adding a special closing word for else clauses, it is possible to let both then and else clauses be statement sequences. The special word that closes the else clause also closes the entire selection construct. This is the situation with the ALGOL 68, FORTRAN 77, Modula-2, and Ada languages. For example, in Modula-2, one could have:

```
IF a > b
  THEN sum := sum + a
  ELSE sum := sum + b
END
```

or

```
IF a > b
  THEN
    sum := sum + a;
    acount := acount + 1
  ELSE
    sum := sum + b;
    bcount := bcount + 1
END
```

This design is more regular than that of Pascal and ALGOL 60, because the form is the same regardless of the number of statements in the then and else clauses. Moreover, the design solves the problem of the ambiguity of nested two-way selection statements. The Pascal example at the beginning of Section 6.3.4 can be written in Modula-2 as:

```
IF  sum = 0
   THEN IF count = 0
            THEN result : = 0
            ELSE result : = 1
         END
END
```

Because the END reserved word closes the nested IF, it is very clear that the else clause is matched to the inner then clause.

In FORTRAN 77 and Ada the closing special word for selection constructs is END IF. For other control constructs, different closing special words are used. Modula-2 closes all control constructs with the same reserved word: END. Although Modula-2 thus accomplishes the same result with fewer special words, that result is less readable than if unique special words were used for different constructs, especially when different control constructs are embedded in one another. When used to close an IF control construct, END carries only part of the information that END IF connotes.

6.4   Multiple Selection Constructs

The **multiple selection** construct allows the selection of any one of any number of statements or statement groups. It is, therefore, a simple generalization of a selector. In fact, single-way and two-way selectors can be built with a multiple selector. The original forms of multiple selection are from FORTRAN, as you might have suspected.

6.4.1   Design Issues

The primary design issues for multiple selection constructs are similar to those of selection constructs:

1. What is the form and type of the expression that controls the selection?
2. Can a single statement, a sequence of statements, or a compound statement be selected?
3. Should the entire construct be encapsulated?
4. How should unrepresented selector expression values be handled, if at all?
5. Should the selectable segments be followed by implicit branches out of the entire construct?

Unrepresented selector expression values arise when both non-Boolean expressions are used for the selector and selectable segments are identified by attached constant values. An unrepresented value is one that can be the value of the selector expression, but that does not appear as a constant attached to a selectable segment.

6.4.2 Three-Way Selectors

A **three-way selector** is considered a special case of a multiple selection statement. Because only three or fewer statement collections can be selected, however, it is not, strictly speaking, a multiple selection statement.

The only example of a three-way selector is the arithmetic IF, which was introduced in FORTRAN I and is still a part of FORTRAN. It is based on the trichotomy of numbers, which means that a given integer or real value is either greater than zero, equal to zero, or less than zero. The arithmetic IF has the form:

IF (arithmetic expression) N1, N2, N3

where N1, N2, and N3 are statement labels to which control is to transfer if the expression's value is negative, zero, or greater than zero, respectively. This form of selector is now considered detrimental to readability because it promotes—indeed demands—a proliferation of goto statements. For example, if an arithmetic IF is used to select among three statement sequences, its general form is often the following:

```
IF (expression) 10, 20, 30
10 ...
   ...
   GO TO 40
20 ...
   ...
   GO TO 40
30 ...
   ...
40 ...
```

Actually, this selector type could be much more harmful to readability than the example illustrates, because the statement sequences to be selected can literally be anywhere in the program units. They are not encapsulated into a single construct.

6.4.3 Early Multiple Selectors

The first two multiple selection statements appeared in FORTRAN I, and, like that language's other control statements, were based directly on IBM 704 instructions. The statements continue to be part of FORTRAN 77. The FORTRAN-computed GOTO has the form:

GO TO (label 1, label 2, ..., label n), expression

where the expression has an integer value and the labels are all defined as statement labels in the program. The semantics of the statement is that the expression's value is used to choose a label to which control is to transfer. The first label is associated with the value 1, the second label with 2, and so forth. If the value is outside the range of 1 to n, the statement does nothing. There is no built-in error detection.

Unlike the two-way selectors, which have an implicit branch at the end of the then clause, there are no implicit branches in the computed GOTO. This can lead to very complex structures. For example, consider the following, in which we assume there are also no explicit GOTO statements:

```
20 ...
   ...
   GO TO (10, 20, 30), SELECT
10 ...
   ...
30 ...
```

If SELECT has the value 2, an execution loop occurs (possibly infinite). If SELECT has the value 1, execution control is transferred to the statement labeled 10, and all following code is executed, including the statement labeled 30. If SELECT has the value 3, control transfers to the statement labeled 30.

FORTRAN's second multiple selector, the assigned GOTO, has the form:

GO TO integer_variable (label 1, label 2, . . . , label n)

In this form, the integer variable stores a label value, which it acquires only through an ASSIGN statement, which has the form:

ASSIGN label TO integer_variable

In this case, the label must be defined in the program unit (main program or subprogram) of the ASSIGN statement. Once again, there are no implicit branches, so very complex structures can result from the use of the assigned GOTO.

Both the computed and assigned GOTOs can lead to highly unreadable programs, for the reason stated above and because the target labels are not restricted to being near the GOTO itself. The probem is that the entire construct is not encapsulated. This also leads to the possibility that execution can continue anywhere after the selected code has been executed. This is a violation of the single-entry/single-exit principle of good control structures.

6.4.4 Modern Multiple Selectors

A much better form of multiple selection was suggested by Hoare and included in ALGOL-W (Wirth and Hoare, 1966), where the special word **case** was first used. In Hoare's **case**, the selectable statements or compound statements are encapsulated in a single construct. Implicit branches to the end of the whole construct are also included. These are the two primary advances made thus far in multiple selector constructs.

Pascal introduced the technique of labeling the targets in Hoare's multiple selection form. Pascal's **case** has the form:

```
case expression of
    constant_list_1: statement_1;
    ...
    constant_list_n: statement_n
end
```

where the expression is of ordinal type (integer, Boolean, character, or enumeration type). As is usual in other Pascal control statements, the selectable statements can be either single statements or compound statements.

The semantics of the Pascal **case** is the following: The expression is evaluated and the value is compared with the constants in the constant lists. If a match is found, control transfers to the statement attached to the matched constant. When statement execution is completed, control transfers to the first statement following the whole **case** construct.

The constant lists must be of the same type as the expression, of course. They must be mutually exclusive but need not be exhaustive; that is, a constant may not appear in more than one constant list, but not all values in the range of the expression type need be present in the lists.

Oddly, Pascal's first widely used definition (Jensen and Wirth, 1974) was not concerned with the possibility of the expression taking on a value that did not appear in any of the constant lists. Such occurrences were said to cause undefined results. Such vagueness, however, meant that the problem was simply ignored. The later ANSI/IEEE Pascal Standard (Ledgard, 1984) is more concrete; it specifies that such occurrences are errors, presumably to be detected and reported during execution by the code generated by Pascal compilers.

Many implementations of Pascal now include an optional clause to be executed when the expression value does not appear in any constant list in the **case**, as in:

```
case index of
    1, 3: begin
            odd := odd + 1;
            sumodd := sumodd + index
          end;
    2, 4: begin
            even := even + 1;
            sumeven := sumeven + index
          end;
    otherwise: writeln ('Error in case, index =', index)
end
```

Whenever index is not in the range of 1 to 4 when this **case** statement is executed, the error message will be printed.

Figure 6.3
Flowgraph of the Pascal **case** statement

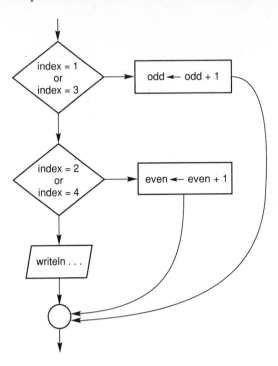

Note that the **otherwise** clause need not be used exclusively for error conditions. It is also sometimes convenient to use it for the normal condition, and use the other cases for the unusual circumstances.

A flowgraph description of the preceding **case** statement is shown in Figure 6.3.

The C multiple selection construct, **switch**, is a relatively primitive design. Its general form is:

```
switch (expression)
    {
    case constant_expression_1: statement_1;
    ...
    case constant_expression_n: statement_n;
    [default: statement_n + 1]
    }
```

where the control expression and the constant expressions are integer type. As is the case with statements in other C constructs, the selectable statements in a **switch** construct can be statement sequences, compound statements, or blocks.

The **switch** encapsulates the selectable code segments, as does the Pascal **case**, but like the FORTRAN-computed GOTO, it does not provide implicit branches at the end of those code segments. Consider the following example, which is similar to the Pascal **case** construct above:

```
switch (index)
  {
  case 1:
  case 3: odd += 1;
          sumodd += index;
  case 2:
  case 4: even += 1;
          sumeven += index;
      default: printf("Error in switch, index = %d\n",
                      index);
  }
```

Because the implicit branches are absent, this code prints the error message on every execution. Likewise, the code for the 2 and 4 constants is executed every time the code at the 1 and 3 constants is executed. To logically separate these segments, an explicit branch must be used. C includes a special statement—**break**—for exiting both **switch** and the bodies of C's loop structures. The **break** statement is actually a restricted branch.

The following C **switch** construct uses **break** and matches the semantics of the Pascal **case** example above:

```
switch (index)
  {
  case 1:
  case 3: odd += 1;
          sumodd += index;
          break;
  case 2:
  case 4: even += 1;
          sumeven += index;
          break;
      default: printf("Error in switch, index = %d\n",
                      index);
  }
```

Occasionally, one chooses convenience over reliability and leaves the implicit **break** out of the **switch** construct. When one selectable code segment needs all the code of another segment, then it is convenient to juxtapose them so that control flows from the first to the second. The reliability problem arises when the absence of a **break** statement in a segment mistakenly allows code from the following segment to be included. Because the **break** is most often required, it is better to include it as part of the construct.

The Ada **case** allows subranges, such as 10..15, and also OR operators specified by the symbol |, as in 10 | 15 | 20 in the constant lists. An **others** clause is available for unrepresented values. The additional Ada restriction that the constant lists be exhaustive provides a bit more reliability, because it disallows the error of inadvertent omission of some constant value. Only integer and enumerated types are allowed for the **case** expression. Most Ada **case** statements include an **others** clause because that is the best way to ensure that the constant list is exhaustive.

Note that while the constant lists of the multiple selection statements in Pascal have a form similar to that of labels, they are not the legal targets of branch statements.

In ALGOL 68, Modula-2, FORTRAN 77, and Ada, two-way selectors can be extended to become multiple selectors. Part of the motivation for this variation concerns the fact that when selectors are nested to a depth of more than about three, they become difficult to read. One solution to this problem is to abbreviate away some of the special words. In particular, **else-if** sequences are replaced with a single special word, and the closing special word on the nested **if** is dropped. The nested selector is then called an **else-if clause.** Consider the following Ada selector construct:

```
if FLAG < 10 then BAG1 : = TRUE;
elsif FLAG < 100 then BAG2 : = TRUE;
elsif FLAG < 1000 then BAG3 : = TRUE;
end if;
```

which is equivalent to:

```
if FLAG < 10
   then BAG1 : = TRUE;
   else if FLAG < 100
           then BAG2 : = TRUE;
           else if FLAG < 1000
                   then BAG3 : = TRUE;
                end if;
        end if;
end if;
```

The else-if version is clearly the more readable of the two. Notice that this example is not easily simulated with a **case** statement, because each selectable statement is chosen on the basis of a Boolean expression. Therefore, the else-if construct is not a redundant form of **case**. A flowgraph description of a selector statement with else-if clauses is shown in Figure 6.4.

6.5   Repetition Statements

A **repetitive statement** is one that causes a statement or collection of statements to be executed repeatedly. Every programming language, from Plankalkül on, has included some method of forming code repetitions. Repetition is the very essence of the power of the computer: If repetition were

Figure 6.4
Flowgraph of a selector with else-if clauses

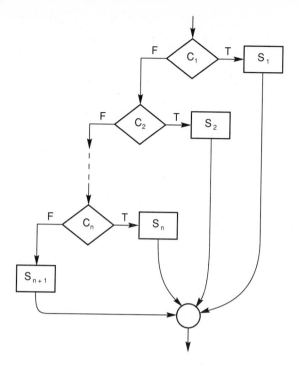

not possible, programmers would be required to state every action in sequence. In that case, useful programs would be huge, both in the amount of time required to write them, and the amount of memory required to store them.

Repetition can be accomplished either by iteration or recursion. In the imperative languages, iteration is the most common method. Recursion in imperative languages is discussed in Chapter 8, and recursion in nonimperative languages is discussed in Chapter 13. Because recursion is a form of program unit control, not statement control, in this chapter we discuss only iteration.

The first iterative constructs were directly related to arrays. This resulted from the fact that in the early years of the computer era, computing was overwhelmingly numerical. Nearly all iterative constructs, or loops, were used to process or compute values in arrays.

Several categories of iteration control statements have been developed. The primary categories are defined by how designers answered two fundamental design questions:

1. How is the iteration controlled?
2. Where should the control mechanism appear in the loop?

The primary possibilities for iteration control are: logical, counting, or a combination of logical and counting. The main choices for the location of the control mechanism are the top of the loop or the bottom of the loop. A third option, which allows the user to decide where to put the control, is discussed in Section 6.5.3. In the following we use the term **pretest** to mean that the test for loop completion is at the top of the loop, and **posttest** to mean it is at the bottom. The **body** of a loop is the collection of statements whose execution is controlled by the iteration statement. The iteration statement and the associated loop body together form an **iteration construct.**

In addition to the primary iteration statements, we discuss another form, which is in a class by itself: user-defined iteration control.

6.5.1   Counter-Controlled Loops

A counting iterative control statement has a variable, called the **loop variable,** in which the count value is maintained. It also includes some means of specifying the **initial** and **terminal values** of the loop variable, as well as the difference between adjacent loop variable values, often called the **stepsize.** The initial, terminal, and stepsize specifications of a loop are called the **loop parameters.**

6.5.1.1   Design Issues

There are a large number of design issues for iterative counter-controlled statements:

1. What is the type and scope of the loop variable?
2. What value does the loop variable have at loop termination?
3. Can the loop variable or loop parameters be changed in the loop, and if so, does the change affect loop control?
4. Is it legal to branch into the loop?
5. Should the test for completion be at the top or the bottom of the loop?
6. Are the loop parameters evaluated only once, or once for every iteration?

6.5.1.2   The FORTRAN IV DO

FORTRAN I introduced the first iterative control statement, which remained the same in FORTRAN II and IV. We include a description of it here to illustrate the differences between it and the corresponding statement in FORTRAN 77. It is interesting to see how designs of constructs evolve, especially within a specific language. The FORTRAN IV counting posttest loop construct has the form

    DO label variable = initial, terminal [, stepsize]

Figure 6.5
Flowgraph of the
FORTRAN IV DO

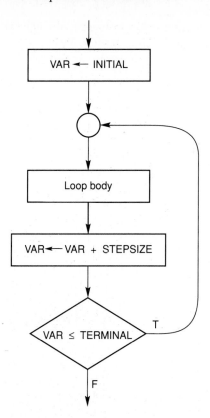

The label is that of the last statement in the loop body. The stepsize parameter is optional; when absent, it defaults to 1. The initial, terminal, and stepsize parameters are restricted to unsigned integer constants or simple integer variables with positive values. This disallows loops with descending loop variables. A flowgraph description of the FORTRAN IV DO statement is shown in Figure 6.5.

The FORTRAN IV DO design answers the above design choices as follows. The loop variable type is restricted to integer and its scope is that of the program unit in which it appears, unless it is in COMMON, in which case its scope also includes any program unit that requests access to the particular COMMON block it is in. The value of the loop variable is undefined upon normal loop termination because that sometimes makes it slightly easier to implement efficiently. The value of the loop variable upon abnormal termination (which can be caused by a branch statement) is its most recently assigned value. The loop variable and loop parameters cannot be changed in the loop body, so there is no reason to evaluate the loop parameters more than once.

A DO construct can be exited and reentered from points outside the loop under certain circumstances. The acceptable circumstances are when a GO

TO is used to exit the loop to a code segment called an **extended loop body.** At the end of the extended loop body, another GOTO transfers control back into the DO body. This is a dangerous capability. First, understanding such potentially complex control, which is a direct violation of the concept of single-entry/single-exit control structures, can be difficult. Moreover, the capability poses a serious problem for compiler designers: How can illegal entries to loops be distinguished from legal entries from extended loop bodies? The answer is usually that no illegal entries are detected. When control transfers into a loop, the values used are those that the loop variable and loop parameters happen to have at that time.

Finally, as stated above, the DO is a posttest loop construct.

6.5.1.3   The FORTRAN 77 DO

Although the basic form of the FORTRAN 77 DO statement remained the same as FORTRAN IV's DO, the designers of FORTRAN 77 changed many of the basic design decisions. The loop variable, for example, is allowed to be integer, real, or double-precision type. The loop parameters are allowed to be expressions, and can have positive or negative values. They are evaluated at the beginning of the execution of the DO statement, and the value is used to compute an **iteration count,** which then has the number of times the loop is to be executed. The loop is controlled by the iteration count, not the loop parameters, so even if the parameters are changed in the loop, which is legal, those changes cannot affect loop control. The iteration count is an internal variable that is inaccessible to the user code.

DO constructs can only be entered through the DO statement, thereby making the statement a single-entry structure. When a DO terminates—and regardless of how it terminates—the loop variable always has its most recently assigned value. Thus, the usefulness of the loop variable is independent of the method by which the loop terminates.

Perhaps the most significant change from one version of the language to another, however, has been the move of the test for completion from the bottom to the top of the loop. FORTRAN I's DO loop was posttest because IBM 704 had a single machine language instruction to implement it that way. Having the test at the top prevents the error of executing loop statements when the loop parameters specify that they should be skipped. A flowgraph description of the FORTRAN 77 DO statement is shown in Figure 6.6.

6.5.1.4   The ALGOL 60 **for** Statement

ALGOL 60's **for** statement is a generalization of the FORTRAN 77 DO and allows far more complexity than necessary, as shown in its EBNF description:

<for_stmt> → **for** var := <list_element>
                        {, <list_element>} **do** <statement>
<list_element> → <expression>

Figure 6.6
Flowgraph of the
FORTRAN 77 DO

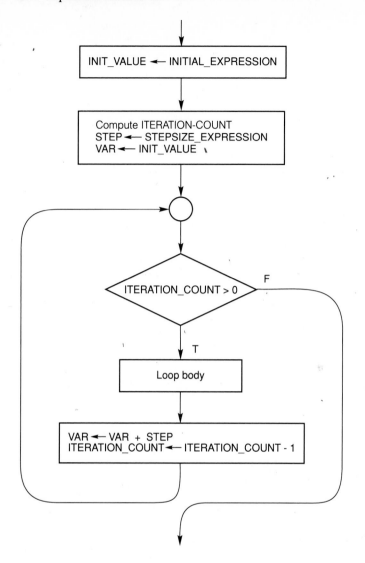

$$| \text{<expression>} \ \textbf{step} \ \text{<expression>}$$
$$\textbf{until} \ \text{<expression>}$$
$$| \text{<expression>} \ \textbf{while} \ \text{<Boolean\_expr>}$$

The most significant difference between this and the FORTRAN 77 DO is that this construct can combine a counter and a Boolean expression for loop control. The three simplest forms are exemplified by:

```
for count := 1, 2, 3, 4, 5, 6,  7, 8, 9, 10 do
     list[count] := 0

for count := 1 step 1 until 10 do list[count] := 0
```

```
for count := 1, count + 1 while (count <= 10) do
   list[count] := 0
```

This statement is far more complex when its different simple forms are combined, as in the following:

```
for index := 1, 4, 13,
              41 step 2 until 47,
              3 * index while index < 1000,
              34, 2, -24  do
   sum := sum + index
```

The statement adds the following values to sum:

```
1, 4, 13, 41, 43, 45, 47, 141, 423, 34, 2, -24
```

Although there may be occasions when such a complicated statement is convenient, those occasions occur too rarely to justify the inclusion of such complexity in a language.

The ALGOL 60 **for** statement is even more difficult than it first appears, since all the expressions in the **for** lists are evaluated for every iteration, or execution, of the loop statements. Thus, if a **step** expression includes a reference to the variable count, for example, and the loop statements change the value of count, the stepsize will change with each iteration. For example, consider the loop:

```
i := 1;
for count := 1 step count until 3 * i do
   i := i + 1
```

This **for** statement causes the assignment (i := i + 1) to be executed while the values of count double with each iteration. Because count is increasing faster than the **until** clause expression (3 * i), the loop is not infinite, although that is not obvious at first glance.

The design choices of the ALGOL 60 **for** are the following. The loop variable can be either integer or real type, and it is declared like any other variable, so its scope is that of its declaration. As is the case in FORTRAN 77, the loop variable has its most recently assigned value after loop termination, regardless of the cause of that termination. Loop parameters, but not the loop variable, can be changed in the loop body. The result of branching into the loop body is undefined; it is legal, but the effect is unpredictable. It is a pretest loop, and, as stated above, the loop parameters are evaluated for every iteration.

It is not feasible to present a flowgraph of the complete ALGOL 60 **for** statement with all of its options. Instead, we present here a flowgraph of a **for** statement with only the step-until form, shown in Figure 6.7.

Figure 6.8 is a flowgraph of the following example **for** statement:

```
for count := 10 step 2 * count until init * init,
              3 * count while sum <= 10000 do
   sum := sum + count
```

Figure 6.7
Flowgraph of the
ALGOL 60 **step-until-for**
statement

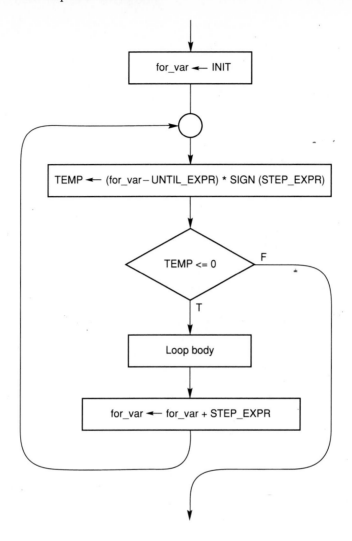

6.5.1.5   The Ada **for** Statement

The Ada **for** statement is a relatively simple counter-controlled pretest loop
with the form:

> **for** variable **in** [**reverse**] discrete_range
> **loop**
>   ...
> **end loop**

A discrete range is a subrange of an integer or enumeration type, such as
1..10.

The design choices of the Ada **for** statement are the following. The
scope of the loop variable is the range of the loop. The variable is implicitly

Figure 6.8
An example of an
ALGOL 60 **for**
statement

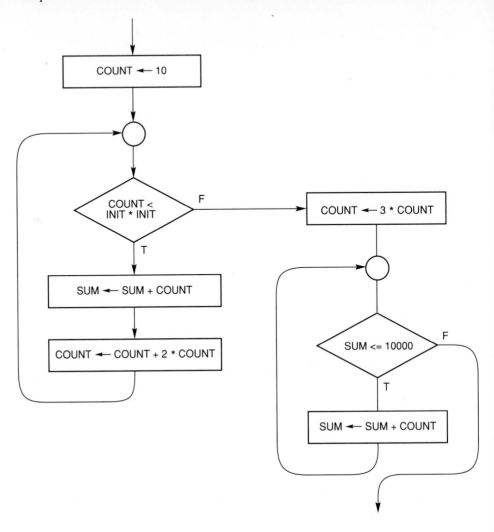

declared at the **for** statement, and implicitly undeclared after loop termination. For example, in:

```
COUNT : FLOAT := 1.35;
for COUNT in 1..10
  loop
   SUM := SUM + COUNT;
  end loop
```

the FLOAT variable COUNT is unaffected by the **for** loop. Upon loop termination, the variable COUNT is still FLOAT type with the value of 1.35. Also,
the FLOAT-type variable COUNT is hidden from the code in the body of the
loop, being masked by the loop counter COUNT, which is implicitly declared
to be the type of the discrete range, INTEGER.

The Ada loop variable cannot be assigned in the loop body. Because the
loop variable does not exist outside the loop body, the question of its value

Figure 6.9
Flowgraph of the Ada
for loop

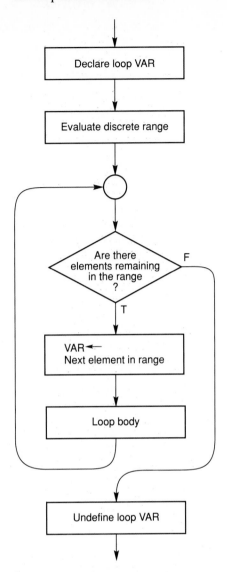

after loop termination is moot. Variables in the discrete range can be changed in the loop, but because the range is evaluated only once, these changes do not affect loop control. The Ada **for** statement has a pretest control, and it is not legal to branch into the **for** loop body. Figure 6.9 is a flowgraph description of the Ada **for** loop.

6.5.1.6 The C **for** Statement

The C language **for** statement forms a pretest counting loop structure. Its general form is:

> **for** (expression_1; expression_2; expression_3)
>   statement

The controlled statement can be a single statement, a compound statement, or a null statement.

Because statements in C produce results and thus can be considered expressions, the expressions in a **for** statement are often statements. The first expression is for initialization, and is evaluated only once: when **for** statement execution begins. The second expression is the loop control, and is evaluated before each execution of the loop body. As is usual in C, a zero value means false and all nonzero values mean true. Therefore, if the value of the second expression is zero, the **for** is terminated; otherwise, the loop statements are executed. The last expression in the **for** is executed after each execution of the loop body. A flowgraph describing the C **for** statement is shown in Figure 6.10.

A typical C counting loop is:

```
for (index = 0; index <= 10; index++)
    sum = sum + list[index];
```

All of the expressions of C's **for** are optional. An absent second expression is considered true, and a potentially infinite loop is thus formed. If the first

Figure 6.10
Flowgraph of the C
for statement

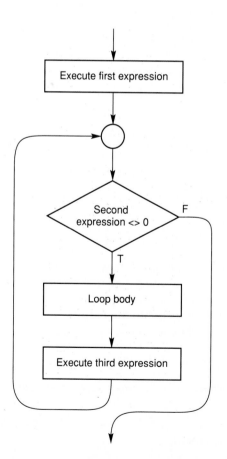

and/or third expressions are absent, no assumptions are made. For example, if the first expression is absent, it simply means that no initialization takes place.

The C **for** design choices are the following. There is no explicit loop variable or loop parameters. All involved variables can be changed in the loop body. The expressions are evaluated in the order stated above. Despite the fact that it can cause havoc, it is legal to branch into a C **for** loop body.

C's **for** is more flexible than that of the other languages we have discussed because each of the expressions can comprise multiple statements, which in turn allows multiple loop variables that can be of any type. When multiple statements are used in a single expression of a **for** statement, they are separated by commas. All C statements have values, and this form of multiple statement is no exception. The value of such a multiple statement is the value of the last component.

Consider the following **for** statement:

```
for  (sum = 0.0,  count = 0;
      count <= 10 && sum < 1000.0;
      sum = sum + count++);
```

The equivalent Pascal code for this is:

```
sum  : = 0.0;
count  : = 0;
while (count <= 10) and (sum < 1000.0) do
   begin
   sum  : = sum + count;
   count  : = count + 1
   end
```

The C version of this **for** statement does not need and thus does not have a loop body. All the desired actions are part of the **for** statement itself. The first expression is a multiple statement; its value is not used in this case. If the same two statements formed the second expression of the **for** statement, the value would be used for the loop control. If it were, it would always be zero, or false.

Note that C's **for** need not count. It can easily model counting and logical loop structures, as demonstrated in the next section.

6.5.2 Logically Controlled Loops

In many cases collections of statements must be repeatedly executed, but the repetition control is based on a Boolean expression. In some of these cases a counter is needed, but in many others, it is not. For the latter situation, a logically controlled loop is convenient. In fact, logically controlled loops are more general than counter-controlled loops. Every counting loop can be built with a logical loop, but the reverse is not true. Also, recall that only selection and logical loops are essential to express the control structure of any flowchart.

6.5.2.1　Design Issues

The primary design issues for logically controlled loops are the following:

1. Should the control be pretest or posttest?
2. Should the logically controlled loop be a special form of a counting loop, or a distinct statement?
3. Is it legal to branch into the body of the loop?

6.5.2.2　Examples

Some imperative languages—for example Pascal, Modula-2, and C—include both pretest and posttest logically controlled loops that are not parts of their counter-controlled iterative statements. In C, the pretest and posttest logical loops have the forms:

```
while (expression) statement
do statement while (expression)
```

In the pretest version (**while**), the statement, which can of course be compound, is executed as long as the expression evaluates to true (non-zero). In the posttest version (**do**), the statement is executed until the expression evaluates to false (zero). In both cases the expression has a numerical value. The flowgraph descriptions of those two statements is shown in Figure 6.11.

It is legal in C to branch into either a **while** or a **do** loop body.

FORTRAN 77 has neither a pretest nor a posttest logical loop. Ada has a pretest logical loop into which it is illegal to branch, but the language includes no posttest version of the logical loop. ALGOL 60 combined its pretest logical statement with its general loop statement, **for**, as we discussed in Section 6.5.1.4. The pretest and posttest logical loops of Pascal and Modula-2 are

Figure 6.11
The pretest and post-test logical loops of C

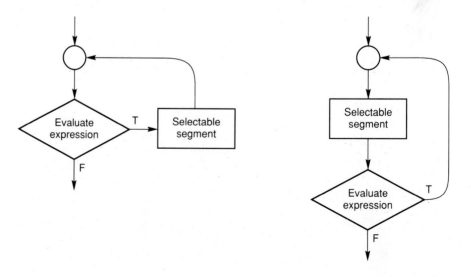

called while and repeat, respectively. It is not legal to branch into either loop in either language.

Pascal's posttest logical loop is called the **repeat-until**. This loop is odd because its body can be either a compound statement or a statement sequence. It is the only control structure in Pascal with this flexibility. This is another example of the lack of orthogonality in the design of Pascal.

6.5.3   User-Located Loop Control Mechanisms

In some situations it is convenient to be able to place the control for a loop at positions other than the top or bottom of the loop. The design choices for such a mechanism are the following:

1. Should the mechanism be conditional or unconditional?
2. Can the mechanism appear in a controlled loop, or only in one without any other control?
3. Should only one loop body be exited, or can enclosing loops also be exited?

Both Modula-2 and Ada have loop statements that have no iteration control; they are infinite loops unless controls are added by the user. The forms of these infinite loops in Modula-2 and Ada are

```
LOOP
. . .
END
```

and

```
loop
. . .
end loop
```

respectively.

Modula-2 has a loop control statement, EXIT, that is not conditional and causes termination of only the uncontrolled loop in which it appears. For example, one could have:

```
LOOP
   . . .
   sum := sum + index;
   IF sum >= 10000
      THEN EXIT
   END
   . . .
END
```

As you might expect, the Ada model of exit is more complex. It can be either unconditional or conditional, and it can terminate one or more of the nested loops in which it is placed. Furthermore, Ada's **exit** can terminate a **for** loop, a **while** loop, or an otherwise infinite loop. The general form of the Ada **exit** statement is:

> **exit** [loop_name] [**when** condition]

The reserved word **loop** can be labeled, and when a loop label is included on the **exit**, the exit is to the statement immediately following the referenced loop. The **when** condition is used in place of the **if** construct to make the **exit** conditional. If the loop name is omitted, control leaves the innermost loop in which the **exit** is placed. For example, consider the following two code segments:

```
OUTER_LOOP:
  for ROW in 1 .. MAX_ROWS loop
INNER_LOOP:
    for COL in 1 .. MAX_COLS loop
      SUM := SUM + MAT(ROW, COL);
      exit OUTER_LOOP when SUM > 1000.0;
      end loop INNER_LOOP ;
    end loop OUTER_LOOP;

loop
  GET (VALUE);
  exit when VALUE = LAST_VALUE;
  SUM := SUM + VALUE;
  end loop;
```

In the first example, the **exit** is a conditional branch to the first statement after the outer loop. If the **exit** were instead

> **exit when** SUM > 1000.0;

it would be a conditional branch to the first statement after the inner loop.

The second example illustrates a loop in which the only control is formed with the conditional **exit**. This is an example of a loop in which the position of the only control mechanism is chosen by the user.

Note that exit statements are often used for handling unusual or error conditions.

The C language contains an unconditional control mechanism similar to Modula-2's EXIT, **break**. As was demonstrated in Section 6.4.4, **break** can also be used in the C multiple selection structure, **switch**. The **break** statement causes the termination of the smallest enclosing loop or **switch** construct.

C also includes a control mechanism, **continue**, that is related to **break**. The **continue** statement transfers control to the end of the smallest enclosing loop. This is not an exit, but rather a way to skip the rest of the loop statements on the current iteration without terminating the loop structure. For example, consider the following:

```
while (sum < 1000)
  {
```

```
    getnext (value);
    if (value < 0) continue;
    sum = sum + value;
    }
```

A negative value causes the assignment statement to be skipped, and control is given instead to the conditional at the top of the loop. On the other hand, in:

```
while (sum < 1000)
    {
    getnext (value);
    if (value < 0) break;
    sum = sum + value;
    }
```

a negative value terminates the loop.

Both **exit** and **break** provide for multiple exits from loops, which is somewhat of a hindrance to readability. However, unusual conditions that require loop termination are so common that such a construct is justified. Furthermore, readability is not seriously harmed if the target of all such loop exits is the first statement after the loop—which it is in these cases—rather than just anywhere in the program.

6.5.4   Iterators

Only one additional kind of looping structure remains for us to consider: iterators. Rather than have a counter or Boolean expression control the iterations, these loops use the number of elements in a user-defined data structure. Iterators are found only in certain experimental languages, such as CLU.

An iterator construct is a loop construct similar to a **for**, except that the control mechanism is specified as a user-defined function. The function is called at the beginning of each iteration, and each time it is called, the function returns an element from a particular data structure in some particular order. For example, suppose we have a linked list of data nodes and wish to process the data in each node. An iterator loop for the list might successively set the loop variable to point to the nodes in the linked list, one at a time. The initial execution of the iterator construct needs to issue a special call to the function to get the first element. The user must provide the function to produce the next node address each time it is called. This routine must always remember which node it presented last so that it visits all nodes without visiting any more than once. An iterator loop terminates when the function that is getting elements finds that the structure from which it is getting those elements has no more elements.

The C **for** construct, because of its high degree of flexibility, can be used to simulate an iterator. For example, suppose the nodes of a binary tree are to be processed. If the tree root is pointed to by root, and traverse is a

function that sets its parameter to point to the next element of a tree, in the
desired order, we could use:

```
for (ptr := root;  ptr != NUL; traverse(ptr))
   { ... }
```

6.6   Unconditional Branching

An **unconditional branch statement** transfers execution control to a specified place in the program.

6.6.1   Problems with Unconditional Branching

One of the most heated debates in language design has been whether
unconditional branching should be part of any high-level language, and if
so, whether its use should be restricted.

The unconditional branch, or goto, is the most powerful statement for
controlling the flow of execution of a program's statements. However,
although the goto has stunning power and great flexibility (all other control
structures can be built with goto and a selector), it is this very power that
makes its use dangerous. Without restrictions on use, imposed either by
language design or programming standards, goto statements can make programs virtually unreadable, and as a result highly unreliable and difficult
to maintain.

These problems follow directly from a goto's capability of forcing any
program statement to follow any other in execution sequence, regardless
of whether that statement precedes or follows the first in textual order.
Readability is best when the execution order of statements is nearly the
same as the order in which they are written—in our case this would mean
top to bottom, which is the order we are accustomed to. Thus, restricting
goto's so they can transfer control only downward in a program partially
alleviates the problem. It allows goto's to transfer control around code sections in response to errors or unusual conditions, but disallows any sort of
goto loop formation.

Although suggested earlier by several thoughtful people, it was Edsgar
Dijkstra who gave the computing world the first widely read exposé on the
evils of the goto; in it he noted, "The goto statement as it stands is just too
primitive; it is too much an invitation to make a mess of one's program"
(Dijkstra, 1968). During the first few years after publication of Dijkstra's
views on the goto, a large number of people argued publicly for either

outright banishment or at least restriction of the goto. Among those who did not favor complete elimination was Donald Knuth, who argued that there were occasions when the efficiency of the goto outweighed its harm to readability (Knuth, 1974).

A few languages have been designed without a goto—for example, Modula-2, Bliss (Wulf et al., 1971), and the experimental languages CLU (Liskov et al., 1981), Euclid (Lampson et al., 1977), and Gypsy (Ambler et al., 1977). However, most currently popular languages include a goto statement. Kernighan and Ritchie (1978) call the goto infinitely abusable, but it is nevertheless included in Ritchie's language, C. Those languages that have eliminated the goto have provided additional control statements, usually in the form of loop and subprogram exits, to replace many of the typical applications of the goto.

6.6.2 Label Forms

Some languages, such as ALGOL 60 and C, use their identifier forms for labels. FORTRAN and Pascal use unsigned integer constants for labels. The Ada language uses its identifier form as the target part of its goto statement, but when the label appears on a statement, it must be delimited by the symbols << and >>. For example, consider the following:

```
goto FINISHED;
    . . .
<<FINISHED>> SUM := SUM + NEXT;
```

The bracketing makes labels easier to find when one is reading a program, and also somewhat simplifies the compiler writer's job. In some other languages, such as ALGOL 60 and Pascal, labels are attached to statements by colons, as in:

```
finished: sum := sum + next
```

In its design of labels, PL/I, once again, takes a construct to its limit of flexibility and complexity. Instead of treating labels as mere constants, PL/I allows them to be variables. In their variable form, they can be assigned values and used as subprogram parameters. This allows a goto to be targeted to virtually anywhere in a program. Although this vast flexibility is sometimes useful, it is far too detrimental to readability to be worthwhile. Imagine trying to read and understand a program that has branches whose targets depend on values assigned at run time. Consider a subprogram that has several labels and a goto whose target label is a formal parameter. To determine the target of the goto, one must know the calling program unit and the actual parameter value used in the call. The implementation of variable labels is also complex, primarily because of all the possible ways label variables can be bound to values.

6.6.3 Restrictions on Branches

Recognizing the problem inherent with goto's, some languages restrict their use. As an example of how the unconditional branch can be restricted, we examine the rules that Pascal applies to its goto statement. Pascal labels must be declared as if they were variables, but they cannot be passed as parameters, stored, or modified. As part of the goto statement, they must be simple constants—not expressions or variables with labels as values.

The target of a Pascal goto must be one of the following:

1. Another statement in the compound statement that contains the **goto**

2. A statement in a compound statement that contains the compound statement that contains the **goto**. In this case, the target statement must be at the outermost level of nesting in the statement part in which it appears. This prevents jumping into a compound statement at a higher level. For example, the following code segment is illegal:

```
while ...  do
  begin
  . . .
  while ...  do
    begin
    . . .
100:  . . .
    . . .
    end;
  while ...  do
    begin
    . . .
    goto 100;
    . . .
    end;
  end
```

The problem is that the label 100 is on a statement that is not at the outermost level of nesting within the compound statement that contains the **goto**; rather, it is in a nested **while**.

The **goto** in the following code segment is legal:

```
while ...  do
  begin
  . . .
 100:  . . .
  . . .
  while ...  do
    begin
    . . .
    goto 100;
    . . .
    end;
  end;
```

3. A statement in a procedure that contains the procedure that contains the `goto`. Once again, the target statement must be at the outermost level of nesting in the statement part in which it appears.

The major problem with Pascal's restrictions is that it is still legal to branch into a different procedure. The target procedure, because it must be enclosing, is already activated. So the `goto` can terminate one or more procedure activations, or executions, but can start one only if the target is a procedure call.

Branching from one procedure to another is highly detrimental to program readability, and is therefore an unreliable programming practice. Although Pascal's design attempts, through its restrictions, to prevent some problems with unconditional branching, it still allows what many consider unsafe use of the powerful `goto` control statement.

On the positive side—in defense of Pascal's `goto` target rules—the ability to branch from a procedure to its parent or grandparent can be a convenient method of propagating error conditions to ancestor procedures for possible corrective action.

Some languages include statements that are actually camouflaged goto statements. The exit statements of Modula-2 and Ada, discussed in Section 6.5.3, fall into this category—they are actually restricted and disguised goto's.

6.7 Guarded Commands

Alternative and quite different forms of selection and loop structures were suggested by Dijkstra (1975). His motivation was to provide control statements that would support a program design methodology that ensured correctness during development, rather than relying on verification or testing of completed programs to ensure their correctness. This methodology is described in Dijkstra (1976).

Dijkstra's selection construct has the form:

```
if <Boolean expression> → <statement>
 ▯  <Boolean expression> → <statement>
   ...
 ▯  <Boolean expression> → <statement>
fi
```

Note the somewhat odd appearance of the closing reserved word, `fi`. It is the opening reserved word spelled backwards. This form of closing reserved word is taken from ALGOL 68. The small blocks are used to separate the guarded clauses, which allows the clauses to be statement sequences.

This selection construct has the appearance of a multiple selection, but its semantics is quite different. All of the Boolean expressions are evaluated each time the construct is reached during execution. If more than one expression is true, one of the corresponding statements is nondeterministically chosen for execution. If none is true, it is a run-time error that causes program termination. This forces the programmer to consider and list all possibilities, as with Ada's **case** statement. Consider the following example:

```
if i = 0 → sum := sum + i
□  i > j → sum := sum + j
□  j > i → sum := sum + i
fi
```

If i = 0 and j = 1, this construct chooses nondeterministically between the first and third assignment statements. If i is equal to j and is not zero, a run-time error occurs because none of the conditions is true. This construct may not appear to be useful, especially in this example, but it can be an elegant way of allowing the programmer to state that the order of execution, in some cases, is irrelevant. For example, to find the largest of two numbers, one can use:

```
if x >= y → max := x
□  y >= x → max := y
fi
```

This computes the desired result without overspecifying the solution. In particular, if x and y are equal, it does not matter which is assigned to max. This is a form of abstraction provided by the nondeterministic semantics of the statement.

Figure 6.12 is a flowgraph description of Dijkstra's selector statement. The loop structure proposed by Dijkstra has the form:

```
do <Boolean expression> → <statement>
□   <Boolean expression> → <statement>
      .
      .
□   <Boolean expression> → <statement>
od
```

The semantics of this construct is that all Boolean expressions are evaluated on each iteration. If more than one is true, one of the associated statements is nondeterministically chosen for execution, after which the expressions are again evaluated. When all expressions are simultaneously false, the loop terminates. Once again the programmer is forced to consider all possibilities.

Consider the following code, which appears in slightly different form in Dijkstra (1975). The four variables q1, q2, q3, and q4 are to be assigned the values of the four variables Q1, Q2, Q3, and Q4 so that q1 <= q2 <= q3 <= q4.

```
q1 := Q1;   q2 := Q2;   q3 := Q3;   q4 := Q4;
do q1 > q2 → temp := q1;   q1 := q2;   q2 := temp;
□  q2 > q3 → temp := q2;   q2 := q3;   q3 := temp;
□  q3 > q4 → temp := q3;   q3 := q4;   q4 := temp;
od
```

A flowgraph description of Dijkstra's loop statement is shown in Figure 6.13.

Figure 6.12
Flowgraph of Dijk-
stra's selector
statement

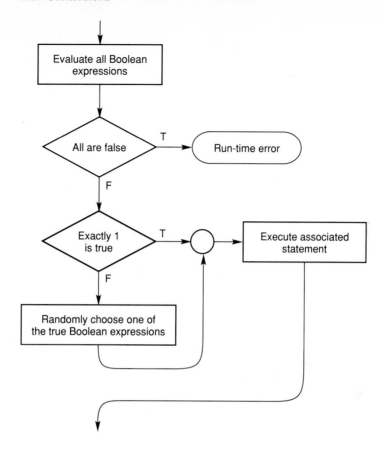

A form of Dijkstra's **do** is used in the concurrency control in the Ada language, as we discuss in Chapter 11.

Dijkstra's guarded commands, as these two constructs are known, are interesting in part because they illustrate how the syntax and semantics of statements can have an impact on program design methodologies, and vice versa. Program verification is virtually impossible when goto statements are used. Verification is possible when only logical loops and selections such as those of Pascal are used. It is greatly simplified when only guarded commands are used.

6.8 Conclusions

We have described and discussed a variety of control structures. A brief evaluation now seems to be in order.

First, we have the theoretical result that only sequence, selection, and pretest logical loops are absolutely required to express computations (Bohm

Figure 6.13
Flowgraph of Dijk-
stra's loop statement

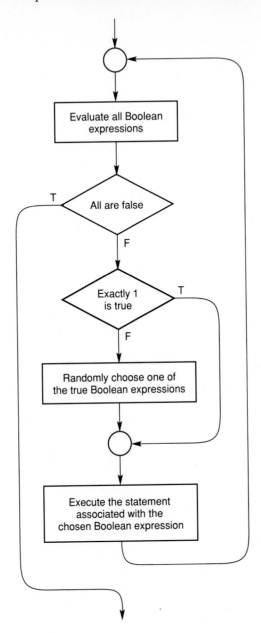

and Jacopini, 1966). This result has been widely used by those who wish to ban unconditional branching altogether. Of course, there are already sufficient practical problems with the goto to condemn it without reliance on any theoretical finding.

Perhaps the more interesting use of the Bohm and Jacopini result is to argue against the inclusion of *any* control structures beyond selection and pretest logical loop. No widely used language has yet taken that step. Further, we doubt that any ever will. The reason is writability. It is easier and more convenient to write programs when other control structures are available. In most uses of the goto, however, the negative readability factor clearly outweighs the positive writability factor. The one possible exception is its use to allow premature exits from loops in languages that do not have exit statements. But in some other cases, the increased writability gained by an additional control structure is not counterbalanced by negative baggage. For example, the Ada multiple selection structure is a great boost to Ada writability, with no clear negatives. Another example is the counting loop structure of many languages, especially when the loop is simple, as in Pascal.

It is not so clear that the utility of many of the other control structures that have been proposed is worth their inclusion in languages (Ledgard and Marcotty, 1975). This question rests to a large degree on the fundamental question of whether the size of languages must be minimized. Both Wirth (1975) and Hoare (1973) strongly endorse simplicity in language design. In the case of control structures, simplicity means a few control statements that are simple.

The rich variety of statement-level control structures that have been invented shows the diversity of opinion among language designers. After all the invention, discussion, and evaluation, however, there is little unanimity on syntax design. No single set of control structures has been widely accepted. There is agreement that the set should be rather small, and that there must be sufficient variety that the goto should be rarely necessary. Beyond that, the debate continues.

SUMMARY

The control statements of the imperative languages occur in several categories: selection, multiple selection, iterative, and unconditional branching.

FORTRAN IV has a single-way single statement selector, the logical IF. ALGOL 60's selector is more advanced, allowing selection of compound statements and including an optional else clause. Most control structures benefited from the compound statement that ALGOL 60 introduced.

FORTRAN's arithmetic IF is a three-way selector that usually requires other unconditional branches.

FORTRAN introduced two forms of multiple selection statement: the computed GOTO and the assigned GOTO. True to their names, both are actually multiple-way branches. The Pascal **case** is representative of modern multiple selection statements; it includes both encapsulation of the selectable segments and implicit branches at the end of each.

A large number of different loop statements have been invented, starting with FORTRAN's counting DO. The **for** statement of ALGOL 60 was far too complex, combining logic and counter controls in a single statement. Pascal's **for** statement is, in terms of complexity, the opposite. It elegantly implements only the most commonly needed counting loop forms. C's **for** statement is the most flexible iteration construct.

The Modula-2, C, and Ada languages have exit statements for their loops; these statements take the place of one of the most common uses of goto statements.

Iterators are user-defined loop constructs for processing user-defined data structures such as linked lists and trees.

Dijkstra's guarded commands are alternative control constructs with positive theoretical characteristics. Although they have not been adopted as the control constructs of a language, part of the semantics appear in Ada's concurrency mechanism.

The unconditional branch, or goto, has been part of most imperative languages. Its problems have been widely discussed and debated. The current consensus is that it should remain in most languages, but that its dangers should be minimized through programming discipline.

BIBLIOGRAPHY

Ambler, A.L., D.I. Good, J.C. Browne, W.F. Burger, R.M. Cohen, C.G. Hoch, and R.E. Wells. (1977) "Gypsy: A Language for Specification and Implementation of Verifiable Programs." Proceedings of the ACM Conference on Language Design for Reliable Software. *ACM SIGPLAN Notices,* Vol. 12, No. 3, pp. 1–10.

Bohm, C., and G. Jacopini. (1966) "Flow Diagrams, Turing Machines, and Languages with Only Two Formation Rules." *Commun. ACM,* Vol. 9, No. 5, pp. 366–371.

Dijkstra, E.W. (1968) "Goto Statement Considered Harmful." *Commun. ACM,* Vol. 11, No. 3, pp. 147–149.

Dijkstra, E.W. (1975) "Guarded Commands, Nondeterminancy, and Formal Derivation of Programs." *Commun. ACM,* Vol. 18, No. 8, pp. 453–457.

Dijkstra, E.W. (1976) *A Discipline of Programming.* Prentice-Hall, Englewood Cliffs, NJ.

Hoare, C.A.R. (1973) "Hints on Programming Language Design." SIGACT/SIGPLAN Symposium on Principles of Programming Languages, keynote address.

Jensen, K., and N. Wirth. (1974) *Pascal Users Manual and Report.* Springer-Verlag, Berlin.

Kernighan, B.W., and D.M. Ritchie. (1978) *The C Programming Language.* Prentice-Hall, Englewood Cliffs, NJ.

Knuth, D.E. (1974) "Structured Programming with GOTO Statements." *ACM Computing Surveys,* Vol. 6, No. 4, pp. 261–301.

Lampson, B.W., J.J. Horning, R.L. London, J.G. Mitchell, and G.J. Popek. (1977) "Report on the Programming Language Euclid." *ACM SIGPLAN Notices,* Vol. 12, No. 2. (Revised Report, XEROX PARC Technical Report CSL78-2.)

Ledgard, H.F. (prepared by) (1984) *The American Pascal Standard.* Springer-Verlag, New York.

Ledgard, H.F., and M. Marcotty. (1975) "A Genealogy of Control Structures." *Commun. ACM,* Vol. 18, No. 11, pp. 629–639.

Liskov, B.H., E. Moss, C. Schaffert, R. Scheiffer, and A. Snyder. (1981) "CLU Reference Manual." In *Computation Structures Group Memo 161*, MIT Laboratory for Computer Science, Cambridge, MA, July.

Wirth, N. (1975) "On the Design of Programming Languages." *Information Processing 74* (Proceedings of IFIP Congress 74), North Holland, Amsterdam, pp. 386–393.

Wirth, N., and C.A.R. Hoare. (1966) "A Contribution to the Development of ALGOL." *Commun. ACM*, Vol. 9, No. 6, pp. 413–431.

Wulf, W.A., D.B. Russell, and A.N. Habermann. (1971) "BLISS:A Language for Systems Programming." *Commun. ACM*, Vol. 14, No. 12, pp. 780–790.

PROBLEM SET

1. Write a defense of the claim that the three-way selection statement of FORTRAN I was the best choice, given the circumstances of the time.

2. Devise a situation in which the label variable of PL/I would be a great advantage.

3. Describe three situations in which a combined counting and logical looping construct is needed.

4. Compare the FORTRAN-computed GOTO with the Pascal **case** statement, especially in terms of readability and reliability.

5. What are the possible reasons why Pascal has a logical posttest loop, while ALGOL 60 did not?

6. Study the iterator feature of CLU in Liskov et al.(1981), and determine its advantages and disadvantages.

7. Compare the set of Ada control statements with those of FORTRAN 77 and decide which are better and why.

8. What are the pros and cons of using unique closing reserved words on compound statements?

9. Analyze the potential readability problems with using closure reserved words for control statements that are the reverse of the corresponding initial reserved words, such as the **case-esac** reserved words of ALGOL 68. For example, consider common typing errors such as the reversal of two adjacent characters.

10. Consider the ALGOL 60-style **for** statement:

    for i := j + 1 **step** i * j **until** 3 * j **do** j := j + 1

    Assume that the initial values of i and j are both 1. List the sequence of values for the variable i used, assuming the following semantics:
    a. All expressions are evaluated once at the loop entry.
    b. All expressions are evaluated before each iteration.
    c. **step** expressions are evaluated once at loop entry and **until** expressions are evaluated before each iteration.
    d. **until** expressions are evaluated once at loop entry and **step** expressions are evaluated before each iteration.
    In all cases, when more than one expression is evaluated at the same time, they are evaluated in left-to-right order. Also, the assignment is always done as soon as its RHS is evaluated. In c and d, the RHS is evaluated as in b.

11. Use the *Science Citation Index* to find an article that refers to Knuth (1974). Read the article and Knuth's paper and write a paper that summarizes both sides of the goto argument.

Handwritten margin notes:

4. FORTRAN – less readable because:

case is encapsulated. (reader need look only at case construct)

FORTRAN – less reliable because gotos in general less reliable

explicit GOTO at end of each selectable group (of computed GOTO) easily forgotten

10.
a) $i = 2$
b) $i = 2, 4$
c) $i = 2, 4, 6, 8 ...$
d) $i = 2$

Key Concepts

- Type compatibility by name and structure
- Character string types
- Enumeration and subrange types
- Arrays and their operations
- Records and their operations
- Discriminated and free unions
- Mathematical sets as a data type
- Dangling pointers
- Garbage
- Implementation methods for data types
- Array access functions
- Reference counters and garbage collection

7

DATA TYPES

Contents

The concept of a data type and the characteristics of some elementary data types were introduced in Chapter 4. We now investigate the design of the more complex data types in imperative languages.

Type compatibility is an important part of the data type design of a language, and is therefore discussed in detail.

For each of the various categories of data types we will state the design issues and explain the design choices made by the designers of the important imperative languages. We will also evaluate these designs.

Implementation methods for data types often have a significant, if not crucial, impact on their design. Therefore, implementation of the different data types is another important part of this chapter.

7.1   Introduction

Computer programs produce results by manipulating data. The ease with which they can perform this task depends on how well the data types match the real-world problem space. It is therefore extremely important that the language support the proper variety of data types and structures. The designers of PL/I attempted to include types for a large range of applications. A much better approach, introduced in ALGOL 68, is to provide a few basic types and a few flexible combining methods that allow a programmer to tailor a structure to the problem at hand. This approach, which results in an orthogonal data type design, is followed in the Pascal, C, Modula-2, and Ada languages.

The contemporary concepts of data typing have evolved over the last 30 years. In the earliest languages, all problem space data structures had to be modeled with only a few basic language-supported data structures. For example, in FORTRAN, linked lists, nonlinked lists, and binary trees are all commonly modeled with arrays.

The data structures of COBOL took the first step away from the FORTRAN model by allowing programmers to specify the accuracy of decimal data values, and also by providing a structured data type for records of information. PL/I extended the capability of accuracy specification to integer and floating-point types. As mentioned above, ALGOL 68 advanced data structure design by allowing programmers to construct new data types from the built-in types.

The Ada language embodies the latest concepts in data type design. The philosophy of this design is that the user should be allowed to create a unique type for each unique class of variables in the problem space. Moreover, the language must enforce the uniqueness of the types, which are in fact abstractions of the problem space variables. This is a powerful concept, and it has a significant impact on the overall process of software design. Taking this concept a step farther, one arrives at abstract data types, which are discussed in detail in Chapter 10.

7.2 Type Compatibility

Before we begin our foray into the various data type categories, we must introduce and discuss the concept of **type compatibility.** The design of the type compatibility rules of a language is important, because it influences the design of the data types and the operations provided for objects of those types. Perhaps the most important result of two variables being of compatible types is that either one can be assigned to the other.

There are two primary type compatibility methods: name compatibility and structure compatibility. Type **compatibility by name** means that two variables have compatible types if they are in either the same declaration or in declarations that use the same type name. Type **compatibility by structure** means that two variables have compatible types if their types have identical structures.

Name type compatibility is easy to implement, but is highly restrictive. Under a strict interpretation, a variable that is a subrange of the integers would not be compatible with an integer type variable. For example, suppose Pascal used strict name type compatibility and we had the following:

```
type indextype = 1..100;
var
  i : integer;
  j : indextype;
```

The variables i and j would not be compatible; we could not assign i to j or vice versa.

Another problem with name compatibility arises when a structured type is passed among procedures through parameters. Such a type must be defined only once, globally. A procedure cannot state the type of such a formal parameters in local terms.

Structure compatibility is more flexible than name compatibility, but more difficult to implement. Under name compatibility, only the two type names need be compared to determine compatibility. Under structure compatibility, however, the entire structures of the two types must be compared. This comparison is not always simple. Consider a data structure that refers to itself. Other questions can also arise. For example, are two record types that have the same structure, but different field names, compatible? Are two single-dimensioned array types with the same element type but subscript ranges 0..10 and 1..11 compatible? Are two enumeration types that have the same number of components, but spell the literals differently, compatible?

Another difficulty with structure compatibility is that it disallows differentiating between types with the same structure. For example, if we have:

```
type celsius = real;
     fahrenheit = real;
```

variables of these two types are considered compatible under structure type compatibility, allowing them to be mixed in expressions, which is surely undesirable in this case. In general, types with different names are likely to be abstractions of different problem objects, and should not be considered equivalent.

The original definition of Pascal (Wirth, 1971) does not specify clearly when name or structure compatibility is to be used. This is highly detrimental to portability, because a program that is correct in one implementation could be illegal in another. The ISO Standard Pascal (ISO, 1982) clearly states the type compatibility rules of the language, which are neither completely by name nor completely by structure. Structure is used in most cases, while name is used for formal parameters and a few other situations.

Under the compatibility rules usually adopted by Pascal implementors, subranges of ordinal types are compatible with their parent ordinal types.

The Ada language uses a restricted form of name compatibility. Ada provides a new construct for building types with identical structure that are not compatible. These are called **derived types.** Derived types inherit all the properties of their parent types. In the following example:

```
type celsius is new FLOAT;
type fahrenheit is new FLOAT;
```

variables of these two derived types are not compatible, although their structures are identical. Derived types can also include constraints on the parent type.

Variables can be declared in many languages without using type names. Consider the following Ada example:

```
A : array (1..10) of INTEGER;
```

In this case, A has an anonymous type, though it is still unique. If we also had

```
B : array (1..10) of INTEGER;
```

A and B would be of anonymous but distinct and incompatible types, though they are structurally identical. The multiple declaration

```
C, D : array (1..10) of INTEGER;
```

creates two anonymous types, one for C and one for D, which are incompatible. This declaration is actually treated as if it were the two declarations:

```
C : array (1..10) of INTEGER;
D : array (1..10) of INTEGER;
```

The result of this is that C and D are not compatible. If we had instead

```
type LIST_10 is array (1..10) of INTEGER;
   C, D : LIST_10;
```

then C and D would be compatible.

7.3   General Design Issues for Data Types

In the following sections we discuss seven categories of data types. Design issues particular to each are stated and a number of example designs are discussed. Two design issues are fundamental to all data types. Rather than repeat them for all seven categories, we state them here at the beginning; they are as follows:

1. What is the syntax of references to variables of the type category?
2. What operations are provided for variables of types in the category and how are they specified?

7.4   Character String Types

A **character string type** is one in which the objects consist of sequences of characters. Character strings are fundamental to many computer applications. Character string constants are used to label output, and input and output of all kinds is often done in terms of strings.

7.4.1   Design Issues

The two most important design issues that are specific to character string types are:

1. Should strings be a primitive type, or simply a special kind of character array?
2. Should strings have static or dynamic length?

7.4.2   Strings and Their Operations

If strings are not defined as a primitive type, string data is usually stored in arrays of single characters. This is the approach taken by the Pascal, Modula-2, and Ada languages. In Pascal, although string is not a primitive type, **char** arrays that have the **packed** attribute can be assigned and compared with the relational operators. In Modula-2, strings in CHAR arrays can be assigned string constants, but that is the only operation provided by the language.

In Ada, STRING is a type that is predefined to be single-dimensioned arrays of CHARACTER elements. Substring reference, catenation, relational operators, and assignment are provided for STRING types. Substring reference allows any substring of a given string to be treated as a value in a reference or as a variable in an assignment. A substring reference is denoted by a parenthesized integer range, which indicates the desired substring by character position. For example,

NAME1(2:4)

specifies the substring consisting of the second, third, and fourth characters of the value in NAME1.

Character string catenation in Ada is an operation specified by the ampersand (&). For example,

NAME1 := NAME1 & NAME2;

catenates NAME2 to the right end of NAME1. For example, if NAME1 has the string "CHRIST" and NAME2 has "MAS", then after the assignment statement is executed, NAME1 will have the string "CHRISTMAS".

PL/I, FORTRAN 77, and BASIC are languages that treat strings as a primitive type and provide assignment, relational operators, catenation, and substring reference operations for them.

Pattern matching is another fundamental character string operation. Typically, it is provided by a library function rather than as an operation in the language. The exception is SNOBOL4 (Griswold et al., 1971), which has an elaborate pattern-matching operation built into the language.

7.4.3 String Length Options

There are several design choices regarding the length of string values that can be stored in string variables. First, the length can be static and specified in the declaration. Such a string is called a **static length string.** This is the choice in the FORTRAN 77, COBOL, and Ada languages. For example, the following FORTRAN 77 statement declares NAME1 and NAME2 to be character strings of length 15:

CHARACTER*15 NAME1, NAME2

The second option is to allow strings to have varying length up to a declared and fixed maximum, as exemplified by the strings in PL/I with the VARYING attribute. These are called **limited dynamic length strings.** Such string variables can store any number of characters between zero and the maximum.

The third option is to allow strings to have varying length with no maximum, as in SNOBOL4. These are called **dynamic length strings.** This option requires the overhead of dynamic storage allocation and deallocation, but provides maximum flexibility. SNOBOL4 is probably the ultimate string manipulation language. It includes elaborate capabilities for pattern matching in strings. Primarily because of the relative inefficiency of its implementations, however, SNOBOL4 has never become a commercial success.

7.4.4 Evaluation

String types are important to the writability of a language. Dealing with strings as arrays can be more cumbersome than dealing with a primitive string type. The addition of strings as a primitive type to a language is not costly, either in terms of language or compiler complexity. Therefore, it is difficult to justify the omission of primitive strings types in some contemporary imperative languages.

String operations such as simple pattern matching and catenation are essential, and should be included for string type objects. Although dynamic length strings are obviously the most flexible, the overhead of their implementation must be weighed against that additional flexibility.

7.5 User-Defined Ordinal Types

An **ordinal type** is one in which the range of possible values can be easily associated with a set of positive integers. In Pascal, for example, the built-in ordinal types are integer, char, and boolean. Users can define two kinds of ordinal types: enumeration and subrange.

7.5.1 Enumeration Types

An **enumeration type** is one in which the user enumerates all of the possible values, which are symbolic constants. A typical enumeration type is shown in the following Ada example:

```
type DAYS is (MON, TUE, WED, THU, FRI, SAT, SUN);
```

The primary design issue that is specific to enumeration types is the following: Is a literal constant allowed to appear in more than one type definition, and if so, how is the type of an occurrence of that literal in the program checked?

7.5.1.1 Designs

In Pascal, a literal constant is not allowed to be used in more than one enumeration type definition in a given referencing environment. Enumeration type variables can be used as array subscripts, **for** loop variables, and **case** selector expressions, but can be neither input nor output. Two enumeration type variables and/or literals can be compared with the relational operators, with their relative positions in the declaration determining the result. For example, if we have

```
type colortype = (red, blue, green, yellow);
var color : colortype;
...
color := blue;
if (color > red) ...
```

the Boolean expression of the **if** will evaluate to true.

The enumeration types of Ada are similar to those of Pascal, except that the literals are allowed to appear in more than one declaration in the same referencing environment. These are called **overloaded literals.** The rule for resolving the overloading—that is, deciding the type of an occurrence of such a literal—is that it must be determinable from the context of its appearance. For example, if a literal and an enumeration variable are compared, the literal's type is, obviously, resolved to be that of the variable.

In some cases, the programmer must indicate some type specification for an occurrence of an overloaded literal. Suppose, for example, that a program has the following two enumeration types:

```
type LETTERS is (A, B, C, D, E, F, G, H, I, J, K, L, M,
                 N, O, P, Q, R, S, T, U, V, W, X, Y, Z);
type VOWELS is (A, E, I, O, U);
```

Further suppose the program uses a **for** loop whose variable is to take on the values of the VOWELS type, as in

```
for LETTER in A..U loop
```

The problem is that the compiler cannot determine the correct type for LETTER. The solution is to use a type qualifier on the literals in the discrete range, as in

```
for LETTER in VOWELS'(A)..VOWELS'(U) loop
```

Enumeration variables can be output and enumeration literals can be input using Ada's TEXT_IO package. These operations require the instantiation of a built-in generic package for the specific enumeration type. Generic instantiations are discussed in Chapter 8.

In Ada, both the BOOLEAN and CHARACTER types are actually predefined enumeration types.

7.5.1.2 Evaluation

Enumeration types provide greater readability in a very direct way: Named values are easily recognized, whereas coded values are not. It is a simple matter of using commonly understood names instead of codings that are meaningless to everyone except the program's author. For example, suppose a program being written in FORTRAN required a variable to store the days of the week. Most likely the names of the days would be coded as integers using the values 1, 2, ... , 7. There are three distinct problems with this approach. First, any one of many arithmetic operations between the coded day and any integer would be legal, because their types would match. This eliminates compiler detection of many logic and typographical errors involving coded data.

Second, the integer values used for codes are rarely connotative. If the constant 4, for example, denotes Wednesday, and is assigned to a variable, that fact is not apparent to the reader of the program.

Third, if an integer variable is used for a coding that used only a very small subrange of the integer values, range errors could occur but could not be detected by the run-time system.

To write a program requiring the same day names as values in Pascal, one could use an enumerated type like the Ada DAYS type defined above. This restricts the assignable values to a small range, is more readable, and provides type checking. Languages like Pascal that have enumeration types clearly allow the programmer to model the problem more naturally.

7.5.2 Subrange Types

A **subrange type** is an ordered contiguous subsequence of an ordinal type. For example, 12..14 is a subrange of the integer type. Subrange types were introduced by Pascal, and are included in Modula-2 and Ada as well. No design issues are specific to subrange types.

7.5.2.1 Designs

In Pascal, typical subrange type declarations are:

```
type
   uppercase = 'A'..'Z';
   index = 1..100;
```

The connection of a subrange type to its parent type is established by matching the values in the subrange definition to those in previously declared or built-in ordinal types. In the example above, the type uppercase is defined to be a subrange of the built-in type for single characters. The type index is defined to be the integers 1, 2, ... , 100.

In Ada, subranges are included in the class of types called subtypes. Subtypes are not new types at all, but rather only new names for possibly restricted, or constrained, versions of existing types. For example, we could have:

```
subtype WEEKDAYS is DAYS range MON..FRI;
subtype INDEX is INTEGER range 1..100;
```

In these examples, the restriction on the existing types is in the range of possible values. All of the operations defined for the parent type are also

defined for the subtype, except assignment of values outside the specified range. For example, in the following:

```
DAY1 : DAYS;
DAY2 : WEEKDAYS;
. . .
DAY2 : = DAY1;
```

the assignment is legal unless the value of DAY1 is SAT or SUN. As in Ada, the subrange types in Pascal and Modula-2 inherit all the operations of the parent.

One of the most common uses of user-defined ordinal types is for the indices of arrays, as discussed in Section 7.6. They can also be used for loop variables in Pascal, Modula-2, and Ada. In fact, subranges of ordinal types are the only way the range of Ada **for** loop variables can be specified.

7.5.2.2 Evaluation

Subrange types enhance readability by making it clear to readers that variables of subtypes can store only certain ranges of values. Reliability is increased with subrange types because values outside the specified range, if assigned to the subrange variable, are detected as errors by the run-time system.

7.6 Array Types

An **array** is an aggregate of homogeneous data elements in which the individual elements are identified by their position in the aggregate, relative to its first element. A majority of computer programs need to model collections of objects in which the objects are of the same type and must be processed in the same way. Thus, the universal need for arrays is obvious.

7.6.1 Design Issues

The primary design issues specific to arrays are the following:

1. What types are legal for subscripts?
2. When are subscript ranges bound?
3. When does array allocation take place?
4. How many subscripts are allowed?
5. Can arrays be initialized when they have their storage allocated?
6. What kinds of slices are allowed, if any?

In the following sections, examples of the design choices made for the arrays of the most common imperative languages are discussed.

7.6.2   Arrays and Indices

Specific elements of an array are referenced by means of a two-level syntactic mechanism, where the first part is the aggregate name and the second part is a possibly dynamic selector consisting of one or more items known as **subscripts** or **indices.** If all of the indices in a reference are constants, the selector is static; otherwise, it is dynamic. The selection operation can be thought of as a mapping from the array name and the index values to an element in the aggregate. Indeed, arrays are sometimes called "finite mappings." Symbolically, this mapping can be shown as:

map (array_name, index_value_list) → element

The syntax of array references is fairly universal: the array name followed by the list of indices, which is surrounded by either parentheses or brackets. A problem with using parentheses is that they are also used to enclose the parameters in subprogram calls; this makes references to arrays appear exactly like those calls. For example, consider the following FORTRAN assignment statement:

```
SUM = SUM + B(I)
```

If parentheses are used for both subprogram parameters and array subscripts, as they are in FORTRAN, both program readers and compilers are forced to use other information to determine whether the reference B(I) in this assignment is a function call or an array element. This can be frustrating for the reader and it requires slightly more effort by the compiler to identify what is being specified.

The designers of FORTRAN and PL/I chose parentheses for array subscripts because no other suitable characters were available at the time. When an identifier followed by a parenthesized expression or list of expressions is found in a FORTRAN or PL/I program, the compiler determines whether it is an array reference or a function call by matching the name against all arrays declared in the referencing environment. If no match is found, such a reference is assumed to be a function call. If it is not a locally defined subprogram, it is assumed to be defined externally. This cannot be determined by the compiler, because these languages have separate compilation, and subprograms that are used in a program but defined elsewhere need not be declared to be external.

In Ada the compiler can always determine whether a reference is to an array or a function, because it has access to information about all names that can be referenced in a program unit that is being compiled. The designers of Ada specifically chose parentheses to enclose subscripts so that there would be uniformity between array references and function calls in expressions, in spite of the potential readability problem. They made this choice based on the fact that both array element references and function calls are mappings. Array element references map the subscripts to a particular element of the array. Function calls map the actual parameters to the function definition and, eventually, a functional value.

The ALGOLs, Pascal, C, and Modula-2 use brackets to delimit their array indices.

Two distinct types are involved in an array type: the element type and the type of the subscripts. The type of the subscripts is often a restricted range of integers, but Pascal, Modula-2, and Ada allow some other types to be used as subscripts. Pascal and Modula-2 allow any ordinal type, which includes Boolean, character, subrange, and enumeration types. Ada is more restrictive, allowing only integer or enumeration types to be used.

7.6.3 Subscript Bindings and Array Categories

The binding of the subscript type to an array is usually static, but the subscript value ranges are sometimes dynamically bound.

Four categories of arrays can be defined based on the binding to subscript value ranges and the binding to storage. A **static array** is one in which the subscript ranges are statically bound and storage allocation is static (done before run time). A **semistatic array** is one in which the subscript ranges are statically bound, but the allocation is done at declaration elaboration time during execution. A **semidynamic array** is one in which the subscript ranges are dynamically bound and the storage allocation is dynamic (done during run time). Once the subscript ranges are bound and the storage is allocated, however, they remain fixed during the lifetime of the variable. A **dynamic array** is one in which the binding of subscript ranges and storage allocation is dynamic, and can change any number of times during the array's lifetime. Examples of the four categories are given in the following paragraphs.

In FORTRAN 77, the subscript type is bound to an array at language design time; all subscripts are integer type. The subscript ranges are statically bound; therefore, FORTRAN 77's arrays are static.

The arrays declared in Pascal procedures are examples of semistatic arrays. Ada arrays can be semidynamic, as in:

```
GET (LENGTH);
declare
 LIST : array (1..LENGTH) of INTEGER;
end;
```

In this example, the user inputs the number of desired elements in the array list, which are then allocated in the declaration in the **declare** block.

ALGOL 68 and FORTRAN 8x have dynamic arrays. In the case of ALGOL 68, the assigning of aggregate values to an array type variable can change the subscript range. ALGOL 68's dynamic arrays are called **flex** arrays. The following ALGOL 68 code demonstrates how a **flex** array can change:

```
flex [1:0] int list;
...
list := (3, 5, 7);
list := 67
```

The declaration sets the type attributes of list to a single-dimensioned flexible array of integer type elements with an initial index range of [1:0], so that it has no storage. The first assignment statement causes the dynamic allocation of memory for three integers, binds list to that storage, and sets the index range to [1:3]. The last assignment causes the deallocation of the last two of the array's elements, leaving an array with index range [1:1] and the single element with the value 67.

The index range of list could be converted back to [1:0] by assigning an "empty row display," as in:

```
list := ()
```

To allow the program to determine the current index ranges of a flexible array, the binary operators **lwb** (lower bound) and **upb** (upper bound) are provided. For example,

```
upperbd := 1 upb list
```

sets the variable upperbd to the upper bound of the first dimension of list.

Ada has similar capabilities for its arrays, although they are not dynamic. Rather than operations, though, in Ada they are attributes of variables. For example, LENGTH is an attribute of arrays. If a program has an array named LIST, LIST'LENGTH returns the number of elements in the first subscript range of LIST.

FORTRAN 8x has dynamic arrays in addition to the static arrays of earlier FORTRANS. For example, one can declare an array to be dynamic with

```
INTEGER, ALLOCATABLE, ARRAY (:,:) :: MAT
```

which declares that MAT is a matrix of INTEGER type elements that can be dynamically allocated. The allocation is specified with an ALLOCATE statement, such as

```
ALLOCATE (MAT(10, NUMBER_OF_COLS))
```

Note that the subscript ranges can be specified by program variables. Lower bounds of subscript ranges default to 1.

Dynamic arrays can be destroyed by the DEALLOCATE statement, as in

```
DEALLOCATE (MAT)
```

To make an existing dynamic array larger or smaller, the array must be destroyed and reallocated, and its elements saved in another array temporarily.

7.6.4 The Number of Subscripts in Arrays

FORTRAN I limited the number of array subscripts to three, because at the time of the design execution efficiency was a large concern. The FORTRAN designers had developed a very fast method for accessing the elements of arrays of up to three dimensions, but not beyond three. FORTRAN 77 restricts the number of array dimensions to seven, but most other contemporary languages enforce no such limits. There is no justification for FORTRAN's limitation. A programmer who wishes to use a variable with ten dimensions and is willing to pay for the cost of references to the elements of such an array should be allowed to do it.

C arrays can have only one subscript, but arrays can have arrays as elements, thus supporting multidimensioned arrays. This is an example of orthogonality. For example, consider the following C declaration:

```
int mat [5] [4];
```

It creates an integer variable, mat, which is an array of five elements, each of which is an array of four elements. The difference between this and a matrix in another language, say FORTRAN, is minimal. The user can nearly always ignore the fact that mat is not really a matrix, except that the syntax for references requires a set of brackets for each subscript.

7.6.5   Array Initialization

Some languages provide the means to initialize arrays at the time their storage is allocated. All data storage in FORTRAN 77 is statically allocated, so that language provides for load-time initialization, using the DATA statement. For example, in FORTRAN 77 one could have:

```
INTEGER LIST (3)
DATA LIST /0, 5, 5/
```

The array LIST is initialized to the values from the list delimited by slashes.

The C language also allows initialization of its static arrays, but with one new twist. In the declaration:

```
int list[] = {4, 5, 7, 83}
```

the compiler sets the length of the array. This is meant to be a convenience, but is not without cost. It effectively removes the possibility that the system could detect programmer errors, such as mistakenly leaving a value out of the list.

Character strings in C are implemented as arrays of **char**. Such arrays, when static (in C, arrays can be either static or semistatic), can be initialized to string constants, as in:

```
char name[] = "freddie"
```

in which name will have eight elements, because in C all strings are terminated by the system with a null character (zero).

Pascal and Modula-2 do not allow array initialization in the declaration sections of programs.

Ada provides two mechanisms for initializing arrays in the declaration statement: by listing them in the order in which they are to be stored, or by directly assigning them to an index position using the => operator. For example, consider the following:

```
LIST : array (1..5) of INTEGER := (1, 3, 5, 7, 9);
BUNCH : array (1..5) of INTEGER := (1 => 3, 2 => 4,
                                    others => 0);
```

In the first statement, all the elements of the array LIST have initializing values, which are assigned to the array element locations in the order in which they appear. In the second, the first and second array elements are initialized using direct assignment, and the **others** clause is used to initialize the remaining elements.

7.6.6 Array Operations

Some languages provide operations that deal with arrays as units; this is not the case with FORTRAN 77, in which only individual elements of arrays can be manipulated.

Arrays and their operations are the heart of APL; it is the most powerful array-processing language ever devised. Because of its relative obscurity and its lack of effect on subsequent languages, however, we do not cover any of the APL array operations. Rather, we discuss those of PL/I, Ada, and FORTRAN 8X.

PL/I arrays can be assigned to other arrays as long as the element types are either the same or the element type of the source array is coercible to the type of the destination array. Furthermore, the number of dimensions and the index ranges must be identical. As we discuss in Section 7.6.7, however, the number of dimensions can be made to appear different in a given array reference, so the number of dimensions restriction does not always apply.

All the operators that apply to a scalar data type in PL/I can also be applied to arrays of those scalar type elements. The compatibility restrictions that apply to array assignment statements also apply to all array names that appear in the expression on the right side. In PL/I, all array operations in expressions are actually only a shorthand for multiple scalar operations. For example, consider the following PL/I code:

```
DECLARE (A(1:5, 1:6), B(1:5, 1:6), C(1:5, 1:6)) FIXED;
. . .
A = 2 * B + C - 1;
```

The assignment statement is simply expanded by the compiler into the nested loop construct:

```
DO ROW = 1 TO 5 BY 1;
  DO COL = 1 TO 6 BY 1;
    A(ROW, COL) = 2 * B(ROW, COL) + C(ROW, COL) - 1;
  END;
END;
```

Ada allows array assignments, including those where the right side is an aggregate value rather than an array name. In the case of an aggregate value, the form of the aggregate is like that of the initialization of an array, as we discussed in Section 7.6.5.

The only operation on arrays is catenation, specified by the ampersand (&), which is defined between two single-dimensioned arrays and between a single-dimensioned array and a scalar. All types in Ada have the built-in relational operators for equality and inequality.

FORTRAN 8x includes a number of array operations that are called **elemental** because they are operations between pairs of array elements. For example, the add operator (+) between two arrays results in an array of the sums of the element pairs of the two arrays. The assignment, arithmetic, relational, and logical operators are all overloaded for arrays of any size or shape. FORTRAN 8x also includes intrinsic, or library, functions for matrix multiplication and vector dot product.

7.6.7   Slices

A **slice** of an array is some substructure of that array. For example, if A is a matrix, the first row of A is one possible slice, as is the last row, and the first column. It is important to realize that a slice is not a new data type. Rather, it is only a mechanism for referencing part of an array as a unit. If arrays cannot be manipulated as units in a language, that language has no use for slices.

One of the design questions for slices is the syntax of specifying a reference to a particular slice. A reference to a particular element of a complete array is the array name and an expression for each subscript. Because a slice is a substructure of an array, instead of an expression for each subscript, a slice reference requires fewer subscript expressions. Somehow, however, the missing subscript expressions must be denoted, so that the present expressions are associated with the correct subscripts. The missing subscript or subscripts of slice references are sometimes specified by asterisks. For example, consider the following PL/I declaration:

```
DECLARE MAT(1:3, 1:3) FIXED;
```

MAT(*, 2) refers to the second column of MAT, and MAT(3, *) refers to the third row of MAT. Both of these references can be used as single-dimensioned arrays. References to all array slices are treated as if they were arrays of the remaining dimensionality. Thus a slice reference such as BLOCK(2, *, *) could be legally assigned to a two-dimensional array. Slices can also appear as the destinations of assignment statements. For example, a single-dimensioned array could be assigned to a slice of a matrix.

In Ada only highly restricted slices are allowed: those that consist of consecutive elements of a single-dimensioned array. For example, if LIST is an array with index range (1..100), then LIST(5..10) is a slice of LIST consisting of the six elements indexed from 5 to 10. As discussed in Section 7.4.2, a slice of a STRING type is called a substring reference.

FORTRAN 8x includes slices of arrays. Suppose MAT is declared to be a matrix with the subscript ranges (1:10, 1:20). A slice of MAT can be simple, such as MAT(1, 1:5), or more complex, such as MAT(1:10:2, 5:11:3). The former reference is a single-dimensioned array containing the first five elements of the first row of MAT. The latter reference is a matrix containing the first, third, fifth, seventh, and ninth rows, each of which contains the fifth, eighth, and eleventh column elements of MAT.

Although it is sometimes convenient to allow the programmer to specify a particular substructure of a multidimensional array, the increased difficulty of implementation and readability is not necessarily worth the convenience.

7.6.8 Evaluation

Arrays have been included in every imperative language. They are simple and have probably been developed to their optimum. The only significant advance since their introduction in FORTRAN I has been the inclusion of all ordinal types as possible subscript types. Although they are essential and fundamental, there is little controversy involved in their design.

7.7 Record Types

A **record** is a possibly heterogeneous aggregate of data elements in which the individual elements are identified by names.

There is frequently a need in programs to model collections of data that are not homogeneous. For example, information about a college student might include name, student number, grade point average, and so forth. A data type for such a collection might use a character string for the name, an integer for the student number, a floating-point for the grade point average, and so forth. Records meet exactly this kind of need.

Records have been part of all of the most popular programming languages, except FORTRAN, since the early 1960s, when they were introduced by COBOL. There are no design issues that are particular to records.

7.7.1 The Structure of Records

The fundamental difference between a record and an array is the homogeneity of elements in arrays versus the possible heterogeneity of elements in records. One important result of this difference is that record elements, or fields, are not usually referenced by indices. Instead, the fields are named with identifiers, and references are made using these identifiers.

The COBOL form of a record declaration, which is part of the data division of a COBOL program, is illustrated in the following example:

```
01   EMPLOYEE-RECORD.
     02   EMPLOYEE-NAME.
          05   FIRST      PICTURE IS X(20).
          05   MIDDLE     PICTURE IS X(10).
          05   LAST       PICTURE IS X(20).
     02   HOURLY-RATE     PICTURE IS 99V99.
```

The EMPLOYEE-RECORD record consists of the EMPLOYEE-NAME record and the HOURLY-RATE field. The PICTURE clauses show the formats of the field storage locations, with X(20) specifying 20 alphanumeric characters and 99V99 specifying four decimal digits with the decimal point in the middle.

Pascal, Modula-2, and Ada use a different form of records; rather than using the level numbers of COBOL, they indicate nested structures as records themselves. Consider the following Ada declaration:

```
EMPLOYEE_RECORD :
  record
    EMPLOYEE_NAME :
      record
        FIRST : STRING (1..20);
        MIDDLE : STRING (1..10);
        LAST : STRING (1..20);
      end record;
    HOURLY_RATE : FLOAT;
  end record;
```

7.7.2 References to Record Fields

References to the individual fields of records are syntactically specified by several different methods, two of which name the desired field and its enclosing records. COBOL field references have the form

field_name OF record_name_1 OF ... OF record_name_n

where the first record named is the smallest record that contains the field. The next record name in the sequence is that of the record that contains the last record, and so forth. For example, the MIDDLE field in the COBOL record example above can be referenced with

MIDDLE OF EMPLOYEE-NAME OF EMPLOYEE-RECORD

PL/I, Pascal, Modula-2, C, and Ada use dot notation, where the components of the reference are connected with periods. Names in dot notation have the opposite order of COBOL references: They use the name of the largest enclosing record first and the field name last. For example, the following is a reference to the field MIDDLE in the Ada record example above:

```
EMPLOYEE_RECORD.EMPLOYEE_NAME.MIDDLE
```

A **fully qualified reference** to a record field is one in which all intermediate record names, from the largest enclosing record to the specific field, are named in the reference. Both the COBOL and the Ada field references above are fully qualified. As an alternative to fully qualified references, COBOL and PL/I allow **elliptical references** to record fields. In an elliptical reference, the field is named, but any or all of the enclosing record names can be omitted, as long as the resulting reference is unambiguous in the referencing environment. For example, FIRST, EMPLOYEE_NAME.FIRST, and EMPLOYEE_RECORD.FIRST are elliptical references to the employee's first name in the record declared above. Although elliptical references are a programmer convenience, they require a compiler to have elaborate data structures and procedures in order to correctly identify the referenced field. They are also somewhat detrimental to readability.

7.7.3　Operations on Records

PL/I allows operations on records that are similar to its array operations. Expressions can reference records as units, as can assignments. However, whereas PL/I arrays in such references are treated as if they were in loops, record references are effectively replaced by sequences of assignments and expressions with the individual fields. As long as the corresponding fields have coercible types, the operations are legal.

In Pascal and Modula-2, records can be assigned, but cannot be involved in expressions. Furthermore, in such assignments, the types of the two sides must be the same.

Ada allows record assignment and comparison for equality and inequality as the only record operations. These operations are legal only if the two records have compatible types. Additional record operations can be defined in both ALGOL 68 and Ada as overloaded operators. User-defined operator overloading is discussed in Chapter 8.

Record initialization at compile time is possible in ALGOL 68 and Ada, where data aggregates are used as the initial values. An Ada data aggregate is a collection of data values, separated by commas, with the whole collection delimited by parentheses. Aggregate values can also be assigned to records by assignment statements in these languages.

COBOL provides the MOVE CORRESPONDING statement for moving records. This statement copies a field of the specified source record to the destination record only if the destination record has a field with the same name. This is a frequently useful operation in data-processing applications, where input records are moved to output files after some modifications.

Because input records often have many fields that have the same names and purposes as fields in output records, but not necessarily in the same order, the move corresponding operation can save many statements. For example, consider the following COBOL structures:

```
01  INPUT-RECORD.
    02  NAME.
          05  LAST            PICTURE IS X(20).
          05  MIDDLE          PICTURE IS X(15).
          05  FIRST           PICTURE IS X(20).
    02  EMPLOYEE-NUMBER       PICTURE IS 9(10).
    02  HOURS-WORKED          PICTURE IS 99.

01  OUTPUT-RECORD.
    02  NAME.
          05  FIRST           PICTURE IS X(20).
          05  MIDDLE          PICTURE IS X(15).
          05  LAST            PICTURE IS X(20).
    02  EMPLOYEE-NUMBER       PICTURE IS 9(10).
    02  GROSS-PAY             PICTURE IS 999V99.
    02  NET-PAY               PICTURE IS 999V99.
```

The statement:

```
MOVE CORRESPONDING INPUT-RECORD TO OUTPUT-RECORD.
```

copies the FIRST, MIDDLE, LAST, and EMPLOYEE-NUMBER fields from the input record to the output record.

7.7.4 Evaluation

Records are frequently valuable data types in programming languages. The design of record types is straightforward and their use is safe. The only aspect of records that is not clearly readable is the elliptical references allowed by COBOL and PL/I.

Records and arrays are closely related structural forms, and it is therefore interesting to compare them. Arrays are used when all the data objects have the same type and are processed in the same ways. This processing is easily done when there is a systematic way of sequencing through the structure. Such processing lends itself to the use of dynamic subscripting as the addressing method.

Records are used when the collection of data objects is heterogeneous and the different fields are not processed in the same way. Also, the fields of a record often need not be processed in a particular sequential order. Field names are like literal, or constant, subscripts. Because they are static, they provide very efficient access to the fields. Dynamic subscripts could be used to access record fields, but it is not considered worth the required additional access time.

Records and arrays represent thoughtful and efficient methods of fulfilling two separate but related applications of data structures.

7.8 Union Types

A **union** is a type that is allowed to store different type values at different times during program execution. Occasionally in programming it is convenient to have union type variables. For example, consider a table of constants for a compiler, in which are stored the constants found in a program being compiled. One field of each table entry is for the value of the constant. Suppose that for a particular language being compiled the types of constants were integer, floating-point, and Boolean. In terms of table management, it would be convenient if the same location, or table field, could store a value of any of these three types. The type of such a location is, in a sense, the union of the three value types it can store.

7.8.1 Design Issues

The problem of type checking union types, which is discussed in Chapter 4, leads to one major design issue. The other fundamental question is the form of union types. In some cases the forms are confined to be parts of record structures, but in others they are not. So, the primary design issues that are particular to union types are the following:

1. Should there be a provision for type checking? Note that any such type checking must be dynamic.
2. What form should union types take?

7.8.2 FORTRAN Union Types

The most primitive form of union is FORTRAN's EQUIVALENCE, with which one can have:

```
INTEGER X
REAL Y
EQUIVALENCE (X, Y)
```

This EQUIVALENCE declaration specifies that both X and Y are to cohabit the same storage location; that is, they are aliases. There is no mechanism whereby the user program or the system can determine the type of the value currently stored in such a FORTRAN shared location, so no type checking is done. Chapter 4 notes several reasons why EQUIVALENCE was included in FORTRAN.

7.8.3   ALGOL 68 Union Types

Although the merit of unions was recognized by the designers of ALGOL 68, they determined that it would be better if the run-time system could detect the current type value in a union. Thus was born the discriminated union.

A **discriminated union** is a union with which is associated an additional value, called a **tag,** or **discriminant,** that identifies the current type value stored in the union. Consider the following example of an ALGOL 68 discriminated union:

```
union (int, real) ir1, ir2
```

In this case, the two variables ir1 and ir2 are declared to be of a **union** type that can have either **int** or **real** type values. Although it is legal to assign values of either of the possible types to such a variable, it is not so simple to reference them. For example, in the following:

```
union (int, real) ir1;
int count;
. . .
ir1 := 33;
. . .
count := ir1;
```

the first assignment statement is legal, but the second is not, because the system cannot statically check the type of ir1. The compiler cannot guarantee that ir1 will actually contain an integer value. To alleviate this problem, ALGOL 68 provides **conformity clauses** for such references. For example, consider the following:

```
union (int, real) ir1;
int count;
real sum;
. . .
case ir1 in
  (int intval): count := intval,
  (real realval): sum := realval
esac
```

This **case** statement executes the assignment that is currently valid—that is, the one in which the value type of the union variable ir1 matches the type of the destination (count or sum). Therefore, the different types are handled individually. The correct choice is made by testing a type tag maintained by the run-time system for the variable. The parenthesized clauses that introduce the assignments specify the current type of ir1, and the following identifier is the means by which the value of ir1 is referenced. For example, (**int** intval) specifies that if the current type of the case variable (ir1) is **int**, the following statement is to be executed; the variable intval refers to the current value of ir1. This is a safe way of implementing discriminated union, because it allows static type checking of user code and dynamic checking of system discriminants in order to disallow erroneous uses of values. The dummy variables, intval and realval, can be thought of as implicitly declared variables whose scope is the statement following their specifications.

The only direct operation provided in ALGOL 68 for discriminated unions is assignment. Other operations can be constructed by user-defined overloaded operators.

7.8.4   Pascal Union Types

Pascal introduced the concept of integrating discriminated unions with a record structure. This design carried over into Modula-2 and Ada. In all of these, the discriminated union is called a **record variant,** or variant part of a record. The discriminant is a user-accessible variable in the record that stores the current type value in the variant. The following example illustrates a Pascal record with only a variant part:

```
type shape = (circle, triangle, rectangle);
     object =
       record
         case form : shape of
           circle:      (diameter : real);
           triangle:    (leftside : integer;
                         rightside : integer;
                         angle : real);
           rectangle:   (side1 : integer;
                         side2 : integer)
       end;
  var thing : object;
```

The variable thing consists of the tag, which is named form, and sufficient storage for its largest variant. In this case the largest variant is for triangle, which consists of two integers and a real. At any time during execution, the tag should indicate which variant is currently stored. If the variant must be printed, one could use:

```
case thing.form of
   circle:      writeln ('It is a circle; its diameter=',
                          thing.diameter);
   triangle:    begin
                writeln ('It is a triangle');
                writeln ('its sides are:', thing.leftside,
                          thing.rightside);
                writeln ('angle between the sides is:',
                          thing.angle);
                end;
```

```
rectangle: begin
              writeln ('It is a rectangle');
              writeln ('its sides are:', thing.side1,
                             thing.side2)
           end
  end
```

There are two distinct problems with the Pascal and Modula-2 variant record design that can make their use unsafe. The first problem is that the user program can change the tag without making a corresponding change in the variant. Therefore, even if the run-time system checks the type of the variant by examining the tag before using the variant, it could not detect all type errors; the user program may have changed the tag so that its value is now inconsistent with the type of the current variant. This is one reason why implementors typically ignore type checking of variant record references in these languages.

The second problem is that the programmer can simply omit the tag from the variant record structure. Then the structure is no longer a discriminated union, but is instead called a **free union.** For example, we could have:

```
type
  object =
    record
      case shape of
        circle :    (diameter : real);
        triangle : (leftside : integer,
          . . .
      end
```

With this structure, neither the user nor the system has any way to determine the current variant type. There is no way to guard against incorrect references such as

```
thing.diameter := 2.73;
side := thing.leftside;
```

in which the second assignment is rarely useful because there is currently a floating-point value in that part of the variant where leftside resides.

Variant records in Pascal are frequently used to get around some of the restrictions of the language. They provide a convenient loophole in the type-checking rules. For example, pointer arithmetic is not allowed in Pascal, although some applications need to manipulate pointer values. To circumvent the restrictions against pointer arithmetic, a pointer can be placed in a variant with an integer, and the integer form can be manipulated as desired. This particular application of variant records is not necessary in C, Modula-2, or Ada, as they all provide other methods for doing pointer, or address, arithmetic.

7.8.5 Ada Union Types

The Ada language extends the Pascal form of variant records so they are safer. Both of the problems associated with Pascal and Modula-2 variant records are avoided. The tag cannot be changed without the variant also being changed, and the tag is required on all variant records. Furthermore, Ada systems are required to check the tag for all references to variants.

The Ada design allows the user to specify variables of a variant record type that will store only one of the possible type values in the variant. In this way the user can tell the system when the type checking can be static. Such a restricted variable is called a **constrained variant.**

The tag of a constrained variant variable is treated like a named constant. Unconstrained variant records are more like their Pascal counterparts in that the values of their variants can change types during execution. However, the type of the variant can be changed only by assigning the entire record, including the discriminant. This disallows inconsistent records because if the newly assigned record is a constant data aggregate, the value of the tag and the type of the variant can be statically checked for consistency. If the assigned value is a variable, it must also be consistent.

The following example shows the Ada version of the Pascal variant record defined above:

```
type SHAPE is (CIRCLE, TRIANGLE, RECTANGLE);
type OBJECT (FORM : SHAPE) is
  record
    case FORM is
      when CIRCLE =>
        DIAMETER : FLOAT;
      when TRIANGLE =>
        LEFT_SIDE : INTEGER;
        RIGHT_SIDE : INTEGER;
        ANGLE : FLOAT;
      when RECTANGLE =>
        SIDE_1 : INTEGER;
        SIDE_2 : INTEGER;
    end case;
  end record;
```

The following two statements declare variables of type OBJECT:

```
THING_1 : OBJECT;
THING_2 : OBJECT (FORM => TRIANGLE);
```

THING_1 is declared to be an unconstrained variant record that has no initial value. Its type can change by assignment of a whole record, including the discriminant, as in the following:

```
THING_1 := (FORM => RECTANGLE,
            SIDE_1 => 12,
            SIDE_2 => 3);
```

The right side of this assignment is a data aggregate.

The variable THING_2 declared above is constrained to be a `triangle`, and cannot be changed to another variant.

This form of discriminated union is perfectly safe, because it always allows type checking, although the references to fields in unconstrained variants must be dynamically checked.

7.8.6   Evaluation

Unions are unsafe constructs in many languages. They are the reason we defined "strongly typed" the way we did. And they are one of the reasons why Pascal and Modula-2 are not strongly typed: They do not allow type checking of references to variant parts of records. The unions of FORTRAN are one of the reasons why FORTRAN is more error-prone than some later languages.

7.9   Set Types

A **set** type is one whose variables can store unordered collections of distinct values from some ordinal type called its **base type.** Set types are often used to model mathematical sets. For example, text analysis often requires that small sets of characters, such as punctuation characters or vowels, be stored and conveniently searched.

A variable of a set type can store any subset of the range of the base type. The set of all subsets of a given base set is often called the **powerset** of that base set. The maximum number of elements in a set is called its **cardinality.**

The only design issue that is particular to set types is: What should be the maximum number of elements in a set base type?

7.9.1   Sets in Pascal and Modula-2

Pascal and Modula-2 are two languages that include sets as a data type. We now briefly describe Pascal's set data type.

The cardinality of Pascal base sets is implementation-dependent. Many implementations severely restrict the set cardinality, often to much less than 100. They do so because sets and their operations are most efficiently implemented by representing set variables as bit strings that fit into machine words.

One problem with letting machine wordsize determine the base set cardinality is that users are restricted to modeling only very small sets. This is a deficiency in writability. Furthermore, different machines have different wordsizes, so programs developed on machines with larger wordsizes that use larger sets may not be portable to machines with smaller wordsizes. These problems both result from letting base set cardinality be chosen by implementors, rather than making it part of the language design.

Pascal allows the following set operations:

:=	assignment of compatible set types
+	set union
*	set intersection
−	set difference
=	set equality
<>	set inequality
<=	set included in (subset)
>=	set includes (superset)
in	element inclusion in a set

The last five of these are predicate operations that return a Boolean value. The operations =, <>, >=, and <= have two sets as operands, whereas the **in** operator has a set element as its first operand and a set as its other operand.

The following examples should help clarify the Pascal set operations. Suppose that the types colors and colorset and the variables set1, set2, and set3 are defined as:

```
type colors = (red, blue, green, yellow, orange, white);
     colorset = set of colors;
var set1, set2, set3 : colorset;
```

We can assign constant values to set1 and set2, as in:

```
set1 := [red, blue, yellow, white];
set2 := [blue, yellow];
```

The following assignments illustrate the union, intersection, and difference operations:

```
set3 := set1 + set2;  {set3 is now [red,blue,yellow,white] }
set3 := set1 * set2;  {set3 is now [blue, yellow] }
set3 := set1 - set2;  {set2 is now [red, white] }
```

The following Boolean expressions illustrate the set predicates:

```
set1 = set2 is false
set1 <> set2 is true
set1 <= set2 is false
set1 >= set2 is true
red in set1 is true
red in set2 is false
```

Modula-2 includes the set type of Pascal, with a few minor changes in syntax and some additional operations. Set constants for user-defined set types must be preceded by the type name, which clarifies occurrences of those constants. For example, consider the following set type declarations:

```
TYPE setype1 = SET OF [red, blue, green, yellow];
     setype2 = SET OF [blue, yellow]
```

The type of the constant:

```
setype1 {blue}
```

is very clear. In Pascal, the constant would simply be [blue], which does not convey its type.

Modula-2 includes two procedures for inserting and removing elements from sets; these are, respectively, INCL and DECL. If setvar1 were a variable of type setype1 as defined above, INCL (setvar1, green) would insert green into setvar1. Similarly, DECL (setvar1, blue) would remove blue from setvar1.

There is a predefined set in Modula-2 named BITSET, whose base type is the subrange 0..k, where k is one less than the wordsize of the implementation computer, or a small multiple of the wordsize, say 2 or 3. On most machines, the wordsize is either 16 or 32, so the subrange is often either 0..15 or 0..31. One purpose of BITSET is to provide a set type for which set operations can be efficiently implemented. If the wordsize of the machine is the set cardinality, then all operations can usually be done by using single machine instructions. Another application of the BITSET type is for bit string operations, which can be done in limited ways on BITSET objects.

Modula-2, like Pascal, does not specify a maximum cardinality of sets, so it is again implementation-dependent. Set type variables, like enumeration type variables, can be neither input nor output in Pascal or Modula-2.

7.9.2   Evaluation

The Ada language does not include set types, although Ada was based on Pascal. Instead, Ada's designers added a set membership operator for its enumeration types. This provides for the most commonly needed set operation.

In other languages without set types, set operations must be done with arrays or enumeration types, and the user must write the code to provide the operations. This is not difficult although it is indeed more cumbersome and less efficient. For example, if the set of vowels were represented as a **char** array in Pascal, determining whether a given character variable stored a vowel would require a loop to search the vowel array. If the vowels were represented as a set, however, the same determination could be made with one application of the **in** operator. This is not only programmer-efficient, but also computer-efficient. In both cases, it is better because the whole set can be dealt with as a unit, whereas the array must be searched one element at a time.

Arrays are, of course, far more flexible than sets; they allow many more operations, more complex shapes, and more options for element types. In fact, if arrays were restricted to a maximum length of 32, as sets in many Pascal implementations are, users would not consider them acceptable. Sets provide an alternative that trades flexibility for efficiency for a certain class of type applications.

7.10   Pointer Types

A **pointer** type is one in which the variables have a range of values that consists of memory addresses and a special value, nil. The value nil indicates that a pointer does not have a valid address as its current value.

Pointers have been designed for two distinct kinds of uses. First, pointers provide some of the addressing flexibility of the indirect addressing that is heavily used in assembly language programming.

Second, pointers provide a method of dynamic storage management. A pointer can be used to access a location in the area where storage is dynamically allocated, which is usually called a **heap.** The name heap comes from the complex organization that may occur because of randomly ordered dynamic allocations and deallocations.

Variables that are dynamically allocated from the heap are called **dynamic variables.** They usually do not have identifiers associated with them, and thus can be referenced only by pointer variables. Variables without names are called **anonymous variables.** It is in this latter application area of pointers that the most important design issues arise.

7.10.1   Design issues

The primary design issues particular to pointers are the following:

1. What are the scope and lifetime of a pointer variable?
2. What is the lifetime of a dynamic variable?
3. Are pointers restricted as to the type of object to which they can point?

7.10.2   Pointer Operations

Languages that provide a pointer type usually include two fundamental pointer operations. The first operation sets a pointer variable to the address of some object. If pointer variables are used only to manage dynamic storage, the allocation mechanism, whether by built-in procedure or otherwise, serves to initialize the pointer variable. If pointers are used for general addressing, then there should be an explicit operator or built-in procedure for fetching the address of a variable, which can then be assigned to the pointer variable.

A reference to a pointer variable in a program can be taken to be either a reference to the contents of the memory cell to which the variable is bound, which is an address, or a reference to the value in the memory cell whose address is in the memory cell to which the variable is bound. The former case is a normal pointer reference; the latter is the result of **dereferencing** the pointer. Dereferencing is the second fundamental pointer operation. To clarify dereferencing, consider a pointer variable, ptr, which is bound to a memory cell with the value 7080. Suppose that the memory cell whose address is 7080 has the value 206. A normal reference to ptr yields 7080, but a dereferenced reference to ptr yields 206.

Dereferencing can be either explicit or implicit. In ALGOL 68 it is implicit, but in most other contemporary languages, it occurs only when explicitly specified. In Pascal it is explicitly specified, with the circumflex (ˆ), as a postfix unary operation. For example, if ptr is a pointer variable with the value 7080, as in the above example, and the cell whose address is 7080 has the value 206, then the assignment:

    j := ptr^

sets j to 206. This process is shown in Figure 7.1.

Languages that use pointers in the management of a heap must include an explicit allocation operation. Some also provide an explicit deallocation operation. These two operations are often in the form of built-in procedures. For example, in Pascal, the allocation and deallocation procedures are called new and dispose, respectively. As we discuss later, C alone includes more than these basic operations for pointer types.

7.10.3   Pointers and Pointer Problems in PL/I

The first high-level programming language to include pointer variables was PL/I, in which pointers can be used to refer to both dynamic variables and other program variables. As was the case with PL/I's generalization of goto statements by allowing label variables, the pointers of PL/I are highly flexible but can lead to several kinds of programming errors.

Our primary purpose in discussing PL/I pointers is to introduce the main programming problems that can occur with pointers.

7.10.3.1   Type Checking

The type of object to which a pointer can point is called its **domain type**. For example, if a pointer is allowed to point only at integer type objects, its domain type is integer. A PL/I pointer is not restricted to a single domain

Figure 7.1
The assignment oper-
ation j: =ptr^

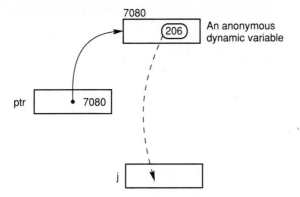

type. The problem with this approach is that it makes static type checking
of pointer references impossible, which thus lowers the reliability of PL/I
programs that use pointers. All subsequent imperative languages that include
pointers restrict them to single type domains, so this problem occurs only
in PL/I.

7.10.3.2 Dangling Pointers

A **dangling pointer,** or **dangling reference,** is a pointer that contains the
address of a dynamic variable that has been deallocated. Dangling pointers
are dangerous because the location being pointed to either contains invalid
data, or may even be the value of a more recently allocated variable. However, because the system cannot detect the fact that the pointer is no longer
pointing at useful data, it can still be used by the program—producing
incorrect results.

In PL/I there are two ways to create dangling pointers. First, a dangling
pointer can be created if the scope of a pointer is smaller than that of the
object to which it points. For example, consider the following PL/I code
segment:

```
BEGIN;
DECLARE POINT POINTER;
. . .
  BEGIN;
  DECLARE SUM FIXED;
  POINT = ADDR(SUM);
  . . .
  END;
. . .
END;
```

After exit from the inner block, the pointer POINT still exists, but the object
to which it pointed, SUM, has been deallocated. POINT is dangling after the
exit from the inner block.

The second way a PL/I program can create dangling pointers is by including an explicit deallocation operation for dynamic variables. In PL/I, dynamic variables, which are called **based** variables, can be explicitly allocated with the ALLOCATE statement and deallocated with the FREE statement. Such a variable is declared to be BASED, and a pointer variable name to be used to reference it can be specified in the declaration.

The following code segment illustrates how dangling pointers can be created using FREE:

```
DECLARE SUM FLOAT BASED (POINT);
DECLARE POINT2 POINTER;

. . .

ALLOCATE SUM;
POINT2 = POINT;
FREE SUM;
```

After execution of the FREE statement, POINT2 is a dangling pointer. No attempt is made, because of the difficulty of the process, to find all pointers pointing to a dynamic variable when a FREE statement is executed.

7.10.3.3 Dangling Objects

A **dangling object** is an allocated dynamic object that is no longer accessible, but may still contain useful data. Such variables are often called **garbage** because both the user and the system have lost access to them; they cannot be recovered and the storage they occupy cannot be reused. For example, consider the following code segment:

```
DECLARE SUM FLOAT BASED (POINT);

. . .

ALLOCATE SUM;

. . .

ALLOCATE SUM;
```

The first ALLOCATE dynamically allocates a FLOAT type anonymous variable that can be referenced through the pointer, POINT. After the second ALLOCATE is executed, however, the first anonymous variable still exists, but it is no longer accessible. If both versions of SUM are required, a second pointer variable can be used to store POINT's value, which is the only access path to that first dynamic variable, before the second ALLOCATE is executed.

In the following we investigate how later language designers dealt with these problems.

7.10.4 Pointers in ALGOL 68

ALGOL 68 includes pointers that are less error-prone than those of PL/I. As a result of its orthogonal design, ALGOL 68 pointers are a natural part of the data-typing structure. A "normal" integer variable X is declared in ALGOL 68 with the statement

```
int X;
```

X is said to be of **ref int** type, because its usual use is as an address. When it appears in an expression, its value is needed and it must be dereferenced. A variable Y that is to be used as a pointer is declared:

```
ref int Y;
```

and is said to be of **ref ref int** type. Consider the following example:

```
int X;
ref int Y;
```

Now, the assignments

```
X := 5;
Y := X;
```

require no implicit conversion or dereferencing. In the first case, the constant is of **int** type. In the second, no conversions are required because the types of both identifiers are exactly what is required. The address of X— not its value (5)—is moved to Y. A constant cannot be assigned to Y because constants cannot be of **ref** type.

In the assignment:

```
X := Y
```

Y is implicitly dereferenced twice. The integer at the address pointed to by Y is moved to the address specified by X. For example, if the other two assignment statements above were executed, the 5 would be assigned to X by this statement.

Another interesting result of the orthogonality of ALGOL 68's type structure is that one can easily declare pointers to pointers. For example,

```
ref ref int ptr;
```

declares ptr to be a pointer to a pointer to an integer variable.

Most occurrences of the dangling pointer problem are avoided in ALGOL 68 by the following restriction: When an assignment is made to a pointer, the scope of the object being pointed to must be at least as large as the scope of the pointer variable that points at it. This specifically disallows code like that in the PL/I example of dangling pointers in Section 7.10.3.2. The restriction can be statically checked in most cases because of the static scoping of ALGOL 68. One exception is when a pointer and an object are passed as parameters to a procedure and then the object is assigned to the pointer. In this case, the legality of the assignment depends on the actual parameters that are passed. Although it is possible to check this dynamically, it is so costly that most ALGOL 68 implementations ignore the potential problem.

The other method of creating dangling pointers in PL/I—using explicit deallocation—is not a problem in ALGOL 68: ALGOL 68 has no explicit deallocation of heap-allocated objects.

The dangling object problem is, in a sense, worse in ALGOL 68 than in PL/I. In ALGOL 68, data objects can be dynamically allocated from either the stack or the heap. The appearance of the reserved word **heap** causes a heap object to be allocated, and the appearance of the reserved word **loc** causes a stack object to be allocated. Dangling objects can be created, therefore, in either the heap or the stack. For example, we could have:

```
ref int ptr;
. . .
ptr := heap int;
ptr := heap int;
```

which creates a garbage object on the heap, or:

```
ref int ptr;
. . .
ptr := loc int;
ptr := heap int;
```

which creates a garbage object on the stack.

7.10.5   Pointers in Pascal

In Pascal, pointers are used only to access dynamically allocated anonymous variables.

Dangling pointers can easily be created in Pascal with explicit deallocation, as in PL/I, because of the design of most Pascal run-time systems. A Pascal programmer creates dynamic variables with new and destroys them with dispose. To do so safely, the function dispose must find and alter all pointers pointing at the dynamic variable being destroyed. Unfortunately, because in general the procedure is complex and costly, the function does not always find and alter all pointers. The result is that some of the pointers to disposed variables are left dangling. This is a problem for all explicit deallocation processes in programming languages.

Several dialects of Pascal provide an alternative method of deallocating dynamic variables. Instead of dispose, which is difficult to implement, two other procedures are provided: mark and release. Dynamic storage is allocated in sequential order from the heap, using a system pointer to point at the next available location. The mark procedure allows the user to access the value of the heap pointer. The release procedure resets the heap pointer to a previously saved value. At the beginning of a section of code that uses dynamic variables, a program can use mark to record the heap pointer. Then, after the section has completed execution, all dynamic storage allocated by the section can be returned by using release to set the heap pointer back to the value it had before the section began execution.

Although mark and release are easy to implement, they have their own problems. For one, they effectively turn the heap into a stack, thus lowering its flexibility. Indeed, heaps were invented to provide more flexibility than stacks by allowing allocation/deallocation sequences that are not nested. Furthermore, it is cumbersome for the user to need to release dynamic objects at the end of their usefulness. Also, the use of the mark/release method can lead to dangling pointers by allowing the scope of dynamic objects to be smaller than pointers that point to them.

7.10.6 Pointers in Ada

Ada provides pointers, called access types, that are similar to those of Pascal. In Ada the dangling pointer problem is partially alleviated, however, by the language's design. A dynamic variable is implicitly deallocated at the end of the scope of its pointer, thus dramatically lessening the need for explicit deallocation. This helps alleviate the problem because improperly implemented explicit deallocation is the major source of dangling pointers. Unfortunately, the Ada language also has an explicit deallocation, UNCHECKED_DEALLOCATION. Its name is meant to discourage its use, or at least warn the user of its potential problems.

The dangling object problem is not eliminated by Ada's design of pointers. Dangling objects can be created in the same way as they can in PL/I.

One other small improvement in Ada pointers over those of Pascal and Modula-2 is the language's requirement that all pointers be implicitly initialized to **null** (Ada's version of nil). This prevents inadvertent accesses to random locations in memory because the user forgot to initialize a pointer before using it.

7.10.7 Pointers in C

In the C language pointers can be used much like addresses are used in assembly languages. Overall, this means they are extremely flexible but must be used with great care. C's pointers do not offer any solutions to the dangling pointer or dangling object problems. However, the fact that pointer arithmetic is possible in C makes its pointers more interesting than those of the other imperative languages.

The asterisk (∗) denotes the dereferencing operation and the ampersand (&) denotes the operator for producing the address of a variable. For example, in the code:

```
int *ptr;
int count, init;
...
ptr = &init;
count = *ptr;
```

the two assignment statements are equivalent to the single assignment:

```
count = init;
```

The assignment to the variable ptr sets ptr to the address of init. The first assignment to count dereferences ptr to produce the value at init, which is then assigned to count. So the effect of the first two assignment statements is to assign the value of init to count. Notice that the declaration of a pointer specifies its domain type.

In C, pointers can be assigned the constant zero, which is used for nil, or the address value of any object of the correct domain type.

Pointer, or address, arithmetic is also possible in some restricted forms. For example, if `ptr` is a pointer variable that is declared to point at some object of some data type,

```
ptr + index
```

is a legal expression. The semantics of such an expression in C is as follows. Instead of simply adding the value of `index` to `ptr`, the value of `index` is first scaled by the size of the object (in memory units) to which `ptr` is pointing. For example, if `ptr` points to an object of size four memory units, then `index` is multiplied by 4 and the result is added to `ptr`. The primary purpose of this sort of address arithmetic is array manipulation. The following discussion is related to single-dimensioned arrays only.

In C, all arrays use zero as the lower bound of their subscript ranges, and array names without subscripts always refer to the address of the first element. In fact, an array name without a subscript is treated exactly like a pointer, except that it is a constant, and therefore cannot be assigned. Suppose we have the following declarations:

```
int list [10];
int *ptr;
```

If we have the initializing assignment

```
ptr = list;
```

which assigns the address of `list[0]` to `ptr`, then

```
*(ptr + 1)  is equivalent to list[1],
*(ptr + index)  is equivalent to list[index], and
ptr[index] is equivalent to list[index]
```

So the pointer operations include the same scaling that is used in indexing operations. This is useful if one wants to access array elements rapidly and in orders other than row sequential.

Pointers in C can point to functions. This feature is used to pass functions as parameters to other functions. Pointers are also used for parameter passing, as we discuss in Chapter 8.

In C, pointers can be used to reference fields of records. For example, if a pointer variable p points to a record with a field named age, *p. age can be used to refer to that field.

7.10.8 Evaluation

The problems of dangling pointers and garbage have already been discussed at length. The problems of heap management are discussed in Section 7.11.7.

Pointers have been compared with the goto. The goto statement widens the range of statements that can be executed next. Pointer variables widen the range of memory cells that can be referenced by a variable.

Pointers are essential in imperative languages. They provide the means by which recursively defined data structures, such as linked lists and binary trees, can be represented. Although they have their problems, no one has yet suggested a retreat back to the old FORTRAN method of representing such structures, which is to use static arrays in place of heap management and indexing in place of pointer links between structure cells.

7.11 Implementing Data Types

We now take a brief look at implementation methods for the data types described in this chapter. The discussion will be general; we will not focus on language variations and specific implementation approaches.

It is convenient, both logically and concretely, to think of variables in terms of descriptors. A descriptor stores the attributes of a variable. If the attributes are all static, descriptors are required only at compile time. For dynamic attributes, however, part or all of the descriptor must be maintained during execution.

7.11.1 Character String Types

Character string types are sometimes supported directly in hardware. In other cases, software is used to implement string storage, retrieval, and manipulation. When character string types are actually character arrays, the language often supplies few operations. In C, for example, operations for string moves and string comparisons are provided outside the language, through a standard library of functions.

Character string types often require descriptors with a field for length, as shown in Figure 7.2.

Figure 7.2
Descriptor for static strings

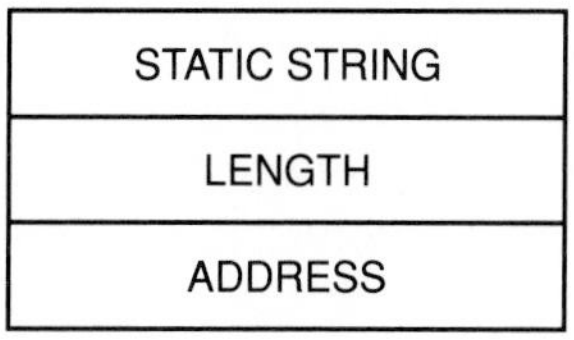

Figure 7.3
Descriptor for limited
dynamic strings

LIMITED DYNAMIC STRING
MAXIMUM LENGTH
CURRENT LENGTH
ADDRESS

Static strings require a descriptor only during compilation. Limited dynamic strings require a run-time descriptor to store both the fixed maximum length and the current length, as shown in Figure 7.3. Dynamic length strings require a simpler run-time descriptor because only the current length needs to be stored.

In C, as discussed in Section 7.6.5, strings are stored as character arrays, and their length is not stored anywhere. Rather, a special character is used to mark the end of the current contents of a character array. This special value, which is a numeric zero, is automatically maintained by the system.

Static length and limited dynamic length strings require no special dynamic storage allocation. In the case of limited dynamic length strings, sufficient storage for the maximum length is allocated when the string variable is bound to storage, so only a single allocation process is involved. The maximum length is fixed at compile time.

Dynamic length strings require more complex storage management. The length of a string, and therefore the storage to which it is bound, must grow and shrink dynamically.

There are two possible approaches to the dynamic allocation problem. First, strings can be stored in a linked list, so that when a string grows, the newly required cells can come from anywhere in the heap. The drawback to this method is the large amount of storage occupied by the links in the list representation. The alternative is to store complete strings in adjacent storage cells. The problem with this method occurs when a string grows: How can storage that is adjacent to the existing cells continue to be allocated for the string variable? The usual situation is that such storage is not available. Instead, a new area of memory is found that can store the complete new string, and the old part is moved to this area. Then the memory cells used for the old string are deallocated.

Although the linked list method requires more storage, the associated allocation and deallocation processes are simple. However, some string operations are slowed by the required pointer chasing. On the other hand, using adjacent memory for complete strings results in faster string operations and requires significantly less storage. However, the allocation process is slower. The adjacency method involves the general problem of managing allocation and deallocation of variable size segments. This problem is discussed in Section 7.11.7.2.2.

7.11.2 User-Defined Ordinal Types

Enumeration types are usually implemented by associating a positive integer value with each symbolic constant in the type. As long as the association is constant, the integers can be used in place of the enumeration constants. Of course, the operations allowed are dramatically different from those of integers, except for the relational operators, which are identical.

Subrange types are implemented in exactly the same way as their parent types, except that range checks must be included in every access. This increases code size and execution time, but is usually considered well worth the cost. Also, a good optimizing compiler can optimize some of the checking away.

7.11.3 Array Types

Implementing arrays requires more compile-time effort than does implementing simple built-in types such as integer. The code to allow accessing of array elements must be constructed at compile time. At run time, this code must be executed to produce element addresses. Accesses to array elements, especially in arrays with several subscripts, are prohibitively expensive if the access code is not carefully constructed. This is true regardless of whether the array is statically or dynamically bound to memory. There is no way to precompute the address to be accessed by a reference such as:

```
list(k)
```

Array elements are stored in contiguous memory locations. A single-dimensioned array is a list of adjacent memory cells. Suppose the array `list` is defined to have a subscript range lower bound of 1. The access function for `list` is often of the form:

$$\text{address}(list(k)) = \text{address}(list(1)) + (k-1) * \texttt{element\_size}$$

This simplifies to:

$$\text{address}(list(k)) = (\text{address}(list(1)) - \texttt{element\_size}) +$$
$$(k * \texttt{element\_size})$$

If the element type is statically bound and the array is statically bound to storage, then the value of the difference between the address of the first array element and the element size can be computed before run time. At run time, then, only the addition and multiplication operations remain to be done. If the base, or beginning address, of the array is not known until run time, the subtraction must also be done then. The compile-time descriptor for single-dimensioned arrays can have the form shown in Figure 7.4.

This is the information required to construct the access function. If runtime checking of index ranges is not done and the attributes are all static,

ARRAY
ELEMENT TYPE
INDEX TYPE
INDEX RANGE

then only the access function is required during execution; no descriptor is needed. If run-time checking of index ranges is done, then those index ranges may need to be stored in a run-time descriptor. If the subscript ranges of a particular array type are static, the ranges may be incorporated into the code that does the checking, thus eliminating the need for the run-time descriptor. If any of the descriptor entries are dynamically bound, then those parts of the descriptor must be maintained at run time.

Multidimensional arrays are more complex to implement than single-dimensioned arrays, although the extension to more dimensions is fairly straightforward. There are two common ways in which multidimensional arrays can be implemented: row major order and column major order. In **row major order,** the elements of the array that have as their first subscript the lower bound value of that subscript are stored first, followed by the elements of the second value of the first subscript, and so forth. If the array is a matrix, it is stored by rows. For example, if the matrix had the values:

       3   4   7
       6   2   5
       1   3   8

it would be stored in row major order as

    3, 4, 7, 6, 2, 5, 1, 3, 8

In **column major order,** the elements of an array that have as their last subscript the lower bound value of that subscript are stored first, followed by the elements of the second value of the last subscript, and so forth. If the array is a matrix, it is stored by columns. If the example matrix above were sorted in column major order, it would have the following order in memory:

    3, 6, 1, 4, 2, 3, 7, 5, 8

Column major order is used in FORTRAN, but the other imperative languages use row major order. FORTRAN is the only language in which it is important for the user to know the storage order of multidimensional arrays—for example, when an array is EQUIVALENCEd to another array with a different shape, as is illustrated in Chapter 4 (Section 4.4.2.1).

The access function for two-dimensional arrays stored in row major order can be developed as follows. The address of an element is the base

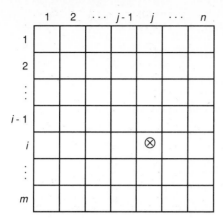

Figure 7.5
The location of the [i,j] element in a matrix

address of the structure plus the element size times the number of elements that precede it in the structure. For a matrix in row major order, the number of elements that precedes an element is the number of rows above the element times the size of a row, plus the number of elements to the left of the element. This is illustrated in Figure 7.5, in which we made the simplifying assumption that subscript lower bounds are all 1.

To get an actual address value, the number of elements that precede the desired element must be multiplied by the element size. Now, the access function can be written as

location(a[i,j]) = (address of a[1,1]) +
((((number of rows above the $i\mathit{th}$ row) ∗ (size of a row))
+ (number of elements left of the $j\mathit{th}$ column)) ∗ element size)

or

location(a[i,j]) = (address of a[1,1]) + (((i − 1) ∗ n)
+ (j − 1)) ∗ element_size

where n is the number of elements per row. This can be generalized relatively easily to an arbitrary number of dimensions.

For each dimension of an array, additional add and multiply instructions are usually required for the access function. Therefore, accesses to elements of arrays with several subscripts are costly. The compile-time descriptor for a multidimensional array is shown in Figure 7.6.

Slices add another layer of complexity to storage mapping functions. To illustrate this, consider a program in which there is a matrix and an array, and a column of the matrix is assigned to the array, as in:

```
var
  mat : array [1..10, 1..5] of integer;
  list : array [1..10] of integer;
  ...
list := mat[*, 3];
```

MULTIDIMENSIONED ARRAY
ELEMENT TYPE
INDEX TYPE
NUMBER OF DIMENSIONS
INDEX RANGE 1
⋮
INDEX RANGE n

The storage mapping function for the matrix, mat, assuming row major order and an element size of 1, is:

$$\begin{aligned} \text{location}(\text{mat}[i, \; j]) &= (\text{address of mat}[1,1]) \\ &\quad + ((i-1)*5 + (j-1))*1 \\ &= (\text{address of mat}[1,1]) + (5*i) + j - 6 \end{aligned}$$

The storage mapping function for the slice reference mat[*, 3] is:

$$\begin{aligned} \text{location}(\text{mat}[i, \; 3]) &= (\text{address of mat}[1,1]) \\ &\quad + ((i-1)*5 + (3-1))*1 \\ &= (\text{address of mat}[1,1]) + (5*i) - 3 \end{aligned}$$

The elements of mat that are to be assigned to list are found by letting i take on the values in the subscript range of the first dimension of mat.

7.11.4   Record Types

The fields of records are stored in adjacent memory locations. But because the size of the fields is not necessarily the same, the access method used for arrays is not used for records. Instead, the offset address, relative to the beginning of the record, is associated with each field. Field accesses are all handled using these offsets. The compile-time descriptor for a record has the general form shown in Figure 7.7. Run-time descriptors for records are unnecessary.

7.11.5   Discriminated Union Types

Discriminated unions are implemented by simply using the same address for every possible variant. Sufficient storage for the largest variant is allocated. In the case of constrained variants in the Ada language, the exact

Figure 7.7
A compile-time
descriptor for a
record

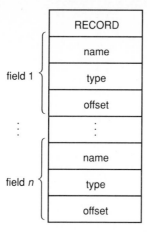

amount of storage can be used because there is no variation. The tag of a discriminated union is stored with the variant in a recordlike structure.

At compile time, the complete description of each variant must be stored. This can be done by associating a case table with the tag entry in the descriptor. The case table has an entry for each variant, which points to a descriptor for that particular variant. To illustrate this arrangement, consider the following example:

```
type NODE (TAG : BOOLEAN) is
  record
    case TAG is
      when true  => COUNT : INTEGER;
      when false => SUM : FLOAT;
    end case;
  end record;
```

The descriptor for this type could have the form shown in Figure 7.8.

7.11.6 Set Types

Sets are usually stored as bit strings in memory. For example, if a set has the ordinal base type:

```
['a'..'o']
```

then variables of this set type can use the first 15 bits of a machine word, with each set bit (1) representing a present element, and each clear bit (0) representing an absent element. Using this scheme, the set value:

```
['a', 'c', 'h', 'o']
```

Figure 7.8
A compile-time
descriptor for a dis-
criminated union

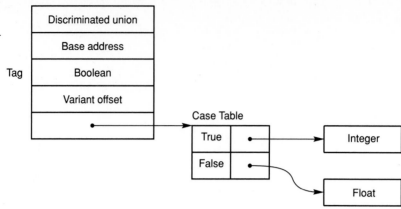

would be represented as:

    101000010000001

The payoff in this approach is that a typical operation such as set union can
be computed as a single machine instruction, a logical OR. Set membership
can also be done in a single instruction when the base set cardinality is less
than or equal to the machine's wordsize. For example, if we had a set variable named `setchars`, and the membership test was

    'g' in setchars

the process could be done with an exclusive OR operation between the bit
string representations of the two operands.

7.11.7   Pointers and Heap Management

In most languages, pointers are used in heap management, so it is difficult
to treat these two features separately. First, we discuss two possible solutions to the dangling pointer problem. Then we briefly describe the major
problems with heap management techniques.

7.11.7.1   Solutions to the Dangling Pointer Problem

Dangling pointers are those that point to storage that has been deallocated.
They are often created by explicit deallocation of dynamic variables. Explicit
deallocation creates dangling pointers because the deallocation statement

Figure 7.9
Implementing
dynamic variables
with and without
tombstones

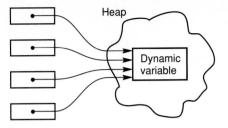

a. **Without tombstones**

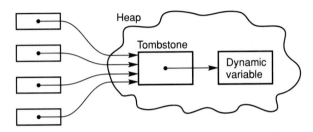

b. **With tombstones**

names only one pointer to the dynamic variable to be deallocated. Any other pointers to the disposed dynamic variable are made dangling by the process, because the run-time system was not informed that other such pointers exist.

Two separate but related solutions to the dangling pointer problem have been either proposed or actually implemented. First, there is the proposal that uses extra heap cells called tombstones.

7.11.7.1.1 Tombstones Tombstones were proposed by Lomet (1975). The idea is to have all dynamic variables include a special cell called a tombstone, which is itself a pointer to the dynamic variable. The actual pointer variable points only at tombstones, and never to dynamic variables. When a dynamic variable is deallocated, the tombstone remains, but is set to nil, indicating that the dynamic variable no longer exists. This prevents a pointer from ever pointing to a deallocated variable. Any reference to a pointer that points to a nil tombstone can be detected as an error. The difference between the tombstone and nontombstone methods is shown in Figure 7.9.

The cost of using tombstones occurs in both time and space. Because tombstones are never deallocated, their storage is never reclaimed. Every access to a dynamic variable through a tombstone requires one more level of indirection, which requires an additional machine cycle on most computers. Apparently none of the designers of the more popular languages have found the additional safety to be worth this additional cost, because no widely used language includes tombstones.

7.11.7.1.2 Locks and Keys   An alternative to tombstones is the locks and keys approach used in the implementation of UW-Pascal (Fischer and LeBlanc, 1977, 1980). In this compiler, pointer values are represented as ordered pairs (key, address), where the key is an integer value. Dynamic variables are represented as the storage for the variable plus a header cell that stores an integer lock value. When a dynamic variable is allocated, a lock value is created and placed both in the lock cell of the dynamic variable and in the key cell of the pointer that is specified in the call to new. Every access to the dereferenced pointer compares the key value of the pointer to the lock value in the dynamic variable. If they match, the access is legal; otherwise, the access is treated as a run-time error. Any copies of the pointer value to other pointers must copy the key value. Therefore, any number of pointers can reference a given dynamic variable. When a dynamic variable is deallocated with dispose, its lock value is cleared to an illegal lock value. Then if a pointer other than the one specified in the dispose is dereferenced, although its address value will still be intact, its key value will no longer match the lock, so the access will not be allowed.

7.11.7.2   Heap Management

Heap management can be a very complex run-time process. We examine the process in two separate situations: one in which all heap storage is allocated and deallocated in a single size of cells, and one in which variable-size segments are allocated and deallocated. Our discussion will be brief and far from comprehensive since a thorough analysis of these processes and their associated problems is beyond the scope of this book.

7.11.7.2.1 Fixed-Size Cells   The simplest situation is when all allocation and deallocation is of a single size cell. It is further simplified when every cell includes a pointer in a fixed position within the cell. This is the scenario of the implementation of LISP, where the problems of dynamic storage allocation were first encountered on a large scale. All LISP programs and most LISP data consist of cells connected into linked lists. There are also some string management processes involved, but we will ignore them here.

In a fixed-size allocation heap, all available cells can be linked together, forming a list of available space. Allocation is a simple matter of taking the required number of cells from this list when they are needed. Deallocation is a much more complex process. In LISP, several of the most frequent operations in user programs create garbage, or cells that are no longer accessible to the program. One of the fundamental design goals of LISP was to ensure that reclamation of garbage would not be the task of the programmer but rather that of the run-time system.

Dynamic variables can be pointed to by more than one pointer, and because of this, it is not simple to determine when a cell has become garbage. Simply because one pointer is disconnected from a cell obviously does not make it garbage. There are two distinct and in some ways opposite processes for reclaiming garbage cells: reference counters and garbage collection.

Reference Counters   The **reference counter** method of garbage reclamation accomplishes its goal by maintaining a counter in every cell, which stores the number of pointers that are currently pointing at the cell. Embedded in the decrement operation for the reference counters, which occurs when a pointer is disconnected from the cell, is a check for a zero value. If the reference counter reaches zero, it means that no program pointers are pointing at the cell and it has thus become garbage and can be returned to the list of available space in the heap.

There are three distinct problems with the reference counter method. First, a counter in each memory cell adds a great deal of overhead in terms of storage requirements. A significant fraction of all used storage will be taken by the counters. Second, a great deal of execution time is required to maintain the counter values. Every time a pointer value is changed, the cell to which it was pointing must have its counter decremented, and the cell to which it is now pointing must have its counter incremented. In a language like LISP, in which nearly every action involves changing pointers, that can be a significant portion of the total execution time of a program. Third, the method does not always work. In fact, it fails completely when a collection of cells is connected circularly. The problem here is that each cell in the circular list has a reference counter value of at least 1, which prevents it from being collected and placed back on the list of available space. Therefore, such cells are uncollectable garbage.

Garbage Collection   The primary alternative to reference counters is called **garbage collection.** With this method, the run-time system allocates storage cells as requested, without regard for storage reclamation, until it has allocated all available cells. At this point, a garbage collection process is begun to gather all the garbage left floating around in the heap. To facilitate the garbage collection process, every heap cell has an extra indicator bit or field, which is used by the collection algorithm.

The collection process consists of three distinct phases. First, all cells in the heap have their indicators set to indicate they are garbage. This is, of course, a good assumption for only some of the cells. The second part of the process is the most difficult. Every pointer in the program is traced into the heap and all reachable cells are marked as not being garbage. After this, the third phase is executed, in which all cells in the heap that have not been specifically marked as not being garbage are returned to the list of available space.

To illustrate the flavor of algorithms used to mark the cells that are currently in use, we provide a simple version of a marking algorithm. We assume that all dynamic variables, or heap cells, consist of an information part, a part for the mark, named tag, and two pointers named llink and rlink. These cells are used to build binary trees. The marking algorithm traverses all trees, marking all cells that are found. Like other tree traversals, the marking algorithm uses recursion.

Marking Algorithm:

```
for every tree root pointer r do
   mark(r)
procedure mark(ptr)
   if ptr^.tag is not marked then
      set ptr^.tag
      mark(ptr^.llink)
      mark(ptr^.rlink)
   end if
```

This is a simple marking algorithm that suffers the problem of using too much storage (for stack space to support recursion). More complex algorithms avoid this problem, but are beyond the scope of this book. A comprehensive discussion of garbage collection algorithms can be found in Cohen (1981).

The most serious problem with garbage collection can be summed up as: When you need it most, it works the worst. You need it most when the program actually needs most of the cells in the heap. Garbage collection in that situation takes a good deal of time, because most of the cells must be traced and marked as being useful. But in that case, the process yields only a small number of cells that can be placed on the list of available space. In addition to this problem, there is the cost of the additional space of the cell markers, which need only be a bit, and the execution time required to execute the collection process.

7.11.7.2.2 Variable-Size Cells   Managing a heap from which variable-size cells are allocated is much more difficult than one from which only single size cells are allocated. Unfortunately, this is the situation of the imperative languages. The additional problems posed by variable-size cell management depend on the method used. If garbage collection is used, the following additional problems occur:

1. The initial setting of the indicators of all cells in the heap to indicate that they are garbage is very difficult. Because the cells are different sizes, scanning them becomes a problem. One solution to this is to require each cell to have the cell size as its first field. Then the scan-

ning can be done, although it takes more space and more time than its counterpart for fixed-size cells.

2. The marking process, in which all cells reachable from program pointers are marked as being in use, is extremely difficult. How can a chain be followed from a pointer if there is no predefined location for the pointer in the pointed-to cell? Cells that do not contain pointers at all are also a problem. Adding a system pointer to each cell will work, but it must be maintained in parallel with the user-defined pointers. This adds a great deal of both space and execution time overhead to program running time.

3. Maintaining the list of available space is also difficult. The list can begin with a single cell consisting of all available space. Requests for segments simply reduce the size of this block. Reclaimed cells are added to the list. The problem is that before long, the list becomes a long list of various sized segments, or blocks; this greatly complicates allocation since requests cause the list to be searched for sufficiently large blocks. Eventually, the list may consist of a large number of very small blocks that are not large enough for most requests. At this point, adjacent blocks may need to be collapsed into larger blocks, which is a complex process. Alternatives to using the first sufficiently large block on the list can shorten the search, but require the list to be ordered by block size. In either case, maintaining the list is complicated and costly.

The problem here is that the cells need to be linked together, but there is no predefined location within the cells where a pointer is always found. An additional system pointer may once again seem to be the most obvious solution, thus adding space overhead for the extra pointer in every cell.

If reference counters are used, the first two problems are avoided, but the available space list maintenance problem remains.

SUMMARY

The data types of a language are a large part of what determines that language's style and use. Along with control structures, they form the heart of a language.

The type compatibility rules of a language have an important effect on the operations provided for the objects in the language. Type compatibility is generally defined in terms of name compatibility or structure compatibility. Name compatibility is easiest to implement, and is also better for several other reasons.

The user-defined enumeration and subrange types are convenient and add to the readability and reliability of programs.

Arrays are part of most programming languages. The relationship between a reference to an array element and the address of that element is given in an access function, which is an implementation of a mapping. Arrays can be either static, as in FORTRAN; semistatic, as in Pascal procedures; semi-dynamic, as in Ada blocks; or dynamic, as in ALGOL 68 **flex** arrays. Most languages allow only a few operations on complete arrays.

Records are now included in most languages. Fields of records are specified in a variety of ways. In the cases of COBOL and PL/I, they can be referenced without naming all of the enclosing records, although this is messy to implement and harmful to readability.

Discriminated unions are locations that can store different type values at different times. They include a tag to record the current value type. A free union is one without the tag. It has proven difficult to design discriminated unions safely, although the designers of the Ada language have succeeded in doing so.

Sets are sometimes convenient and are relatively easy to implement. The applications that usually use sets, however, can be done without too much difficulty using other data types.

Pointers are used for addressing flexibility and to control dynamic storage management. PL/I introduced pointers and allows the maximum flexibility but minimal safety in their use. Pascal and Modula-2 offer less flexibility and more safety through restrictions. Pointers have some inherent dangers: Dangling pointers and garbage creation are difficult to avoid.

The level of difficulty in implementing a data type has a strong influence on whether the type will be included in a language. Elementary types, enumeration types, subrange types, and record types are all relatively easy to implement. Arrays are also straightforward, although array element access is an expensive process when the array has several subscripts. The access function requires an additional addition and multiplication for each subscript after the first.

Pointers are costly to implement if they are used for dynamic storage management and steps are taken to avoid dangling pointers. Heap management is relatively easy if all cells have the same size, but is severely complicated by variable-size cell allocation and deallocation.

BIBLIOGRAPHIC NOTES

A wealth of computer science literature exists that is concerned with data type design, use, and implementation. Hoare gives one of the earliest systematic definitions of structured types in Dahl et al. (1972). Tanenbaum compares the type design of ALGOL 68 and Pascal (Tanenbaum, 1978). Feuer and Gehani (1982) compare C and Pascal, including their type structures. A discussion of the insecurities of the Pascal data type design is included in Welsh et al. (1977).

Implementing run-time checks on the possible insecurities of Pascal data types is discussed in Fischer and LeBlanc (1980). Most compiler design books, such as Fischer and LeBlanc (1988) and Aho et al. (1986), describe implementation methods for data types, as do the other programming language texts, such as Pratt (1984) and Ghezzi and Jazayeri (1987). Garbage collection methods are described by Schoor and Waite (1967) and Deutsch and Bobrow (1976).

BIBLIOGRAPHY

Aho, A.V., R. Sethi, and J.D. Ullman. (1986) *Compilers: Principles, Techniques, and Tools.* Addison-Wesley, Reading, MA.

Cohen, J. (1981) "Garbage Collection of Linked Data Structures." *ACM Computing Surveys*, Vol. 13, No. 3, pp. 341–368.

Dahl, O.-J., E.W. Dijkstra, and C.A.R. Hoare. (1972) *Structured Programming.* Academic Press, New York.

Deutsch, L.P., and D.G. Bobrow. (1976) "An Efficient Incremental Automatic Garbage Collector." *Commun. ACM*, Vol. 11, No. 3, pp. 522–526.

Feuer, A., and N. Gehani. (1982) "A Comparison of the Programming Languages C and Pascal." *ACM Computing Surveys*, Vol. 14, No. 1, pp. 73–92.

Fischer, C.N., and R.J. LeBlanc. (1977) "UW-Pascal Reference Manual." Madison Academic Computing Center, Madison, WI.

Fischer, C.N., and R.J. LeBlanc. (1980) "Implementation of Runtime Diagnostics in Pascal." *IEEE-TSE*, SE-6, No. 4, pp. 313–319.

Fischer, C.N., and R.J. LeBlanc. (1988) *Crafting a Compiler.* Benjamin/Cummings, Menlo Park, CA.

Ghezzi, C., and M. Jazayeri. (1987) *Programming Language Concepts.* 2d ed. Wiley, New York.

Griswold, R.E., F. Poage, and I.P. Polonsky. (1971) *The SNOBOL4 Programming Language.* 2d ed. Prentice-Hall, Englewood Cliffs, NJ.

ISO. (1982) *Specification for Programming Language Pascal.* ISO7185-1982. International Organization for Standardization, Geneva, Switzerland.

Lomet, D. (1975) "Scheme for Invalidating References to Freed Storage." *IBM J. of Research and Development*, Vol. 19, pp. 26–35.

Pratt, T.W. (1984) *Programming Languages: Design and Implementation.* 2d ed. Prentice-Hall, Englewood Cliffs, NJ.

Schoor, H., and W. Waite. (1967) "An Efficient Machine Independent Procedure for Garbage Collection in Various List Structures." *Commun. ACM*, Vol. 10, No. 8, pp. 501–506.

Tanenbaum, A.S. (1978) "A Comparison of Pascal and ALGOL 68." *Computer Journal*, Vol. 21, pp. 316–323.

Welsh, J., M.J. Sneeringer, and C.A.R. Hoare. (1977) "Ambiguities and Insecurities in Pascal." *Software—Practice and Experience*, Vol. 7, No. 6, pp. 685–696.

Wirth, N. (1971) "The Programming Language Pascal." *Acta Informatica*, Vol. 1, No. 1, pp. 35–63.

PROBLEM SET

1. What are the required entries in a Pascal array descriptor, and when must they be stored (compile time or run time)?

2. What are the main advantages of user-defined enumeration types?

3. Differentiate clearly among static, semistatic, semidynamic, and dynamic arrays.

4. How is readability affected by dynamic binding of type?

5. What is an aggregate constant?

6. What are the differences between the slices of PL/I and those of Ada?

7. What is the worst aspect of elliptical references to fields of a record?

8. What is the main problem with designing discriminated union structures?

9. In what ways are the variant records of the Ada language safer than those of Pascal?

10. Why are there usually severe restrictions on the size of sets in Pascal implementations?

11. What problems can occur with Pascal pointers?

12. Why are the pointers of most languages restricted to pointing at a single type object?

13. Compare the tombstones and keys and locks methods of avoiding dangling pointers, from the points of view of safety and implementation cost.

14. Design a set of simple test programs to determine the type compatibility rules of the Pascal compiler to which you have access. Write a report of your findings.

15. Determine whether some Pascal compiler to which you have access implements the dispose procedure.

16. Suppose that a language includes user-defined enumeration types and that the enumeration values could be overloaded; that is, the same literal value could appear in two different enumeration types, as in:

type
```
    colors = (red, blue, green);
    mood = (happy, angry, blue);
```

Use of the constant blue cannot be type checked. Propose a method of allowing such type checking without completely disallowing such overloading.

17. Multidimensional arrays can be stored in row major order, as in Pascal, or in column major order, as in FORTRAN. Develop the access functions for both of these arrangements for three-dimensional arrays.

18. In the Burroughs Extended ALGOL language, matrices are stored as a single-dimensioned array of pointers to the rows of the matrix, which are treated as single-dimensioned arrays of objects. What are the advantages and disadvantages of such a scheme?

19. Write a program that does matrix multiplication in some language that does subscript range checking and for which you can obtain an assembly language or machine language version from the compiler. Determine the number of instructions required for the subscript range checking and compare it with the total number of instructions for the matrix multiplication process.

[Handwritten margin notes:]

16. require all refs to enumeration constants to be qualified with the type name, as in colors.blue

13. tombstones –
simple & easy to implement
wastes stg
all access indirect

lock + key –
less stg wasted (lock need not be full word)
access has overhead to checking keys
a little more complex to implement

17.

20. Write a Pascal program that includes the following declarations:

```
var
  A, B : array [1..10] of integer;
  C : array [1..10] of integer;
  D : array [1..10] of integer;
```

Include code in the program that determines, for each of the arrays, which of the other three arrays are compatible with it.

21. If you have access to a compiler in which the user can specify whether subscript range checking is desired, write a program that does a large number of matrix accesses and times their execution. Run the program with subscript range checking and without it and compare the times.

1. a) # of dimensions
   b) type + upper + lower bounds for each subscript
   c) type of elements
   compile time only

2) readability
   also reliability of enumeration types instead of a type with larger than necessary range of possible values

3) p.241

4) more difficult, because readers must trace execution to determine the type of a specific reference to a variable

5) aggregate cost is one for a structured type, thus requiring more than one simple typed value to be involved

7) readability reduced by absence of parts of the record. 2nd, compiler must do extensive analysis to see if it's legal + to which field they refer

8) finding suitable mechanism for type checks. not too much bother and implementable in some efficient way

9) a) tag can't be changing without also changing variant value
   b) tag is mandatory
   c) Ada compilers must generate code that checks the tag in all references to the variant

10) for efficient implementation. Since Pascal a teaching tool, thought not to need large sets

11) Pascal pointers can be left dangling. Pascal also allows creation of garbage

12) pointers of most langs most are restricted to pointing at a single type so use can be type-checked

Key Concepts

- Process abstraction
- Local referencing environments
- Parameter-passing methods
- Aliasing with parameters
- Value versus access path transmission
- Nonlocal referencing environments
- Static versus dynamic scope
- Overloaded subprograms
- User-defined overloaded operators
- Generic subprograms
- Separate compilation

8

SUBPROGRAMS

Subprograms are the fundamental building blocks of programs, and are therefore among the most important concepts in programming language design. We now explore the design of subprograms, including parameter-passing methods, local and nonlocal referencing environments, overloaded subprograms, generic subprograms, separate compilation, and the aliasing and side effects problems that are associated with subprograms.

Coroutines and concurrent subprograms are not covered in this chapter; they are such important forms of subprograms that they have their own chapter, Chapter 11. Implementation methods for subprograms are discussed in Chapter 9.

8.1   Introduction

Two fundamental abstraction facilities can be included in a programming language: process abstraction and data abstraction. In the early history of high-level programming languages, process abstraction was held to be the more important of the two since it was a central concept in all programming languages. It was the first of the two to be recognized and exploited. Recently, however, more people are beginning to believe that data abstraction is equally important. Data abstraction is discussed in detail in Chapter 10.

The first programmable computer, Babbage's Analytical Engine, built in the 1840s, had the capability of reusing collections of instruction cards at any number of spots in a program where they were needed. Already, the idea of process abstraction was being employed: When a collection of instructions is needed more than once in a program, we reuse a single instance of the collection rather than repeating it. Such a mechanism is an abstraction because the collection is replaced in a program by a statement that "calls" that collection. Instead of explaining how it is to be done, that explanation (the collection of instructions) is enacted by a "call" instruction, effectively abstracting away the details. This increases the readability of a program by exposing its logical structure while hiding the small-scale details.

8.2   Fundamentals of Subprograms

8.2.1   General Subprogram Characteristics

Before discussing the fundamentals of subprograms, we must clarify the basic characteristics of the kinds of subprograms that are discussed in this chapter. These are:

1. Each subprogram has a single entry point.
2. The calling program unit is suspended during the execution of the called subprogram, which implies that there is only one subprogram in execution at any given time.

3. Control always returns to the caller when the subprogram execution terminates.

Although FORTRAN subprograms can have multiple entries, that particular kind of entry is relatively unimportant because it does not provide any fundamentally different capabilities. Therefore, in this chapter, we will ignore the possibility of multiple entries in FORTRAN subprograms.

Other alternatives to the above assumptions result in coroutines and concurrent units, which are explored in Chapter 11.

8.2.2 Basic Definitions

A **subprogram definition** describes the actions of the subprogram abstraction. A **subprogram call** is the explicit request that the subprogram be executed. A subprogram is said to be **active** if it has begun execution after having been called, but has not yet completed that execution.

A **subprogram header**, which is the first line of the definition, serves several purposes. First, it specifies that the following syntactic unit is a subprogram definition of some particular kind. This is often accomplished with a special word. Second, it provides a name for the subprogram. Third, it may optionally specify a list of parameters. They are optional because not all subprogram definitions have parameters. Consider the following header examples:

SUBROUTINE ADDER (parameters)

This is the header of a FORTRAN subroutine type subprogram named ADDER. In Ada we could have:

procedure ADDER (parameters) **is**

as the header of a procedure type subprogram named ADDER. No special word appears in the header of a C subprogram. C has only one kind of subprogram, the function, and the header of a function is recognized by context rather than by a special word. For example, we could have:

adder (parameters)

as the header of a function named adder.

8.2.3 Parameters

The parameters in the subprogram header are called **formal parameters.** They are sometimes thought of as dummy variables because they are not variables in the usual sense: They are only bound to storage when the subprogram is enacted, and that binding is through some other program variables.

Subprogram call statements must include the name of the subprogram and a list of parameters to be bound to the formal parameters of the subprogram. These parameters are called **actual parameters.** They must be differentiated from formal parameters because the two can have different restrictions on their forms, and their uses are quite different.

In nearly all programming languages, the correspondence between actual and formal parameters—or the binding of actual parameters to formal parameters—is done by simple position: The first actual parameter is bound to the first formal parameter, and so forth. Such parameters are called **positional parameters.** This is a good method for relatively short parameter lists. When lists are long, however, it is easy for the program writer to make mistakes in the order of parameters in the list. One solution to this problem is to provide **keyword parameters**, in which the formal parameter to which an actual parameter is to be bound is specified with the actual parameter. The advantage of keyword parameters is that they can appear in any order in the actual parameter list. Ada procedures can be called using this method, as in:

```
SUMER  (LENGTH => MY_LENGTH,
        LIST => MY_ARRAY,
        SUM => MY_SUM) ;
```

where the definition of SUMER has the formal parameters LENGTH, LIST, and SUM.

The chief disadvantage to keyword parameters is that the user of the subprogram must know the names of formal parameters.

In addition to keyword parameters, Ada allows positional parameters. The two can be mixed in a call, as in:

```
SUMER  (MY_LENGTH,
        SUM => MY_SUM,
        LIST => MY_ARRAY) ;
```

The only restriction with this is that after a keyword parameter appears in the list, all remaining parameters must be keyworded. This is necessary because position may no longer be well defined after a keyword parameter has appeared.

One other feature of Ada parameters that is different from other common languages is that there can be default values for formal parameters that receive information into the subprogram. A default value is used if no actual parameter is passed to the formal parameter in the subprogram header. Consider the following partial Ada procedure header:

```
procedure COMPUTE_PAY (INCOME : FLOAT;
                       EXEMPTIONS : INTEGER : = 1;
                       TAX_RATE : FLOAT;
                       ... ) is
```

The EXEMPTIONS parameter can be eliminated in a call to COMPUTE_PAY; when it is, the value 1 is used. No comma is included for an absent actual parameter in an Ada call. Thus, all actual parameters after an absent actual parameter must be keyworded, for obvious reasons. For example, we could have:

```
COMPUTE_PAY (20000.0, TAX_RATE => 0.8, ...);
```

In most languages, the number of actual parameters in a call must match the number of formal parameters in the subprogram definition header. C is one language in which this is not required. When there are fewer actual parameters in a call than formal parameters in a C program definition, it is the programmer's responsibility to ensure that the parameter correspondence, which is always positional, and the subprogram execution are sensible.

8.2.4 Procedures and Functions

There are two distinct categories of subprograms: procedures and functions, both of which can be viewed as methods of extending the language. Procedures are collections of statements that define parameterized, user-defined statements in the form of calls. For example, because Pascal does not have a sort statement, a user can build a procedure to sort lists of data and use that procedure in place of the unavailable sort statement.

Procedures can produce results in the calling program unit by two methods. First, if there are variables that are not formal parameters but they are visible in both the procedure and the calling program unit, the procedure can change them. Second, if the subprogram has formal parameters that allow the transfer of data to the caller, those parameters can be changed.

Functions are modeled after mathematical functions. If they are faithful models, they produce no side effects; that is, they modify neither their parameters nor any other variables declared outside the function or declared in the function and visible outside the function. The result of a call to a function that does not produce side effects is returned to the calling code, effectively replacing the call.

Functions are collections of statements that define new user-defined operations. For example, if a language does not have an exponentiation operator, a function can be written that returns the value of one of its parameters raised to the power of another parameter. Its header in Pascal may be:

```
function power (base, exp : real)
```

which could be called, as in:

```
result := 3.4 * power (10.0, x)
```

Compare this with the same operation in FORTRAN, where exponentiation is a built-in operation:

```
RESULT = 3.4 * 10.0 ** X
```

FORTRAN procedures are called **subroutines,** and we use that term when referring to those units.

8.3   Design Issues for Subprograms

The following are the primary design issues for subprograms in general. Additional issues that are specifically associated with functions are discussed in Section 8.10.

1. Are local variables statically or dynamically allocated?
2. What parameter-passing method or methods are used?
3. Are the types of the actual parameters checked against the types of the formal parameters?
4. Are the types of parameters checked in calls to subprograms that are passed as parameters?
5. What is the referencing environment of a subprogram that has been passed as a parameter?
6. Can subprograms be overloaded?
7. Can subprograms be generic?
8. Is either separate or independent compilation possible?

These issues and example designs are discussed in the following sections.

8.4   Local Referencing Environments

Subprograms are generally allowed to declare their own variables, thereby defining local referencing environments. Variables that are declared inside subprograms are called **local variables,** because access to them is usually restricted to the subprogram in which they are declared.

Local variables can be either statically or dynamically bound to storage. In Chapter 4 we called these two static and semidynamic variables, respectively. If local variables are semidynamic, they are bound to storage when the subprogram begins execution and unbound from storage when that execution terminates. There are several advantages of semidynamic local variables, the primary one being the flexibility they provide the subprogram. It is essential that recursive subprograms have semidynamic local variables. Another advantage of semidynamic locals is that the storage for local variables of all subprograms in a system that are never active at the same time can be shared. This is not as great an advantage as it was when computers had smaller memories.

The main disadvantages of semidynamic local variables are the following. First, there is the cost of the time required to allocate and deallocate such variables for each call. Second, references to semidynamic local variables must be indirect, whereas references to static variables can be direct. On most computers indirect references are slower than direct references. Finally, with semidynamic local variables, subprograms cannot be history-sensitive; that is, they cannot retain data values of local variables between calls.

The primary advantage of static local variables is that they are very efficient—they can usually be accessed faster, and there is no run-time overhead of allocation and deallocation. Furthermore, they allow subprograms to be history-sensitive.

In ALGOL 60 and its descendant languages, local variables in a subprogram are usually semidynamic. ALGOL 60 also allows users to specify that a local variable is to be static. They can do this by attaching the reserved word **own** to such a declaration. Without the **own** specification, ALGOL 60 local variables are semidynamic. C is like ALGOL 60 in that locals are semidynamic unless specifically declared to be static. Pascal, Modula-2, and Ada subprograms have only semidynamic local variables.

As discussed in Chapter 4, FORTRAN 77 implementors can choose whether local variables are to be static or semidynamic. Most implementors stay with the tradition of earlier FORTRANs and make them static. And actually, since FORTRAN does not allow recursion, there is no compelling reason to make them semidynamic. The savings in storage is not thought to be worth the loss in efficiency. FORTRAN 77 users can force one or more local variables to be static regardless of the implementation by listing their names on a SAVE statement.

8.5   Parameter-Passing Methods

Parameter-passing methods are the ways in which parameters are transmitted to and/or from an enacted subprogram. We first focus on the primary semantics models of parameter-passing methods. Then we discuss the various implementation models invented by language designers for these semantics models. Next, we survey the design choices of the various imperative languages. Then we discuss the actual methods used to implement the implementation models. Finally, we consider the design considerations that face a language designer in choosing among the methods.

8.5.1   Semantics Models of Parameter Passing

Most formal parameters can be categorized into one of three distinct semantics models: (1) They can receive data from the corresponding actual parameter, (2) they can transmit data to the actual parameter, or (3) they can do both. These three models are called **in mode, out mode,** and **inout mode,** respectively.

There are two conceptual models of how data transfers take place in parameter transmission: Either an actual value is physically moved between the caller and the callee, or vice versa, or an access path is moved. Most commonly, the access path is a simple pointer.

8.5.2   Implementation Models of Parameter Passing

A variety of models has been developed to guide the implementation of the three basic parameter transmission modes. In the following sections we discuss several of these and evaluate their strengths and weaknesses.

8.5.2.1   Pass by Value

When a parameter is **passed by value,** the value of the actual parameter is used to initialize the corresponding formal parameter, which then acts as a local variable in the subprogram, thus providing only in mode, or one-way communication.

Pass by value could be implemented by transmitting an access path to the value of the actual parameter in the caller, but that would require that the value be in a write-protected cell (or in one that can only be read). Because accesses are usually more efficient with actual data transfer, this is the method normally used.

The main disadvantage of the pass by value method, if physical moves are done, is that additional storage is required for the formal parameter, either in the called subprogram or in some area outside both the caller and the called subprogram. In addition, the actual parameter must be physically moved to the storage area for the corresponding formal parameter. The storage and the move operations can be costly if the parameter is large, such as a long array.

8.5.2.2   Pass by Result

Pass by result is an implementation model for out mode parameters. When a parameter is passed by result, no value is transmitted to the subprogram. The corresponding formal parameter acts as a local variable, but just before control is transferred back to the caller, its value is passed back to the caller's actual parameter, which must be a variable. If actual values are transmitted, as they typically are, pass by result also requires the extra storage and the same copy operations that are required by pass by value.

One problem with the pass by result model is that there can be an actual parameter collision, such as is created with the call:

```
sub (p1, p1)
```

In sub, assuming the two formal parameters have different names, the two can obviously be assigned different values. Then whichever of the two is assigned to their corresponding actual parameter last becomes the value of p1. Thus the order in which the actual parameters are assigned determines their value. Because the order is usually implementation-dependent, portability problems can occur that are difficult to diagnose.

The procedure call shown in this section can also create problems when another parameter-passing method is used, as is discussed in Section 8.5.2.4.

8.5.2.3 Pass by Value-Result

Pass by value-result is an implementation model for inout mode parameters in which actual values are moved. It is in effect a combination of pass by value and pass by result. The value of the actual parameter is used to initialize the corresponding formal parameter, which then acts as a local variable. At subprogram termination, the value of the formal parameter is transmitted back to the actual parameter.

Pass by value-result is sometimes called pass by copy, because the actual parameter is copied to the formal parameter at subprogram entry, and then copied back at subprogram termination.

Pass by value-result shares with pass by value and pass by result the disadvantages of requiring multiple storage for parameters and the time required to copy values. It shares with pass by result the problems associated with the order in which actual parameters are assigned.

8.5.2.4 Pass by Reference

Pass by reference is another implementation model for inout mode parameters. Rather than transmitting data values back and forth, however, as in pass by value-result, the pass by reference method transmits an access path, usually just an address, to the called subprogram. This provides the access path to the cell storing the actual parameter. Thus, the called subprogram is allowed to access the actual parameter in the calling program unit. In effect, the actual parameter is shared with the called subprogram.

The advantage of call by reference is that the passing process itself is efficient, in terms of both time and space. Duplicate space is not required, nor is any copying.

There are several disadvantages to the pass by reference method. First, accesses to the formal parameters may be somewhat slower because indirect addressing is needed, whereas direct addressing can be used when data values are transmitted, as with pass by value-result. Second, if only one-way communication to the called subprogram is required, inadvertent and erroneous changes may be made to the actual parameter.

Another serious problem of pass by reference is that aliases can be created. This should be expected, because pass by reference makes access paths available to the called subprograms, thereby broadening their access to nonlocal variables. There are several ways aliases can be created when parameters are passed by reference.

First, collisions can occur between actual parameters. Suppose we have a Pascal procedure that has two parameters that are to be passed by reference, as in:

```
procedure SUB (var FIRST, SECOND : integer)
```

If the call to SUB happens to pass the same variable twice, as in:

```
SUB (TOTAL, TOTAL)
```

FIRST and SECOND in SUB will be aliases.

Collisions between array elements can also cause aliases. For example, suppose the subprogram SUB is called with two array elements that are specified with variable subscripts, as in:

```
SUB (LIST[I], LIST[J])
```

If I happens to be equal to J, FIRST and SECOND are again aliases.

Collisions between array element parameters and elements of arrays passed as array name parameters are another possible cause of aliases. If two of the formal parameters of a subprogram are a scalar and an array of the same type, then a call such as:

```
SUB1 (LIST[I], LIST)
```

could result in aliasing in SUB1, since SUB1 can access all elements of LIST through the second parameter, and access a single element through its first parameter.

Still another way to get aliasing with pass by reference parameters is through collisions between formal parameters and nonlocal variables that are visible.

These aliases are possible when a language provides more nonlocal access than is necessary, such as with static scoping. For example, consider the following Pascal code:

```
procedure BIGSUB;
  var GLOBAL : integer;
  procedure SMALLSUB (var LOCAL : integer);
    begin
      . . .
    end;    { SMALLSUB }
  begin
    . . .
  SMALLSUB (GLOBAL);
    . . .
  end;    { BIGSUB }
```

Inside SMALLSUB, LOCAL and GLOBAL are aliases. As stated above, the main reason for the aliasing is that static scoping provides too much access to nonlocal variables. The problem with these kinds of aliasing is the same as in other circumstances: It is harmful to readability and thus to reliability. It also makes program verification extremely difficult.

All of these possible aliasing situations are eliminated if pass by value-result is used instead of pass by reference. However, in place of aliasing, other problems sometimes arise, as were discussed in Sections 8.5.2.2 and 8.5.2.3.

Lastly, a subtle but fatal error can occur with pass by reference parameters. Suppose a program contains two references to the constant 10, the first being as an actual parameter in a call to a subprogram. Further suppose that the subprogram mistakenly changes the formal parameter that corresponds to the 10 to the value 5. The compiler for this program may have built a single location for the value 10 during compilation, as compilers often do, and may use that location for all references to the constant 10 in the program. But after the return from the subprogram, all subsequent occurrences of 10 will actually be references to the value 5. This can happen in some systems, and it creates a programming problem that is very difficult to diagnose. This did in fact happen with many implementations of FORTRAN IV.

8.5.2.5 Pass by Name

Pass by name is a parameter transmission method that does not correspond to a single semantics mode, as we explain below. When parameters are passed by name, the actual parameter is, in effect, textually substituted for the corresponding formal parameter in all of its occurrences in the subprogram. This is quite different from the methods discussed thus far. In those cases, formal parameters are bound to actual values or addresses at the time of the subprogram call. A pass by name formal parameter is bound to an access method at the time of the subprogram call, but the actual binding to a value or an address is delayed until the formal parameter is assigned or referenced.

The objective of the late binding in pass by name parameters is flexibility. This is consistent with other situations in which we have encountered differences in binding time. For example, binding a variable to a type occurs at a later point in APL than it does in FORTRAN, thus yielding more flexible uses of variables.

The form of the actual parameter affects the semantics of pass by name parameters. This distinguishes pass by name parameters from those passed by other methods. If the actual parameter is a scalar variable, then pass by name is equivalent to pass by reference. If the actual parameter is a constant expression, then pass by name is equivalent to pass by value. If the actual parameter is an array element, pass by name may be different from any other method because the value of the actual subscript can change during execution between the times of the call and a reference, thus allowing different appearances of the formal parameter in the called subprogram to refer to different array elements. This is discussed in greater detail later in this section.

If the actual parameter is an expression that contains references to a variable, pass by name is again different from any other method. The difference occurs because the expression is evaluated for each reference to the formal parameter at the time the reference is reached. If any of the variables in the expression are themselves accessible and are changed by the subprogram, the value of the expression can change with each reference to the formal parameter.

Consider the following example program, written in an ALGOL-like language:

```
procedure BIGSUB;
  integer GLOBAL;
  integer array LIST [1:2];
  procedure SUB (PARAM);
   integer PARAM;
   begin
   PARAM := 3;
   GLOBAL := GLOBAL + 1;
   PARAM := 5
   end;
  begin
  LIST[1] := 2;
  LIST[2] := 2;
  GLOBAL := 1;
  SUB (LIST[GLOBAL])
  end;
```

After execution, the array LIST has the values 3 and 5, both set in SUB. Access to LIST[2] is provided after GLOBAL is incremented by 1 in SUB to produce the value 2.

Some rather clever trickery can be played with pass by name parameters. The most famous example of this was proposed by J. Jensen of the Regnecentralen in Copenhagen in 1960, and has since been called *Jensen's Device*. Consider the following ALGOL 60 procedure:

```
real procedure SUM (ADDER, INDEX, LENGTH);
  value LENGTH;
  real ADDER;
  integer INDEX, LENGTH;
  begin
  real TEMPSUM;
  TEMPSUM := 0.0;
  for INDEX := 1 step 1 until LENGTH do
   TEMPSUM := TEMPSUM + ADDER;
  SUM := TEMPSUM
  end;
```

If A is a scalar, the call:

```
SUM (A, I, 100)
```

simply produces the value 100 * A by adding A to an initially cleared location 100 times. Suppose that A is an array of 100 reals and we called SUM with:

    SUM (A[I], I, 100)

Now, the **for** statement effectively becomes:

    for I := 1 **step** 1 **until** 100 **do**
      TEMPSUM := TEMPSUM + A[I]

So this call produces the sum of an array. If we instead wanted the sum of the squares of the elements of the A array, we could call it with:

    SUM (A[I]*A[I], I, 100)

The inner product of the two vectors in arrays A and B, each of length 100, could be gotten from:

    SUM (A[I]*B[I], I, 100)

These different uses of the procedure SUM show that the pass by name mechanism provides a large degree of flexibility: A single procedure can be used for a variety of different purposes. The cost of this flexibility lies in two areas: readability and execution speed. Procedures that use the pass by name feature to achieve the flexibility demonstrated above are difficult to understand. The many possible uses of such procedures are not always apparent from their listings. The cost of pass by name parameters, in terms of execution efficiency, is discussed in Section 8.5.5.

One surprising problem with pass by name is that it cannot be used to perform the simple task of interchanging the values of two given actual parameters. A simple implementation of the interchange is:

    procedure SWAP (FIRST, SECOND);
      integer FIRST, SECOND;
      begin
      integer TEMP;
      TEMP := FIRST;
      FIRST := SECOND;
      SECOND := TEMP
      end;

The procedure SWAP performs correctly if the two arguments are scalars, and in most other cases. However, if an array element and its subscript are sent, it fails—for example, if we called SWAP with the actual parameters I and A[I]. In this case the statements of SWAP become, in effect:

    TEMP := I;
    I := A[I];
    A[I] := TEMP;

The problem is that the new value of I is used to compute the address of the destination of the last assignment. The assignment to A[I] is to a different location than the value referenced in the second statement, which assigns the value of A[I] to I. It has been proven that it is not possible to write a general ALGOL 60 function that correctly interchanges the values of its two parameters.

In summary, the primary advantage of pass by name is the flexibility it affords the programmer. The main disadvantage is the slowness of the process, relative to other parameter-passing methods. Also, it is difficult to implement and may confuse both readers and writers of programs that use it.

8.5.3   Parameter-Passing Methods of the Major Languages

FORTRAN implementations use the inout mode semantics model of parameter passing. In most FORTRAN implementations before FORTRAN 77, parameters were passed by reference. In recent years, however, value-result has been frequently used for simple variable parameters. Formal parameters in FORTRAN subprograms are declared as if they were local parameters, although these declarations do not cause storage allocation.

As stated in the previous section, ALGOL 60 introduced the pass by name method. It also allows pass by value as an option.

Primarily because of the difficulty in implementing pass by name parameters, they were not carried from ALGOL 60 to the design of ALGOL 68. The passing method used in ALGOL 68 is pass by value. A pointer type actual parameter can give the effect of pass by reference. ALGOL 68 introduced the syntax of attaching the type of a formal parameter to its name in the formal parameter list. For example, the ALGOL 68 header for the ADDER example above could have the form:

```
proc adder = (ref int a, int b, ref real c) ...
```

Both the a and c parameters are inout mode, and are therefore passed as access paths, in this case simply pointers. The C language uses the same parameter-passing method as ALGOL 68. ALGOL W (Wirth and Hoare, 1966) introduced the value-result method of parameter passing as an answer to the inefficiency of pass by name and the problems of pass by reference.

In Pascal and Modula-2, the default parameter-passing method is pass by value, and pass by reference can be specified by prefacing formal parameters with the reserved word **var**. For example, the Pascal header for the ALGOL 68 ADDER example above could be

```
procedure adder (var a : integer;
                      b : integer;
                 var c : real);
```

The designers of Ada defined versions of the three semantics modes of parameter transmission, in, out, and inout. The three modes are appropriately named with the reserved words: **in**, **out**, and **in out**, where **in** is the default method. For example, the ADDER example could have the following Ada header:

```
procedure ADDER (A :  in out INTEGER;
                 B :  in INTEGER;
                 C :  in out FLOAT) ;
```

Ada formal parameters declared to be **out** mode can be assigned but not referenced. Parameters that are **in** mode can be referenced but not assigned. Unlike **in** mode and **out** mode parameters, however, **in out** mode parameters can be both referenced and assigned.

8.5.4 Type-Checking Parameters

It is now widely accepted that software reliability demands that the types of actual parameters be checked for consistency with the corresponding formal parameters. Without such type checking, small typographical errors can lead to program errors that may be difficult to diagnose because they are not detected by the system. For example, in the function call

```
RESULT  : =  SUB1 (1)
```

the actual parameter is an integer constant. If the formal parameter of SUB1 is a floating-point type, no error will be detected without parameter type checking. Yet, SUB1 cannot produce a correct result given an actual parameter that is not near the expected value of a floating point 1.0.

FORTRAN 77 and C do not require parameter type checking; Pascal, Modula-2, FORTRAN 8x, and Ada do require it.

8.5.5 Implementing Parameter-Passing Methods

We now address the question of how the primary implementation models of parameter passing are actually implemented.

In ALGOL 60 and its descendant languages, parameter communication takes place through the run-time stack. In the following discussion we assume that the stack is used for all parameter transmission.

Pass by value parameters have their values copied into stack locations. Pass by result parameters are implemented as the opposite of pass by value. The values assigned to the pass by result actual parameters are placed in the stack, where they can be retrieved by the calling program unit upon termination of the called subprogram. Pass by value-result parameters can be implemented directly from their semantics: as a combination of pass by value and pass by result.

Pass by reference parameters are perhaps the simplest to implement. Regardless of the type of the actual parameter, its address is all that must be transmitted. In the case of constants, the address of the constant could be transmitted. However, because of the potential problem with constant actual parameters, described in Section 8.5.2.4, a better method is to pass the address of a temporary copy of such a constant. In the case of an expression, the compiler must build code to evaluate the expression just before the transfer of control to the called subprogram. The address where that code places the result of that evaluation is then transmitted. Access to the formal parameters in the called subprogram is by indirect addressing.

Pass by name parameters are usually implemented with parameterless procedures or code segments that are run-time resident, called **thunks**. A thunk must be called for every reference to a pass by name parameter in the called subprogram. The thunk evaluates the reference in the proper referencing environment, which is that of the subprogram in which the passed ~~subprogram~~ parameter was declared, and returns the address of the actual parameter. If the parameter reference is in an expression, the code of the reference must include the necessary dereference. Altogether, this is a costly process, relative to the simple indirect addressing used by pass by reference parameters. Recall that for actual parameters that are scalar variables, pass by name and pass by reference are semantically equivalent. The cost of implementing pass by reference is that of indirect addressing, whereas pass by name requires a subprogram call—albeit without parameters—and its execution to accomplish the same thing.

The Ada language definition specifies that simple (nonstructured) parameters are to be passed by copy; that is, **in** and **in out** mode parameters are to be local variables that are initialized by copying the value of the corresponding actual parameter. Simple parameters that are **out** or **in out** mode are to have their values copied back to the corresponding actual parameter at subprogram termination.

In the case of formal parameters that are arrays, records, or tasks, implementors are given the choice between pass by value-result and pass by reference. By failing to specify the implementation method for passing structured parameters, the Ada designers left open the possibility of a subtle problem. The problem is that the two implementation methods can lead to different program results in the presence of certain program errors. This difference can arise because the pass by reference method provides access to a location in the calling program that can also be provided if the actual parameter is also available as a global, thereby creating an alias. If pass by value-result is used in place of pass by reference, this dual access to the actual parameter is not possible.

An additional problem is the following: Suppose the subprogram terminates abnormally (via an exception); in this case the actual parameter in the pass by value-result implementation will be unchanged, whereas the pass by reference implementation may have changed the corresponding actual parameter before the error occurred. Once again, there can be a difference between the two implementation methods.

Ada programs that produce different results depending on how the **in out** method is implemented are termed **erroneous.** Despite this label, however, there is no way the compiler can detect the erroneous condition. So the error is usually detected only when the user moves the program from one implementation to another and realizes that it no longer produces the same result, and in fact is therefore incorrect. The Ada design philosophy here is that programmers must guard against aliasing: If they create aliases, they must contend with the potential problems.

8.5.6 Design Considerations

Two important considerations are involved in choosing parameter-passing methods: efficiency and whether one-way or two-way data transfer is desired.

Contemporary software engineering principles dictate that access to parameters be minimized. With this goal in mind, in mode parameters should be used whenever no data is to be returned through a parameter to the caller. Out mode should be used when no data is transferred to the called subprogram, but the subprogram must transmit data back to the caller. Finally, inout mode should be used only when data must move in both directions between the caller and the called subprogram.

There is a practical consideration that is in conflict with this principle. Sometimes it is justifiable to pass access paths for one-way parameter transmission. For example, when a large array is to be passed to a subprogram that does not modify it, a one-way method may be preferred. However, pass by value would require that the entire array be moved to a local storage area of the subprogram. This would be costly in both time and space. In these situations, then, arrays are often passed by reference.

The choice of a parameter-passing method for functions is related to another design issue: functional side effects. These two issues are discussed in Section 8.10.

8.6 Parameters That Are Subprogram Names

A number of situations occur in programming that are most conveniently handled if subprogram names can be sent as parameters to other subprograms. One of the more common of these occurs when a subprogram must sample some mathematical function. For example, a subprogram that does numerical integration estimates the area under the graph of a function by sampling the function at a number of different points. When such a subprogram is written, it should be usable for any given function—it should not need to be rewritten for every function that must be integrated. It is therefore natural that the name of a program function that evaluates the mathematical function to be integrated be sent to the integrating subprogram as a parameter.

Although the idea is natural and seemingly simple, understanding how it works can be difficult. If only the transmission of the subprogram code were necessary, it could be done by passing a single pointer. However, several complications arise.

First, the description of the subprogram's parameters must be sent, along with the subprogram name, assuming that the types of the actual parameters are to be checked at run time against the types of the formal parameters. The original definition of Pascal (Jensen and Wirth, 1974) allowed subprograms to be passed as parameters without including their parameter type information. If separate compilation is possible, this disallows the compiler from even checking for the correct number of parameters. In the absence of separate compilation, checking for parameter consistency is possible, but is a very complex task, and is usually not done in practice. FORTRAN 77 suffers the same problem, but because parameter consistency is never checked in FORTRAN 77, it is not a serious additional problem.

When a subprogram name is passed as a parameter in ALGOL 68 or in the later versions of Pascal, the formal parameter types are included in the formal parameter list of the receiving subprogram, so parameter consistency in the actual call to the passed subprogram can be statically checked. For example, consider the following Pascal code:

```
procedure integrate (function fun (x : real) : real;
                     lowerbd, upperbd : real;
                     var result : real);
  . . .
  var funval : real;
  begin
  . . .
  funval := fun (lowerbd);
  . . .
  end;
```

The actual parameter in the call to fun in integrate can be statically checked for consistency with the type of fun's formal parameter, which appears in the formal parameter list of integrate.

In Modula-2, procedure types are used to pass procedures as if they were variables. This method allows consistency checking of the parameters of passed subprograms, because the types of the parameters are part of the procedure type. FORTRAN 8x has a mechanism for providing types of parameters for subprograms that are passed as parameters, and they must be checked. Ada does not allow subprograms to be passed as parameters. The functionality of passing subprograms as parameters is instead provided by Ada's generic facility, which is discussed in Section 8.8.

A more difficult aspect of subprogram names that are passed as parameters is the question of what is the correct referencing environment for executing of the passed subprogram. The three possibilities are (1) the environment of the subprogram that enacts the passed subprogram, (2) the environment of the subprogram in which the passed subprogram is declared, or (3) the environment of the subprogram that passed the subprogram as an actual parameter. The following example skeletal program illustrates these choices:

(handwritten margin notes: "shallow binding", "deep binding")

```
procedure SUB1;
   procedure SUB2;

      . . .
   end;
   procedure SUB3;

      . . .
      SUB4 (SUB2) ;

      . . .
   end;
   procedure SUB4 (SUBX) ;

      . . .
      SUBX;

      . . .
   end;
   . . .
   SUB3;

   . . .
end;
```

The referencing environment of the execution of SUB2 when called from SUB4 for choice (1) is SUB4; for choice (2) it is SUB1; for choice (3) it is SUB3.

In some cases the subprogram that declares a subprogram also passes that subprogram as a parameter, so that choices (2) and (3) are the same. Choice (1) is called **shallow binding,** and choice (2) is called **deep binding.** Choice (3) has never been used.

Shallow binding is not appropriate for block-structured languages because of static binding of variables. For example, suppose the procedure SENDER passes the procedure SENT as a parameter to the procedure RECEIVER. The problem is that RECEIVER may not be in the static environment of SENT, thereby making it very unnatural for SENT to have access to RECEIVER's variables. On the other hand, it is perfectly normal for any subprogram, including one sent as a parameter, to have its referencing environment determined by the lexical position of its definition. It is therefore more logical for block-structured languages to use deep binding. Some dynamic scoped languages like SNOBOL use shallow binding.

8.7 Overloaded Subprograms

An overloaded operator is one that has multiple meanings. The meaning of a particular instance of an overloaded operator is determined by the types of its operands. For example, if the ∗ operator has two floating-point operands in a Pascal program, it specifies floating-point multiplication.

An **overloaded subprogram** is a subprogram that has the same name as another subprogram in the same referencing environment. Every incarnation of an overloaded procedure must be unique in the types of its parameters. In the case of functions, the uniqueness can be either in the types of its parameters or in the type of the returned value. The meaning of a call to an overloaded subprogram is determined by the actual parameter list (and/or the type of the returned value, in the case of a function).

Ada allows both functions and procedures to be overloaded. For example, it is not only possible, but usually true that Ada programs have several versions of the output function PUT available to them. The most common versions are those that accept string, integer, and floating-point type values as parameters. Because each version of PUT has a unique parameter type, the compiler can disambiguate occurrences of calls to PUT by the different type parameters.

Users are also allowed to write multiple versions of subprograms with the same name. Although it is not necessary for such subprograms to provide basically the same process, they usually do. For example, a particular program may require two sorting procedures, one for integer arrays and one for floating-point arrays. They both can be named SORT, as long as the types of their parameters are different. In the following skeletal Ada program, two procedures named SORT are included:

```
procedure MAIN is
  type FLOAT_VECTOR is array (INTEGER range <>) of FLOAT;
  type INT_VECTOR is array (INTEGER range <>) of INTEGER;
  . . .
  procedure SORT (FLOAT_LIST : in out FLOAT_VECTOR;
                  LOWER_BOUND : in INTEGER;
                  UPPER_BOUND : in INTEGER) is
  . . .
  end SORT;
  procedure SORT (INT_LIST   : in out INT_VECTOR;
                  LOWER_BOUND : in INTEGER;
                  UPPER_BOUND : in INTEGER) is
  . . .
  end SORT;
  . . .
end MAIN;
```

8.8 Generic Subprograms

The Ada language provides a construct that supports the construction of multiple versions of program units to deal with different data types. The same mechanism is used to allow different versions of a single subprogram to include uses of different subprograms. This is useful in providing the functionality of subprograms passed as parameters. Because program units of this sort are generic in nature, they are called **generic units.**

The following example illustrates a procedure that is generic in the type of its parameter. It is an exchange sort procedure that is designed to work on any array with elementary numeric type elements, using any ordinal type subscript range:

```ada
generic
type ELEMENT is private;
type INDEX is (<>);
type VECTOR is array (INDEX) of ELEMENT;
procedure GENERIC_SORT (LIST : in out VECTOR) is
  TEMP : ELEMENT;
  LOWER_BOUND : LIST'FIRST;
  UPPER_BOUND : LIST'LAST;
  INDEX_1 : LIST'RANGE;
  INDEX_2 : LIST'RANGE;
  OUTER_LIMIT : LIST'RANGE;
  INNER_BEGIN : LIST'RANGE;
begin
OUTER_LIMIT : UPPER_BOUND - 1;
for INDEX_1 in LOWER_BOUND .. OUTER_LIMIT loop
  INNER_BEGIN := INDEX_1 + 1;
  for INDEX_2 in INNER_BEGIN .. UPPER_BOUND loop
    if LIST(INDEX_1) > LIST(INDEX_2)
      then
      TEMP := LIST(INDEX_1);
      LIST(INDEX_1) := LIST(INDEX_2);
      LIST(INDEX_2) := TEMP;
    end if;
    end loop; -- for INDEX_1 ...
  end loop; -- for INDEX_2 ...
end GENERIC_SORT;
```

Parts of this generic procedure may appear rather odd if you are not familiar with Ada. That is not a major problem, however, because you need not understand all the details of the syntax. The private type ELEMENT is the variable in this generic. Private types are discussed thoroughly in Chapter 10. The array is declared to have any type subscript with any range.

This generic sort is nothing more than a template for a procedure; no code is generated for it by the compiler and it has no effect on a program, unless it is instantiated for some type. Instantiation is accomplished with a statement such as the following:

```
procedure INTEGER_SORT is new GENERIC_SORT (INTEGER);
```

The compiler reacts to this statement by building a version of GENERIC_SORT named INTEGER_SORT that sorts INTEGER type variables.

The generic program units of Ada are a kind of poor cousin to a subprogram in which the types of the formal parameters are dynamically bound to the types of the actual parameters in a call. In this case only a single copy of the code is needed, whereas with the Ada method a copy must be created, at compile time, for each different type that is required. The Smalltalk language supports the dynamic type binding necessary to allow truly generic subprograms. Smalltalk is discussed in Chapter 15.

Recall that Ada does not allow subprograms to be passed as parameters to other subprograms. To provide that functionality, Ada allows generic formal subprograms. In a language such as Pascal, subprograms are passed as parameters so that a particular call of a subprogram can execute using the specific passed subprogram to compute its result. In Ada the same result is achieved by allowing the user to instantiate a generic subprogram any number of times, each with a different subprogram that can be used. For example, the procedure integrate as defined in Section 8.6 can be written in Ada as:

```
generic
  with function FUN(X : FLOAT) return FLOAT;
  procedure INTEGRATE (LOWERBD :  in FLOAT;
                       UPPERBD :  in FLOAT;
                       RESULT : out FLOAT) is
    FUNVAL : FLOAT;
    begin
    . . .
    FUNVAL := FUN (LOWERBD);
    . . .
    end;
```

This could be instantiated for a user-defined function FUN1 with:

```
INTEGRATE_FUN1 is new INTEGRATE (FUN => FUN1);
```

Now, INTEGRATE_FUN1 is a procedure for integrating the function FUN1.

8.9 Separate Compilation

The capability of compiling program units separately is essential to the construction of large software systems. Thus, all languages that were designed for such use provide for some kind of separate compilation. With separate compilation, only the modules of a system that are being changed need to be recompiled during development or maintenance. Newly compiled and previously compiled units are collected by a program called the linker, which is a part of the operating system. Without separate compilation, every change to a system requires a complete recompilation.

To provide reliable separate compilation of a program unit, information about program entities (variables, types, and subprograms) that it uses that are declared elsewhere must be available. Information about the entities of an Ada package that can be visible in other program units, which are called the exported entities, is called the interface of the package. The interface of a separately compiled procedure is just the number and types of its parameters. In the case of a function, the type of the returned value is included. Ada implementations maintain unit interface information in a library that is accessible to the compiler. Every compilation that specifies a certain library name causes the interface information of that compilation to be placed in that library.

During compilation of an Ada program unit, all externally declared entities that are used are type checked against their local uses. Not all library information is available to a particular program unit compilation. The names of those units that provide required external entities are listed on a **with** statement at the beginning of the unit being compiled. For example, the following procedure uses entities from two external units, GLOBALS and TEXT_IO, and thus specifies those two:

```
with GLOBALS, TEXT_IO;
procedure EXAMPLE is
    . . .
    end EXAMPLE;
```

Modula-2 provides separate compilation that is similar to that of Ada. FORTRAN 8x also allows separate compilation of its subprograms and modules. We discuss the separate compilation of Modula-2 and Ada in greater detail in Chapter 10, after we have discussed the data abstraction facilities of those languages.

In some languages, most notably FORTRAN 77, independent but not separate compilation is allowed. **Independent compilation** means that program units can be compiled without information about any other program units. Such compilation allows the construction of large program systems, but does so in a less secure way than separate compilation. The only requirement of FORTRAN 77's independent compilation is that the names and types of the variables in COMMON storage must be specified in the program unit being compiled.

An important characteristic of independent compilation is that the interfaces between the separately compiled units are not checked for consistency. An important part of the interface of a FORTRAN 77 subroutine is its parameter list. When a subroutine is independently compiled, the types of its parameters are not stored with the compiled code or in a library. Therefore, when another program that calls that subroutine is compiled, the types of the actual parameters in the calls cannot be checked against the types of the formal parameters of the subroutine, even if the machine code for the called subroutine is available.

This is not surprising in FORTRAN 77. Even when the program that calls a subprogram and the subprogram are compiled from the same file, they are in effect, if not actually, compiled independently. So the parameter interface between FORTRAN 77 program units is never checked for type compatibility.

Pascal specifically does not allow for separate compilation, although many implementations of it do provide a form of independent compilation.

8.10   Design Issues for Functions

The following two design issues are specific to functions:

1. Are side effects allowed?
2. What types of values can be returned?

8.10.1   Functional Side Effects

Because of the problems of side effects of functions that are called in expressions, as described in Chapter 5, parameters to functions should always be one-way in the direction of the function. Some languages in fact require this; for example, Ada functions can have only **in** mode formal parameters. This effectively prevents a function from causing side effects through its parameters, or through aliasing of parameters and globals. In Pascal, functions can have either pass by value or pass by reference parameters, thus allowing functions that cause side effects and aliasing.

None of the popular imperative languages disallow functions from accessing nonlocals, which is a prime method of producing side effects.

8.10.2   Types of Returned Values

One of the fundamental reasons why many imperative languages cannot be used effectively for functional programming is that they have restrictions on the types of values that can be returned by functions. FORTRAN 77 functions allow only unstructured types to be returned. In Pascal and Modula-2 only simple types can be returned by functions. These are integer, real, char, boolean, pointers, and enumeration types. The C language allows any type except arrays and functions to be returned by its functions. Both of these can be handled by pointer type return values. The Ada language is alone among current imperative languages in that its functions can return values of any type. Although this alone does not make Ada an ideal functional language, it is better suited for it than the other popular imperative languages.

8.11   Accessing Nonlocal Environments

Although much of the required communication between subprograms can be accomplished through parameters, most languages provide some other method of accessing variables from external environments.

The **nonlocal variables** of a subprogram are those that are visible within the subprogram but are not locally declared. **Global variables** are those that are visible in all of the program units in a program. Two methods of accessing nonlocal variables are discussed in Chapter 4: static scoping and dynamic scoping. The problems with these designs are reviewed in the following paragraphs.

The primary problem of using static scoping as the means of nonlocal variable sharing is the following: A good deal of program structure in such languages may be dictated by the accessibility of procedures and nonlocal variables to other procedures, rather than dictated by well-engineered problem solutions. Additionally, in all cases, more access to nonlocals is provided than is necessary. Recall our examples of this problem in Chapter 4.

Two kinds of programming problems follow directly from dynamic scoping. First, during the time span beginning when a subprogram begins its execution and ending when that execution ends, the local variables of the subprogram are all visible to any other executing subprogram regardless of its textual proximity. There is no way to protect local variables from this accessibility. Subprograms are always executed in the immediate environment of the caller. Because of this, dynamic scoping results in less reliable programs than static scoping.

A second problem that results from dynamic scoping is an inability to statically type check references to nonlocals. This results specifically from the inability to statically determine the declaration for a variable referenced as a nonlocal.

8.11.1   FORTRAN COMMON Blocks

FORTRAN provides access to blocks of global storage through its COMMON statement. There can be any number of these blocks, and all but one must be named. Any subprogram that wishes to access or create a common block has a COMMON statement that names the block and provides a list of the variables that it can use to access storage in the block. A common block is created when the first COMMON statement that mentions the block's name is found by the compiler.

The primary problem with using COMMON is that each of two subprograms can include a COMMON statement that specifies the same block name as the COMMON statement in the other, and thus refers to the same block. Further, each can specify a different list of variables, whose number and types can be unrelated to those in the other list. For example, it is perfectly legal to have the declarations:

```
REAL  A(100)
INTEGER  B(250)
COMMON  /BLOCK1/  A,  B
```

in one subprogram, and the declarations:

```
REAL  C(50),  D(100)
INTEGER  E(200)
COMMON  /BLOCK1/  C,  D,  E
```

in another subprogram. The identifier delimited by slashes, BLOCK1, is the block name. The two views of the variables in BLOCK1 are shown in Figure 8.1.

This can only make sense if BLOCK1 is merely used as shared storage, not shared data. In fact, storage sharing is the main reason for allowing this. In most cases, data in a COMMON block is to be shared, using the same variable names and types. A simple ordering error in the list of variables on a COMMON statement in this situation can cause inadvertent storage sharing between variables of different types, which can cause an error that is difficult to locate.

FORTRAN subprograms cannot be nested, so there is no other means of access to external data.

8.11.2   External Declarations and Modules

The Modula-2 and Ada languages use static scoping as a means of sharing data among program units. They both also provide an alternative method of data sharing, which is by allowing units to specify the external modules to which access is required. Using this method, every module can specify exactly the other modules to which access is needed, no more and no fewer. In Modula-2, this access can be restricted to only specific procedures, variables, and data types from a given external module. Ada allows the user to specify only an external module's name, which then provides access to all of its types, variables, and procedures. This method is also possible in Modula-2. The approach of specifying each entity to which access is desired is certainly more tedious to use, because the lists of desired types, variables, and procedures can become long. It is, however, a safer method than simply specifying a module's name.

FORTRAN 8x also includes modules that can provide for selective and type-checked sharing of nonlocal data.

Figure 8.1
Two views of a
COMMON block

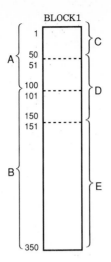

We discuss these language features more thoroughly in Chapter 10 in connection with data abstraction.

In the C language, there is no nesting of subprograms, so there is only a single level of scoping. Global variables can be created by placing their declarations outside function definitions. Access is provided to such a variable in a function that declares the variable to be external with an **external** statement. All functions whose definitions follow globally declared variables in a code file have access to those variables without declaring them to be external. This method is cumbersome and provides far more access than is usually needed.

Global variables that are defined in other files of C code that are included in a program can also be accessed by functions declaring them to be external. Thus, separate, nonshared scopes can be introduced by separate compilation of modules. By this method, access to variables in those separately compiled modules is restricted to those other functions that declare the variables to be external.

8.12 User-Defined Overloaded Operators

Operators can be overloaded by the user in Ada and C++ programs. A popular example of this is the overloading of the asterisk operator for matrix multiplication, which can be done in Ada with the following:

```
function "*" (A, B : in MATRIX) return MATRIX is
   RESULT : MATRIX (A'FIRST(1)..A'LAST(1),
                    B'FIRST(2)..B'LAST(2))
```

```
        SUM : integer;
        begin
        for ROW in A'RANGE(1) loop
          for COL in B'RANGE(2) loop
          SUM := 0.0;
          for INNER in A'RANGE(2) loop
            SUM := SUM + A(ROW ,INNER) * B(INNER, COL):
            end loop;   -- for INNER ...
          RESULT(ROW, COL) := SUM;
          end loop;   -- for COL ...
        end loop;   -- for ROW ...
      end "*";
```

Note that this function does not check to see if the two input matrices are of dimensions that allow them to be multiplied.

Matrix multiplication, as specified in this function definition, will be done whenever the asterisk appears with two operands of MATRIX type. The asterisk can be further overloaded any number of times, as long as the parameters or return types are in some way different.

The question naturally arises: How much operator overloading is good, or can you have too much of this? The answer is, to a large degree, a matter of taste. The argument against too much operator overloading is largely one of readability. In many cases it is more readable to call a function to carry out an operation than to use an operator that is more frequently used for other type operands. Even in the case of matrix multiplication, it may be too easy to forget what is involved when a simple assignment statement, such as:

```
C := A * B
```

is encountered in a program. It looks too much as though A, B, and C are simple scalars.

Another consideration is the situation of attempting to construct a software system from modules created by different groups. If the different groups overloaded the same operators in different ways, a great deal of difficulty will occur in putting the system together.

SUMMARY

Process abstractions are represented in programming languages by subprograms. A subprogram definition describes the actions represented by the subprogram. A subprogram call enacts those actions.

Formal parameters are the names that subprograms use to refer to the actual parameters given in subprogram calls.

Subprograms can be either functions, which model mathematical functions and are used to define new operations, or procedures, which define new statements.

Local variables in subprograms can be dynamically allocated from a stack, providing support for recursion, or statically allocated, providing efficiency and history-sensitive local variables.

There are three fundamental semantics models of parameter passing—in mode, out mode, and inout mode—and a number of implementation models can be used to implement them. The implementation models can actually be implemented in a variety of ways.

Aliasing can occur when pass by reference parameters are used, both among two or more parameters and between a parameter and an accessible nonlocal variable.

Access to nonlocal variables is provided in several different ways: through external declarations, global data blocks, external modules, and through static and dynamic scoping.

Parameters that are subprogram names provide a necessary service, but are sometimes difficult to understand. The opaqueness lies in the referencing environment that is available when a subprogram that has been passed as a parameter is executing.

Ada has several capabilities for overloading. Subprograms can be overloaded as long as the various versions can be disambiguated by the types of their parameters or returned values. Function definitions can be used to build additional meanings for operators. Program units can be generic, so that the desired types of their data objects can be passed to the compiler, which then can construct units for the requested types. Also, different instantiations of generic subprograms can use different subprograms, providing the functionality of subprograms passed as parameters.

BIBLIOGRAPHY

Jensen, K., and N. Wirth. (1974) *Pascal User Manual and Report.* 2d ed. Springer-Verlag, New York.

Wirth, N., and C.A.R. Hoare. (1966) "A Contribution to the Development of ALGOL." *Commun. ACM*, Vol. 9, No. 6, pp. 413–431.

PROBLEM SET

1. What are arguments for and against a user program building additional definitions for existing operators, as can be done in Ada? Do you believe such user-defined operator overloading is good or bad? Support your answer.

2. Suppose someone designed a programming language in which all parameters were passed by reference, using access path transmission only. State both the advantages and disadvantages of this design choice.

3. Argue in support of the Ada designers' decision to allow the implementor to choose between implementing **in out** mode parameters by copy or by reference.

4. FORTRAN has two slightly different kinds of COMMON: blank and named. One difference between them is that blank COMMON cannot be initialized at compile time. See if you can determine the reason why blank COMMON was designed this way. *Hint*: This design decision was made early in the development of FORTRAN, when computer memories were quite small.

5. Suppose you wish to write a subprogram that prints a heading on a new output page, along with a page number that is 1 in the first activation, and that increases by 1 with each subsequent activation. Can this be done without parameters and without reference to nonlocal variables in Pascal? Can it be done in FORTRAN?

6. FORTRAN allows a subprogram to have multiple entry points. Why is this sometimes a valuable capability?

7. Write a Pascal procedure ADDER that adds two integer arrays together. It must have only two parameters, which have the two arrays to be added. The second array is also to hold the sum array on exit. Both parameters must be passed by reference. Test ADDER with the call:

ADDER (A, A)

where A is an array to be added to itself. Explain the results of running this program.

8. Consider the program in Section 8.5.2.5. Change the two assignments to the LIST array to:

```
LIST [1]  : = 3
LIST [2]  : = 1
```

Hand execute the new program under the following assumptions and compare the resulting values in the array LIST in BIGSUB after the return from SUB:
   a. parameters are passed by value
   b. parameters are passed by reference
   c. parameters are passed by name
   d. parameters are passed by value-result

9. Present one argument against providing both static and dynamic local variables in subprograms.

10. Argue against the C design of providing only function subprograms.

11. From a textbook on FORTRAN, learn the syntax and semantics of statement functions. Justify their existence in FORTRAN.

12. Study the methods of user-defined operator overloading in C++ and Ada and write a report comparing the two, using our criteria for evaluating languages.

Key Concepts

- Subprogram linkage
- Activation records
- Static chains
- Displays
- Deep access versus shallow access
- Referencing environments for subprograms passed as parameters

9

IMPLEMENTING
SUBPROGRAMS

We now explore methods for implementing subprograms in the major imperative languages. The discussion will provide the reader with some insight into how such languages "work," and also why ALGOL 60 was a challenge to the unsuspecting compiler authors of the early 1960s. We begin with the simplest kind of subprograms—those in FORTRAN 77—and progress to the more complicated subprograms of the static scoped languages, such as Pascal. The difficulty of implementing subprograms in these languages is increased by the mechanisms needed to access nonlocal variables. Recursion is another complicating factor.

Two methods of accessing nonlocals in static scoped languages, static chains and displays, are discussed in detail and compared. Implementing blocks is covered briefly. Several methods of implementing nonlocal variable access in a dynamic scoped language are discussed. Finally, a method is described for implementing parameters that are subprogram names.

9.1   The General Semantics of Calls and Returns

The subprogram call and return operations of a language are together called its **subprogram linkage.** Any implementation method for subprograms must model the semantics of subprogram linkage.

A subprogram call in Pascal has numerous actions associated with it. The call must include the parameter-passing mechanism for whatever method is used. It must cause storage to be allocated for the local variable declarations in the called subprogram and bind those variables to that storage. It must save the execution status of the calling program unit. It must arrange to transfer control to the code of the subprogram and ensure that control can return to the proper place when subprogram execution terminates. Finally, if static scoping is used, the call must cause some mechanism to be created to provide access to nonlocal variables that are visible to the called subprogram.

The required actions of a subprogram return are also complicated. If the subprogram has parameters that are out mode and are implemented by copy, the first action of the return process is to move the local values of the associated formal parameters to the actual parameters. Next it must deallocate the storage used for local variables. It must also remove whatever else was stored as a result of the subprogram execution. Some action must then be taken to return the mechanism used for nonlocal references to the configuration it had before the call. Finally, control must be returned to the calling program unit.

9.2   Implementing FORTRAN 77 Subprograms

We begin with the relatively simple situation of FORTRAN 77 subprograms. All referencing of nonlocal variables in FORTRAN 77 is through COMMON. COMMON is not connected to the subprogram linkage mechanism, so it is not

Figure 9.1
A FORTRAN 77 activation record format

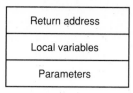

| Return address |
| Local variables |
| Parameters |

addressed here. Other simplifying characteristics of FORTRAN 77 include the facts that local variables in subprograms are usually statically allocated and subprograms cannot be recursive.

The semantics of a FORTRAN 77 subprogram call in this situation includes the following actions:

1. Save the execution status of the current program unit.
2. Carry out the parameter-passing process.
3. Pass the return address to the callee.
4. Transfer control to the callee.

The semantics of a FORTRAN 77 subprogram return requires the following actions:

1. If pass by value-result parameters are used, the current values of those parameters are moved to the corresponding actual parameters.
2. If the subprogram is a function, the functional value is moved.
3. The execution status of the caller is restored.
4. Control is transferred back to the caller.

The call and return actions require storage for the following:

1. Status information about the caller
2. Parameters
3. Return address
4. Functional value for function subprograms

These, along with the local variables and the subprogram code, form the complete set of information a subprogram needs to execute and then return control to the caller.

A FORTRAN 77 subprogram consists of two separate parts: The actual code of the subprogram, which is static, and the local variables and data listed above, which can change when the subprogram is executed. Note that both of these parts have fixed sizes.

The noncode part of a subprogram is associated with a particular execution, or activation, of the subprogram, and is therefore called an **activation record.** Because FORTRAN disallows recursion, there can be only one active version of a given subprogram at a time. Therefore, there can be only a single instance of the activation record for a subprogram. One possible layout for FORTRAN 77 activation records is shown in Figure 9.1. The saved

Figure 9.2

The code and activation records of a FORTRAN 77 program

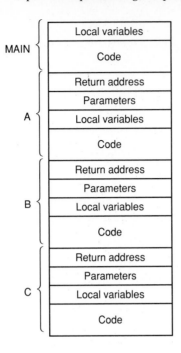

execution status of the caller is omitted, simply because it is not relevant to our discussion.

Because the activation record for a FORTRAN 77 subprogram has fixed size, it can be statically allocated. In fact, it could be attached to the code part of a subprogram.

Figure 9.2 shows a FORTRAN 77 program consisting of a main program and three subroutines: A, B, and C. The construction of the FORTRAN 77 software system shown in the figure is not done entirely by the compiler. In fact, because of independent compilation, the four program units—MAIN, A, B, and C—may have been compiled on different days or even in different years. At the time each is compiled, the machine code for it, along with a list of references to external subprograms within the code, is written to a file. The executable image shown in Figure 9.2 is built by the loader, which is part of the operating system. (Sometimes loaders are called linkers, loader/ linkers, or link editors.) When the loader is called with a particular program unit, its task is to find the files that contain the translated subprograms referenced in the program unit being loaded, and load them into memory. Then it must set the addresses of all references to those units in the program being loaded to the entry addresses of those units. In the example above, the loader may have been called for MAIN. The loader had to find the machine code programs for A, B, and C, and load them into memory with the code for MAIN. Then it had to patch in the addresses of all references to A, B, and

C in MAIN. Furthermore, any references in A, B, or C to the other subprograms must also be patched. Note that we assume that no other subprograms are referenced by the code of MAIN, A, B, and C.

9.3 Implementing Subprograms in ALGOL-like Languages

We now examine the implementation of the subprogram linkage in ALGOL-like languages, focusing on the call and return actions required for increasingly complicated situations. Two related but different approaches to handling nonlocal variable access, static chains and displays, are discussed.

9.3.1 More Complex Activation Records

Subprogram linkage in ALGOL-like languages is more complex than the linkage of FORTRAN 77 subprograms for the following reasons:

1. Parameters are usually passed by two different methods. For example, in Modula-2 they are passed by value or reference.

2. Variables declared in subprograms are often dynamically allocated.

3. Recursion adds the possibility of multiple simultaneous activations of a subprogram, which means there can be more than one instance (incomplete execution) of a subprogram at a given time, with one call from outside the subprogram and one or more recursive calls. Recursion therefore requires multiple instances of activation records, one for each subprogram activation that can exist at the same time. Each activation requires its own copy of the formal parameters and the dynamically allocated local variables.

4. Finally, ALGOL-like languages use static scoping to provide access to nonlocal variables. Support for these nonlocal accesses must be part of the linkage mechanism.

The format of an activation record for a given subprogram in a static scoped language is known at compile time. In Pascal procedures, the size is also known for activation records since all data local to a Pascal procedure is of fixed size. That is not the case in some other languages, in which the size of a local array can depend on the value of an actual parameter. In those cases, the format is static, but the size can be dynamic. An activation record format is a template for instances of the activation record. The form of the template is static; instances of it must be created dynamically. The typical activation record format for an ALGOL-like language is shown in Figure 9.3.

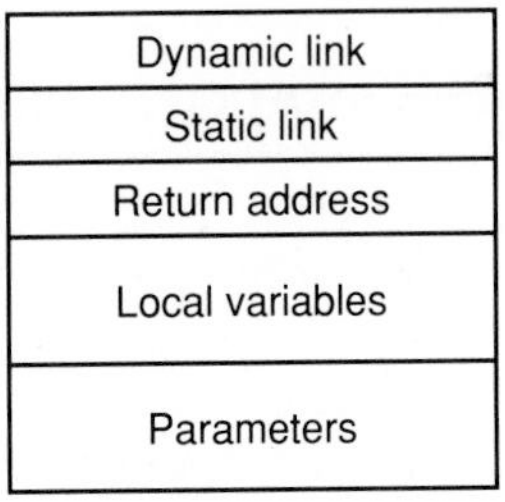

Dynamic link
Static link
Return address
Local variables
Parameters

Figure 9.3
A typical activation record format for
an ALGOL-like language

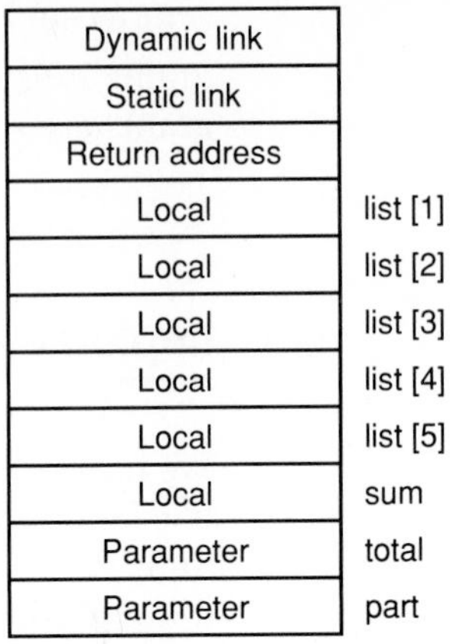

Dynamic link	
Static link	
Return address	
Local	list [1]
Local	list [2]
Local	list [3]
Local	list [4]
Local	list [5]
Local	sum
Parameter	total
Parameter	part

Figure 9.4
The activation record format for procedure sub

Local scalar variables are bound to storage within an activation record instance. Local variables that are structures are sometimes allocated elsewhere, and only their descriptors and a pointer to that storage are part of the activation record. The static link, which is sometimes called a static scope pointer, is explained later, in Section 9.3.4. The dynamic link is a pointer to an instance of the activation record of the caller. In static scoped languages, this link is used in the destruction of the current activation record instance when the procedure completes its execution. The dynamic link is required because in some cases there are other allocations from the stack above an activation record. So, although the size of the activation record may be known, the size cannot simply be subtracted from the stack top pointer to remove the activation record. The return address often consists of a pointer to the code segment of the caller and an offset address in that code segment of the instruction following the call. The actual parameters in the activation record are the values or addresses provided by the caller.

Consider the following skeletal Pascal procedure:

```
procedure sub (var total : real; part : integer);
   list : array [1..5] of integer;
   sum : real;
   begin
   . . .
   end;
```

The activation record format for sub is shown in Figure 9.4.

Activating a procedure requires the dynamic creation of an instance of the activation record for the procedure. As stated earlier, the format of the activation record is fixed at compile time, although its size may depend on the call. (In the case of the example, sub, the size of the activation record is fixed.) Because the call and return semantics specify that the last called subprogram is the first to complete, it is reasonable to create instances of these activation records on a stack. Every procedure activation, whether recursive or nonrecursive, creates a new instance of an activation record on the stack. This provides the required separate copies of the parameters, local variables, and the return address.

A procedure in an ALGOL-like language has a single entry point and is active until its execution is completed. At that time it becomes inactive, along with its local scope and its referencing environment, and therefore its activation record instance is destroyed.

9.3.2   An Example without Recursion and Nonlocal References

Because of the complexity of implementing subprogram linkage, we consider it in several stages. First, we examine an example program that does not reference any nonlocal variables and has no recursive calls. For this example, the static link is not used. We later consider how recursion and nonlocal referencing can be implemented.

Consider the following skeletal example program:

```
program MAIN;
  var P : real;
  procedure A (X : integer);
    var Y : boolean;
    procedure C (Q : boolean);
      begin
      . . .                ◄─────────────────────── 3
      end; { of procedure C }
    begin
    . . .                  ◄─────────────────────── 2
    C (Y);
    . . .
    end; { of procedure A }
  procedure B (R : real);
    var S, T : integer;
    begin
    . . .                  ◄─────────────────────── 1
    A (S);
    . . .
    end; { of procedure B }
  begin { MAIN program body }
  . . .
  B (P);
  . . .
  end. { of MAIN program }
```

The sequence of procedure calls in this program is:

MAIN calls B
B calls A
A calls C

The stack contents for the points labeled 1, 2, and 3 are shown in Figure 9.5.

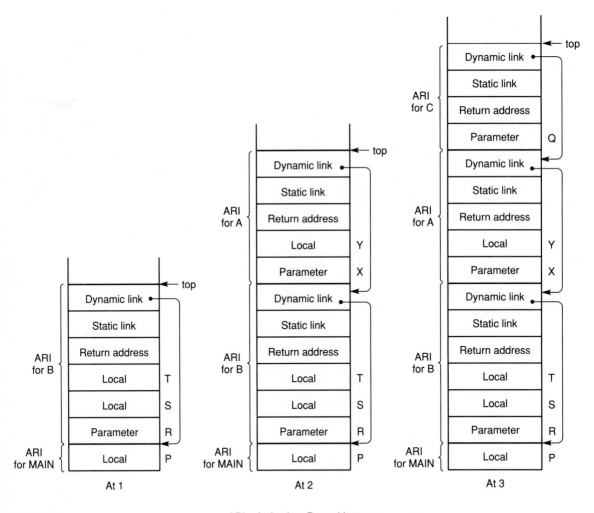

ARI = Activation Record Instance

Figure 9.5
Stack contents for three points in a program

At point 1, only the activation record instances for program MAIN and procedure B are on the stack. When B calls A, an instance of A's activation record is created on the stack. When A calls C, an instance of C's activation record is created on the stack. When C's execution ends, the instance of its activation record is removed from the stack, and the dynamic link is used to reset the stack top pointer. A similar process takes place when procedures A and B terminate. After the return to the call to B from MAIN, the stack has only the instance of the activation record of MAIN. Note that some implementations do not actually use an activation record such as the one shown for the main program. However, it can be done this way, and it simplifies both the implementation and our discussion.

The collection of dynamic links present in the stack at a given time is called the **dynamic chain,** or **call chain.** It links together the dynamic history of how execution got to its current position, which is always in the procedure code whose activation record instance is on the top of the stack. References to local variables can be represented in the code as offsets from the beginning of the activation record of the local scope. Such an offset is called a **local_offset.**

The local_offset of a variable in an activation record can be determined at compile time, using the order, types, and sizes of variables declared in the procedure associated with the activation record. To simplify the discussion, assume that all variables take one position in the activation record. The first local variable declared in a procedure would be allocated in the activation record three positions from the top (the first three positions are for the dynamic and static links and the return address). The second local variable declared would be four positions from the top, and so forth. For example, consider the preceding example program. In MAIN, the local_offset of X is 3; for P it is 4. Likewise, in B, the local_offset of S is 3; for T it is 4.

incorrect

9.3.3 Recursion

Consider the following example program, which uses recursion to compute the factorial function:

```
program TEST (OUTPUT);
  var VALUE : integer;

  function FACTORIAL (N : integer);
  begin   ◄─────────────────────────1
  if N <= 1
    then FACTORIAL := 1
    else FACTORIAL := N * FACTORIAL (N - 1);
  end;   ◄─────────────────────────2
```

```
begin { beginning of body of TEST }
VALUE := FACTORIAL (3);
writeln ("factorial of 3 is:", VALUE)
end.
```

The activation record format for the function factorial is shown in Figure 9.6. Notice that it has an additional entry for the returned value of the function.

Figure 9.7 shows the contents of the stack for the three times that execution reaches position 1 in the function FACTORIAL. Each shows one more activation of the function, with its functional value undefined. The first activation record instance has the return address to the calling program, TEST. The others have a return address to the function itself; these are for the recursive calls.

Figure 9.8 shows the stack contents for the three times that execution reaches position 2 in the function FACTORIAL. The functional value grows with each deactivation, from 1 to the final value, 6.

9.3.4 Mechanisms for Implementing Nonlocal References

There are two major implementation mechanisms for creating accesses to nonlocal variables in a static scoped language: static chains and displays. Both of these are examined in detail in the following sections.

A reference to a nonlocal variable requires a two-step access process. All variables that can be nonlocally accessed are in activation record instances, and therefore are somewhere in the stack. The first step of the access process is to find the instance of the activation record in the stack where the variable was allocated. The second part is to use the local_offset of the variable to actually access it. So, accessing a nonlocal variable requires the address of the correct instance of the correct activation record and the variable's local_offset.

9.3.4.1 Static Chains

A **static chain** is a chain of static links that connect certain activation record instances.

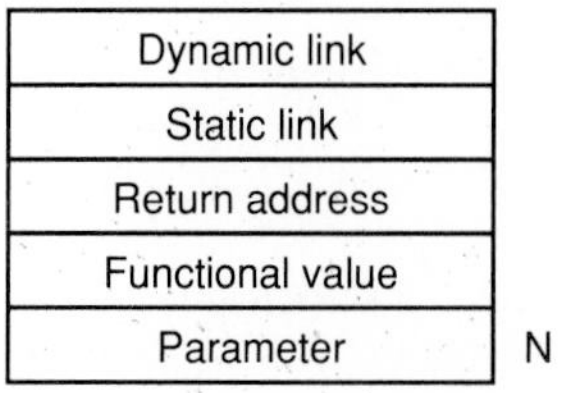

Figure 9.6
The activation record format for factorial

| Dynamic link |
| Static link |
| Return address |
| Functional value |
| Parameter | N

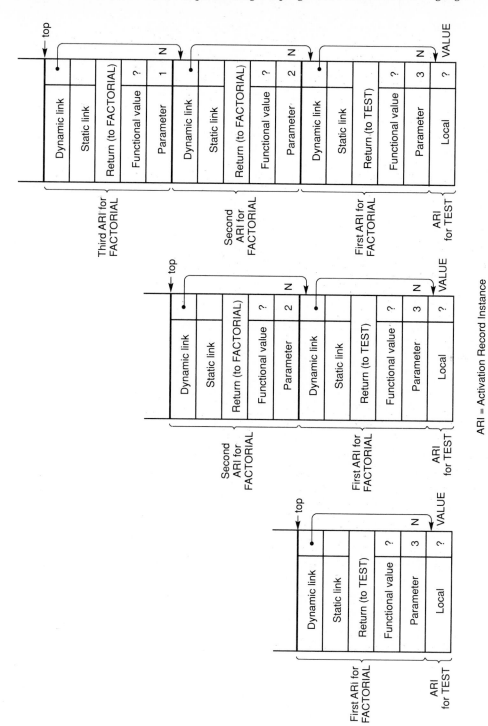

Figure 9.7
Stack contents at position 1 in factorial

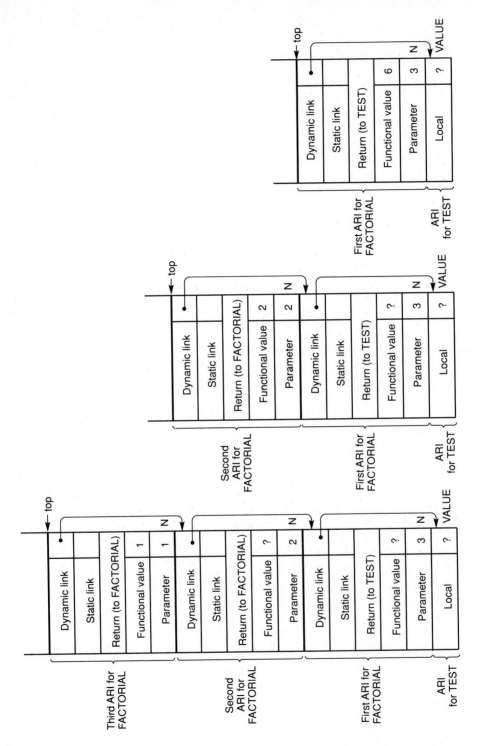

Figure 9.8

Stack contents at position 2 in factorial

ARI = Activation Record Instance

During the execution of a procedure P, the static link of its activation record instance points to an activation record instance of P's static parent procedure. That instance's static link points, in turn, to the static parent procedure's activation record instance, if there is one. So the static chain links all the static ancestors of an executing subprogram, in order of static parent first. This chain can be used to implement a method of accessing nonlocal variables in static scoped languages.

9.3.4.1.1 References   Recall that references to nonlocal variables require two steps: (1) Find the activation record instance of the nonlocal variable and (2) find that variable's relative position in that instance. This second part is simply the local_offset of the variable.

We now examine the problem of finding the correct activation record instance. The static link of each activation record instance points to an instance of an activation record of the smallest enclosing scope, the static parent. In the case of Pascal, this is the most closely nested enclosing procedure that contains the definition of the procedure whose activation record is in question. Thus, if procedure A contains a single procedure named B, every activation record instance of B will have a static link that points to an activation record instance of A (there can be more than one if recursion is allowed). Note that an instance of the static parent's activation record always exists on the stack when it is to be referenced by the activation of a nested procedure. This is guaranteed by the semantic rules of the ALGOL-like languages: A procedure is callable only when its static parent procedure is active. This rule is necessary because the nested procedure can access the variables of all static ancestor procedures. If the parent procedure were not active, its local variables would not be bound to storage. However, note that although the parent scope activation record must have an instance on the stack, it need not appear adjacent to the child's activation record instance. This is illustrated in an example below.

The problem of finding the correct activation record instance of a nonlocal variable when the implementation uses static links is relatively straightforward. When a reference is made to a nonlocal variable, the activation record instance containing the variable could be found by searching the static chain until a static ancestor activation record instance were found that contains the variable. However, in fact, it is much easier than that. Because the nesting of scopes is known at compile time, the compiler can determine not only that a reference is nonlocal, but also the length of the static chain needed to reach the activation record instance that actually contains the nonlocal object.

Let **static_depth** be an integer associated with a static scope that indicates how deeply it is nested in the outermost scope. The main program has a nesting level of 0. If procedure A is the only procedure defined in a main program, its static_depth is 1. If procedure A contains the definition of a nested procedure B, then B's static_depth is 2.

The length of the static chain needed to reach the correct activation record instance for a nonlocal reference to a variable x is exactly the difference between the static_depth of the procedure containing the reference to x and the static_depth of the procedure containing the declaration for x. This difference is called the **nesting_depth,** or **chain_offset,** of the reference. The actual reference can be represented by an ordered pair of integers (chain_offset, local_offset), where chain_offset is the number of links to the correct activation record instance and local_offset is as described in Section 9.3.2. For example, consider the following situation:

```
program A;                0
  procedure B;            1
    procedure C;          2
      . . .
    end; { of procedure C }
      . . .
  end;  { of procedure B }
    . . .
end;  { of program A }
```

The nesting levels of A, B, and C are 0, 1, and 2, respectively. If procedure C references a variable declared in A, the chain_offset of that reference will be 2 (nesting level of C minus the nesting level of A). If procedure C references a variable declared in B, the chain_offset of that reference will be 1. References to locals can be handled using the same mechanism, with a chain_offset of zero.

To illustrate the complete process of nonlocal accesses, consider the following skeletal program in Pascal:

```
program MAIN;
  var X : integer;
  procedure BIGSUB;
    var A, B, C : integer;
    procedure SUB1;
      var A, D : integer;
      begin
      A := B + C;        ◄───────────────────1
      . . .
      end; { of procedure SUB1 }
    procedure SUB2;
      var B, E : integer;
      procedure SUB3;
        var C, E : integer;
        begin
        . . .
        SUB1;
        . . .
        E := B + A;      ◄───────────────────2
        end; { of procedure SUB3 }
```

```
      begin
      . . .
      SUB3;
      . . .
      A := D + E;        ◄─────────────────3
      end; { of procedure SUB2 }
    begin { BIGSUB }
    . . .
    SUB2;
    . . .
    end;   { of procedure BIGSUB }
  begin
  . . .
  BIGSUB;
  . . .
  end. { of MAIN }
```

The sequence of procedure calls is:

MAIN calls BIGSUB
BIGSUB calls SUB2
SUB2 calls SUB3
SUB3 calls SUB1

The stack situation at this first arrival at point 1 in this program is shown in Figure 9.9.

At position 1 in procedure SUB1, the reference to A is local; it is not to the nonlocal variable A from BIGSUB. The correct A has the chain_offset/local-offset pair (0, 3). The reference to B is to the nonlocal B from BIGSUB. It can be represented by the pair (1, 4). The local_offset is 4 because a 3 offset would be the first variable, as explained above. Notice that if the dynamic link were used to do a simple search for an activation record instance with a declaration for the variable B, it would find the variable B declared in SUB2, which would be incorrect. If the (1, 4) pair were used with the dynamic chain, the variable E from SUB3 would be used. The static link, however, points to the activation record for BIGSUB, which has the correct version of B. The variable B in SUB2 is not in the referencing environment at this point, and is (correctly) not accessible.

After SUB1 completes its execution, the activation record instance for SUB1 is removed from the stack and control returns to SUB3. The reference to the variable E at position 2 in SUB3 is local, and uses the pair (0, 4) for access. The reference to the variable B is to the one declared in SUB2, because that is the nearest static ancestor that contains such a declaration. It is accessed with the pair (1, 3). The reference to the variable A is to the A declared in BIGSUB, because neither SUB3 nor its static parent SUB2 has a declaration for a variable named A. It is referenced with the pair (2, 3).

Figure 9.9
Stack contents at
position 1 in the
program

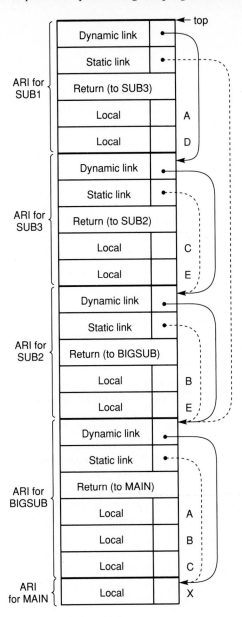

ARI = Activation Record Instance

After SUB3 completes its execution, the activation record instance for SUB3 is removed from the stack, leaving only the activation record instances for MAIN, BIGSUB, and SUB2. At position 3 in SUB2, the reference to the variable A is to the A in BIGSUB, which has the only declaration of A among the active routines. This access is made with the pair (1, 3). At this position, there is no visible scope containing a declaration for the variable D, so this reference to D is a syntax error. The error would be detected when the compiler attempted to compute the chain_offset/local_offset pair. The reference to E is to the local E in SUB2.

9.3.4.1.2 Maintenance   It is reasonable at this point to ask how the static chain is maintained during program execution. If its maintenance is excessively costly, the fact that it is simple and effective will be nullified. In this section we assume that pass by name parameters and parameters that are subprogram names and label names are not implemented.

The static chain must be changed for each subprogram call and exit. The exit part is trivial: When the subprogram terminates, its activation record instance is removed from the stack. This is accomplished by setting the stack top pointer to the value of the dynamic link of the top activation record instance. No other action is necessary because all other stack information is still relevant.

The action required at a subprogram call is more complex. The activation record instance must be created on the stack. The dynamic link is simply a copy of the value of the stack top pointer before the new activation record instance is created on the stack. The static link is not to a fixed place, however. The static link in a new activation record instance must point to the most recently created activation record instance of the parent scope. The correct parent scope is easily determined at compile time.

At execution time, when the activation record instance is created, the most recent activation record instance of the parent scope must be found. This could be done by a search down the stack, using the dynamic chain, until the first activation of the parent scope were found. However, this search can be avoided by treating procedure declarations and references exactly as variable declarations and references. When the compiler encounters a procedure call, among other things, it determines the procedure that declared the called procedure, which must be a static ancestor of the calling routine. It then computes the nesting_depth, or number of enclosing scopes between the caller and the procedure that declared the called procedure. This information is stored with the procedure call for use at run time. At the time of the call, during execution, the static link of the called procedure's activation record instance is determined by moving down the static chain of the caller the number of links equal to the nesting depth computed at compile time.

Figure 9.10 shows the stack contents of the example program above, as it appeared in Figure 9.9, except before the call to SUB1 by SUB3. At the call to SUB1 in SUB3, the compiler would determine the nesting_depth of SUB3

Figure 9.10
Stack contents just
before the call of
SUB1 in SUB3

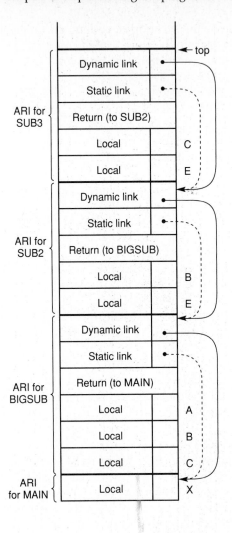

(the caller) to be two levels inside the procedure that declared the called
procedure, SUB1, which is BIGSUB. When the call to SUB1 in SUB3 is executed, the static link of the activation record instance for SUB1 is computed
to be two links down the static chain from the activation record instance
for SUB3.

This method works for all procedure linkage, except when parameters
that are subprogram names are involved. That situation is discussed in
Section 9.6.

9.3.4.1.3 Evaluation   One criticism of using the static chain to access nonlocal variables is that if there are a large number of references to variables
in scopes beyond the static parent, a great deal of time is required to move
down the chain. Also, it is difficult for a programmer working on a time-

critical program to estimate the costs of references, since the cost of each reference depends on the depth of nesting between the reference and the scope of declaration. In addition, although the nesting_depth of a reference can be statically determined, it is tedious to need to do it for every nonlocal reference. And finally, code modifications may change nesting depths, thereby changing the timing of some existing code.

9.3.4.2 Displays

One solution to the problems of using a static chain is to implement nonlocal references by the display method. With this method, the static links are collected in a single array called a **display,** rather than being stored in the activation records. The contents of the display at any time are a list of addresses of the accessible activation record instances in the stack—one for each active scope—in the order in which they are nested.

9.3.4.2.1 References   References to nonlocals using a display are accomplished by finding the link to the correct activation record in the display; using a value called the display_offset, which is closely related to the static chain chain_offset; and using the local_offset to access the variable there. In this situation, nonlocal references can be represented by the ordered pair of integers (display_offset, local_offset). This can be done conveniently and quickly with two applications of an offset-indirect addressing mode, which many contemporary computers have.

9.3.4.2.2 Maintenance   Every subprogram call and exit requires that the display be modified to reflect the new scope situation. We now investigate the actions required to maintain the display. Once again, we assume that parameters cannot be subprogram names and that pass by name parameters are not involved. The more complex case is discussed in Section 9.6.
      First, note that the display_offset depends only on the static_depth of the procedure. If the static_depth of procedure P is 2, then the link from the display to P's activation record instance will always appear in position 2 in the display.
      Let the display entries begin at the subscript of 0. Then the pointer at position k of the display points to an activation record instance for a procedure with a static_depth of k. The display modification required for a call to procedure P, which has a static_depth of k, is:

1. Save, in the new activation record instance, a copy of the pointer at position k in the display.
2. Place the link to the activation record instance for P at position k in the display.

Subprogram termination requires the saved pointer in the activation record instance of the terminating subprogram to be placed back in the display.

Then the activation record instance is removed from the stack, as with the static chain implementation.

To see that the two simple steps of display modification for procedure calls are correct, we examine the three possible situations defined by considering a call to procedure P by procedure Q. Let Psd be the static_depth of P and Qsd be the static_depth of Q. The three cases are defined as:

1. Qsd = Psd
2. Qsd < Psd
3. Qsd > Psd

We use the following program, which is a skeletal version of the program of our earlier example, to examine these three cases.

```
program MAIN;
  procedure BIGSUB;
    procedure SUB1;
         . . .
      end;  { SUB1 }
    procedure SUB2;
      procedure SUB3;
           . . .
        end;  { SUB3 }
         . . .
      end;  { SUB2 }
       . . .
    end;  { BIGSUB }
  end.  { MAIN }
```

The first case would occur if SUB2 called SUB1, because they are both at a depth level of 2. The stack and display for the situation for just before and just after the call are shown in Figure 9.11.

The call, as always, requires that the new activation record instance for SUB1 be added to the stack. The new referencing environment includes only SUB1, BIGSUB, and MAIN. Because the static_depth values of SUB1 and SUB2 are equal, their display links must occupy the same position in the display; that is, their display offsets are equal. In this case, therefore, the display entry for SUB2 must be removed. The new display entry for SUB1 is then inserted into its proper position, which is always the static_depth of the procedure. When SUB1 completes its execution and returns control to SUB2, the display entry for SUB2 must be restored. The display entry that is temporarily removed can be stored in the new activation record instance. Just before the activation record instance is removed from the stack, the saved display entry is moved from the instance to the display.

The second case would occur if SUB2 called SUB3. The static_depth value of SUB2 is 2, and for SUB3 it is 3. The stack and display for the situations just before the call and just after the call are shown in Figure 9.12.

In this case, the new activation record instance is created on the stack, as usual, but the referencing environment simply grows by one new scope,

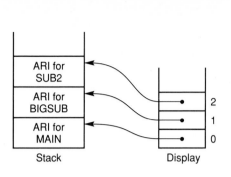

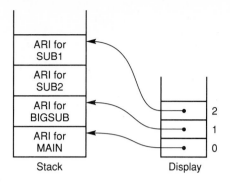

a. MAIN calls BIGSUB; BIGSUB calls SUB2　　**b.** SUB2 calls SUB1

Figure 9.11
Display modification for callers and callees with equal depth values

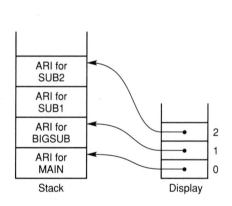

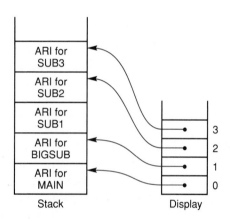

a. MAIN calls BIGSUB; BIGSUB calls SUB1;
SUB1 calls SUB2　　**b.** SUB2 calls SUB3

Figure 9.12
Display modifications for callers with smaller depth values
than the callee

that of the called subprogram. Thus, the new pointer can be simply added to the display. This example does not require that the existing pointer in the display at the position of the new pointer be saved. However, this is not true in general. Other situations of the same case do require that the existing display pointer be saved. For example, suppose there were a subprogram, SUB4, defined in SUB1 in our example, as shown below:

```
program MAIN;
    procedure BIGSUB;
        procedure SUB1;
            procedure SUB4;
```

```
        . . .
      end;

        . . .
    end;  { SUB1 }
  procedure SUB2;
    procedure SUB3;

        . . .
      end;  { SUB3 }

        . . .
    end;  { SUB2 }

    . . .
  end;  { BIGSUB }
end.  { MAIN }
```

Now suppose execution produced the following sequence of subprogram calls:

```
MAIN calls BIGSUB
BIGSUB calls SUB2
SUB2 calls SUB3
SUB3 calls SUB1
```

The result would be the stack and display contents shown in Figure 9.13.

Now, suppose SUB1 calls SUB4. This is an example of a subprogram calling a subprogram with a larger static_depth. In this case, the display pointer for SUB3 is at the position where SUB4's pointer must be placed in the display. They both have a static_depth of 3. Therefore, in this situation, the existing display pointer must be saved before the new pointer is placed in the display. The correct stack and display for the execution of SUB4 is shown in Figure 9.14.

The third case is illustrated by a call to SUB1 from SUB3. The procedure SUB3 has a static_depth of 3, and that of SUB1 is 2. The stack and display values for just before the call and just after the call are shown in Figure 9.15.

Figure 9.13
Stack and display before SUB1 calls SUB4. Dashed lines indicate inactive pointers

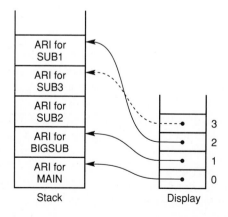

ARI = Activation Record Instance

Figure 9.14
Stack and display
after SUB1 calls
SUB4

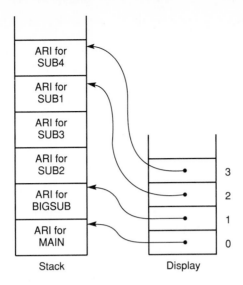

Figure 9.15
Display modification for callers with larger depth values
than their callees

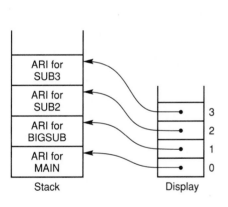

a. MAIN calls BIGSUB; BIGSUB calls SUB2;
SUB2 calls SUB3

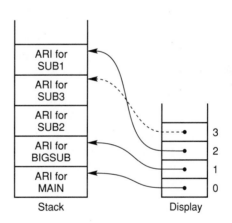

b. SUB3 calls SUB1

In this case, it appears that two display elements must be temporarily removed: those for SUB2 and SUB3, which are not in the referencing environment of SUB1. However, only one must actually be removed, the one for SUB2. The pointer for SUB3 can remain in the display. Variable references in SUB1 will not use the SUB3 display pointer because the SUB3 variables are not visible to SUB1; thus, leaving the pointer in the display cannot cause problems. The compiler cannot generate code that will access display entries above the entry for the current active subprogram.

The display can be stored as a run-time static array in memory. The maximum size, which is the maximum static_depth of any subprogram in the program, can be determined by the compiler. Storing the display in memory works reasonably well as long as the machine has indirect addressing through memory locations. Nonlocal accesses, then, cost one more memory cycle than local accesses, which can use direct addressing. An alternative is to place the display in registers, assuming the machine has a sufficient number of registers. In this case, accesses do not require the extra memory cycle.

9.3.4.2.3 Evaluation   We can now compare the static chaining and display methods. References to local variables will be slower with a display than with static chains if the display is not stored in registers, because all references must go through display entries, a procedure that adds a level of indirection. This indirection in local accesses can easily be avoided when static chains are used. References to nonlocals that are only one static level away take the same time for both methods, but if they are more than one static level away they will be faster with a display, since no chain needs to be followed.

The maintenance at a procedure call is faster with static chains, unless the called procedure is more than a few static levels away. The extra time required in that case is due to the need to find all the activation record instances in the chain. The maintenance of a procedure return has fixed cost with both methods, with static chaining always being slightly faster. With a display, the display must be restored when the subprogram terminates.

Overall, displays are better if there is deep static nesting and many references to distant nonlocal variables. Static chaining is better if there are few nesting levels, and many local references compared to the number of distant nonlocal references. This is the more common situation. Note that experiments indicate that nesting levels rarely exceed 3 in practice.

9.4 Blocks

Several languages, including ALGOL 60 and C, provide for highly localized scopes for variables. In Pascal, a new scope can be introduced only with a new procedure declaration. In these other languages, however, a new scope can be introduced with each compound statement, which is then called a **block.** In ALGOL 60, that means that any **begin** can be followed by variable declarations that create objects that are dynamically bound to storage when the block is entered during execution, and deallocated when that block is

exited. The same is true in C. For example, consider the following C code
segment:

```
{ int index;
  for (index = 0; index <= last; index++)
  {
    . . .
  }
}
```

The lifetime of the variable index begins when the **for** begins execution
and ends when the loop terminates. This example creates a local counting
variable, index, for the **for** statement. The advantage of using such a local
is that it cannot interfere with any other variable with the same name that
is declared elsewhere in the program.

Blocks can be implemented by using the process we described for implementing Pascal procedures. However, they can also be implemented in a
much simpler way. The variables declared in blocks can be allocated from
the top of the stack, which adds them to the current activation record instance.
One can imagine a number of allocations and deallocations of such local
variables at the stack top during the execution of a given procedure. This
method requires a different access method than the one required by the
locals of the subprogram, because locals are at fixed offsets in the activation
record. Although it should not be slower, it may be more complex for the
compiler writer. Because the execution sequence of enclosing blocks is known
at compile time, all references to variables declared anywhere in a procedure
can be determined at that time. All references to variables outside the procedure are handled in the usual way. There is, therefore, no need for actual
activation records for blocks.

9.5 Implementing Dynamic Scoping

There are at least two distinct ways in which nonlocal references in a dynamic
scoped language can be implemented: deep access and shallow access. Note
that deep and shallow access are not concepts related to deep and shallow
binding. For one thing, deep and shallow bindings result in different
semantics; deep and shallow access result in the same semantics.

9.5.1 Deep Access

When a program in a language that uses dynamic scoping refers to a nonlocal variable, the reference can be resolved by searching through the declarations in the other subprograms that are currently active, beginning with

the one most recently activated. This concept is somewhat similar to that of accessing nonlocal variables in a static scoped language, except that the dynamic—rather than the static—chain is followed. The dynamic chain links together all subprogram activation record instances in the reverse of the order in which they were activated. Therefore, the dynamic chain is exactly what is needed to reference nonlocal variables in a dynamically scoped language. This method is called **deep access** because accesses may require searches deep in the stack.

There are two important differences between the deep access method for nonlocal access in a dynamic scoped language and the static chain method for static scoped languages. First, in a dynamic scoped language there is no way to determine at compile time the length of the chain that must be searched. Every activation record instance in the chain must be searched until the first instance of the variable is found. This is one reason why dynamic scoped languages typically have slower execution speeds than static scoped languages. Second, activation records must store the names of variables, whereas in static scoped language implementations only the values are required. The names are needed for the search process.

9.5.2 Shallow Access

Shallow access is an alternative implementation method, not an alternative semantics. As stated above, the semantics of deep access and shallow access are identical. In the shallow access method, variables declared in subprograms are not stored in the activation records of those subprograms. Because with dynamic scoping there is at most one visible version of a variable of any specific name at a given time, a very different approach can be taken. One variation of shallow access is to have a separate stack for each variable name in a complete program. Every time a new variable with a particular name is created by a declaration at the beginning of a subprogram activation, it is placed on the stack for its name. Every reference to the name is to the variable on top of the stack, because it is the most recently created. When a subprogram terminates, the lifetime of its local variables ends and the stacks for those variable names are popped. This method allows very fast references to variables, but maintaining the stacks at the entrances and exits of subprograms is quite expensive.

Another option is to use a central table that has a location for each different variable name in a program. Along with each entry, a bit is maintained that indicates whether the name has a current binding, or variable association. Any access to any variable can then be to an offset into the central table. The offset is static, so the access can be fast.

Maintenance of a central table is straightforward. A subprogram call requires that all of its local variables be logically placed in the central table.

If the position of the new variable in the central table is already active—
that is, if it contains a variable whose lifetime has not yet ended—that value
must be saved somewhere during the lifetime of the new variable. Whenever a variable begins its lifetime, the active indicator in its central table
position must be set.

There have been several variations in the design of the central table and
in the way values are stored when they are temporarily replaced. One
variation is to have a "hidden" stack on which all saved objects are stored.
Because subprogram calls and returns, and thus the lifetimes of local variables, are nested, this works well.

The second variation is perhaps the cleanest and most inexpensive to
implement. In this variation a central table of single cells is used, and replaced
variables are stored in the activation record of the subprogram that created
the replacement variable. This is a stack mechanism, but one that already
exists, so the new overhead is minimal.

In all of these alternatives, note that the central table or stack position
for the variables is usually pointer type, and the actual objects are allocated
from a heap. The reason for this is that objects of the same name are often
of different sizes, and will not fit conveniently into any fixed stack or table
structure.

9.6 Implementing Parameters That Are Subprogram Names

Parameters that are subprogram names were discussed at length in Chapter
8. Recall that static scoped languages use a method called deep binding to
associate a referencing environment with the activation of a subprogram
that was passed as a parameter. We now investigate how deep binding can
be implemented using the static chain and display methods.

9.6.1 Static Scoping

Suppose static chaining is used in the implementation. A subprogram that
passes a subprogram name as a parameter must have in its static ancestry
the unit in which that subprogram was declared; if it does not, the name
of the subprogram to be passed will not be visible. If it does, the compiler
can simply pass the link to the static parent of the subprogram to be passed,
along with the subprogram name. The activation record instance of the
subprogram that is passed has this link in its static link field. Terminating
the passed subprogram does not require any actions different from those
for any other subprogram activation.

9.6.2 Displays

Suppose a display is used. Recall that we specifically stated that the display maintenance process described in Section 9.3.4.2.2 was correct only in the absence of subprogram name parameters (and some other features). Maintenance for calls without these involves the simple replacement of a single display pointer. When a parameter is a subprogram name, pointers to all of the static ancestors of that subprogram must be placed in the display, thus requiring that that number of old display pointers be saved. Because the static environment of an activation of a subprogram that has been passed as a parameter may have little relationship to the static environment of the subprogram in which it is called, in many cases the entire display needs to be replaced. In many implementations, the entire existing display is saved for every call, often in the activation record instance of the subprogram in execution. When the passed subprogram terminates, the complete saved display replaces the display used for the passed subprogram's execution.

9.6.3 Referencing Environment Confusion, Revisited

Now that activation records and implementation methods have been covered, we can expand somewhat on a problem introduced in Chapter 8: the possible misunderstanding concerning which referencing environment is correct when a subprogram that was passed as a parameter is executed. For example, consider the following skeletal program, which is a variation of one found in Ghezzi and Jazayeri (1987):

```
program MAIN;
  procedure SUB1;
  . . .
  end; { of procedure SUB1 }
  procedure SUB2 (procedure SUBX);
    var SUM : real;
    procedure SUB3;
      . . .
      begin
      SUM := 0.0;
      . . .
      end; { of procedure SUB3 }
    begin { of procedure SUB2 }
    SUBX;
    SUB2 (SUB3);
    . . .
    end; { of procedure SUB2 }
  begin { MAIN }
  . . .
  SUB2 (SUB1);
  . . .
  end. { MAIN }
```

Figure 9.16
Stack contents for the
example program with
a parameter that is a
subprogram

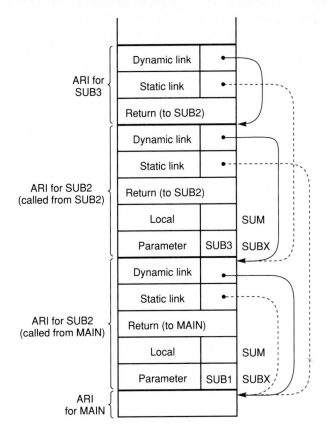

MAIN calls SUB2, sending SUB1 as a parameter. SUB2 then calls the passed procedure, SUB1. Upon return from SUB1, SUB2 calls itself, sending its own procedure SUB3 as a parameter. There are now two instances of the activation record for SUB2 on the stack, with the topmost being for the recursive call. The topmost activation of SUB2 then calls SUB3. When SUB3 uses the variable SUM, there are two versions of it, one for each activation of SUB2, where it is declared. Because the referencing environment of SUB3 is that of the caller that sent SUB3 as a parameter, it is the first activation of SUB2, not the most recent. This is indeed not apparent to the casual reader of the program.

This is admittedly a contrived example. However, the same thing could occur in more realistic programs. The problem is that, although intuitively it may seem that the most recent activation should be the referencing environment, that is not always the case.

Figure 9.16 shows the stack during the execution of SUB3 of the preceding example program.

SUMMARY

Subprogram linkage semantics requires many actions by the implementation. In the case of FORTRAN, these actions are relatively simple because of the lack of nonlocal references, other than through COMMON; the fact that local variables are usually static; and the absence of recursion. In the ALGOL-like languages, subprogram linkage is far more complex. This follows from the requirements of nonlocal accesses through static scoping, semidynamic local variables, and also from recursion.

Subprograms have two components: the actual code, which is static, and the activation record, which is dynamic. Activation records contain the formal parameters and local variables, among other things.

Static chains and displays are the two primary methods of implementing accesses to nonlocal variables in static scoping languages. In both methods, access paths can be established to variables in all static ancestor scopes.

Access to nonlocal variables in a dynamic scoped language can be implemented by use of the dynamic chain or through some central variable table method. Dynamic chains provide slow accesses but fast calls and returns. The central table methods provide fast accesses but slow calls and returns.

Parameters that are subprograms provide a necessary service, but are sometimes difficult to understand. The opaqueness lies in the referencing environment that is available when a subprogram that has been passed as a parameter is executing. Subprograms that are passed as parameters can be implemented with either static chains or displays.

BIBLIOGRAPHIC NOTES

Implementation of both static and dynamic scoping is covered in Pratt (1984) and Ghezzi and Jazayeri (1987), but it is discussed more thoroughly in books on compiler design, such as Fischer and LeBlanc (1988).

BIBLIOGRAPHY

Fischer, C.N., and R.J. LeBlanc. (1988) *Crafting a Compiler.* Benjamin/Cummings, Menlo Park, CA.

Ghezzi, C., and M. Jazayeri. (1987) *Programming Language Concepts.* 2d ed. J. Wiley, New York.

Pratt, T. (1984) *Programming Languages: Design and Implementation.* 2d ed. Prentice-Hall, Englewood Cliffs, NJ.

PROBLEM SET

1. Write an algorithm to perform the display maintenance required upon entry to a subprogram in a language that uses static scoping and also allows subprogram names as parameters.

2. Write an algorithm to perform the display maintenance required upon exit from a subprogram in a language that uses static scoping and also allows subprogram names as parameters.

3. Show the stack with all activation record instances, including static and dynamic chains, when execution reaches position 1 in the following skeletal program:

```
procedure BIGSUB;
  procedure A;
    procedure C;
      ...
    begin
      ...
      B;
      ...
      end; { of procedure C }
    begin { of procedure A }
    ...
    C;
    ...
    end; { of procedure A }
  procedure B;
    ...
    begin
    ...       <----------------- 1
    end; { of procedure B }
  begin { of BIGSUB }
  ...
  A;
  ...
end; { of procedure BIGSUB }
```

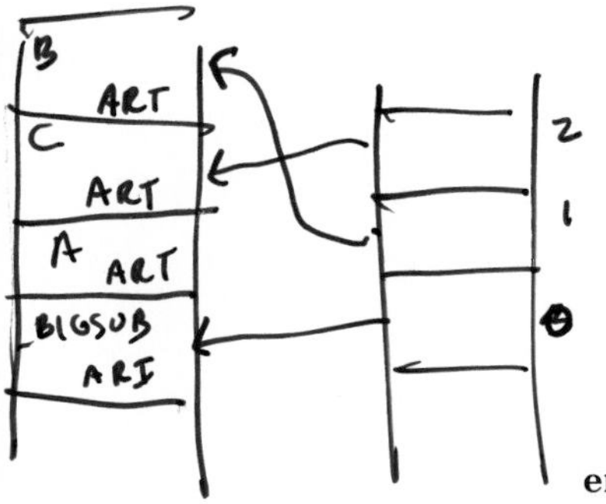
B
ART
C
ART
A
ART
BIGSUB
ARI
2
1

note this also shows return

4. For the skeletal program in Problem 3, show the display that would be active at position 1, along with the activation record instances on the stack.

5. Although local variables in Pascal procedures are dynamically allocated at the beginning of each activation, under what circumstances could the value of a local in a particular activation retain the value of the previous activation?

5- 2 consecutive calls to the same procedure would use the same stack location for a given local variable

6. It is stated in this chapter that when nonlocal variables are accessed in a dynamically scoped language using the dynamic chain, variable names must be stored in the activation records with the values. If this were actually done, every nonlocal access would require a sequence of costly string comparisons on names. Design an alternative to these string comparisons that would be faster.

6. assign integer values to all variable names used in the program. then the integer values could be used in activation recds.

7. Pascal allows goto's with nonlocal targets. How could such statements be handled if static chains were used for nonlocal variable access? [*Hint*: Consider the way the correct activation record instance of the static parent of a newly enacted procedure is found (Section 9.3.4.1.2).]

8. Repeat Problem 7, using a display instead of static chains.

9. How could the display mechanism described in this chapter be modified to make local variables accessible without indirect addressing?

7. represent target of every goto as an address + a nesting-depth, where nesting depth is the difference between the nesting level of the proc containing the goto and that of proc containing targ. then go down static chain that # of links ....

Key Concepts

- Abstraction in programming languages
- Data abstraction
- Encapsulation
- Information hiding
- Class hierarchies
- Transparent versus opaque export
- Name qualification
- Private types
- Generic packages

8. as in 7, except that nesting-depth is used to ~~com~~ move display top pointer, as well as stack top pointer

9. assume i'en access mechanism, that 0th entry in display indicates a local + const bother forks display pointer

10

DATA ABSTRACTION

Contents

In this chapter we explore the concept of data abstraction as a supported feature in programming languages, from its origins in SIMULA 67 to its more advanced form in Modula-2 and Ada. Among the new ideas of the last 20 years in programming methodologies and programming language design, data abstraction is one of the most profound.

We begin by discussing the general concept of abstraction in programming and programming languages. Data abstraction is then defined and illustrated with an example. Linguistic support for data abstraction is discussed in terms of three specific languages: SIMULA 67, Modula-2, and Ada. An implementation of the same example data abstraction is shown in each language. This illuminates the similarities and differences in the design of the language facilities that support data abstraction.

10.1   The Concept of Abstraction

The concept of **process abstraction** is among the oldest in programming language design. Even Plankalkül had a method for constructing subprograms. All subprograms are process abstractions: They are a way of allowing a program to specify that some process is to be done, without spelling out how it is to be done (at least in the calling program). For example, when a program needs to sort an array of numeric data objects of some type, it would most likely use a subprogram for the process. Then, when the sorting process is required, a statement such as:

```
SORT_INT (LIST, LENGTH)
```

is placed in the program. This call is an abstraction of the actual sorting process, whose algorithm is not specified. The call is independent of the algorithm implemented in the called subprogram.

Process abstraction is absolutely essential to the programming process. The ability to abstract away many of the details of procedures makes it possible to construct and comprehend large programs.

In general, the concept of abstraction holds that some class of processes or objects can be represented by only a subset of its attributes. These are the essential attributes of the class, with all the other attributes abstracted away. In the case of the subprogram SORT_INT, the only essential attributes are the name of the array to be sorted, the type of its elements, and the array's length. The particular algorithm that SORT implemented is an attribute that was nonessential to the user.

10.2   Introduction to Data Abstraction

Data abstraction as a programming method was discovered much later than process abstraction. The concept of data abstraction is similar to that of process abstraction, as far as its usefulness to programming is concerned.

It is a weapon against complexity, a means of making complicated programs manageable.

10.2.1 Floating-Point as an Abstract Data Type

Some forms of data abstraction have been present in all programming languages. Perhaps the best example is the floating-point data type. Built into most languages, this type provides a means of creating variables for floating-point data, and also provides a set of arithmetic operations for manipulating objects of the type.

Floating-point types in high-level languages often employ a key concept in data abstraction: information hiding. The actual format of the data value in a floating-point memory cell is usually hidden from the user. The only operations available are those provided by the system. The user is not allowed to create new operations on data of the type, except those that can be constructed using the built-in operations. In particular, the user is not allowed to directly manipulate the actual representation of floating-point objects. This makes it possible to have a flexible data representation, rather than one fixed in some particular format. It is this feature that allows program portability between implementations, even though the implementations may use different representations of floating-point values.

10.2.2 User-Defined Abstract Data Types

A user-defined abstract data type should provide the same characteristics provided by floating-point types: (1) a type definition that allows program units to declare variables of the type, and (2) a set of operations for manipulating objects of the type.

We now formally define an abstract data type. An **abstract data type** is a data type that satisfies the following two conditions:

1. The representation, or definition, of the type and the operations on objects of the type are described in a single syntactic unit.
2. The representation of objects of the type is hidden from the program units that use the type, so that the only direct operations possible on those objects are those provided in the type's definition.

The primary advantage of packaging the representation and operations in a single syntactic unit is that it cleanly localizes modifications. There are several advantages of hiding representation details. The most important of these is that program units that use the type are not able to "see" the representation details, and thus their code cannot depend on that representation. The result of this is that the representation can be changed at any time without affecting the program units that use the type.

Another distinct and important benefit of information hiding is increased reliability. Program units cannot change underlying representations directly, either by accident or by intent, thus increasing the integrity of such objects. Section 10.4.3 contains an illustration of the danger of not including the information hiding part of data abstraction. It is difficult to overstate the importance of hiding the representation details of an abstract data type.

10.2.3   An Example

Suppose an abstract data type is constructed for a stack, consisting of the abstract operations:

empty (stack) —a predicate function that returns TRUE if the
                specified stack is empty and FALSE otherwise
push (stack, element) —pushes the specified element on the
                specified stack
pop (stack) —removes the top element from the specified stack
top (stack) —returns a copy of the top element from the specified
                stack

Now suppose that a large software system uses an implementation of this abstraction, having STK1 and STK2 as variables of the abstract stack type. Then we might have code sequences like the following:

```
. . .
push (STK1,  COLOR1) ;
push (STK1,  COLOR2) ;
. . .
if (not empty (STK1))
   then TEMP : = top (STK1) ;
. . .
push (STK2,  TEMP) ;
. . .
```

Further suppose that the original definition of the stack abstraction uses an adjacency representation (one that implements stacks in arrays). At a later time, because of memory management problems with the adjacency representation, it is changed to a linked list representation. Because data abstraction was used, this change can be made in the code that defines the stack type, but no changes will be required in any of the program units that use the stack abstraction. In particular, the code sequence above does not need to be changed.

In the absence of data abstraction, such a change would require that all the program units that used the stack type be modified to conform to the new representation. Suppose, for example, that the stack operations had been implemented in Pascal to operate on arrays. The change to linked list representation would require that user programs be modified to send pointers instead of array names as parameters to the stack operation procedures.

In summary, the goal of data abstraction is to provide the facilities so that programs can be written that depend only on the abstract properties, not on the representation of data objects. In the stack example, the main abstract property is the order of access, and the operations are push, top, pop, and the predicate empty.

10.3 Design Issues

An ideal facility for defining abstract data types in a language must provide a syntactic unit that can encapsulate the type definition and subprogram definitions of the abstraction operations. It must be possible to make the type names and subprogram headers visible to other program units that use the abstraction. Although the type names must have external visibility, the type definitions must be hidden.

Few, if any, operations should be provided for objects of abstract data types, other than those provided with the type definition. Assignment and comparison for equality are the only operations that should be built in.

The encapsulation requirement of abstract data types can be met in two distinct ways. First, an encapsulation construct can be designed to provide a single data type and its operations. This is the approach of Concurrent Pascal (Brinch Hansen, 1975) and Smalltalk (Goldberg and Robson, 1983). The alternative to this is to provide a more generalized encapsulation construct that can define any number of entities, any of which can be selectively specified to be visible outside the encapsulating unit. This is the approach of Modula-2 and Ada.

The primary design issues beyond this fundamental one of encapsulation include the questions of what types can be abstract and whether abstract data types can be generic. Another design issue is how imported types, or other entities if the encapsulation construct is generalized, can be qualified to prevent collisions between local and nonlocal names.

Because of the popularity of Modula-2 and Ada, we focus mainly on languages in the same category as these, which provide generalized encapsulation constructs. But first, we briefly discuss the class concept of SIMULA 67, which provided the first support of any kind for data abstraction.

10.4 SIMULA 67 Classes

The first language facilities for the direct support of data abstraction, although incomplete by our definition, appeared in the class construct in the SIMULA 67 programming language.

10.4.1   Encapsulation

A class, like a procedure in Pascal, can include variable declarations, procedure definitions, and a section of code. The difference in SIMULA 67 is that a class instance can only be referenced indirectly through a pointer, and when used to define an abstract data type, the code section is executed only once, at instantiation time. In this situation, the code section is used only for initialization of variables declared at the top of the class definition. After instantiation, the variables and procedures of a class object can be used by any other unit in a program.

SIMULA 67's contribution to data abstraction is to have the class construct allow data declarations and the procedures that manipulate them to be syntactically encapsulated. Interestingly, the significance of this aspect of the class construct was not recognized until several years after the design of SIMULA 67 was completed. The importance of data abstraction was not generally realized until the early 1970s.

10.4.2   Information Hiding

The variables that are declared in a SIMULA 67 class are not hidden from other program units that allocate class objects using the class. These variables can be accessed through the operations provided by the class subprograms, or directly through their names. This violates one of the two major characteristics of the definition of a data abstraction because multiple access paths are possible. The impact of the violation is that a class used as a data abstraction is far less reliable than a true abstraction. Furthermore, because program units that use the class can be designed to depend on the variable definitions in the class, changes to those variable definitions require changes in the other program units. This makes such programs more difficult to modify.

10.4.3   An Example

As an example of a data abstraction in SIMULA 67, consider the following class, which implements stacks for integer elements:

```
class stack;
  begin
comment ** GLOBAL VARIABLES FOR THE CLASS **;
  integer array list(1..100);
  integer topsub;
comment ** PROCEDURE DEFINITIONS **;
  boolean procedure empty;
    empty := topsub == 0;
```

```
    procedure push (element);
      integer element;
      begin
      if topsub >= 100
        then outtext ("ERROR - Stack overflow")
        else
          begin
          topsub := topsub + 1;
          list(topsub) := element
          end
      end push;

    procedure pop;
      if empty
        then outtext ("ERROR - Stack is empty")
        else topsub := topsub - 1;

    integer procedure top;
      top := list(topsub);

  comment ** CODE SECTION OF THE stack CLASS **;
      topsub := 0
  end stack;
```

This code should be self-explanatory because of its simplicity and its relatively close relationship with that of other ALGOL-like languages.

A class definition is a template for a type. Instances of a class, called **class objects,** are created dynamically at the request of the user program. Class objects can only be referenced with pointer type variables. For example, to use a stack as defined previously, one would first declare a pointer that can point to a stack class object, and then instantiate such an object, which could be done with:

```
ref (stack) stack1;
. . .
stack1 :- new stack
```

Now, stack can be used as follows:

```
stack1.push (17);
stack1.push (42);
. . .
stack1.pop
```

The class mechanism of SIMULA 67 allows one to build constructs that are similar to abstract data types, as the stack example shows. It does not, however, hide the representation of those data types. In the example, both the array list that implements the stack and the stack top subscript topsub are visible outside the class definition. For example, there is no safeguard against a programmer using:

```
stack1.topsub := 0
```

which effectively empties the stack. Furthermore, the following statement is also legal:

```
stack1.list (42) : = 99999
```

Therefore, none of the information in the stack abstraction is hidden—and one of the main advantages of the abstraction is missing.

10.4.4   Class Hierarchies

In addition to the simple kind of class construct used above, SIMULA 67 also allows the construction of a sort of cascaded class construct. The underlying concept is that any class can be built as the child of an existing class object. Such a class inherits the attributes of the parent class, which are its data and procedure declarations. In effect, what happens is that the new class literally has the attributes of the parent copied into its definition. It is possible in this way to build hierarchical arrangements of class definitions, which can model the hierarchical decomposition of a problem into a solution program.

Although the inheritance of class attributes was introduced in SIMULA 67, because of that language's obscurity, we will not discuss it further here. Smalltalk includes a similar kind of inheritance, as we discuss in Chapter 15.

10.4.5   Evaluation

The SIMULA 67 class construct provides for the syntactic encapsulation of data objects and the procedures that manipulate them. However, it does not provide information hiding, which allows representation details to be kept from the program modules that use them. Furthermore, SIMULA 67 does not allow user-defined types.

SIMULA 67 was revolutionary in its development of the class construct. However, because the language never enjoyed widespread use, we cover it primarily for its historic interest. We now turn our attention to two popular contemporary languages that implement a more complete form of data abstraction: Modula-2 and Ada.

10.5   Abstract Data Types in Modula-2

Modula-2 provides facilities for data abstraction, including the ability to hide the representations of abstract data types.

10.5.1   Encapsulation

The program unit of Modula-2 that provides the facilities for data abstraction is the module. Like the SIMULA 67 class construct, the module is, at least in part, meant to break away from the limitations of static scoping. Both SIMULA 67 and Modula-2 retain static scoping, but offer other methods of sharing data among program units.

Modula-2 was designed to revise some of the syntax of Pascal, and, more importantly, to extend it so that it could be used for systems programming and for large software systems. Recall that the original Pascal did not provide for separate compilation, which makes the language inadequate for constructing large systems.

The most important advance of Modula-2 over Pascal is the module. A module is a program unit that can include definitions of types, objects, and subprograms that may be accessed by other program units. Access to the types, objects, and subprograms of a module is gained by specifically requesting that access to the other units, which are then called **clients** of the module.

Modules can be either local or library modules. Local modules are not useful for designing abstract data types, so we focus on library modules here. A **library module** consists of two syntactic entities—the definition and implementation units, which are also called modules. The **definition module** contains at least partial specifications of the types and objects, and also the headers of the subprograms that are visible to client units. These specifications define the **interface** of the module. The **implementation module** contains the complete definitions of any types that were only partially defined in the corresponding definition module. Also, the implementation module contains the complete definitions of the subprograms whose headers appear in the corresponding definition module.

A definition module and its associated implementation module share the same name. The syntactic difference between the two lies in the use of the reserved words DEFINITION and IMPLEMENTATION, which appear in their respective headers.

Modules are separately compilable; even the two parts, the definition and implementation modules, can be separately compiled as long as the definition module is compiled first. When a definition module is compiled, its interface information is kept. This allows precompiled modules to be included in a program, with complete interface checking possible. The interfaces are checked by the loader at the time the program is assembled for execution. This is a great advance over a language such as FORTRAN 77, in which no interface checking is done among units.

Early implementations of Modula-2 required that the types, objects, and procedures that are visible outside a definition module be listed on an EXPORT statement. In more recent implementations, however, all names defined in the definition module are implicitly exported to client units, obviating the need for the EXPORT statement.

10.5.2   Information Hiding

The types that are declared in a definition module can have their representation, or complete definition, included in or excluded from the definition module. If the representation is included, the type is said to be **transparent,** and its representation is not hidden from the modules that import it. If the representation is not included, but rather is placed in the associated implementation module, that type is said to be **opaque,** and its representation is not available to client units.

An important aspect of the design of Modula-2 modules is that only pointer types can be opaque. The design decision to require this restriction is partially based on the efficiency of software development. If client modules are allowed to declare variables of an opaque type, they need to be able to determine the size of objects of that type. If they see only the type name, this can be a problem, unless all opaque types have the same size—and all pointers do have the same size. Perhaps more importantly, changes to the representation details of opaque types do not require recompilation of client modules if they are always pointers. If other types are opaque and exported, changes in their representation will require recompilation of client modules.

The restriction of opaque types to pointers is not a severe one from the user's point of view, because a pointer can point to any data structure. It does, however, create some problems, as we discuss in Section 10.5.5.

10.5.3   An Example

As an example of a specification module, consider the following:

```
DEFINITION MODULE stackmod;
  TYPE stacktype;
  PROCEDURE empty (s : stacktype) : BOOLEAN;
  PROCEDURE push (VAR s : stacktype;
                      element : INTEGER);
  PROCEDURE pop (VAR s : stacktype);
  PROCEDURE top (s : stacktype) : INTEGER;
  PROCEDURE initialize (VAR s : stacktype);
END stackmod.
```

This definition module describes the external view of a stack type for integer elements, similar to the SIMULA 67 stack we defined in an earlier section. One important difference is that the actual representation of the stack type is not present. The type, stacktype, is opaque, so the details of its representation will be visible only in the implementation module; they will not be visible to any client modules. One of the results of restricting opaque types to pointers is that the stack in our example must be dynamically allocated before it can be used. Therefore, an initialization procedure must be included so the user can create a stack for use.

The implementation module for stacks is as follows:

```
IMPLEMENTATION MODULE stackmod;
  FROM Terminal IMPORT WriteString, WriteLn;
  FROM Storage IMPORT ALLOCATE;
  CONST max = 100;
  TYPE stacktype = POINTER TO
                      RECORD
                      list : ARRAY [1..max] OF INTEGER;
                      topsub : [0..max]
                      END;
  PROCEDURE empty (s : stacktype) : BOOLEAN;
    BEGIN
    IF s^.topsub = 0
      THEN RETURN TRUE
      ELSE RETURN FALSE
    END
    END empty;

  PROCEDURE push (VAR s : stacktype;
                    element : INTEGER);
    BEGIN
    IF s^.topsub = max THEN
      WriteString ("ERROR - Stack overflow");
      WriteLn
    ELSE
      s^.topsub := s^.topsub + 1;
      s^.list[s^.topsub] := element
    END
    END push;

  PROCEDURE pop (VAR s : stacktype);
    BEGIN
    IF empty (s) THEN
      WriteString ("ERROR - Stack underflow");
      WriteLn
    ELSE
      s^.topsub := s^.topsub - 1
    END  (* of IF empty... *)
    END pop;

  PROCEDURE top (s : stacktype) : INTEGER;
    BEGIN
    IF empty (s) THEN
      WriteString ("ERROR - Stack underflow");
      WriteLn
    ELSE
      RETURN s^.list[s^.topsub]
    END  (* of IF empty ... *)
    END top;
```

```
      PROCEDURE initialize (VAR s : stacktype);
         BEGIN
         NEW (s);
         s^.topsub := 0
         END initialize;
   END stackmod.
```

The second two statements of the implementation module import the necessary processes for displaying error messages and for allocation of the stack in the initialize procedure. The rest of the code should be relatively self-explanatory.

The following skeletal module demonstrates how the facilities of stack-mod can be used:

```
MODULE usestacks;
   FROM InOut IMPORT WriteInt, WriteLn, WriteString;
   FROM stackmod  IMPORT stacktype,  empty,  push,  pop,
                         top, initialize;
   VAR stack : stacktype;
   VAR stuff : INTEGER;          really a pointer
   ...
   BEGIN
   ...
   initialize (stack);
   push (stack, 42);
   push (stack, 27);
   pop (stack);
   stuff := top (stack);
   ...
   END usestacks.
```

This code creates and initializes a stack, pushes two values on it, 42 and 27, and pops the 27, leaving the stack with the value 42.

10.5.4 Name Qualification

An imported name is **qualified** in a client module if it indicates the source module of the name so that there are no conflicts with other entities of the same name that are either declared locally or imported from other modules. Client modules can qualify references to those imported entities in two ways: explicitly or implicitly.

If the client module needs all of the exported entities from a module, it can simply import the entire module by naming the module on an IMPORT statement. This obviates the need to list each entity to be imported. In this case, every reference to the imported entities needs to be explicitly qualified by attaching the exporting module's name, as in:

```
stackmod.push (stack, 22)
```

The alternative to this form of qualification is the method used in our module usestacks, in which we imported specific entities from stackmod. In this case, which is called implicit qualification, no explicit qualification is required on references to the imported entities. Implicit qualification is better in the sense that it restricts access to entities that are not needed. However, the use of implicitly qualified references to imported entities has two drawbacks. First, it prevents the compiler from detecting some mistaken uses of variables, types, and processes. For example, suppose there was a local variable and an imported variable with similar names. A minor keying error might replace one with the other, leading to a subtle but fatal program error, and the system would not be able to detect the error. Of course, this problem can occur with any use of similar names, not just imported names. Second, it is more readable to have imported variables explicitly qualified with their source module names. This advantage is lost when implicit qualification is used.

10.5.5 Evaluation

The restriction of opaque types to pointers in Modula-2 causes some problems. First, it means that every module that provides an abstract data type must include a procedure for creating objects of that abstract type. The process of providing the procedure is not difficult, but the need to use it clearly detracts from the model's simplicity and "abstractness." Users must always be concerned with object creation—a process that can easily be forgotten. If it is forgotten, the imported pointer could be used before it points to anything meaningful. Compounding the problem is the fact that Modula-2 pointer variables are not always automatically initialized to nil.

Another problem with the restriction to pointers is that it forces a good deal of unnecessary use of pointers, which are far less safe to use than nonpointer variables. Recall our discussion in Chapter 7 of the problems related to pointers.

The fact that definition modules can be separately compiled has a profound impact on constructing software systems in Modula-2. True top-down design can be used, and an entire system can be built initially with only definition modules. All module interfaces can then be automatically checked for consistency by the compiler, before any implementation code is written.

Let us now reiterate one of the primary reasons why abstract data types like stacktype are so attractive. Regardless of the number of client modules of stackmod, the representation of stacks in its implementation module can be changed without even requiring recompilation of those client modules. For example, we could rewrite the implementation module to represent stacks as linked lists of dynamically allocated elements. If we did this, not even the definition module for stackmod would need to be recompiled. Of course, this assumes that the element type is not changed.

10.6   Abstract Data Types in Ada

The method of constructing abstract data types in Ada is similar to that of doing so in Modula-2, although there are a few critical differences.

10.6.1   Encapsulation

The encapsulating constructs, or modules, in the Ada language are called **packages.** As with Modula-2 modules, packages can have two parts, which are also called packages. In this case they are called the specification package and the body package, although not all packages have body parts (packages that contain only data sometimes do not have bodies).

A specification package and its associated body package share the same name. The reserved word **body** in a package header identifies it as being a body package. Specification and body packages may be compiled separately, provided the specification package is compiled first.

10.6.2   Information Hiding

The most important difference between Modula-2 modules and Ada packages is that the types that are exported are not restricted to pointers in Ada. Any type that can be defined anywhere can be defined in a specification package and thus exported.

Recall that the advantage of the Modula-2 restriction that exported types can only be pointers is that client modules do not have to be recompiled when the representation of the exported type is changed. Because the client modules see only a pointer, whose size is fixed regardless of the structure to which it points, the modules do not depend in any way on that structure.

In Ada packages, these problems are partially overcome by allowing a kind of visible/invisible specification for types. A type that is to be exported from a package, but whose representation details are to be hidden, is declared twice in the specification package. The specification has two sections, one that is entirely visible, and one that is only partially visible outside the package. The part that is only partially visible is called the **private** part. It is introduced by the reserved word **private**.

Suppose a type named NODE_TYPE is to be exported by a package but its representation is to be hidden. NODE_TYPE is declared in the visible part of the specification package without its representation details, as in:

```
type NODE_TYPE is private;
```

In the private clause, the declaration of NODE_TYPE is repeated, but this time with the complete type definition, as in:

```
package LINKED_LIST_TYPE is
   type NODE_TYPE is private;
```

```
    . . .
private
  type NODE_TYPE;
  type PTR is access NODE_TYPE;
  type NODE_TYPE is
    record
    INFO : INTEGER;
    LINK : PTR;
    end record;
end LINKED_LIST_TYPE;
```

The part of a specification before the private clause, which is always at
the end of a specification package, is visible outside the package. However,
the private clause declarations are hidden to all other program units except
the matching implementation package.   *+ compiler at compile time ?*

When client program units are being compiled, the compiler can "see"
enough of a private type specification to get the size, thus allowing such
units to declare variables of the type. However, client units cannot access
any of the entities described in the private part of the specification. Types
that are declared to be private are called **private types.**

A client program unit that imports a type that is declared private can
use several built-in operations on objects of that type. The objects can be
assigned and compared for equality and inequality with operations specified by the usual operators = and / = (not equal). Any other operation must
be defined in the specification package that defined the type.

An alternative to private types is a more restricted form, limited private
types. **Limited private types** are described in the private section of a specification package, just as private types are. The only syntactic difference is
that limited private types are declared to be **limited private** in the visible
part of the package specification.

Objects of a type that is declared limited private have no built-in operations. If assignment or equality comparisons are required, they must be
provided by the specification package. The assignment operation needs to
be in the form of a normal procedure, whereas the equal and not equal
operators can be provided by overloading those operators for the new type.

10.6.3   An Example

To allow easy comparison, we have once again chosen the stack to illustrate
an abstract data type, this time in the Ada language:

```
package STACKPACK is
  type STACKTYPE is limited private;
  function EMPTY (S : in STACKTYPE) return BOOLEAN;
  procedure PUSH (S        : in out STACKTYPE;
                  ELEMENT : in INTEGER);
  procedure POP (S : in out STACKTYPE);
  function TOP (S : in STACKTYPE) return INTEGER;
```

```
    private
      type LIST_TYPE is array (1..100) of INTEGER;
      type STACKTYPE is
      record
        LIST  : LIST_TYPE;
        TOPSUB : INTEGER range 0..100 := 0;
      end record;
  end STACKPACK;
```

The package body for the specification package for the stack type is as follows:

```
with TEXT_IO; use TEXT_IO;
package body STACKPACK is
  function EMPTY (S : in STACKTYPE) return BOOLEAN is
    begin
    if S.TOPSUB = 0
      then return TRUE;
      else return FALSE;
    end if;
    end EMPTY;

  procedure PUSH (S : in out STACKTYPE;
                  ELEMENT : in INTEGER) is
    begin
    if S.TOPSUB >= 100
      then
        PUT_LINE ("ERROR - Stack overflow");
      else
        S.TOPSUB := S.TOPSUB + 1;
        S.LIST(TOPSUB) := ELEMENT;
    end if;
  end PUSH;

  procedure POP (S : in out STACKTYPE) is
    begin
    if S.TOPSUB = 0
      then PUT_LINE ("ERROR - Stack underflow");
      else S.TOPSUB := S.TOPSUB - 1;
    end if;
    end POP;

  function TOP (S : in STACKTYPE) return INTEGER is
    begin
    if S.TOPSUB = 0
      then PUT_LINE ("ERROR - Stack underflow");
      else return S.LIST(S.TOPSUB);
    end if;
    end TOP;
  end STACKPACK;
```

The first line of the code of this package contains two statements: a **with** and a **use**. The with statement imports external packages, in this case TEXT_IO, which provides functions for input and output of text. The **use** statement eliminates the need for explicit qualification of the references to entities from the named package. Thus, in our package, we use the function PUT_LINE from TEXT_IO without explicit qualification. The **use** statement is, therefore, a means of creating implicit qualification for the entities in the package it lists.

There must be procedure definitions in the implementation package with headings that match the procedure headings in the associated specification package. The specification package, in a sense, promises this.

The following procedure is an example of how the package STACKPACK might be used. It is identical in effect to the Modula-2 module usestacks in the previous section.

```
with STACKPACK, TEXT_IO;
use STACKPACK, TEXT_IO;
procedure USE_STACKS is
   TOPONE :  INTEGER;
   STACK :  STACKTYPE;
   begin
   . . .
   PUSH (STACK, 42);
   PUSH (STACK, 17);
   POP (STACK);
   TOPONE := TOP (STACK);
   . . .
   end USE_STACKS;
```

The only significant difference between this and the Modula-2 version is that here it was not necessary to initialize the stack; that was done automatically when we declared the variable stack to be of stacktype. This again points out the difference between exporting only pointers versus exporting any type. Exporting only a pointer to a data type always requires the extra process of initialization.

10.6.4 Generic Packages

Generic procedures in Ada are discussed and illustrated in Chapter 8. Packages can also be generic, however, so we can also construct generic abstract data types.

The stack abstract data type example of the previous section suffers two restrictions: (1) stacks of its type can store only integer type elements, and (2) the stacks can have only up to 100 elements. Both of these restrictions can be eliminated by using a generic package, which can be instantiated for other element types and any desirable size. The following specification package describes the interface of a generic stack abstract data type with these features:

```
generic
  SIZE : POSITIVE;
  type ELEMENT_TYPE is private;
package GENERIC_STACK is
  type STACKTYPE is limited private;
  function EMPTY (S : in STACKTYPE) return BOOLEAN;
  procedure PUSH (S : in out STACKTYPE;
                  ELEMENT : in ELEMENT_TYPE) ;
  procedure POP (S : in STACKTYPE) ;
  function TOP (S : in STACKTYPE) return ELEMENT_TYPE;
private
  type LIST_TYPE is array (1..SIZE) of ELEMENT_TYPE;
  type STACKTYPE is
    record
    LIST : LIST_TYPE;
    TOPSUB : INTEGER range 0..SIZE := 0;
    end record;
  end GENERIC_STACK;
```

The body package for GENERIC_STACK is the same as the package body for the STACKPACK body in previous section except that the 100 is replaced by SIZE and the type of the ELEMENT formal parameter in PUSH and TOP is ELEMENT_TYPE instead of INTEGER.

To get the facilities available in STACKPACK from GENERIC_STACK, the following instantiation could be used:

```
package INTEGER_STACK is new GENERIC_STACK (100, INTEGER);
```

One could also build an abstract data type for a stack of length 500 for floating-point elements, as in:

```
package FLOAT_STACK is new GENERIC_STACK (500, FLOAT);
```

The utility of generic packages in the construction of abstract data types is obvious.

10.6.5 Evaluation

Abstract data types implemented with Ada packages have all of the advantages of those implemented in Modula-2 modules. Several differences exist, however, as has been pointed out in the preceding sections. The most important of these are the following.

Abstract data types in Ada are more flexible than those of Modula-2 because of Modula-2's restriction of opaque export to pointers only. Ada's design lessens the dependence on pointers, which introduce their own batch of insecurities.

Modula-2's design of allowing selected entities to be imported from a module is an advantage over Ada's design, wherein all or none of a package must be imported.

The disadvantage of Ada's design for abstract data types is the need to recompile client modules when the representation of an exported type is changed. But this is necessary only when the exported type is not a pointer. When a pointer is exported from a specification package, the definition of the type to which the pointer points can be declared in the associated package body. Therefore, if Ada is used in the restricted fashion of Modula-2 and exports only pointers, neither it nor Modula-2 will require recompilation of client program units. Only when a nonpointer type is exported in Ada is recompilation of client program units necessary. Thus, the additional cost in Ada arises only from the additional flexibility of allowing any nonpointer type to be exported.

SUMMARY

The concept of data abstraction and its use in program design were milestones in the development of programming as an engineering discipline. Although the concept is relatively simple, its use did not become convenient and safe until languages were designed to implement it.

The two primary features of data abstraction are encapsulation of data objects with their associated operations, and information hiding.

SIMULA 67 provided the first construct for encapsulating data objects with their operations—the class. However, the class construct does not provide for information hiding.

The Modula-2 and Ada languages provide forms of complete data abstraction. The main difference between the two designs is Modula-2's restriction of exported types with hidden representations to pointers. This restriction allows changes to representations that do not require recompilation of definition modules and their clients. The Ada language allows any type to be exported. When nonpointer types are exported, client program units must be recompiled when the representation is changed.

BIBLIOGRAPHY

Birtwistle, G.M., O-J. Dahl, B. Myhrhaug, and K. Nygaard. (1973) *Simula BEGIN.* Van Nostrand Reinhold, New York.

Brinch Hansen, P. (1975) "The Programming Language Concurrent Pascal." *IEEE Trans. on Software Engineering,* SE-1, No. 2, pp. 199–207.

Goldberg, A., and D. Robson. (1983) *Smalltalk-80: The Language and Its Implementation.* Addison-Wesley, Reading, MA.

Goos, G., and J. Hartmanis. (eds.) (1983) *The Programming Language Ada Reference Manual*. Springer-Verlag, New York.

Wirth, N. (1982) *Programming in MODULA-2*. 2d corrected ed. Springer-Verlag, New York.

PROBLEM SET

1. Design the example abstract stack type in Pascal, assuming that the stack definition, its operations, and the code that use it are all in the same program.

2. What critical part or parts of the definition of an abstract data type are missing from a Pascal implementation of the stack type, such as the one in Problem 1?

3. Design the example abstract stack type in FORTRAN 77, using a single subprogram with multiple entries for the type definition and the operations.

4. How does the FORTRAN implementation of Problem 3 compare with the Ada implementation in this chapter, in terms of reliability and flexibility?

5. Modify the Modula-2 implementation module for the abstract stack type to use a linked-list representation, and test it with the same code that appears in this chapter.

6. What operations are built in for the opaque types in Modula-2?

7. What is the main drawback of exporting transparent types in Modula-2?

8. Devise a situation in which it would be advantageous to define a type in a Modula-2 definition module that is not to be exported.

9. How is Modula-2's EXPORT different from FORTRAN's COMMON?

10. Some software engineers believe that all imported entities should be qualified by the name of the exporting program unit. Do you agree? Support your answer.

11. Design a matrix abstraction in a language that you know, including operations for addition, subtraction, and matrix multiplication.

12. Design a queue abstraction in a language you know, including operations for enqueue, dequeue, and empty.

13. Suppose someone designed a stack abstraction in which the function top returned an access path (or pointer), rather than returning a copy of the top element. This is not a true data abstraction. Why? Give an example that illustrates the problem.

Handwritten margin notes:

1. proc usestack
   type stack = record
     stack array [1..100] of integer
     topsub integer;
   proc pop
   proc push ___
   new (stack)

2. Pascal implementation would lack information hiding. Access could be made to the stack other than provided mechanisms or directly

8. 'any type needed internally but not needed outside the module should be defined in a 'definition?' module'

6. only pointer operations

7. information hiding lost

9. EXPORT makes types, objects, + procedures available to other units. Type check. common only allows share stg. not type check

10. yes. for readability.

11. ...

Key Concepts

- Physical and logical concurrency
- Symmetric unit control (coroutines)
- Competition and cooperation synchronization
- Semaphores
- Shared data buffers
- Monitors
- Message-passing model of concurrency
- Nondeterminancy in message receiving

11

SYMMETRIC AND CONCURRENT SUBPROGRAMS

Contents

In Chapter 8 we discussed subprograms whose behavior is restricted by a small set of rules. In particular, such a subprogram has a single entry point and always returns control to the caller when its execution terminates normally. Also, the calling program unit is suspended during execution of the called subprogram, and therefore only a single program unit is executing at any given time.

Symmetric and concurrent subprograms have control semantics that do not follow these rules. Symmetric control allows an equal relationship between units, rather than the master–slave relationship between caller and called subprograms described above. Symmetric control also allows a unit to return control to the caller after partial execution, and then have its execution resumed later from the point where it earlier relinquished control. This provides a sequence of unit entry points.

Concurrent control allows more than one program unit to execute at the same time, either on separate processors or in some time-sliced fashion on a single-processor computer system. On the surface, this may appear to be a simple concept, but it presents serious design problems in a programming language.

Symmetric and concurrent control methods both increase programming flexibility. Both were originally devised for particular problems, but can be used for a variety of other programming applications. Moreover, they provide a framework for approaches to software design that cannot be used with the more restricted form of subprogram control discussed in Chapter 8.

In this chapter we discuss the concepts underlying symmetric and concurrent unit control, and also the design choices for programming languages to support these concepts.

11.1 Introduction

11.1.1 Classes of Concurrency

There are several classes of concurrent unit control. One of those classes is the symmetric unit model; in this model a number of program units, called **coroutines,** can cooperate to intertwine their execution sequence, but only one can be in execution at any given time. The execution of symmetric units is sometimes called **quasi-concurrency.** Another class of concurrency is exhibited in most larger computer systems—that is, the concurrent execution of the central processor and one or more peripheral devices, which allows program code to be executed during input or output operations. The most general class of concurrency is that in which, assuming that more than one processor is available, several program units literally execute simultaneously. This is **physical concurrency.** A slight relaxation of this concept of concurrency allows the programmer and the application software to assume that there are multiple processors providing actual concurrency when, in fact, the actual execution of programs is taking place in interleaved fashion on a single processor. This is **logical concurrency**. It is similar to the illusion of simultaneous execution that is provided to different users of a multiprogrammed computer system. From the programmer and language designer points of view, logical concurrency is the same as physical concurrency. It is the language implementor's task to map the logical concurrency to the underlying hardware. Both logical and physical concurrency allow the concept of concurrency to be used as a program design methodology. For the remainder of this chapter, we will mean logical concurrency whenever we use the word *concurrency* without qualification.

As will become clear later, although logical concurrency and symmetric unit control appear to be similar if not identical, they are in fact significantly different.

There are at least two reasons to consider concurrency as a language design issue. First and foremost, it provides a new method of conceptualizing about program solutions to problems. Many problem domains lend themselves naturally to concurrency, in much the same way that recursion is a natural way to design the solution to some problems. Much of computing involves simulating physical entities. In many cases the system being simulated includes more than one entity, and the entities do whatever they do simultaneously—for example, aircraft in a control area, relay stations in a communications network, and the various machines in a manufacturing facility. To accurately simulate such systems with software, that software must be able to provide for logical concurrency. Therefore, languages should provide the framework for creating problem solutions that use the concept of concurrency, regardless of how the program will actually be executed. The second reason to discuss concurrency is that multiple-processor computers are now becoming readily available, thus creating the need for languages that allow user access to that hardware capability.

There are similar, although far less compelling, reasons to consider symmetric unit control.

11.1.2 Fundamental Concepts

A **task** a program unit that can be in concurrent execution with other program units. A programming language that includes tasks must provide the means to define tasks and control their execution.

A task can communicate with other tasks through shared nonlocal variables, through message passing, or through parameters. If a task does not communicate with or affect the execution of any other task in a program in any way, it is said to be **disjoint**. Because tasks often work together to create simulations or solve problems, and therefore are not disjoint, they must use some form of communication to synchronize their executions.

Two kinds of synchronization are required when tasks share data: **cooperation** and **competition.** A simple form of cooperation synchronization can be illustrated by a common category of applications called the producer–consumer problem. This problem originates in the development of operating systems, where one program unit produces some data value and another uses that value. Access to the memory location, or buffer, that stores the data must be coordinated if the integrity of the data is to be guaranteed. For example, the consumer unit must not be allowed to take a value from the buffer if the buffer is empty. Likewise, the producer unit cannot place a new value in the buffer if the buffer is full. This is called the problem of cooperation synchronization because the users of the shared data structure must cooperate if the integrity of the data is to be maintained.

Note that the need for cooperation synchronization in the producer–consumer application is not restricted to the world of concurrency. Cooperation synchronization is also required for a shared buffer when the producers and consumers are coroutines, whose execution is only quasi-concurrent. This will be made clear in the examples of Section 11.2.

Competition synchronization prevents two tasks from accessing a shared data structure at exactly the same time—a situation that could destroy the integrity of that shared data. To provide competition synchronization, mutually exclusive access to the shared data must be guaranteed.

To clarify the competition problem, consider the following scenario. Suppose task A is in the process of adding 1 to the shared integer variable TOTAL. To do this, it fetches a copy of the current value of TOTAL to do the addition. Before A updates the value of TOTAL, task B begins to increment TOTAL by 1, using the same method. Task B fetches the old value of TOTAL, because A has not yet stored the new value. Then A writes its new value to TOTAL. Finally, B writes its new value to TOTAL. The result of this scenario is that after both A and B are finished incrementing TOTAL, the value of TOTAL is larger by only 1, although it should have been incremented twice, once by A and once by B. Note that this does not occur with coroutines, because only one of them can be in execution at a given time. That is, a coroutine cannot increment a shared variable while another coroutine is in the process of accessing that shared variable.

One general method for providing mutually exclusive access to a resource is to consider the resource to be something that a task can possess and then allow only a single task to possess a shared resource at a time. To gain possession of a shared resource, a task must request it. When a task is finished with a shared resource that it possesses, it must relinquish that resource so that the resource can be made available to other tasks.

Three methods of providing for mutually exclusive access to a shared data structure are semaphores, which are discussed in Section 11.3.2; monitors, which are discussed in Section 11.3.3; and message passing, which is discussed in Section 11.3.4.

Associated with the use of shared resources is the concept of **liveness.** In the environment of sequential programs, a program has the characteristic of liveness if it continues to execute, eventually leading to completion. In more general terms, liveness means that if some event—say program completion—is supposed to occur, it will occur, eventually. That is, progress is continually made. In the environment of concurrency and the use of shared resources, the liveness of a task can cease to exist, meaning that the program cannot continue, and thus will never terminate.

For example, suppose task A and task B both need the shared resources X and Y to complete their work. Further suppose that task A gains possession of X and task B gains possession of Y. After some execution, task A needs resource Y to continue, so it requests Y but must wait until B releases it. Likewise, task B requests X but must wait until A releases it. Neither relinquishes the resource it possesses, and as a result, both lose their liveness, guaranteeing that execution of the program will never complete normally. This particular kind of loss of liveness is called **deadlock.** Deadlock is a serious threat to the reliability of a program, and therefore its avoidance demands serious consideration in both language and program design.

We are now ready to discuss some of the mechanisms for providing symmetric and concurrent unit control.

11.2 Coroutines

The actual origin of the concept of symmetric unit control is difficult to determine. One of the earliest published applications of coroutines was in the area of syntax analysis (Conway, 1963). The first high-level programming language to include facilities for coroutines was SIMULA 67. Recall that the original purpose of SIMULA was system simulation, which often requires the modeling of independent processes. This need was the motivation for the development of coroutines in SIMULA 67.

A coroutine is a subprogram that has multiple entry points, which are controlled by the coroutine itself, and the means to maintain its status between activations. Execution of a coroutine often begins at points other than the beginning of the coroutine. Coroutines often include a segment of code that is executed only at the time the coroutine is created. This code is called the coroutine's initialization code, and its purpose will become clear when we illustrate coroutines with an example.

One of the usual characteristics of subprograms is maintained in coroutines: Only one coroutine actually executes at a given time. Rather than executing to their ends, however, coroutines often partially execute and then transfer control to some other coroutine. When restarted, the first coroutine resumes execution just after the statement that was last active.

Typically, coroutines are created in an application by a program unit called the master unit, which is not a coroutine. When created, coroutines execute their initialization code and then return control back to that master unit. When all of a family of coroutines are constructed, the master program resumes one of the coroutines, and the family of coroutines then resume each other in some order until their work is completed, if in fact it can be completed. If the execution of a coroutine reaches the end of its code section, control is transferred to the master unit that created it. This is the mechanism for ending execution of the collection of coroutines, if that is desirable, which is not always the case.

One example of a problem that can be solved with this sort of collection of coroutines is the simulation of a card game. Suppose the game has four players, who all use the same strategy for playing. Such a game can be simulated by having a master program unit create a family of coroutines, each with a collection, or hand, of cards. The master program could then start the simulation by resuming one of the player coroutines, which, after it had played its turn, could resume the next player coroutine, and so forth until the game ended.

Suppose program units A and B are coroutines. Figure 11.1 shows two ways an execution sequence involving A and B might proceed.

In Figure 11.1a, the execution of coroutine A is started by the master unit. This enacting of coroutine A may be accomplished by the same statement that is used by the coroutines to enact each other, which is often called a resume statement. The initial resume of a coroutine by the master unit is similar to a subprogram call. In the case of the coroutines resuming each other, the resumes cause the execution of the resumed coroutine to be continued. For example, when coroutine B in Figure 11.1a first causes control to return to coroutine A, the semantics is that A is meant to continue from where it ended its last execution. In particular, its local variables have the values left them by the previous activation. Figure 11.1b shows an alternative execution sequence of coroutines A and B. In this case, B is resumed by the master unit.

Rather than have the patterns shown in Figure 11.1, coroutines often have a loop containing a resume. In this scenario, Figure 11.2 more aptly describes the execution sequence.

11.2.1 Design Issues

The following are the primary design issues for coroutines:

1. Should the coroutine control statements be in the language or provided in a library?
2. How should coroutine execution terminate?
3. Should coroutines be created statically or dynamically?

11.2.2 Coroutines in SIMULA 67

SIMULA 67 classes were devised to implement coroutines. Although SIMULA 67 was the first programming language to include coroutines, because of

Figure 11.1
Two possible execu-
tion control
sequences for two
coroutines without
loops

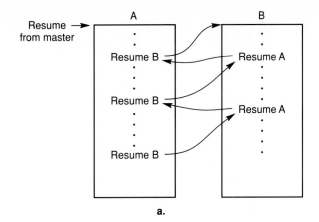

a.

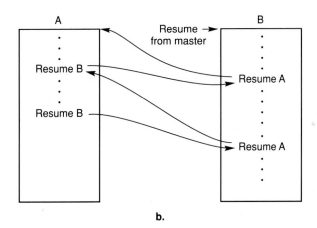

b.

the obscurity of the language, our discussion of its coroutines will be relatively brief.

11.2.2.1   Design

The execution of SIMULA 67 coroutines is controlled, at least in part, by the
resume and **detach** statements. The **detach** statement suspends the execution of a coroutine and returns control to the master unit that created it.
The **detach** statement is usually placed immediately after the initialization
code in a class body. Recall that the class body is executed when the class
is instantiated through the execution of **new**.

The **resume** statement is similar to a procedure call, except that the
execution of the called coroutine begins with the statement following the
statement that was last executed. Because the initial execution of a SIMULA
67 coroutine occurs when it is created, a **resume** can never begin executing

Figure 11.2
Coroutine execution
sequence with loops

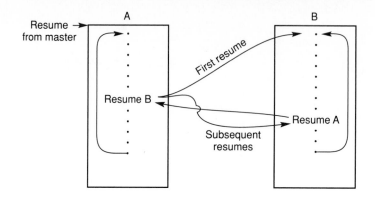

a coroutine at its beginning. Instead, the first resume of a coroutine begins executing at the first statement after its first **detach**.

The designers of SIMULA 67 made the following choices in answering the design questions for coroutines: the coroutine control statements are part of the language, coroutines return control to the master unit if their execution is completed, and coroutines are dynamically created.

11.2.2.2   An Example

The producer–consumer problem described in Section 11.1 can be solved using coroutines because coroutines provide the required cooperation synchronization. A skeletal SIMULA 67 program for a simple version of the producer–consumer problem, where the entity being produced and consumed is a simple integer value, follows. Note that the integer value is transferred between the producer and the consumer through a single element global buffer named buf.

```
begin
COMMENT *** DEFINITION OF THE PRODUCER COROUTINE
   class producer (consumerptr);
     ref (consumer) consumerptr;
     begin
     integer stuff;
     detach;
     while true do
       begin
             -- produce stuff --
       buf := stuff;
       resume (consumerptr);
       end
     end;
```

```
COMMENT *** DEFINITION OF THE CONSUMER COROUTINE
  class consumer (producerptr);
    ref (producer) producerptr;
    begin
    integer value;
    detach;
    while true do
      begin
      value := buf;
      -- consume value --
      resume (producerptr);
      end
    end;


COMMENT *** THE MASTER PROGRAM UNIT
  integer buf;
  ref (producer) prod1;
  ref (consumer) cons1;
  prod1 :- new producer;
  cons1 :- new consumer;
  resume (prod1)
  end;
```

The main program code area of this system, which begins with the declaration of the variable buf, creates the instances of the producer and consumer coroutines and then continues executing the producer with a **resume**, thereby beginning the action of the coroutines. Execution control then alternates between the producer and consumer coroutines. Notice that this program has no way of terminating gracefully. This is not uncommon for coroutine systems, although some are not designed to run forever. If execution is simply allowed to reach the end of any coroutine, control returns to the master program.

The only synchronization of these two coroutines, which is cooperation, guarantees that the producer places a value in the buffer before the consumer removes it, and vice versa. This synchronization is accomplished by the use of the **resume** statements in the two coroutines.

11.2.3   Coroutines in Modula-2

The language design philosophy of Niklaus Wirth is centered on the concept that simplicity is an essential characteristic of a good programming language. His language, Modula-2, clearly reflects this. It is an attempt to design the simplest language possible that has powerful and flexible capabilities.

11.2.3.1   Design

There are no statements, data types, or operators in Modula-2 for either symmetric or concurrent control units. However, that does not disallow those capabilities. Most Modula-2 compilers supply a module, as suggested by Wirth (1983), that provides sufficient facilities for building and using coroutines. This technique allows coroutines to be used without, at the same time, enlarging the language. Furthermore, the facilities for coroutines can be provided at a high level of abstraction.

Two levels of abstraction for coroutine support are typically provided with a Modula-2 compiler: (1) a low-level module, usually called SYSTEM, that provides a data type and procedures for creating and starting and resuming coroutines; and (2) a high-level module that uses the low-level module to provide a data type and procedures for dealing with coroutines, including synchronizing their execution sequences. In the following we briefly describe a version of this higher-level module, which is called Processes.

The coroutines of Modula-2 are called processes. They are constructed from parameterless procedures using the facilities of the SYSTEM module, and can only be called through other facilities of SYSTEM. Because they are actually just procedures, Modula-2 coroutines are statically created.

The Processes module can be designed for a variety of applications because it is not part of the language. In the following we provide an abstract description of a version of Processes that is designed for use in building data abstractions for handling shared data buffers. The definition module for this version of Processes is:

```
DEFINITION MODULE Processes;
    EXPORT QUALIFIED SIGNAL, StartProcess, SEND, WAIT,
                        Awaited, Init;
    TYPE SIGNAL;
    PROCEDURE StartProcess (p : PROCEDURE; n : CARDINAL);
    PROCEDURE SEND (VAR s : SIGNAL);
    PROCEDURE WAIT (VAR s : SIGNAL);
    PROCEDURE Awaited (s : SIGNAL) : BOOLEAN;
    PROCEDURE Init (VAR s : SIGNAL);
    END Processes.
```

The SIGNAL type is for objects that can be associated with a shared buffer, in order to allow cooperation synchronization to be managed for that structure. In this case, the SIGNAL type objects consist of an integer counter and a queue for storing process descriptors. The actual form of a process descriptor is not important here. For our discussion, simply assume a processor descriptor is whatever it takes to be able to refer to a process.

11.2.3.2   An Example

We describe the facilities of Processes in terms of its intended purpose: management of a shared multiposition buffer. The problem of providing cooperation synchronization is somewhat more complex when the shared buffer has more than one position. In this case, rather than simply keeping track of whether the buffer is full or empty, the module must have some way of recording both the number of empty positions and the number of filled positions. The counter component of a SIGNAL type variable can be used for this purpose. We can use one SIGNAL type variable, say emptyspots, to store the number of empty locations in a shared buffer, and another, say fullspots, to store the number of filled locations in the buffer.

We design the buffer as an abstract data type in which all data enters the buffer through the procedure deposit, and all data leaves the buffer through the procedure fetch. Then the deposit procedure only needs to check with the emptyspots SIGNAL to see if there are any empty positions in the buffer. If there are, it can go ahead with the deposit. If the buffer is full, the caller to deposit must be made to wait in the emptyspots queue for an empty spot to become available. When the deposit is complete, the deposit procedure can indicate to the fullspots SIGNAL that there is one more filled location in the buffer.

The fetch procedure has the opposite sequence of deposit. It checks the fullspots SIGNAL to see if the buffer contains at least one item. If it does, the item is removed and the emptyspots SIGNAL has its counter incremented by 1. If the buffer is empty, the calling process is put in the fullspots queue to wait until an item appears.

To clarify the purpose of the queue component of a SIGNAL type variable, in terms of a shared buffer, consider the situation in which several coroutines attempt to place a data value in a shared buffer that is full. In this situation, the system must "remember" all coroutines that attempted to place a data value in the queue but were not allowed, so that when an empty position becomes available, one of the waiting coroutines can be resumed. In our example, references to coroutines waiting for empty positions in the buffer are stored in the queue of the emptyspots SIGNAL variable.

The operations on SIGNAL types are not direct, but rather are done through the WAIT and SEND procedures in Processes. Before we describe them, however, we must discuss the concept of a ready queue for processes. When we have a collection of processes, in this case coroutines, in quasi-concurrent execution and that execution must be synchronized, occasionally one or more of the processes will be suspended while they wait for some event. If more than one process is waiting for the same event, when that event occurs, only one process can be resumed. The others must be stored somewhere until the executing process is suspended, at which time one of the others can be given the processor. The place where these waiting processes are stored is called the **process ready queue,** or simply ready queue. The WAIT and SEND procedures must be able to access the ready queue.

This use of a process ready queue is exactly like the method employed by multiprogramming operating systems. Modula-2 was designed so that such software systems could be written using it.

A brief description of WAIT and SEND are:

```
WAIT (signal1)
  IF signal1's counter > 0
    THEN decrement signal1's counter
    ELSE
     put the caller in signal1's queue
     attempt to transfer control to some ready process
         (If the ready queue is empty, deadlock occurs)
  END

SEND (signal1)
  IF signal1's queue is empty {no process is waiting}
    THEN increment signal1's counter
    ELSE
     put the calling process in the ready queue
     transfer control to a process from signal1's queue
  END
```

Now we can present our Modula-2 data abstraction for the shared buffer, which stores simple integers and has 100 locations in a logically circular structure:

```
DEFINITION MODULE Buffer;
  PROCEDURE deposit (newstuff: INTEGER);
  PROCEDURE fetch (VAR oldstuff: INTEGER)
  END Buffer.

IMPLEMENTATION MODULE Buffer;
  FROM Processes IMPORT SIGNAL, SEND, WAIT, Init;
  CONST BUFSIZE = 100;
  VAR fullspots : SIGNAL;
      emptyspots : SIGNAL;
      in, out : [0..BUFSIZE-1];
      buf : ARRAY [0..BUFSIZE-1] OF INTEGER;
      counter : INTEGER;

  PROCEDURE deposit (newstuff : INTEGER);
    BEGIN
    WAIT (emptyspots);
    buf[in] := newstuff;
    in := (in + 1) MOD BUFSIZE;
    SEND (fullspots)
    END deposit;

  PROCEDURE fetch (VAR oldstuff : INTEGER);
    BEGIN
    WAIT (fullspots);
    oldstuff := buf[out];
    out := (out + 1) MOD BUFSIZE;
    SEND (emptyspots)
    END fetch;
```

```
BEGIN { code body for Buffer }
in : = 0;
out : = 0;
Init (emptyspots);
Init (fullspots);
FOR counter : = 1 TO BUFSIZE DO
  SEND (emptyspots)
END
END Buffer.
```

The declarations of the Buffer implementation module create the buffer, the two signals for synchronizing its use, and the indices for storing the next available element and empty locations in it. The variable counter is used only in the module code body.

The code body of the Buffer implementation module first initializes the indices, in and out, to correspond to the first location in the buffer. Then the Init procedure, which was imported from Processes, initializes the two SIGNAL variables: emptyspots and fullspots. This empties their process queues and sets their counters to zero. SEND is then called with emptyspots as its parameter, once for each position in the new buffer. This simply sets the counter in emptyspots to that value, because initially the buffer is indeed empty. The loop is necessary because the only access to a SIGNAL is through SEND and WAIT; we cannot simply set a SIGNAL's counter to a value. After these initializing actions, the Buffer module is available for use by any number of coroutines that need to share its buffer.

The SIMULA 67 coroutine example given earlier manages a single-entry buffer, whereas the Modula-2 example manages a multiple-entry buffer. We could have written a SIMULA 67 program to manage the same multiple-entry buffer, but the program would have had to include the implementation of some form of the SIGNAL type and the SEND and WAIT operations, similar to those provided by the Modula-2 Processes module.

Keep in mind that the Processes module can be rewritten to make it convenient for other applications. The one given here was designed explicitly to support the shared buffer. The SIGNAL type and the WAIT and SEND procedures can be whatever the user wants them to be.

The following code shows a typical skeletal procedure for a producer coroutine that could use the Buffer module:

```
PROCEDURE Producer;
  VAR stuff : INTEGER;
  BEGIN
    LOOP
    -- produce stuff --
    deposit(stuff)
    END
  END Producer;
```

Note that a coroutine is constructed and its execution is started by procedures provided by the SYSTEM module, the details of which are not discussed here.

A serious deficiency of Wirth's suggested model for the Processes module is that coroutine termination is not considered. Recall that in SIMULA 67, coroutines can return control to their master program units, either by execution of a **detach** statement or by executing to their ends. In the Processes module, as suggested by Wirth, no action is specified when execution reaches the end of a process. In some implementations, the whole program simply terminates if any process ends.

In summary, the design choices for the coroutines of Modula-2 are the following: coroutine control is provided by a library, not language statements; coroutine execution termination is not well-defined; and coroutines are created statically.

11.2.3.3   Evaluation of the Modula-2 Coroutine Model

Use of the SIGNAL type variables to provide cooperation synchronization creates an unsafe programming environment since there is no way to statically check for the correctness of their use, which depends on the semantics of the program in which they appear. In the buffer example, leaving the SEND (fullspots) statement out of the producer procedure in the example above will result in buffer overflow. Leaving out the WAIT (fullspots) statement will result in buffer underflow. These are cooperation synchronization failures.

Another significant problem with the Modula-2 implementation of coroutines is the one discussed in the previous section: No means is provided for returning control to a master unit. To make it a viable system, some method must be devised to handle process termination in a less catastrophic way. One such method has been suggested in Sewry (1984a).

Finally, the decision to relegate coroutine creation and control to a library has the following negative repercussion: There is no strong incentive for Modula-2 implementors to provide Processes modules that are identical to those in other implementations. Therefore, programs that use Processes must provide the Processes code themselves if they are to be portable. That is the price of the simplicity gained by leaving coroutine control out of the language.

We now turn our attention to concurrent unit control.

11.3   Concurrency

One of the fundamental capabilities that are required to support concurrency is competition synchronization. In this section we discuss three methods of providing this capability: semaphores, monitors, and the message-passing model. Of course, any linguistic mechanism that is meant to support concurrency must also provide for cooperation synchronization.

11.3.1   Design Issues

The following are the primary design issues for language support for concurrency:

1. How is competition synchronization provided?
2. How is cooperation synchronization provided?
3. Are tasks statically or dynamically created?

There are several additional design issues for concurrent unit control. Prominent among them is how to provide for task scheduling. However, for simplicity's sake, our discussion of concurrency is intentionally incomplete, and several design issues are neither listed above nor discussed in this chapter.

In the following sections we discuss three alternative answers to the first design issue for concurrency, the question of how to provide competition synchronization. The three approaches are semaphores, monitors, and message passing.

11.3.2   Semaphores

11.3.2.1   Semaphore Design Concepts

In an effort to provide for competition synchronization through mutually exclusive access to shared data structures, Edsger Dijkstra devised semaphores in 1965 (Dijkstra, 1968). The concept of a semaphore is that, to provide limited access to a data structure, one simply places guards around the code that accesses the structure. A guard is a linguistic device that allows the guarded code to be executed only under a specified condition. An integral part of a guard mechanism is a technique for ensuring that all attempted executions of the guarded code actually take place, eventually. This is usually handled by having requests for access stored in a queue. Therefore, a semaphore must have both a counter and a process queue. This should all sound familiar because the SIGNAL data type exported by the Modula-2 module, Processes, is a form of semaphore. Since we have already discussed the use of semaphores to provide cooperation synchronization, we focus here on the use of semaphores to provide competition synchronization.

The only two operations provided for semaphores were originally named *P* and *V* by Dijkstra, after the two Dutch words *proberen* (to try) and *verhogen* (to increase). These correspond to the WAIT and SEND operations of the SIGNAL data type.

Suppose there is a shared data structure named STUFF, and access to it must be mutually exclusive. We provide for such access with a semaphore, which we name SEMASTUFF, if all processes that share STUFF have the following form:

```
process example
  begin
    . . .
  wait (SEMASTUFF)
  -- access STUFF --
  signal (SEMASTUFF)
    . . .
  end
```

The code in this process that accesses STUFF is called the **critical region,** which is protected by the semaphore SEMASTUFF. Whenever a process gets to its critical region, it uses **wait**, which allows the access if the SEMASTUFF counter has the value 1, indicating that STUFF is not currently being accessed. If the SEMASTUFF counter has a value of 0, there is a current access taking place, and the process is placed on the queue of SEMASTUFF. Notice that SEMASTUFF's counter must be initialized to 1. The queues of semaphores must always be initialized to empty.

The concept of a semaphore protecting a critical region is shown in Figure 11.3.

11.3.2.2 A Concurrently Accessed Shared Buffer
with Semaphores

In the example code below, we illustrate the use of semaphores to provide both competition and cooperation synchronization for a concurrently accessed shared buffer.

Two semaphores are used to ensure against buffer underflow or overflow, thus providing cooperation synchronization. A third semaphore is used to control access to the buffer, thus providing competition synchronization. Assume that the buffer has length BUFLEN, and that the routines that actually manipulate it already exist as REMOVE and ENTER. We specify accesses to the counter of a semaphore by dot notation. For example, if semap is a semaphore, its counter is referenced by semap.count.

```
semaphore access, fullspots, emptyspots;
  access.count := 1;
  fullspots.count := 0;
  emptyspots.count := BUFLEN;

process producer;
  loop
  -- produce VALUE --
  wait (emptyspots);  { wait for a space }
  wait (access);  { wait for access }
  ENTER (VALUE);
```

Figure 11.3
Two processes using
a semaphore to syn-
chronize access to a
critical region

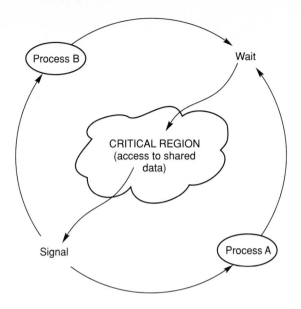

```
       signal (access); { relinquish access }
       signal (fullspots); { increase filled spaces }
       end loop
     end producer;

   process consumer;
     loop
     wait (fullspots);   { make sure it's not empty }
     wait (access);   { wait for access }
     REMOVE (VALUE);
     signal (access); { relinquish access }
     signal (emptyspots); { increase empty spaces }
     end loop
   end consumer;
```

The semaphore fullspots records the number of filled locations in the
buffer. It causes the consumer process to be queued to wait for a buffer
entry if it is currently empty. The semaphore emptyspots stores the number
of empty spaces in the buffer. It causes the producer process to be queued
to wait for an empty space in the buffer if it is currently filled. These two
semaphores are used in exactly the same way that the two SIGNAL type
variables of the same names were used in the Modula-2 coroutine example:
The access semaphore ensures mutually exclusive access to the buffer.
Note that there may be more than one producer and more than one consumer.

ALGOL 68 includes a data type, **sema**, that implements the kind of semaphores used in this example. However, they are used only to achieve
cooperation among statements or blocks that are executed concurrently.

ALGOL 68 does not provide facilities for concurrent execution of program units. Instead of **wait** and **signal**, the ALGOL 68 operations are named **down** and **up**.

11.3.2.3   Evaluation of Semaphores

Semaphores used to provide cooperation synchronization suffer the same problems faced by the SIGNAL type variables in Modula-2. Similar problems arise with using semaphores for competition synchronization. Leaving out the **wait** (access) statement in either process can cause insecure access to the buffer. Leaving out the **signal** (access) statement in either process results in deadlock. These are competition synchronization failures. Lastly, semaphores cannot prevent accesses to shared data structures that are inadvertently placed outside the protected critical regions.

11.3.3   Monitors

11.3.3.1   Monitor Design Concepts

One relatively obvious solution, in retrospect, to some of the problems of semaphores in a concurrent environment is to encapsulate shared data structures with their operations and hide their representations—that is, make shared data structures abstract data types. This solution allows the problem of competition to be solved without semaphores, by transferring responsibility for synchronization to the operating system.

When the concepts of data abstraction were being formulated, the people involved in that effort applied the same concepts to shared data in concurrent programming environments to produce monitors. According to Per Brinch Hansen (Brinch Hansen, 1977, page xvi), Edsger Dijkstra suggested in 1971 that all synchronization operations on shared data be gathered into a single program unit. Brinch Hansen formalized this concept in the environment of operating systems (Brinch Hansen, 1973). The following year, Hoare named these structures monitors (Hoare, 1974).

11.3.3.2   Monitors in Concurrent Pascal

The first programming language to incorporate monitors was Concurrent Pascal (Brinch Hansen, 1975). Modula (Wirth, 1976), CSP/k (Holt et al., 1978), and Mesa (Mitchell et al., 1979) also provide monitors. The following discussion of monitors is based on their incarnation in Concurrent Pascal.

Concurrent Pascal is Wirth's Pascal with three important kinds of constructs added: classes from SIMULA 67, processes, and monitors. Our concern here is with the features that support concurrent programming: processes and monitors. Note that some of the concepts underlying the design of the

Modula-2 coroutine mechanism originated in the processes and monitors of Concurrent Pascal.

A Concurrent Pascal process has a syntactic form that is similar to that of a procedure, but the semantics is quite different. All processes are types, so they are defined in **type** statements of the form:

type process_name = **process** (formal parameters)
-- local declarations --
-- process body --
end

Because they are types, process definitions are merely templates for actual processes, and because variable declarations must be used to create processes, they are created statically. Declaring a variable to be of a process type creates the code for the process, but does nothing else. To cause the allocation of its local data and to begin its execution, an **init** statement is used, which includes actual parameters, as in:

init process_variable_name (actual parameters)

After execution of the **init**, the process remains in the execution state for the duration of the program, except when it is put to sleep by delayed access to the shared data in a monitor.

Before an example of a process can be of value, we must briefly discuss Concurrent Pascal monitors. Monitors are abstract data types for shared data resources. Their general form is:

type monitor_name = **monitor** (formal parameters)
-- declarations of shared variables --
-- definitions of local procedures --
-- definitions of exported procedures --
-- initialization code --
end

The exported procedures of a monitor are syntactically different from local procedures only in that they contain the reserved word **entry** in their **procedure** statements.

Like process types, monitor types are templates. The **init** statement, with actual parameters, is used to create instances of monitors. This causes dynamic allocation of storage for the variables of the process and execution of the initialization code. The lifetime of monitor variables, except those in monitor procedures, is from the time of the **init** until the program terminates. Their scope is only the monitor itself. The exported procedures of a monitor can be called by either processes or procedures in other monitors.

One of the most important features of monitors is that shared data is resident in the monitor rather than in any of the client program units. Thus, the programmer does not synchronize mutually exclusive access to shared data through the use of semaphores or other mechanisms. Because all accesses are resident in the monitor, monitor implementation can be made to guarantee synchronized access by simply allowing only one access at a time. Calls to monitor procedures are queued if the monitor is busy at the time of the call.

Although mutually exclusive access to shared data is intrinsic with a monitor, cooperation between processes is still the task of the programmer. In particular, the programmer must guarantee that a shared buffer does not underflow or overflow. For this task, Concurrent Pascal has a special data type, **queue**, and two operations on it, **delay** and **continue**. The queue type is a form of semaphore and the two operations are very similar to the send and signal semaphore operations.

A variable of queue type stores processes that are waiting to use a shared data structure. This waiting, as we saw, is caused by the need for cooperation synchronization: Either a process tries to place a value in a full storage structure, or a process tries to remove a value from an empty structure. The **delay** operation takes a queue type variable as a parameter. Its action is to place the process that calls it in the specified queue and remove its exclusive access rights to monitor data structures. The process that executes **delay** has its execution suspended. The monitor is then available to other processes. The **continue** operation also takes a queue type parameter. Its action is to disconnect from the monitor the process that calls it, thus freeing the monitor to access by other processes. It then examines the specified queue. If the queue contains a process, that process is removed and its execution, which had been suspended by a **delay** operation, is restarted.

A program containing four processes and a monitor that provides synchronized access to a concurrently shared buffer is shown in Figure 11.4.

Figure 11.4
A program using a monitor to control access to a shared buffer

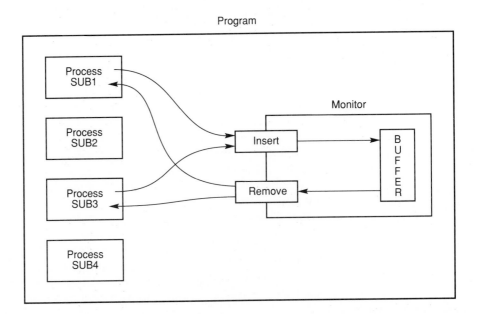

11.3.3.3 A Monitor Implementation of a Concurrently Accessed Shared Buffer

With the **queue** data type and the **delay** and **continue** operations, we can construct a monitor that controls a shared buffer, thus providing both competition and cooperation synchronization. In our example, the shared buffer is the same as that implemented in our Modula-2 coroutine example: a logically circular list of 100 integers.

```
type databuf =
  monitor
    const bufsize = 100;
    var buf : array [1..bufsize] of integer;
      next_in,
      next_out       : 1..bufsize;
      filled         : 0..bufsize;
      sender_q,
      receiver_q     : queue;

  procedure entry insert (item : integer);
    begin
    if filled = bufsize
      then delay (sender_q);
    buf[next_in] := item;
    next_in := (next_in mod bufsize) + 1;
    filled := filled + 1;
    continue (receiver_q)
    end;

  procedure entry remove (var item : integer);
    begin
    if filled = 0
      then delay (receiver_q);
    item := buf[next_out];
    next_out := (next_out mod bufsize) + 1;
    filled := filled - 1;
    continue (sender_q)
    end;

  begin
  filled := 0;
  next_in := 1;
  next_out := 1
  end;
```

An instance of type databuf is an abstraction of a particular kind of buffer for storing integers. Besides storing integers, a databuf type buffer coordinates the activities of adding and removing its values by concurrent processes. The integrity of this buffer is guaranteed by the mechanisms used to construct it. It is protected against underflow and overflow, and concurrent processes using it cannot destructively interfere with each other.

An example of declarations for the processes that can use the databuf monitor is as follows:

```
type producer = process (buffer : databuf);
   var stuff : integer;
   begin
     cycle
     -- produce stuff --
     buffer.insert (stuff)
     end
   end;

type consumer = process (buffer : databuf);
   var stored_value : integer;
   begin
   cycle
   buffer.remove (stored_value);
   -- consume stored_value --
   end
  end;
```

The type declarations of the monitor databuf and the two processes producer and consumer can be included in the declaration section of a program in which they are to be used, as in:

```
-- type declarations --
var new_producer : producer;
    new_consumer : consumer;
    new_buffer  : databuf;
begin
init new_buffer, new_producer (new_buffer),
            new_consumer (new_buffer)


   end;
```

This may appear a bit odd to the reader not familiar with concurrent programs, because it is not obvious how the program either begins or terminates. It begins when the init is executed, creating a buffer and two processes, and the processes begin execution at that time. It never ends.

11.3.3.4 Evaluation of Monitors

Monitors, as implemented in Concurrent Pascal, provide the same capabilities as the coroutines of Modula-2. In addition, they also provide for the mutually exclusive access to shared data structures that is required in a language that supports tasks, or processes as they are called in Concurrent Pascal. Monitors are a better way to provide competition synchronization than semaphores, primarily because of the problems of semaphores, as discussed in Section 11.3.2.3, which are not present with monitors. The use of **queue** type variables to provide cooperation synchronization is, however, subject to the same problems as semaphores used in other languages for this same purpose.

11.3.4 Concurrency through Message Passing

11.3.4.1 Design Concepts of the Message-Passing Model

The monitor construct is a dependable and safe method for providing competition synchronization for shared data access in concurrent systems. It is expected that truly distributed systems, which have multiple processors, each with its own memory, will become readily available in the near future. In such an environment, which may include no shared storage, the monitor concept is less useful. For these systems, cooperation among tasks can be achieved through message passing.

The first efforts to design languages that provide the capability for message passing among concurrent tasks were those of Brinch Hansen (1978) and Hoare (1978). The pioneer developers of message passing also developed methods for handling the problem of what to do when multiple simultaneous requests were made by other tasks to communicate with a given task. It was decided that some form of nondeterminism was required to provide a kind of fairness in choosing among those requests. This "fairness" can be defined in various ways, but in general it means that all requesters be provided an equal chance of communicating with a given task. Nondeterministic constructs for statement-level control, called guarded commands, were introduced by Dijkstra (1975). (Guarded commands are discussed in Chapter 6.) Guarded commands are the basis of the construct design for controlling message passing.

We now briefly explore the process of message passing between tasks. The basic concept of message passing is that tasks are independent program units that are often busy, and when busy are unwilling to be interrupted by other units. Suppose task A and task B are both in execution, and A wishes to send a message to B. Clearly, if B is busy, it is not desirable to allow another task to interrupt it. That would disrupt B's current processing. Furthermore, messages usually cause associated processing in the receiver, which may not be sensible if other processing is incomplete. The alternative is to provide a linguistic mechanism that allows a task to specify to other tasks when it is ready to receive messages. This is somewhat like an executive who instructs his or her secretary to hold all incoming calls until an important activity, perhaps another telephone conversation, is completed. Later, the executive tells the secretary he or she is now willing to receive one of the callers who has been placed on hold.

A task can be designed so it can suspend its execution at some point, either because it is idle, or because it needs information from another unit before it can continue, and is waiting to receive a message. This is like a person who is waiting for an important call. In some cases, there is nothing else to do but sit and wait. In this situation, if task A wants to send a message to B, and B is willing to receive a message, the message can be transmitted. This actual transmission is called a **rendezvous.** Note that a rendezvous can occur only if both the sender and receiver want it to happen. Note also that the information of the message can be transmitted in either or both directions.

Both cooperation and competition synchronization of tasks can be conveniently handled with the message-passing model.

11.3.4.2   The Ada Message-Passing Model

The Ada design for tasks is partially based on the work of Brinch Hansen and Hoare, in that message passing is the design basis and nondeterminism is used to choose among competing tasks.

The full Ada tasking model is complex, so our discussion of tasks must be limited. Our focus will be on the Ada version of the message-passing mechanism.

Monitors are passive entities that provide management services for the shared data they store. They provide their services, however, only when those services are requested. Ada tasks can be more active in nature. When used to manage shared data, they can be thought of as managers that can reside with the resource they manage. They have several mechanisms, some deterministic and some nondeterministic, that allow them to choose among competing requests for access to their resources.

11.3.4.2.1 Simple Ada Tasks   The form of Ada tasks is similar to that of Ada packages. There are two parts, a specification part and a body part, each with the same name. The interface of a task is its entry points, or locations where it can accept messages from other tasks. It is natural that these be listed in the specification part of a task. Because a rendezvous can involve an exchange of information, task entry points can include parameters, which must also be described in the specification part. In appearance, a task specification is very similar to the package specification for an abstract data type.

As an example of an Ada task specification, consider the following, which includes a single entry point named ENTRY_1:

```
task TASK_EXAMPLE is
   entry ENTRY_1 (ITEM :  in INTEGER) ;
   end TASK_EXAMPLE;
```

A task body must include some syntactic form of entry points that correspond to the **entry** clauses in that task's specification part. In the Ada language, these are specified by **accept** clauses, which are introduced by the **accept** reserved word. An **accept** clause is defined as the range of statements beginning with the **accept** reserved word and ending with the matching **end** reserved word. **Accept** clauses are themselves relatively simple, but their surroundings can make their semantics quite complex. A simple **accept** clause has the form:

> **accept** entry_name (formal parameters) **do**
>
> ...
>
> **end** entry_name;

The **accept** entry name matches the name in an **entry** clause in the associated task specification part. The (optional) parameters provide the means of communicating data between the caller and the called tasks. The statements between the **do** and the **end** define the operations that take place during the rendezvous. These statements are together called the **accept clause body.** During the actual rendezvous, the sender task is suspended. After we discuss how **accept** clauses are situated in tasks, we will discuss how the sender and receiver tasks can be put into concurrent execution, immediately after a rendezvous.

Ada tasks communicate with other tasks using the rendezvous mechanism. Whenever a task entry point, or **accept** clause, receives a message that it is not ready to accept, for whatever reason, the sender task must be suspended until the entry point is ready to accept the message. For this purpose, each **accept** clause in a task has a queue associated with it. The queue records a list of other tasks that have attempted to communicate with the associated entry point.

The following is the skeletal body of the task whose specification was given above:

```
task body TASK_EXAMPLE is
  begin
  loop
    accept ENTRY_1 (ITEM : in INTEGER) do
      . . .
      end ENTRY_1;
    end loop;
  end TASK_EXAMPLE;
```

The **accept** clause of this task body is the implementation of the entry named ENTRY_1 in the task specification. If the execution of TASK_EXAMPLE begins and reaches the ENTRY_1 **accept** clause before any other task sends a message to ENTRY_1, TASK_EXAMPLE is suspended. If another task sends a message to ENTRY_1 while TASK_EXAMPLE is suspended at its **accept**, a rendezvous occurs and the **accept** clause body is executed. Then, because of the loop, execution proceeds to the **accept** again. If no additional calling task has sent a message to ENTRY_1, execution is again suspended to wait for the next message.

A rendezvous can occur in two basic ways in this simple example. First, the receiver task, TASK_EXAMPLE, can be waiting for another task to attempt to send a message to the ENTRY_1 entry. When the message is sent, the rendezvous occurs. This is the situation described above. Second, the receiver task can be busy with one rendezvous, or with some other processing not associated with a rendezvous, when another task attempts to send a message to the same entry. In that case, the sender is suspended until the receiver is free to accept that message in a rendezvous. If several messages arrive while the receiver is busy, the senders are queued to wait their turn for a rendezvous.

The two rendezvous just described are illustrated with the time line diagrams in Figure 11.5.

A task need not have any entry points at all. Such tasks are called **actor tasks,** because they do not wait for a rendezvous in order to do useful work. Actor tasks can rendezvous with other tasks by sending them messages. In contrast to actor tasks, a task can have entry points but little or no code besides that associated with accepting messages, so it can only react to other tasks. Such a task is called a **server task.**

An Ada task that sends a message to another task must know the entry name in that task. However, the opposite is not true: A task entry need not know the name of the task from which it will accept messages. This asymmetry is in contrast to the design of the language known as CSP (Commu-

Figure 11.5
Two ways a rendezvous with TASK-EXAMPLE can occur

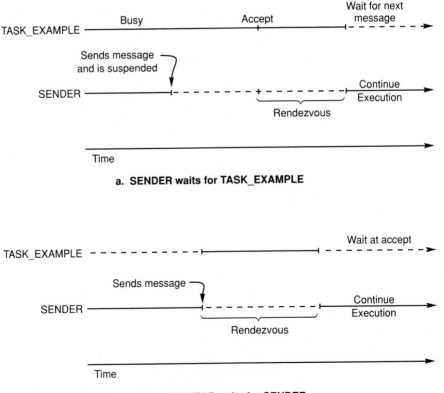

a. **SENDER waits for TASK_EXAMPLE**

b. **TASK_EXAMPLE waits for SENDER**

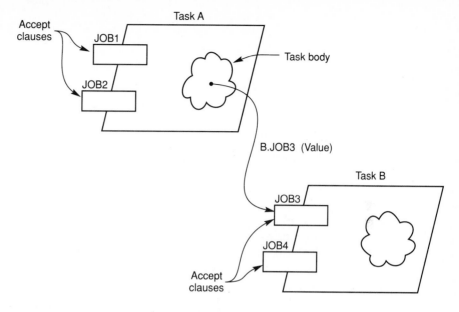

Figure 11.6
Graphical representation of a rendezvous caused by a message sent from task A to task B

nicating Sequential Processes) (Hoare, 1978). In CSP, which also uses the message-passing model of concurrency, tasks accept messages only from explicitly named tasks. The disadvantage of this is that libraries of tasks cannot be built for general use.

The usual graphical method of describing a rendezvous in which task A sends a message to task B is shown in Figure 11.6.

An Ada task that is defined the way TASK_EXAMPLE is defined above is statically allocated. Tasks can be dynamically allocated if they are defined as types, as in the following example:

```
task type BUFFER is
  entry DEPOSIT (STUFF : in INTEGER);
  entry REMOVE (STUFF : in INTEGER);
  end;
type BUF_PTR is access BUFFER;
. . .
BUF_PTR := new BUFFER;
```

11.3.4.2.2 More Complex Rendezvous Control   A task that has more than one entry point uses a **select** statement to enclose the entries, as in:

```
task body TASK_EXAMPLE is
  loop
    select
      accept ENTRY_1 (formal parameters) do
        . . .
      end ENTRY_1;
      . . .
```

```
         or
            accept ENTRY_2 (formal parameters) do
               . . .
            end ENTRY_2;
               . . .
         end select;
      end loop;
   end TASK_EXAMPLE;
```

In this task, there are two entry points, or **accept** clauses, each of which
has an associated queue. The action of the **select** is to examine the queues
associated with the two **accept** clauses. If one of them is empty, but the
other contains at least one waiting message, the associated **accept** clause
has a rendezvous with the task that sent the first message that was received.
If both **accept** clauses have empty queues, the **select** waits until one of
the entries is called. If both **accept** clauses have nonempty queues, one of
the associated **accept** clauses is nondeterministically chosen to have a rendezvous with one of its callers. The loop forces the **select** statement to be
executed repeatedly forever.

The **end** of the **accept** clause marks the end of the code that assigns or
references the formal parameters of the **accept** clause. The code, if there
is any, between an **accept** clause and the next **or** (or the **end select** if the
accept clause is the last one), is called the **extended accept clause.** The
extended **accept** clause is executed only after the associated (immediately
preceding) **accept** clause is executed. This execution of the extended **accept**
clause is not part of the rendezvous, and takes place in parallel with the
calling task. The sender is suspended during the rendezvous, but is restarted
when the end of the **accept** clause is reached. If an **accept** clause has no
formal parameters, the **do-end** is not required, and the **accept** clause can
consist entirely of an extended **accept** clause. The example in Section 11.3.4.3
includes extended **accept** clauses.

Each **accept** clause can have a guard attached, in the form of a **when**
clause, that can delay rendezvous. For example,

```
   when not EMPTY (BUFFER) =>
    accept STORE_NEW (NEW_VALUE) do
```

An **accept** clause with a **when** clause can be either open or closed. If the
Boolean expression of the **when** clause on an **accept** clause is currently true,
that **accept** clause is called **open**; if the Boolean expression is false, the
accept clause is called **closed.** An **accept** clause that does not have a guard
is always open. An open **accept** clause is available for rendezvous; a closed
accept clause cannot rendezvous.

Suppose there are several guarded **accept** clauses in a **select** clause.
Such an **accept** clause is usually placed in an infinite loop. The loop causes
the **select** clause to be executed repeatedly, with each **when** clause evaluated with each repetition. On each repetition a list of open **accept** clauses
is constructed. If exactly one of the open clauses has a nonempty queue, a

message from that queue is selected and a rendezvous takes place. If more than one of the open **accept** clauses have nonempty queues, one queue is chosen nondeterministically, a message is selected from that queue, and a rendezvous takes place. If the queues of all open clauses are empty, the task waits for a message to arrive at one of those **accept** clauses, at which time a rendezvous will occur. After each rendezvous, the **select** execution is repeated. If, on a particular repetition, every **accept** clause is closed, a run-time exception, or error, results. This possibility can be avoided, either by making sure one of the **when** clauses is always true, or by adding an **else** clause in the **select**.

An **else** clause can include any sequence of statements, except an **accept** clause. When an **else** clause execution completes, the loop causes the **select** to be executed again.

The features described so far provide for cooperation synchronization and communication between concurrent tasks. We next discuss how mutually exclusive access to shared data structures can be enforced.

If access to a data structure is to be controlled by a task, then mutually exclusive access can be achieved by declaring the data structure within a task. The semantics of task execution usually guarantees mutually exclusive access to the structure, because only one **accept** clause in the task can be active at a given time. The only exceptions to this occur when tasks are nested in procedures or other tasks. For example, if a task that defines a shared data structure has a nested task, that nested task can also access the shared structure, which could destroy the integrity of the data. Thus, tasks that are meant to control access to a shared data structure should not define procedures or tasks.

11.3.4.3 A Concurrently Accessed Shared Buffer Using Ada Tasks

The following is an example of an Ada task to provide synchronized access to a buffer. It is very similar in effect to our monitor example.

```
task BUF_TASK is
  entry INSERT (ITEM :  in integer);
  entry REMOVE (ITEM :  out integer);
end BUF_TASK;

task body BUF_TASK is
  BUFSIZE :  constant integer  := 100;
  BUF     :  array (1..BUFSIZE) of integer;
  FILLED :  integer range 0..BUFSIZE := 0;
  NEXT_IN,
  NEXT_OUT :  integer range 1..BUFSIZE := 1;
  begin
    loop
      select
```

```
        when FILLED < BUFSIZE =>
          accept INSERT (ITEM :  in integer)  do
            BUF (NEXT_IN) : = ITEM;
            end INSERT;
          NEXT_IN : = (NEXT_IN mod BUFSIZE) + 1;
          FILLED : = FILLED + 1;
      or
        when FILLED > 0 =>
          accept REMOVE (ITEM :  out integer)  do
            ITEM : = BUF (NEXT_OUT);
            end REMOVE;
          NEXT_OUT : = (NEXT_OUT mod BUFSIZE) + 1;
          FILLED : = FILLED - 1;
      end select;
    end loop;
  end BUF_TASK;
```

In this example, both **accept** clauses have extended **accept** clauses. These allow concurrent execution of BUF_TASK with the calling tasks.

The form of the tasks for the producer and consumer that could use the BUF_TASK task is the following:

```
task PRODUCER;
task CONSUMER;
task body PRODUCER is
  STUFF : integer;
  begin
    loop
    -- produce STUFF --
    BUF_TASK. INSERT (STUFF) ;
    end loop;
  end PRODUCER;

task body CONSUMER is
  STORED_VALUE : integer;
  begin
    loop
    BUF_TASK. REMOVE (STORED_VALUE) ;
    -- consume STORED_VALUE --
    end loop;
  end CONSUMER;
```

If access to a data structure is to be controlled and it is not encapsulated in a task, another means must be used to provide mutually exclusive access. One way is to build a semaphore task to use with the task that references the data structure. The semaphore task could have a BOOLEAN variable in which to store whether the structure currently belongs to some task. It could have two entries—one to capture the structure and one to release it. Then, if the user task called the capture entry before accessing the structure and the release entry after using the structure, the system would operate correctly. Because the semaphore would be controlled by entries in a task, its integrity would be ensured. Of course, this use of semaphores suffers all of the potential problems discussed in Section 11.3.2.3.

Like semaphores, monitors can be simulated with the Ada tasking capability. So, the Ada tasking model includes both semaphores and monitors.

11.3.4.4 Evaluation of the Message-Passing Model of Concurrency

In the absence of distributed processors with independent memories, the choice between monitors and message passing as means of providing competition synchronization is somewhat a matter of taste. Cooperation synchronization in message passing is less dependent than semaphores (which are required with monitors) on correct usage. Overall, therefore, message passing is slightly better, even in a shared memory environment.

For distributed systems, however, message passing is a clearly superior model for concurrency, because it naturally supports the concept of separate processes executing in parallel on separate processors.

11.3.5 Concurrency in PL/I

The earliest programming language to provide concurrency was PL/I. The IBM version of PL/I tied its concurrency very closely to the IBM operating system. All independent processes in the original IBM System/360 Operating System (OS) of the 1960s were called tasks.

To start the concurrent execution of a PL/I procedure, a normal procedure call statement with an added TASK clause is used, as in:

CALL SUB2 (actual parameters) TASK (event_variable)

Up to the keyword TASK, this is a typical procedure call. The keyword TASK indicates that SUB2's execution is to begin while the caller unit continues its execution. This split of control is sometimes called a **fork operation.** The event variable is used to monitor the progress of the secondary task. It can be tested as a logical variable, where true indicates that the task is still in execution and false indicates that it has completed its execution. The event variable can also be used in a statement that causes the caller to be suspended until the secondary task is completed, as in:

TASK (event_variable)

Event variables are much like semaphores, except that their use is restricted to signaling completion information between processes. Through event variables, the execution of concurrent tasks can be synchronized.

PL/I's facilities for support of concurrency are incomplete, because they provide no way to have mutually exclusive access to shared data. The data that is shared in PL/I is the local data in the calling unit, which is all available to the activated secondary tasks. This is closely related to dynamic scoping, where the called subprogram is executed in the environment of the caller. But in the presence of concurrent execution, this can be highly unreliable since it is impossible to ensure the integrity of the shared data. Because of the lack of communication between concurrent PL/I tasks, semaphores cannot be implemented in the shared data area.

SUMMARY

There are different categories of concurrency, two of which are of great concern to language design and evaluation: symmetric unit control and concurrent unit control. We use the phrase physical concurrency when multiple processors are actually used to execute concurrent units. If concurrent units are executed on a single processor, we term it logical concurrency. The underlying conceptual model of all concurrency can be referred to as logical concurrency.

Two of the primary facilities that concurrent languages must provide are mutually exclusive access to shared data structures (competition synchronization) and cooperation among tasks.

A coroutine provides quasi-concurrency in the same sense that multiprogramming operating systems provide the illusion of concurrency by concurrently executing several users' programs simultaneously. SIMULA 67 classes serve well as implementations of coroutines.

The Modula-2 language provides no facilities for symmetric or concurrent unit control. However, a module commonly provided with Modula-2 compilers provides a few low-level facilities for support of coroutines. These facilities can be used to build higher-level abstractions to implement coroutines.

Semaphores can be used to provide both competition and cooperation synchronization among concurrent tasks. Semaphores can cause serious problems when not used carefully.

Monitors are data abstractions that provide a natural way of allowing mutually exclusive access to data shared among concurrent tasks. They are included in several programming languages. Cooperation synchronization in languages with monitors must be provided with some form of semaphores.

Ada provides complex but effective constructs based on the message-passing model. The basic concurrent units are tasks, which communicate with each other through the rendezvous mechanism. A rendezvous is the action of a task of accepting a message sent by another task. Ada includes complicated methods of controlling the occurrences of rendezvous among tasks.

PL/I was the first high-level language to have any facilities for concurrency. It includes a limited form of semaphores that can provide cooperation synchronization.

BIBLIOGRAPHIC NOTES

The general subject of concurrency is discussed at great length in Andrews and Schneider (1983), Holt et al. (1978), and Ben-Ari (1982).

The first work on coroutines appears in Conway (1963). Coroutines are also discussed in Knuth (1968). The SIMULA 67 version of coroutines is described in Birtwistle et al. (1979). The implementation of coroutines in Modula-2 is discussed by Wirth (1983). Methods for using Modula-2 for logically concurrent control were developed by Sewry (1984a and 1984b).

The monitor concept is developed and its implementation in Concurrent Pascal described by Brinch Hansen (1977).

The early development of the message-passing model of concurrent unit control is discussed by Hoare (1978) and Brinch Hansen (1978). An in-depth discussion of the development of the Ada tasking model can be found in Ichbiah et al. (1979).

Discussions of many of the topics in this chapter can be found in Marcotty and Ledgard (1986), Pratt (1984), Ghezzi and Jazayeri (1987), and Horowitz (1984).

BIBLIOGRAPHY

Andrews, G.R., and F.B. Schneider. (1983) "Concepts and Notations for Concurrent Programming." *ACM Computing Surveys,* Vol. 15, No. 1, pp. 3–43.

Ben-Ari, M. (1982) *Principles of Concurrent Programming.* Prentice-Hall, Englewood Cliffs, NJ.

Birtwistle, G.M., O-J. Dahl, B. Myhrhaug, and K. Nygaard. (1979) *SIMULA Begin.* Van Nostrand Reinhold, New York.

Brinch Hansen, P. (1973) *Operating System Principles.* Prentice-Hall, Englewood Cliffs, NJ.

Brinch Hansen, P. (1975) "The Programming Language Concurrent-Pascal." *IEEE Transactions on Software Engineering,* Vol. 1, No. 2, pp. 199–207.

Brinch Hansen, P. (1977) *The Architecture of Concurrent Programs.* Prentice-Hall, Englewood Cliffs, NJ.

Brinch Hansen, P. (1978) "Distributed Processes: A Concurrent Programming Concept." *Commun. ACM,* Vol. 21, No. 11, pp. 934–941.

Conway, M.E. (1963) "Design of a Separable Transition-Diagram Compiler." *Commun. ACM,* Vol. 6, No. 7, pp. 396–408.

Dijkstra, E. W. (1968) "Cooperating Sequential Processes." In *Programming Languages,* ed. F. Genuys. Academic Press, New York.

Dijkstra, E.W. (1975) "Guarded Commands, Nondeterminancy, and Formal Derivation of Programs." *Commun. ACM,* Vol. 18, No. 8, pp. 453–457.

Ghezzi, C., and M. Jazayeri. (1987) *Programming Language Concepts.* 2d ed. Wiley, New York.

Hoare, C.A.R. (1974) "Monitors: An Operating System Structuring Concept." *Commun. ACM,* Vol. 17, No. 10, pp. 549–557.

Hoare, C.A.R. (1978) "Communicating Sequential Processes." *Commun. ACM*, Vol. 21, No. 8, pp. 666–677.

Holt, R.C., G.S. Graham, E.D. Lazowska, and M.A. Scott. (1978) *Structured Concurrent Programming with Operating Systems Applications*. Addison-Wesley, Reading, MA.

Horowitz, E. (1984) *Fundamentals of Programming Languages*, 2d ed. Computer Science Press, Rockville, MD.

Ichbiah, J.D., J.C. Heliard, O. Roubine, J.G.P. Barnes, B. Krieg-Brueckner, and B.A. Wichmann. (1979) "Rationale for the Design of the Ada Programming Language." *ACM SIGPLAN Notices*, Vol. 14, No. 6, Part B.

Knuth, D.E. (1968) *The Art of Computer Programming*. Vol. 1. Addison-Wesley, Reading, MA.

Marcotty, M., and H.F. Ledgard. (1986) *Programming Language Landscape*. 2d ed. SRA, Chicago.

Mitchell, J.G., W. Maybury, and R. Sweet. (1979) "Mesa Language Manual." Technical Report CSL-78-1, Xerox Palo Alto Research Center, Palo Alto, CA.

Pratt, T.W. (1984) *Programming Languages: Design and Implementation*. 2d ed. Prentice-Hall, Englewood Cliffs, NJ.

Sewry, D.A. (1984a) "Modula-2 Process Facilities." *ACM SIGPLAN Notices*, Vol. 19, No. 11, pp. 23–32.

Sewry, D.A. (1984b) "Modula-2 and the Monitor Concept." *ACM SIGPLAN Notices*, Vol. 19, No. 11, pp. 33–41.

Wirth, N. (1976) "Modula: A Language for Modular Multi-Programming," *Software—Practice and Experience*, Vol. 7, pp. 3–35.

Wirth, N. (1983) *Programming in Modula-2*. 2d, corrected ed. Springer-Verlag, New York.

PROBLEM SET

1. Describe two problems in which it is most natural to program the solution using coroutines.

2. Explain clearly why competition synchronization is not a problem in a programming environment that has symmetric unit control but no concurrency.

3. Compare the wait and signal operations on semaphores with the SEND and WAIT operations in our Modula-2 Processes module.

4. What is the best action a system can take when deadlock is detected?

5. Write an Ada task to implement semaphores.

6. Write an Ada task to manage a shared buffer such as the one in our example, but using the semaphore task from Problem 5.

7. Busy waiting is a method of having a task wait for a given event by continuously checking for that event to occur. What is the main problem with this approach?

8. In the producer–consumer example of Section 11.3.2.2, suppose that we incorrectly replaced the signal(access) in the consumer process with

`wait(access)`. What would be the result of this error on execution of the system?

9. From a book on VAX assembly language programming, determine what instructions the VAX architecture includes to support the construction of semaphores.

10. From a book on IBM PC (8088) assembly language programming, determine what instructions are provided to support the construction of semaphores.

11. Why do coroutines require local static storage?

12. How do semaphores differ from PL/I event variables?

*In short, exceptions and exception handling
mechanisms are not needed just to deal with errors.
They are needed, in general, as a means of
conveniently interleaving actions belonging to
different levels of abstraction.*

JOHN B. GOODENOUGH

Key Concepts

- Error and nonerror exceptions
- Exception handlers
- Static and dynamic binding of exceptions to handlers
- Exception propagation
- Execution continuation

12

EXCEPTION HANDLING

Contents

Some programming languages have facilities for users to handle run-time errors and other special events that occur during program execution. Designers of these languages face difficult decisions involving trade-offs between complexity and flexibility.

We first define the fundamental concepts of exception handling, and then describe some of the basic design alternatives. The design choices of three of the programming languages that include such facilities—PL/I, CLU, and Ada—are described and evaluated.

12.1   Introduction to Exception Handling

Most computer hardware systems are capable of detecting certain run-time error conditions, such as arithmetic overflow. Many programming languages are designed and implemented in such a way that the user program can neither detect nor attempt to deal with such errors. In these languages, the occurrence of such an error simply causes the program to be terminated and control to be transferred to the operating system. The typical operating system reaction to a run-time error is to print a diagnostic message, which may be very meaningful or highly cryptic, and then terminate the program.

One common exception to this situation is related to errors and conditions associated with input from and output to peripheral storage devices. For example, FORTRAN allows a READ statement to intercept input errors and end-of-file conditions, both of which are detected by the hardware. In both cases, the READ statement can specify a statement label of user code that deals with the condition. In the case of the end-of-file, it is clear that the condition is not always to be considered an error; rather, the condition often requires special handling, but seldom demands program termination. However, FORTRAN handles both errors and end-of-file with the same mechanism. Consider the following FORTRAN READ statement:

```
READ (UNIT=5, FMT=1000, ERR=100, END=999) WEIGHT
```

The ERR clause specifies that control is to be transferred to the statement labeled 100 if an error occurs in the read operation. The END clause specifies that control is to be transferred to the statement labeled 999 if the read operation encounters the end of the file.

12.1.1   Basic Concepts

We term both the errors detected by hardware (such as in the ERR clause of the FORTRAN READ) and also unusual conditions such as end-of-file (which are also detected by hardware) as exceptions. We further extend the concept of an exception to include errors or unusual conditions that are software-

in which they can be raised. The scope of a declared exception is usually the scope of the program unit that contains the declaration.

When a language includes built-in exceptions, several other design issues follow. For example, should the language run-time system provide default handlers for the built-in exceptions, or should the user be required to handle all exceptions. Another question is whether built-in exceptions can be explicitly raised by the user program. This can be convenient if there are software-detectable situations in which the user would like to use a built-in handler.

Finally, there is the question of whether exceptions, either built-in or user-defined, can be temporarily or permanently disabled. This question is somewhat philosophical, particularly in the case of built-in error conditions. For example, suppose a language has a built-in exception that is raised when a subscript range error occurs. Many believe that subscript range errors should always be detected, and therefore it should not be possible for the program to disable detection of these errors. Others argue that subscript range checking is too costly for production software.

12.1.3 Summary of Design Issues

1. How and where are exception handlers specified?
2. How is an exception occurrence bound to an exception handler?
3. Where does execution continue, if at all, after an exception handler completes its execution (the question of continuation)?
4. How are user-defined exceptions specified?
5. Should there be default exception handlers for programs that do not provide their own?
6. Can built-in exceptions be explicitly raised?
7. How can exceptions be disabled, if at all?

12.1.4 History

PL/I (ANSI, 1976) pioneered the concept of allowing user programs to be directly involved in exception handling. The language allows the user to write exception handlers for a long list of language-defined exceptions. Furthermore, PL/I introduced the concept of user-defined exceptions, which allow programs to create software-detected exceptions. These exceptions use the same mechanisms that are used for the built-in exceptions.

Since PL/I was designed, a substantial amount of work has been done to design alternative methods of exception handling. In particular, CLU (Liskov et al., 1981), Mesa (Mitchell et al., 1979), and Ada (Goos and Hartmanis, 1983) include exception-handling facilities. We are now prepared to examine the exception-handling facilities of several programming languages.

12.2 Exception Handling in PL/I

In still another pioneering effort, the designers of PL/I tackled the problem of providing users with the first linguistic mechanisms for exception handling. As was their style in other areas, they provided facilities that are very powerful and highly flexible. But, as is the case with other PL/I constructs, the exception-handling facilities are difficult to understand, implement, and use reliably.

Twenty-two standard conditions cause exceptions in the execution of a PL/I program. These range from arithemetic errors such as ZERODIVIDE to programming errors such as SUBSCRIPTRANGE.

12.2.1 Exception Handlers

User-written exception handlers have the form of executable code blocks. They can appear anywhere an executable statement can appear, and have the form:

        ON condition [SNAP] BEGIN;

                    . . .

                    END;

where condition is the name of the associated exception. In place of the block, the single keyword, SYSTEM, can be used, which specifies that the system-supplied handler is to be used. The optional keyword SNAP, when included, specifies that the dynamic chain of the program at the time the exception was raised is to be printed when the exception occurs. This provides the traceback information that allows the programmer to determine how execution got to the point of the exception. Such information is an aid to debugging.

The referencing environment of a PL/I exception handler is that of the code in which it is embedded. Because exception handlers do not have parameters, it is common to place handlers near the places where their exceptions are likely to be raised.

12.2.2 Binding Exceptions to Handlers

The binding of exceptions to handlers in PL/I is dynamic. The ON statement specifies the binding of an exception to an exception handler. Since it is executable, its position in the program has a critical impact on its effect. If ON were a declarative statement, there could be only one per exception per block. In fact, however, there can be more than one ON statement for a given exception, even within the same block. The ON binding stays in effect until either a new ON statement for the same exception is executed, or the block in which it occurs is exited.

12.2.3 Continuation

As stated in Section 12.1, another important design problem is deciding where execution is to continue, if at all, after an exception handler has completed its execution. In PL/I, different built-in exception handlers provide different actions. For some exceptions, execution returns to the statement that caused the exception; other conditions cause program termination. User-written handlers can go to any part of the program they wish after handling an exception, but there is no mechanism that provides the address of the statement that caused the exception, so it is often impossible to return to it. The choice between the two actions in system handlers was made on the basis of whether it was deemed possible for a handler to fix the cause of the problem and continue successfully. In some cases, such as some arithmetic errors, it was believed that successful continued processing was not possible. In other cases, such as the CONVERSION exception (for errors in converting strings to numerics), it was thought possible to recover, so control returns to the statement that caused the exception after the handler completes its execution. The PL/I design for continuation is often confusing for program readers and writers alike.

12.2.4 Other Design Choices

User-defined exceptions are created in PL/I programs by using a simple declaration, whose form is:

CONDITION exception-name

All built-in exceptions have built-in handlers. These handlers can be preempted by user-written exception handlers. User-defined exceptions must be raised explicitly, which is done with a statement of the form:

SIGNAL CONDITION (exception_name)

Any condition can be explicitly raised with a SIGNAL statement, although the built-in exceptions are normally raised implicitly by hardware or software conditions. A SIGNAL of an exception that is currently disabled does nothing.

Built-in exceptions are divided into three categories: (1) those that are always enabled, (2) those that are enabled by default but can be disabled by user code, and (3) those that are disabled by default but can be enabled by user code.

The process of enabling and disabling conditions is accomplished by prefixing a statement, block, or procedure with the condition name or names, as in:

```
(SUBSCRIPTRANGE, NOOVERFLOW):
    BEGIN;
    . . .
    END;
```

In this case, the SUBSCRIPTRANGE exception is enabled and the OVERFLOW exception is disabled. The prefix NO can be attached to any condition that is not permanently enabled in order to disable it.

12.2.5 An Example

The following example program illustrates two simple but common uses of exception handlers in PL/I. The program computes and prints a distribution of input grades by using an array of counters. Invalid input grades are detected by trapping indexing errors. This trapping occurs when the index computed from a bad grade is used as a subscript in a reference to the frequency array. The special case of a grade of 100 is also handled in the exception handler for invalid input data.

```
GRADE_DISTRIBUTION: PROCEDURE OPTIONS (MAIN);
 DECLARE FREQ(1:10) FIXED INIT ((10) 0),
          NEW_GRADE FIXED,
          LIMIT_1 FIXED,
          LIMIT_2 FIXED,
          INDEX FIXED;
/* Exception Handlers */
 ON ENDFILE (SYSIN) GOTO FINISH;
 ON SUBSCRIPTRANGE
   BEGIN;
   IF NEW_GRADE = 100
     THEN FREQ(10) = FREQ(10) + 1;
     ELSE
       DO;
       PUT LIST ('INPUT GRADE: ' || NEW_GRADE ||
                        'NOT IN RANGE') SKIP;
       GOTO INPUT_LOOP;
       END;
     END;
   /* Main program body */
   INPUT_LOOP:
   DO;
   GET LIST (NEW_GRADE);
```

```
      INDEX = NEW_GRADE / 10 + 1;
      (SUBSCRIPTRANGE) :
      FREQ (INDEX) = FREQ (INDEX) + 1;
      END INPUT_LOOP;

   FINISH:
    PUT LIST ('  LIMITS   FREQUENCY') SKIP(2);
      DO INDEX = 0 TO 9;
      LIMIT_1 = 10 * INDEX;
      LIMIT_2 = LIMIT_1 + 9;
      IF INDEX = 9
        THEN LIMIT_2 = 100;
      PUT LIST (LIMIT_1, LIMIT_2, FREQ(INDEX+1));
      END;
   END GRADE_DISTRIBUTION;
```

This program anticipates that we wish to have three different events trigger exception handling. Among these three, only one is an error; the other two are simply signals that something special has happened. In one case, it is a grade of 100; in the other, the end of the input data has been reached.

Notice that the handler for the SUBSCRIPTRANGE exception allows execution to continue for illegal grades, even though the built-in handler for that exception would cause program termination.

12.2.6 Evaluation

In summary, PL/I offers a powerful and flexible facility for exception detection and handling. The high level of flexibility, however, is not without cost. One of the primary problems with PL/I's exception-handling design is the dynamic binding of exceptions to handlers.

The dynamic nature of this binding causes a problem in writability and readability that is related to the problems of dynamic scoping. Indeed, it is the identical problem: The scope of the exception handler is dynamic, so it is very difficult to determine from a program listing which binding is in effect at any given point in the program. Because of dynamic binding, it is easy to have a handler unintentionally used for an exception that is in fact far from the exception, and also completely inappropriate for that exception in that situation. For example, consider the following simple code segment:

```
   ON SUBSCRIPTRANGE
     BEGIN;
     PUT LIST ('ERROR - BAD SUBSCRIPT ARRAY SUBSUM');
     GO TO FIXIT;
     END;
   . . .
```

```
        ON  SUBSCRIPTRANGE
          BEGIN;
          PUT LIST ('ERROR - THIRD SUBSCRIPT IN BLK IS BAD');
          GO TO QUIT;
          END;
        . . .
   LABEL1;
        . . .
        BLK(I, J, K) = SUM;
        . . .
```

If the code between the two handlers for the exception SUBSCRIPTRANGE happened to include a GO TO LABEL1, then the first handler would be executed if the exception was raised by the assignment to BLK. This would enact the wrong handler, causing at the very least a good deal of confusion for the user.

Another serious problem is posed by the flexibility of the continuation rules of PL/I exceptions. They are difficult to implement, harmful to readability in the same way that the goto is, and are also difficult to learn to use effectively.

Some of the built-in PL/I conditions that can be detected and handled are very useful. For example, the CHECK exception has a parameter that can be an identifier, a label, or a procedure name. If it is an identifier, the CHECK exception is raised every time an assignment is made to the specified variable. If it is a label or procedure name, the exception is raised every time the label is reached or the procedure is entered. Thus, the CHECK condition provided **watch** and **trace** facilities long before symbolic debuggers had been devised.

12.3 Exception Handling in CLU

Because PL/I's mechanisms for exception handling were thought to be too complex, they were not copied by other language designers. A more restricted model was proposed in 1975 by Goodenough (1975) in which exception handlers are statically associated with exceptions. An even more constrained model was designed into the CLU language in the middle 1970s (Liskov et al., 1981).

12.3.1 Exception Handlers

The CLU designer's view was that exceptions are raised in procedures and are normally handled in the calling unit. Therefore, a procedure definition, say sub1, includes exception handlers for those exceptions that can be raised in the procedures called by sub1.

Exception handlers can be attached to any statement in a CLU procedure. When attached to a statement, they handle only exceptions raised by subprograms called by that statement. The general form of an exception handler is:

statement **except** handler-list **end**

Because the placement of handlers on individual statements can reduce code readability, the handlers are often collected at the end of the procedure. In fact, they are usually placed at locations other than the end only if two or more handlers are supplied for the same exception.

The form of the exception handler list is:

when exception_name_1 (parameters): statement_1

. . .

when exception_name_n (parameters): statement_n

The parameters are used to pass information about the exception to the handler.

12.3.2 Bindings of Exceptions to Handlers

Exception handlers are statically bound to exceptions in CLU. If a statement calls a procedure that raises an exception, but that statement has no attached handler for that exception, then the exception is propagated to progressively larger static scopes within the procedure. If no handler is found in the procedure, the built-in default exception **failure** is raised and control returns to the caller. **failure** is the only exception that is implicitly propagated.

The **failure** exception is always handled by the system. If **failure** is raised by the lack of a handler for an exception, its handler prints the name of the unhandled exception. If it is raised explicitly, which is possible, the handler prints a message passed through the raising statement, which is discussed in Section 12.3.4. In both cases, program execution is terminated.

12.3.3 Continuations

CLU procedures that raise exceptions are normally terminated. If a handler is found in the calling program unit, it is executed. After handler execution, control simply flows to the statement following the statement to which the handler is attached. Because handlers are usually at the ends of procedures, continuation is usually to the caller of the caller of the procedure that raised the exception.

An exception can be handled locally in the procedure that raises it. To clearly illustrate that an exception is to be handled locally, it is raised with a different statement, **exit**, which has the form:

exit exception_name

The **exit** statement is similar to an unconditional branch statement, transferring control to the named exception handler. CLU has no goto statement.

The following example illustrates the use of **exit** and multiple handlers for the same exception. The block has separate overflow handlers for two occurrences of integer division:

```
begin
  a := b / c
    except when overflow:
      . . .
      exit done
    end
  b := d / e
    except when overflow:
      . . .
      exit done
    end
  . . .
end % end of block
  except when done:
    . . .
  end
```

Both handlers for the overflow exception raise the local exception, done. In both cases, the done handler is executed.

12.3.4 Other Design Choices

A procedure definition can include a list of exceptions that the procedure may raise (to its callers). These are simply listed at the top of the procedure definition, as in:

```
procedure_name = proc (formal parameters)
                    signals (exception_1 (parameters),
                              . . .
                              exception_n (parameters))
  -- procedure body --
  end procedure_name
```

Note that exceptions can have parameters, which are sent to the handlers.

Except for **failure**, CLU does not include default exception handlers; therefore, most handlers must be provided by the user.

CLU exceptions can be explicitly raised with the **signal** statement, which is syntactically somewhat like a procedure call, and includes optional parameters that can be used to pass information to the handler. Handlers can themselves raise exceptions. A handler can use this capability to reraise an exception that is propagated to it, thereby passing to a higher level in the dynamic chain the problem of handling an exception.

Because the designers thought that one could rarely guarantee that an exception would not occur, CLU does not include a mechanism for disabling an exception condition.

12.3.5 An Example

The following complete procedure example, which appears in Liskov and Snyder (1979), shows the form and use of the CLU exception-handling mechanisms. The purpose of this procedure is to get an integer from an input file. To do this, it uses another procedure, get_field, to get a string of nonblank characters from the input file, and then another procedure, s2i, to convert the string representation of an integer to the corresponding integer value. Both get_field and s2i can raise exceptions that get_number can either handle or pass on to its caller.

```
get_number = proc (s: stream) returns (int)
              signals (end_of_file,
                          unrepresentable_integer (string),
                          bad_format (string))
      field: string := get_field (s)
        except when end_of_file:
                  signal end_of_file
        end
      return (s2i (field))
        except when unrepresentable_integer:
                  signal unrepresentable_integer (field)
               when bad_format, invalid_character (*):
                  signal bad_format (field)
        end % end of exception clause
      end get_number
```

The definition statements for get_field and s2i are:

```
get_field = proc (s: stream) returns (string)
                              signals (end_of_file)
s2i = proc (s: string) returns (int)
                    signals (invalid_character (char),
                             bad_format,
                             unrepresentable_integer)
```

The get_field procedure can raise but one exception, end_of_file, which is simply reraised by the **signal** statement in the handler attached to the call to get_field in get_number. The s2i procedure can raise three different exceptions: unrepresentable_integer, which means the integer gotten from the string was too large to be represented in the form of an integer; bad_format, which means that there was more that one minus sign, or a minus sign followed a digit; or `invalid_character`, which means the string contained a character that was neither a digit nor a minus sign (plus signs are not allowed).

The handler in `get_number` for the `bad_format` and `invalid_character` exceptions, which can be raised in `s2i`, uses the * parameter form to indicate that the two either have no parameters or parameters that do not have the same names among the exception conditions; in either case, none of the parameters are used in the handler. This may seem to be odd syntax, but it is quite appropriate. It specifies that the parameters are not important, either in number or name. Both of these exceptions are propagated to the caller as the single exception, `bad_format`.

12.3.6 Evaluation

CLU's exception-handling design has neither of the main difficulties of PL/I—that is, dynamic binding of handlers to exceptions and continued execution nearly anywhere after an exception has been handled.

CLU's static binding of exceptions to handlers is a great advantage over the dynamic binding of PL/I. A program reader can easily determine the exception bindings in a CLU program, whereas that can be extremely difficult in a PL/I program.

12.4 Exception Handling in Ada

The facilities in Ada for exception handling are partially based on those of CLU.

The Ada language includes five built-in exceptions, which are actually categories of exceptions. For example, the exception CONSTRAINT_ERROR is raised when an array subscript is out of range, when there is a range error in a numeric variable with a range restriction, when a reference is made to a record field that is not present in a discriminated union, and in a few additional situations.

12.4.1 Exception Handlers

Ada exception handlers are usually local to the code in which the exception can be raised. Because this provides them with the same referencing environment, parameters for handlers are not necessary and are not allowed.

Exception handlers have the general form:

```
when exception_choice { | exception_choice} =>
    statement_sequence
```

where exception_choice has the form:

exception_name ¦ **others**

The exception name indicates the particular exception or exceptions that this handler is meant to handle. The statement sequence is the handler body. The reserved word **others** indicates that this handler is meant to handle exceptions not named elsewhere locally, or exceptions that have propagated to this location, which is outside the scope of the original exception. We discuss the propagation of exceptions in the next section.

Exception handlers can be included in blocks, or in the bodies of subprograms, packages, or tasks. Regardless of the block or unit in which they appear, handlers are gathered together in an **exception** clause, which must be placed at the end of the block or unit. For example, the usual form of an exception clause is shown in the following:

```
begin
   -- the block or unit body --
exception
   when exception_name =>
      -- first handler --
   when exception_name =>
      -- second handler --
   -- other handlers --
end;
```

Any statement that is legitimate in the block or unit in which the handler is placed is also legal in the handler.

12.4.2 Binding Exceptions to Handlers

When the block or unit that can raise the exception includes a handler for that exception, the exception is (statically) bound to that handler. If an exception is raised in a block or unit that does not have a handler for that particular exception, the exception is propagated to some other block or unit. The way in which exceptions are propagated depends on the program entity in which the exception occurs.

When an exception is raised in a procedure, whether in the elaboration of its declarations or in the execution of its body, and the procedure has no handler for it, an exception is implicitly propagated to the calling program unit. The exception is reraised in that unit at the point of the call. This policy is reflective of the philosophy that exception propagation should trace back through the control path, not through static ancestors.

If the calling unit to which an exception has been propagated also has no handler for the exception, it is again propagated to that unit's caller. This continues, if necessary, to the main program. If an exception is propagated to the main unit and still does not have a handler, execution is terminated. This is distinctly different from the CLU design, in which only the system exception **failure** is implicitly propagated.

In a discussion of exception handling, Ada blocks can be considered to be parameterless procedures that are "called" by their parent blocks when execution control reaches their beginnings. When an exception is raised in a block, in either its declarations or executable statements, and the block has no handler for it, the exception is implicitly propagated to the next larger enclosing scope, which is the code that "called" it. The point at which the exception is reraised is just after the end of the block in which it occurred, which is its "return" point. In this case, the Ada design of statically binding an exception to a handler is identical to that of CLU.

When an exception is raised in a package body and the package body has no handler for the exception, an exception is implicitly propagated to the unit containing the package declaration. The exception is reraised in the declarative section of that enclosing scope. If the package happens to be a library unit (separately compiled), the program is terminated. Exceptions in package bodies are propagated to the declaring scope because packages are separately compiled units that do not have callers.

If an exception occurs in a task body, the task is immediately marked as being completed. A completed task is, in effect, terminated. If the exception has a local handler, that handler is executed. If not, the exception is not propagated. The control mechanism of a task is too complex to lend itself to a reasonable and simple answer to the question of where to propagate its unhandled exceptions.

Exceptions can also occur during the elaboration of the declarative sections of subprograms, blocks, packages, and tasks. For example, suppose that a function is called to initialize a variable in its declaration statement, as in:

```
procedure RIVER is
   . . .
   CURRENT_FLOW :  FLOAT  : =  GET_FLOW;
   . . .
begin
   . . .
end RIVER;
```

If the function GET_FLOW raises and propagates an exception to its caller, the exception is reraised in this declaration.

In the cases of procedures, packages, and blocks, exceptions that occur in declaration elaborations are propagated exactly as if the exception were raised in the code section. In the case of a task, the task is completed and the built-in exception, TASKING_ERROR, is raised at the point of activation for the task.

If an exception occurs in the specification part of a procedure, package, or task, the exception is propagated to the part of the program that contains the specification.

12.4.3   Continuation

In all of these cases, the block or unit that raises an exception, along with all units to which the exception was propagated but which did not handle it, is terminated. Control never returns implicitly to the raising block or unit after the exception is handled. Control simply continues after the exception clause, which is always at the end of a block or unit. This causes an immediate return to a higher level of control.

In the matter of deciding where execution would continue after exception handler execution was completed, the Ada design team had little choice, because the requirements specification (Department of Defense, 1980) clearly states that program entities that raise exceptions cannot be continued or resumed. However, in the case of a block, a statement can be retried after it raises an exception and that exception is handled. For example, suppose a statement that can raise an exception and a handler for that exception are both enclosed in a block, which is itself enclosed in a loop, as in the following coded segment:

```
for INDEX in 1..10 loop
  begin
  GET (TAPE_FILE, IN_RECORD);
  exit;
  exception
    when TAPE_INPUT_ERROR =>
      if INDEX < 10
        then BACK_SPACE (TAPE_FILE);
        else raise FATAL_TAPE_ERROR;
      end if;
  end;
end loop;
```

In this code, up to ten attempts are made to read a tape file. If the GET procedure propagates the TAPE_INPUT_ERROR exception to this call, that exception is handled in the block that contains the call. The handler simply backspaces the read pointer in the file. Then the block is exited, which causes control to go back to the top of the loop to repeat the GET. Only if the tape read fails ten times is an exception propagated, by the explicit **raise**, to a larger scope.

12.4.4   Other Design Choices

User-defined exceptions can be defined with the declaration:

exception_name_list : **exception**

Such exceptions are treated exactly as built-in exceptions, except that they must be raised explicitly.

There are default handlers for the built-in exceptions, all of which result in program termination.

Exceptions can be explicitly raised with the **raise** statement, which has the general form:

    raise [exception_name]

The only place a **raise** statement can appear without naming an exception is within an exception handler. In that case, it reraises the same exception that caused execution of the handler. This propagates the exception according to the rules stated above. A **raise** in an exception handler is useful when one wishes to print an error message when an exception is raised, but handle the exception elsewhere.

An Ada pragma is a directive to the compiler. Exception conditions can be disabled in Ada programs by use of the SUPPRESS pragma, which has the form:

    pragma SUPPRESS (exception_list)

and which can only appear in declaration sections. When it appears, all listed exceptions are ignored in the associated block or program unit of which the declaration section is a part. Explicit raises are not affected by SUPPRESS.

12.4.5   An Example

The following example has the same intent and use of exception handling as the PL/I program earlier in this chapter. It produces a distribution of input grades by using an array of counters for the ten categories. Illegal grades are detected by checking for invalid subscripts used in incrementing the selected counter.

```
with TEXT_IO; use TEXT_IO;
procedure GRADE_DISTRIBUTION is
 package INTEGER_TEXT_IO is new INTEGER_IO (INTEGER);
 use INTEGER_TEXT_IO;
 FREQ: array (1..10) of INTEGER;
 NEW_GRADE,
 INDEX,
 LIMIT_1,
 LIMIT_2 : INTEGER;
 begin
  loop
  GET (NEW_GRADE);
  INDEX := NEW_GRADE / 10 + 1;
   begin
   FREQ(INDEX) := FREQ(INDEX) + 1;
```

```
      exception
        when CONSTRAINT_ERROR =>
         if NEW_GRADE = 100
           then FREQ (10) := FREQ (10) + 1;
           else
             PUT ("ERROR -- new grade: ");
             PUT (NEW_GRADE) ;
             PUT (" is out of range");
             NEW_LINE;
         end if;
        end;
      end loop;
      exception
        when END_OF_FILE =>
         PUT ("Limits    Frequency");
         NEW_LINE; NEW_LINE;
         for INDEX in 0..9
           loop
           LIMIT_1 := 10 * INDEX;
           LIMIT_2 := LIMIT_1 + 9;
           if INDEX = 9
             then LIMIT_2 := 100;
           end if;
           PUT (LIMIT_1) ;
           PUT (LIMIT_2) ;
           PUT (FREQ (INDEX) ) ;
           NEW_LINE;
           end loop;
    end GRADE_DISTRIBUTION;
```

Notice that the code to handle invalid input grades is in its own local block. This allows the program to continue after such exceptions are handled, as in our earlier example involving a tape read.

12.4.6 Evaluation

As is the case in some other language constructs, Ada's design of exception handling represents something of a consensus of contemporary ideas on the subject. Many believe that it is superior to any previous design in a nonexperimental imperative language. It is doubtful, however, that this design is the ultimate one. Rather, one should expect that exception handling in programming languages will continue to evolve.

SUMMARY

Exception handling has been incorporated in few widely used languages, although many experimental languages designed since the middle 1970s have had such facilities.

PL/I has powerful and flexible exception-handling capabilities, but there are a number of difficulties with the design. Overall, PL/I exception handling is sometimes too complex to be easily used and understood. The dynamic binding of exceptions to their handlers is one of the major causes of these problems.

CLU includes a much more restricted form of exception handling than PL/I. One of the main features of CLU's design is that the binding of exceptions to exception handlers is static.

Ada provides extensive exception-handling facilities and a small but comprehensive collection of built-in exceptions. In this case, the handlers are attached to the program entities, although exceptions can be implicitly or explicitly propagated to other program entities if no local handler is available.

BIBLIOGRAPHIC NOTES

One of the most important papers on exception handling that is not connected with a particular programming language is the work by Goodenough (1975). The problems with the PL/I design for exception handling are covered in MacLaren (1977). The CLU exception-handling design is clearly described by Liskov and Snyder (1979). Exception-handling facilities of the Ada language are defined by Goos and Hartmanis (1983).

BIBLIOGRAPHY

ANSI. (1976) *American National Standard Programming Language PL/I.* (ANS X3.53-1976). American National Standards Institute, New York.

Department of Defense. (1980) "Requirements for High Order Programming Languages, STONEMAN." February.

Goodenough, J.B. (1975) "Exception Handling: Issues and Proposed Notation." *Commun. ACM*, Vol. 18, No. 12, pp. 683–696.

Goos, G., and J. Hartmanis. (1983) *The Programming Language Ada Reference Manual.* Springer-Verlag, New York.

Liskov, B.H., and A. Snyder. (1979) "Exception Handling in CLU." *IEEE Transactions on Software Engineering*, Vol. SE-5, No. 6, pp. 546–558.

Liskov, B.H., R. Atkinson, T. Bloom, E. Moss, J.C. Schaffert, R. Scheifler, and A. Snyder. (1981) *CLU Reference Manual.* Springer-Verlag, New York.

MacLaren, M.D. (1977) "Exception Handling in PL/I." *ACM SIGPLAN Notices*, Vol. 12, No. 3, pp. 101–104.

Mitchell, J.G., W. Maybury, and R. Sweet. (1979) *Mesa Language Manual* (Version 5.0). Xerox Research Center, Palo Alto, CA, CSL-79-3.

PROBLEM SET

1. What run-time errors or conditions, if any, can Pascal programs detect and handle?

2. From textbooks on the PL/I and Ada programming languages, look up the respective sets of built-in exceptions. Do a comparative evaluation of the two, considering both completeness and flexibility.

3. Write a CLU code segment that retries a call to a procedure, tape_read, that reads input from a tape drive and can raise the tape_read error exception.

4. Why does CLU need the built-in exception, **failure**, which is implicitly raised when no handler is found for some other exception, and Ada does not?

5. From *The Programming Language Ada Reference Manual* (Goos and Hartmanis, 1983), determine how exceptions that take place during rendezvous are handled.

6. In languages without exception-handling facilities, it is common to have most subprograms include an "error" parameter, which can be set to some value representing "OK" or some other value representing "error in procedure." What advantage does a linguistic exception-handling facility like that of CLU have over this method?

7. Obtain a textbook on COBOL and determine how exception handling is done in COBOL programs.

8. In a language without exception-handling facilities, one could send an error-handling procedure as a parameter to each procedure that can detect errors that must be handled. What disadvantages are there to this method?

9. Compare the methods suggested in Problems 6 and 8. Which do you think is better, and why?

10. Suppose you are writing an Ada procedure that has three alternate methods for accomplishing its requirements. Write a skeletal version of this procedure so that if the first alternative raises any exception, the second is tried, and if the second alternative raises any exception, the third is executed. Write the code as if the three methods were procedures named ALT1, ALT2, and ALT3.

Functional languages have had a small band of very
enthusiastic advocates for many years now. . . .
However, functional languages are now beginning to
attract a much wider interest and several
developments, not least the development of highly
parallel VLSI architectures, are promising to
translate the theoretical advantages of these
languages into practical reality.

J. DARLINGTON

Key Concepts

- Mathematical functions
- Functional forms
- Lambda notation
- Symbolic computation
- Conditional expressions
- Mapping functional forms
- Run-time code construction
- The functional argument problem
- The FP languages

13

FUNCTIONAL PROGRAMMING LANGUAGES

The first 12 chapters of this book have been primarily concerned with the imperative programming languages. This chapter is the first to focus on a category of nonimperative languages.

The high degree of similarity among the imperative languages arises in part from one of the common bases of their design: the von Neumann architecture, as discussed in Chapter 1. One can think of the imperative languages collectively as a progression of developments to improve the basic model, which was FORTRAN I. All have been designed to make efficient use of von Neumann architecture computers. Although the imperative style of programming has been found acceptable by most programmers, its heavy reliance on the underlying architecture is an unnecessary restriction on the process of software development.

Other bases for language design exist, many of them oriented more to particular programming paradigms than to efficient execution on a particular computer architecture. Thus far, however, the reduced efficiency in executing these languages has prevented them from dominating the software business.

The functional programming paradigm, which is based on mathematical functions and functional composition, is the design basis for one of the most important nonimperative styles of languages. This style of programming is supported by functional, or applicative, programming languages.

LISP began as a purely functional language, but soon acquired some important imperative features that increased its execution efficiency. It is still the most important of the functional languages, and is the only one to achieve widespread use.

The objective of this chapter is to introduce the concept, but not the process of functional programming, and also to describe one way in which a language can be designed to provide convenient facilities for functional programming. Our method is to discuss mathematical functions, functional programming, and then introduce a small subset of LISP to illustrate the functional programming style.

Sufficient material on LISP is included to allow the reader to write a few small, simple LISP programs. It is difficult to acquire an actual feel for functional programming without some actual programming experience, so that is strongly encouraged. Anything beyond the simplest programming, however, will require a good deal more information on LISP than is offered here.

13.1   Mathematical Functions

A mathematical function is a mapping of members of one set, called the domain set, to another set, called the range set. A function definition specifies the domain and range sets, either explicitly or implicitly, along with the mapping. Functions can be applied to a particular element of the domain set. Note that the domain set may be the cross-product of several sets. A function yields, or returns, an element of the range set.

One of the fundamental characteristics of mathematical functions is that the evaluation order of their mapping expressions is controlled by recursion and conditional expressions, rather than by the sequencing and iterative repetition that is common to the imperative programming languages.

13.1.1 Simple Functions

Function definitions are often written as a function name, followed by a list of parameters in parentheses, followed by the mapping. For example:

$$\lambda \text{ cube}(x) \equiv x * x * x, \qquad x \text{ a real number}$$

The domain and range sets are the real numbers. The symbol $\equiv$ is used to mean "is defined as." The parameter, x, can represent any member of the domain set, but is fixed to represent one specific element during evaluation of the function expression.

Function applications are specified by pairing the function name with a particular element of the domain set. The range element is obtained by evaluating the function mapping, which is an expression, with the domain element substituted for the occurrences of the parameter. For example, cube(2.0) yields the value 8.0.

It is not always necessary for functions to have names. Lambda notation, as devised by Alonzo Church (Church, 1941), provides a method for defining nameless functions. A lambda expression specifies both the parameter and the mapping of a function. The value of a lambda expression is the function itself. For example, consider:

$$(x)x * x * x$$

The parameter of a lambda expression is sometimes called a bound variable. Before evaluation, a parameter represents any member of the domain set, but during evaluation it is bound to a particular member. When a lambda expression is evaluated for a given parameter, the expression is said to be applied to that parameter. The mechanics of such an application are the same as for any function evaluation. Lambda expressions, like other function definitions, can have more than one parameter.

13.1.2 Functional Forms

Complex functions in mathematics are defined in terms of other functions. A higher-order function, or **functional form,** is one that either takes functions as parameters or yields a function as its result, or both. One common kind of functional form is function composition, which has two functional parameters and yields a function whose value is the first actual parameter function applied to the result of the second. Function composition is written as an expression, using ∘ as an operator, as in:

$$h \equiv f \circ g$$

For example, if

$$f(x) \equiv x + 2$$
$$g(x) \equiv 3 * x$$

then h is defined as:

$$h(x) \equiv f(g(x)) \quad \text{or} \quad h(x) \equiv (3 * x) + 2$$

Construction is a functional form that takes a list of functions as parameters. When applied to an argument, a construction applies each of its functional parameters to that argument and collects the results in a list or sequence.

Apply-to-all is a functional form that takes a single function as a parameter. If applied to a list of arguments, apply-to-all applies its functional parameter to each of the values in the list argument and collects the results in a list or sequence.

There are many other functional forms, but these examples should illustrate their nature.

13.2   Functional Programming Languages

The objective of the design of a functional programming language is to mimic mathematical functions to the greatest extent possible. This results in an approach to problem solving that is fundamentally different from methods used with imperative languages. In an imperative language, an expression is evaluated and the result is stored in a memory location, which is represented as a variable in a program. This necessary attention to memory cells results in a rather low-level programming methodology. A program in an assembly language often must also store the results of partial evaluations of expressions. For example, to evaluate:

$$(x + y) / (a - b)$$

the value of $(x + y)$ is evaluated first. That value must then be stored while $(a - b)$ is evaluated. To help alleviate this problem, the storage of intermediate results of expression evaluations in high-level languages are handled by the compiler. The storage for intermediate results is still required, however, but the details are hidden from the programmer.

A purely functional programming language does not use variables or assignment statements. This frees the programmer from concerns about the memory cells of the computer on which the program is executed. Programs are function definitions and function application specifications, and executions consist of evaluating the function applications. Futher, although functional languages are sometimes implemented with interpreters, they can also be compiled.

Complex functions are constructed from less complex functions, and so forth, until only primitive functions are involved. A functional language provides a set of primitive functions, a set of functional forms to construct complex functions, a function application operation, and some structure or structures for storing data. A well-defined functional language requires only a few primitive functions.

Imperative languages provide some support for functional programming. Most, for example, include some kind of function definition and enactment facilities. The most serious drawback to using an imperative language to do functional programming is that functions in imperative languages have strong restrictions on the types of values that can be returned. In many languages, such as FORTRAN and Pascal, only simple type values can be returned. More importantly, they cannot return a function. Such restrictions limit the kinds of functional forms that can be provided.

A number of functional programming languages have been developed. The oldest and most widely used is LISP. Studying functional languages through LISP is somewhat akin to studying the imperative languages through FORTRAN: LISP was the first functional language, but some now believe that, although it has steadily evolved over the last 25 years, it no longer represents the latest design concepts for functional languages. In addition, with the exception of the first version, all LISP dialects include imperative language features, such as variables, assignment statements, and iteration. Despite this and its somewhat odd form, however, LISP still represents well the fundamental concepts of functional programming, and is therefore worthy of study. Our discussion of the language is relatively brief, and does not touch on its imperative features.

To investigate LISP as a functional language, we first discuss its history and its fundamental features, and then see how it fulfills the needs of functional programming. Because LISP was designed to deal with data in a particular and unusual (for imperative language programmers) form, we also discuss the development of that form.

13.3 The Early Development of LISP

As was the case with other languages and language features, it is instructive to examine the origins of LISP to gain an appreciation of the factors that influenced the design decisions made during its development.

13.3.1   The Beginnings of Artificial Intelligence and List Processing

LISP was originally designed for the first artificial intelligence (AI) applications, so it was strongly influenced by the environment of the origins of that area. Interest in AI began to appear in the middle 1950s in a number of places. Some of this interest grew out of linguistics, some from psychology, and some from mathematics. Linguists were concerned with natural language processing. Psychologists were interested in modeling human information storage and retrieval, along with other fundamental processes of the brain. Mathematicians were interested in mechanizing certain intelligent processes such as theorem proving. All of these investigations arrived at the same conclusion: Some method must be developed to allow computers to process symbolic data in lists. At the time nearly all computation was on numeric data in arrays.

The concept of list processing was developed by Allen Newell, J.C. Shaw, and Herbert Simon. It was first published in a classic paper that describes one of the first AI programs, the Logical Theorist, and a language in which it could be implemented (Newell and Simon, 1956). The language, named IPL-I (Information Processing Language I), was never implemented. The next version, IPL-II, was implemented on a Rand Corporation Johnniac computer. Development of IPL continued until 1960, when the description of IPL-V was published (Newell and Tonge, 1960). The low level of the IPL languages prevented their widespread use. They were actually assembly languages for a hypothetical computer, implemented by interpreters, in which list-processing instructions were included. The fact that the first implementation was on the obscure Johnniac machine was another factor that kept the IPL languages from becoming popular.

The contributions of the IPL languages were in their list design and their demonstration that list processing was feasible and useful.

IBM became interested in AI in the middle 1950s, and chose theorem proving as a demonstration area. At the time, the FORTRAN project was still underway. The high cost (18 worker-years) of the FORTRAN I compiler convinced IBM that their list processing should be attached to FORTRAN, rather than in the form of a new language. Thus, the FORTRAN List Processing Language (FLPL) was designed and implemented as an extension to FORTRAN. FLPL was used to construct a theorem prover for plane geometry, which was then considered the easiest part of that area of AI.

13.3.2   The Beginnings of LISP

John McCarthy of MIT took a summer position at the IBM Information Research Department in 1958. His goal for the summer was to investigate symbolic computations and develop a set of requirements of doing such computations. As a pilot example problem area, he chose differentiation of algebraic expressions. From this study came a list of perceived language requirements. Among them were the control flow methods of mathematical functions: recursion and conditional expressions. The only available high-level language of the time, FORTRAN I, had neither of these.

Another requirement that grew from the symbolic differentiation investigation was the need for some kind of implicit erasure of abandoned lists. McCarthy simply would not allow his elegant algorithm for differentiation to be cluttered with explicit statements to place unused list structures back into a pool of available storage.

Because FLPL did not support recursion, conditional expressions, or implicit erasure, it was clear to McCarthy that a new language was required.

When McCarthy returned to MIT in the fall of 1958, he and Marvin Minsky formed the MIT AI Project, with funding from the Research Laboratory for Electronics. The first important effort of the project was to produce a system for list processing. It was to be initially used to implement a program proposed by McCarthy called the Advice Taker. This application became the impetus for the development of the list processing language, LISP. The first version of LISP is sometimes called pure LISP, because it is a purely functional language. In the following we describe the development of pure LISP.

13.3.3 Data Types and Structures

There are only two types of data objects in pure LISP: atoms and lists. They are not types in the sense that imperative languages have types. Atoms, which have the form of identifiers, are the symbols of LISP. Numeric constants are also considered atoms.

The concept of storing symbolic information in linked lists is natural, and was used in IPL-II. Such structures allow insertions and deletions at any point, which was then thought to be a necessary part of list processing. As it eventually developed, however, LISP rarely requires these operations.

Lists are specified by delimiting their elements with parentheses. The elements of simple lists are restricted to atoms, as in:

(A B C D)

Nested list structures are also specified by parentheses. For example, the list:

(A (B C) D (E (F G)))

is a list of four elements. The first is the atom A; the second is the sublist (B C); the third is the atom D; the fourth is the sublist (E (F G)), which has as its second element the sublist (F G).

Internally, lists are usually stored as single-linked list structures, in which each node has two pointers and represents an element. A node for an atom has its first pointer pointing to some representation of the atom, such as its symbol or numeric value. A node for a sublist element has its first pointer

Figure 13.1
Internal representa-
tion of two LISP lists

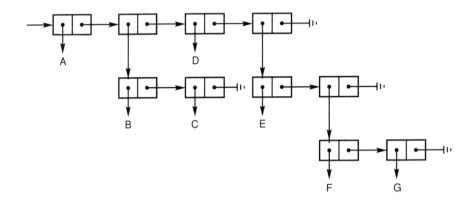

pointing to the first node of the sublist. In both cases, the second pointer
of a node points to the next element of the list. A list is referenced by a
pointer to its first element. The internal representations of the two lists
above are shown in Figure 13.1.

Note that the elements of a list are shown horizontally. The last element
of a list has no successor, so its link is NIL. Sublists are shown with the
same structure.

13.3.4   The First LISP Interpreter

The original intent was to have a notation for LISP programs that would be
as close to FORTRAN's as possible, with additions when necessary. This notation was called M-notation, for meta-notation. There was to be a compiler
that would translate programs written in M-notation into semantically
equivalent machine code programs for the IBM 704.

Early in the development of LISP, McCarthy decided to write a paper
that would promote list processing as a general symbolic processing method.
McCarthy believed that list processing could be used to study computability, which was usually studied using Turing machines. McCarthy thought
that the processing of symbolic lists was a more natural model of computation than Turing machines. One of the common requirements of such
study is to be able to prove certain computability characteristics of the whole
class of whatever model of computation is being used. In the case of the
Turing machine model, one can construct a universal Turing machine that
can mimic the operations of any other Turing machine. From this concept

came the idea of constructing a universal LISP function that could evaluate any other function in LISP.

The first requirement for the universal LISP function was a notation that allowed functions to be expressed in the same way data was expressed. The parenthesized list notation described in Section 13.3.3 had already been adopted for LISP data, so it was decided to invent conventions for function definitions and function calls that could also be expressed in list notation. Function calls were specified in a prefix list form called Cambridge Polish, as in:

(function_name argument_1 ... argument_n)

The lambda notation described in Section 13.1 was chosen to specify function definitions. It had to be modified, however, to allow the binding of functions to names so that functions could refer to themselves. The function name was simply added to the beginning of the lambda notation, and the whole thing was placed in a list, as in:

(function_name LAMBDA (arg_1, ... arg_n) map_expression)

LISP functions specified in this new notation were called S-expressions, for symbolic expressions. Eventually, all LISP structures, both data and code, were called S-expressions. An S-expression can be either a list or an atom.

McCarthy successfully developed a universal function that could evaluate any other function that was in the form of an S-expression. This function was named EVAL, and was itself in the form of an S-expression. One of the people in the AI Project, Steve Russell, noticed that an implementation of EVAL could serve as a LISP interpreter, and promptly constructed such an implementation.

There were several important results of this quick, easy, and unexpected implementation. First, all early LISP systems copied EVAL, and were therefore interpretive. Second, the definition of M-notation was never completed or implemented, so S-expressions became LISP's only notation. The use of the same notation for data and code has important consequences, one of which will be discussed in Section 13.5. Third, much of the original language design was effectively frozen, keeping certain odd features in the language, such as the conditional expression form and the use of 0 for both the NIL address and logical false.

Another feature of early LISP systems that was apparently somewhat accidental was the use of dynamic scoping. Functions were evaluated in the environments of their callers. No one at the time knew much about scoping, and it is doubtful that much thought was given to the choice. We further discuss the scoping rules of LISP in Section 13.6.

As stated earlier, EVAL is often implemented as an interactive interpreter. Such implementations produce a prompt, such as:

EVAL>

and then wait for the user to ask it to evaluate some function for which a definition has previously been given. When a function name and the appropriate parameters are typed in, EVAL applies the requested function to the parameter values, and prints the result of the application. Any parameters that are themselves function calls must be evaluated before the function is applied. These evaluations are identical to that of the other function, and are accomplished by recursive calls to EVAL. We discuss this process in the following section.

13.4 LISP as a Functional Language

As pointed out in Section 13.2, a functional programming language consists of a set of primitive functions, a set of functional forms, a function application operator, and some structures for storing data. The LISP function application operator is EVAL, and its data structures are atoms and lists. In the following sections we describe the primitive LISP functions. We also describe LISP's one functional form, and how others can be added through LISP's extensibility capability.

13.4.1 Primitive LISP Functions

Computer programs manipulate data whether the language is imperative or functional. Because lists are the primary data structure of LISP, the language must include primitives for manipulating lists. In particular, it must provide operations for selecting parts of a list, which in a sense dismantle the list, and an operation for constructing lists. Because the primary operations of functional languages are provided by functions, LISP includes primitive functions for these operations.

The first LISP primitive we describe is neither a selector nor a constructor. Rather, it is a utility function, required by the nature of the LISP function application operation, EVAL. EVAL first evaluates the parameters of the given function. This action is often necessary because the actual parameters in a function call are themselves function calls. In some cases, however, the parameters are data elements, either atoms or lists, rather than function references. When a parameter is not a function reference, it obviously should not be evaluated.

For example, suppose we have a function that has two parameters, an atom and a list, whose purpose is to determine whether the given atom is in the given list. Neither the atom nor the list should be evaluated; they are literal data to be examined. To avoid evaluating parameters, they are first given as parameters to the primitive function QUOTE, which simply returns them as is. For example,

```
(QUOTE A) returns A
(QUOTE (A B C)) returns (A B C)
```

In the remainder of this chapter, we will use the abbreviation of the call to QUOTE. As provided by most LISP systems, the S-expression parameter to QUOTE is preceded by an apostrophe symbol ('). Thus, instead of (QUOTE A), we will use 'A.

There are two primitive list selectors in LISP: CAR and CDR (read "coulder"). The CAR function returns the first element of a given list. The following examples illustrate CAR:

```
(CAR '(A B C)) returns A
(CAR '((A B) C D)) returns (A B)
(CAR 'A) is undefined (A is not a list)
(CAR '(A)) returns A
(CAR '()) is undefined (the list has no first element)
```

The CDR function returns the remainder of a given list after its CAR is removed:

```
(CDR '(A B C)) returns (B C)
(CDR '((A B) C D)) returns (C D)
(CDR 'A) is undefined
(CDR '(A)) returns () or NIL
(CDR '()) is undefined
```

Notice that an empty list can be written either as () or as NIL. NIL is, in effect, both an atom and a list.

The names of the CAR and CDR functions are peculiar at best. The origin of these names lies in the first implementation of LISP, which was on an IBM 704 computer. The 704's memory words had two fields that were named "decrement" and "address" fields, which were used in various operand addressing strategies. Each of these fields could store a machine memory address. The 704 also included two machine code instructions named CAR (contents of address register) and CDR (contents of decrement register), which extracted the associated fields. It was natural to use the two fields to store the two pointers of a list node, so that a memory word could neatly store a node. Using these conventions, the CAR and CDR instructions of the 704 provided efficient list selectors. The names carried over into the LISP primitives, and were never changed.

CONS is the LISP primitive list constructor. It builds a list from its two arguments, the first of which can be either an atom or a list; the second is usually a list. Consider the following examples:

```
(CONS 'A '(B C)) returns (A B C)
(CONS '(A B) '(C D)) returns ((A B) C D)
(CONS 'A '()) returns (A)
(CONS '() '(A B)) returns (() A B)
```

Note that CONS is, in a sense, the inverse of CAR and CDR. CAR and CDR take a list apart, and CONS constructs a new list from given list parts. The two parameters to CONS become the CAR and CDR of the new list.

There are three predicate functions among LISP's primitive functions: EQ, ATOM, and NULL. A predicate function is one that returns a Boolean value (either true or false). In LISP, the two Boolean values are T and NIL.

The EQ function takes two parameters and returns T if both are atoms and the two are the same, and NIL otherwise.

```
(EQ 'A 'A) returns T
(EQ 'A 'B) returns NIL
(EQ 'A '(A B)) returns NIL
(EQ '(A B) '(A B)) returns NIL
```

Lists are usually not duplicated in memory; that is, two equal lists are represented as two pointers to the same list representation. Because most contemporary LISP systems implement EQ as a pointer comparison, EQ will also work for list arguments, returning T for two equal lists. In these implementations, (EQ '(A B) '(A B)) returns T.

The ATOM predicate function returns T if its single argument is an atom and NIL otherwise, as in the following examples:

```
(ATOM '(X Y)) returns NIL
(ATOM 'X) returns T
```

The NULL function tests its parameter to determine whether it is the empty list, and returns T if it is. Consider the following examples:

```
(NULL '(A B)) returns NIL
(NULL '()) returns T
(NULL 'A) returns NIL
(NULL '(())) returns NIL
(NULL NIL) returns T
```

The second last case is NIL because the parameter is not the empty list. Rather, it is a list containing a single element, an empty list. The last case is T because NIL represents both an atom and the empty list.

Functional composition is the only primitive functional form provided by the original LISP. Functions are simply applied to the results of other function calls. Inner function calls, like outer function calls, are parenthesized. The following examples illustrate function composition:

```
(CDR (CDR '(A B C))) returns (C)
(CAR (CAR '((A B) B C))) returns A
(CDR (CAR '((A B C) D))) returns (B C)
(ATOM (CAR '(A B))) returns T
(NULL (CAR '(() B C))) returns T
(CONS (CAR '(A B)) (CDR '(A B))) returns (A B)
```

Notice that inner function names are not quoted; this is because they must be evaluated rather than treated as literal data. Additional functional forms can be constructed by the LISP system implementor and the user. We describe one of the more common of these in Section 13.4.5.

13.4.2   Functions for Constructing Functions

As stated earlier, LISP uses lambda notation in list form to define functions. For example, the lambda expression list:

```
(LAMBDA (lis) (CAR (CDR lis)))
```

is a function that returns the second element of its given parameter, which must be a list. This function can be applied in the same way that named functions are: by placing it in the beginning of a list that contains the actual parameters. For example, we could have:

```
((LAMBDA (lis) (CAR (CDR lis))) '(A B C))
```

which yields B. Notice that actual parameters to LISP functions that are defined as parameters of the lambda expression are not quoted; an example is the parameter lis in the call to CDR in the expression above. lis is called a *bound variable* within the lambda expression, and is not evaluated in the expression after being bound to an actual parameter value at the time the lambda expression is first evaluated.

It is often necessary to bind a function definition to a name, so that it can be easily applied to various arguments, and also so it can be recursive. This is done in LISP with the DEFINE function, whose one parameter is a list of "labeled" lambda expressions. The label on each lambda expression is bound to that expression and serves as its function name. The following example call to DEFINE has only a single element in its argument list.

```
(DEFINE (
   '(second (LAMBDA (lis)
      (CAR (CDR lis))
    ))
 ))
```

Once this function has been evaluated, the function second can be used, as in:

```
(second '(A B C))
```

which yields B.

13.4.3   Control Flow

The control flow mechanisms of LISP are modeled after those of mathematical functions. Control flow in mathematical function definitions is quite different from that in functions in imperative programming languages. Whereas functions in imperative languages are defined as collections of statements that may include several kinds of sequence control flow, mathematical functions do not have multiple statements, and use only recursion and conditional expressions for evaluation flow. For example, the factorial function can be defined with these two operations as:

$$f(n) = \begin{cases} 1 & \text{if } n = 0 \\ n * f(n-1) & \text{if } n > 0 \end{cases}$$

Note that a mathematical conditional expression is in the form of a list of pairs, each of which is a guarded expression. Each guarded expression has a predicate and an expression. The value of such a conditional expression is the value of the expression associated with the predicate that is true. Only one of the predicates is true for a given parameter or parameter list.

The LISP conditional expression is in the form of a call to a function, which in this case is named COND. COND is a slightly generalized version of the mathematical conditional expression that allows more than one predicate to be true at the same time. Because different mathematical conditional expressions have different numbers of parameters, COND does not require a fixed number of actual parameters. Each parameter to COND is a pair of S-expressions, in which the first is a predicate.

The semantics of COND is as follows: The predicates of the parameters are evaluated, one at a time, in order from the first, until one evaluates to true. The S-expression that is the right component of the parameter whose predicate is true is then evaluated and returned as the yield of COND.

As an example of a COND call, assume that LISP allows numeric atoms and has primitives for arithmetic (which all contemporary dialects do), and consider the following function for factorial:

```
(DEFINE (
   '(factorial (LAMBDA (n)
     (COND
        ((EQ n 0)  1)
        (T (TIMES n (factorial (SUB1 n))))
     )
   ))
))
```

TIMES is a built-in function that takes a variable number of numeric atoms as parameters and returns their product. SUB1 is also a built-in function. It returns a value one less than its numeric parameter. Note the close resemblance of the LISP factorial function to the mathematical version.

In most of its uses, COND has T as the predicate of its last parameter. If no parameter to COND has a predicate that evaluates to true, COND returns NIL. Notice the similarity between a COND and the multiple selection statement with an "otherwise" clause at the end, such as the Ada **case** statement.

13.4.4 Example LISP Functions

This section contains several examples of functional programs using LISP. These programs solve simple list-processing problems.

Consider the problem of membership of a given atom in a given simple list. A simple list is one without sublists. If the function is named member, it could be used as follows:

```
(member 'B '(A B C)) returns T
(member 'B '(A C D E)) returns NIL
```

Thinking in terms of iteration, the membership problem is simply to compare the given atom and the individual elements of the given list, one at a time in some order, until either a match is found or there are no more elements in the list. A similar process can be accomplished using recursion. The function can compare the given atom with the CAR of the list. If they match, the value T is returned. If they do not match, then the atom can only be found in the remainder of the list, so the function should call itself with the CDR of the list as the list parameter. In this process, there are two ways out of the recursion: either the list is empty on some call, in which case NIL is returned, or a match is found and T is returned.

Altogether, there are three cases that must be handled in the function: an empty input list, a match between the atom and the CAR of the list, or a mismatch between the atom and the CAR of the list, which causes the recursive call. These three are exactly the three parameters to COND, with the last being the default case, triggered by a T predicate. The complete function follows:

```
(DEFINE (
   '(member (LAMBDA (atm lis)
     (COND
        ((NULL lis) NIL)
        ((EQ atm (CAR lis)) T)
        (T (member atm (CDR lis)))
      )
   ))
))
```

This form is typical of simple LISP functions. LISP is a list-processing language, and the data in lists are usually processed recursively, one element at a time. The individual elements may be gotten by CAR, and the process is continued using recursion on the CDR of the list.

As another example, consider the problem of determining whether two given lists are equal. If the two lists are simple, the solution is relatively easy, although some unfamiliar techniques are involved. A predicate function for comparing simple lists is shown here:

```
(DEFINE (
  . '(equalsimp (LAMBDA (lis1 lis2)
     (COND
        ((NULL lis1) (NULL lis2))
        ((NULL lis2) NIL)
```

```
((EQ (CAR lis1)  (CAR lis2))
            (equalsimp (CDR lis1)  (CDR lis2)))
    (T NIL)
  )
 ))
))
```

The first case, which is handled by the first parameter to COND, is for when the first list parameter is the empty list. This can occur in an external call if the first list parameter is initially empty. Because a recursive call uses the CDRs of the two parameter lists as its parameters, the first list can be empty in such a call if the first list has had all of its elements removed by previous recursive calls. When the first list is empty, the second list must be checked to see if it is also empty. If so, they are equal, and NULL correctly returns T. If the second list is not empty, it was larger than the first list, and NIL should be returned, as it is by NULL.

The next case deals with the second list being empty when the first list is not. This situation occurs only when the second list is smaller than the first. Only the second list must be tested, because the first case catches all instances of the first list being empty.

The third case is the recursive step that tests for equality between corresponding elements in the two lists. It does this by comparing the CARs of the two nonempty lists. If they are equal, then the two lists are equal up to this point, so recursion is used on the CDRs of both. This case fails when two unequal atoms are found. When this occurs, we obviously do not want to continue, so the default case, which is last, takes effect, causing the functional value to be NIL without further comparisons.

Note that equalsimp expects lists as parameters, and does not operate correctly if either or both parameters are atoms.

The problem of comparing general lists is slightly more complex than this, because sublists must be traced completely in the comparison process. This is a situation where the power of recursion is uniquely appropriate, since the form of sublists is the same as that of the given lists. Any time the corresponding elements of the two given lists are lists, they are separated into their two parts, CAR and CDR, and recursion is used on them. This is a perfect example of the usefulness of the divide and conquer approach. If the corresponding elements of the two given lists are atoms, they can simply be compared using EQ.

The definition of the complete function follows:

```
(DEFINE (
  '(equal (LAMBDA (lis1 lis2)
    (COND
      ((ATOM lis1)  (EQ lis1 lis2))
      ((ATOM lis2)  NIL)
      ((equal (CAR lis1)  (CAR lis2))
                  (equal (CDR lis1)  (CDR lis2)))
```

```
            (T NIL)
          )
       ) )
    ) )
```

The first two cases of the COND handle the situation where either of the parameters is an atom, instead of a list. The third COND case is the most interesting. The predicate is a recursive call with the CARs of the lists as parameters. If this call returns T, then recursion is used again on the CDRs of the lists.

This definition of equal works on any pair of S-expressions, not just lists.

Another commonly needed list operation is that of constructing a new list that contains all of the elements of two given list arguments. This is usually implemented as a LISP function named append. It can be constructed by repeated use of CONS to place the elements of the first list argument into the second list argument. To clarify the action of append, consider the following examples:

```
(append '(A B) '(C D R)) returns (A B C D R)
(append '((A B) C) '(D (E F))) returns ((A B) C D ( E F)
```

The definition of append is:

```
(DEFINE (
  '(append (LAMBDA (lis1 lis2)
     (COND
        ((NULL lis1) lis2)
        (T (CONS (CAR lis1) (append (CDR Lis1) lis2)))
     )
  ) )
) )
```

13.4.5 Another Functional Form

Because of its ease of extensibility, LISP need not provide many primitive functional forms. Implementors and users can and have added their own. The most common functional forms added by implementors are variations of mathematical apply-to-all functional forms. The simplest of these is mapcar, which has two parameters, a function, and a list. mapcar applies the given function to each element of the given list, and returns a list of the results of these applications. A definition of a mapcar function is:

```
(DEFINE (
  '(mapcar (LAMBDA (fun lis)
     (COND
        ((NULL lis) ())
```

```
             (T  (CONS  (fun  (CAR  lis))
                               (mapcar  fun  (CDR  lis)))))
       )
     ))
   ))
```

Note the simple form of the LISP function mapcar, which expresses a complex functional form. This is testament to the great expressive power of LISP.

As an example of the use of mapcar, suppose we have a simple list of numeric elements named numlist and we want all of the elements cubed. We can accomplish this with:

```
(mapcar  (LAMBDA  (num)  (TIMES  num  num  num))  numlist)
```

If numlist contained (3 4 2 6), this call would return (27 64 8 216).

Note that the first parameter to mapcar is a LAMBDA expression. It defines the function that is to be applied to each element of the second parameter.

The paucity of functional forms in LISP can be viewed in at least two different ways. On the one hand, it is unsatisfactory to have only composition as a primitive functional form. On the other, it is good that LISP allows users to construct their own functional forms. Some users believe, however, that this kind of extensibility leads to chaos. They feel that the best functional language design should include a rich set of functional forms and disallow users from adding their own. It should be noted that this view is held by a minority of interested people.

FP is a family of purely functional languages designed by John Backus (Backus, 1978). Backus chose to give FP languages a rich set of functional forms and to not allow users to add more. A brief introduction to a few of the FP primitive functions and functional forms is given in Section 13.7.

13.5 LISP Functions That Build LISP Code

The fact that programs and data have the same structure can be exploited in constructing programs. Combined with access to the function EVAL, this fact allows user programs to construct other programs and immediately evaluate them.

One of the simplest examples of this process involves numeric atoms. Most LISP systems include a function for numeric atoms named PLUS, which takes any number of numeric atoms as arguments and returns their sum. For example, (PLUS 3 7 10 2) returns 22.

Our problem is as follows: Suppose that in a program we have a list of numeric atoms and need the sum. We cannot apply PLUS directly on the list, because PLUS can take only atomic parameters, not a list of numeric atoms. We could, of course, write a function that repeatedly adds the CAR of the list to the sum of its CDR, using recursion to go through the list. Such a function follows:

```
(DEFINE (
  'adder (LAMBDA (lis)
    (COND
      ((NULL lis) 0)
      (T (PLUS (CAR lis) (adder (CDR lis))))
    )
  ))
))
```

An alternative solution to the problem is to write a function that builds a call to PLUS with the proper parameter forms. This can be done by using CONS to, in effect, insert the atom PLUS into the list of numbers. This new list can then be submitted to EVAL for evaluation, as in:

```
(DEFINE (
  '(adder (LAMBDA (lis)
    (COND
      ((NULL lis) 0)
      (T (EVAL (CONS 'PLUS lis)))
    )
  ))
))
```

For example, the call:

```
(adder '(3 4 6))
```

causes adder to build the list:

```
(PLUS 3 4 6)
```

which is then submitted to EVAL, which invokes PLUS and returns the result, 13.

Note that complete functions can be built and evaluated by LISP programs.

13.6 The Functional Argument Problem

Until the late 1970s, most LISP systems were interpretive and implemented dynamic scoping, following the lead of the first LISP system, as discussed in Section 13.3.4. The disadvantages of dynamic scoping are discussed in Section 4.8.5.

When functions are sent as actual parameters in a language that uses dynamic scoping, some unusual and often unexpected results can occur. Consider the following scenario. Suppose that function P references a non-local variable X, and that P is sent as a parameter to function Q. The problem arises if Q happens to have another formal parameter, and it happens to be named X. When Q calls P, Q's parameter X will be used in P, rather than the X that was in the environment of P at the time Q was called. Two instances of this situation are shown and further explained with the following skeletal program:

```
(DEFINE (
  '(A (LAMBDA (...)
      ...  (CAR X)  ...
  ))

  '(B (LAMBDA (FUN X)
      ... FUN ...
  ))

  '(C (LAMBDA (X Z)
      ...  A ...
      ...  (B A Z)  ...
  ))
))
```

```
(C '(I J) '(K L M))
```

C's direct call to A causes A to reference the X that is a formal parameter in C, which is bound to the list (I J), so that the call (CAR X) in A yields I. Then C calls B, passing A and Z, the latter being bound to the list (K L M). Then B calls the passed function, A. This execution of A references the X that is the formal parameter in B, which is then bound to (K L M). So this time, (CAR X) in A yields K. This will likely be unexpected by the programmer and will yield odd and probably incorrect results.

As a cure for this problem, which is called the functional argument problem, or simply the funarg problem, a new function named FUNCTION was added to LISP's primitives. FUNCTION takes a function as a parameter and returns both the function and some representation of the current referencing environment (for example, a pointer into the stack). It is used on a function being sent as an actual parameter in order to provide that function with its proper referencing environment and to avoid the possibility of a later binding that would hide the reference to a variable that was in the environment of the sender.

In the example above, the call to B in C could be changed to:

```
(B (FUNCTION A) Z)
```

which would cause A to use C's referencing environment, so that both calls to A in this program would use the same X reference.

An alternative solution to the funarg problem would have been to simply change the semantics of LISP to use static scoping. This solution was rejected at the time because some programmers had become accustomed to dynamic scoping and there was a desire to maintain backward compatibility with earlier implementations of LISP.

Note that the use of FUNCTION does not provide static scoping in the same sense as in Pascal, where bindings of nonlocal references can be made at compile time. The binding of a nonlocal is still dynamic with FUNCTION; it is just earlier in execution time. In fact, the result of using FUNCTION is very similar to the effect of passing parameters by name. The address evaluation procedures for parameters passed by name are evaluated in the referencing environment of the caller, not that of the called procedure.

Recent dialects of LISP, such as Common LISP (Steele, 1984), abandon backward compatibility and adopt static scoping, which not only solves the funarg problem, but also slightly simplifies compilation. Furthermore, as argued in Chapter 4, programs in statically scoped languages are easier to read because the execution sequence does not determine nonlocal variable bindings.

The problem of choosing the correct environment for execution of a subprogram that has been passed as a parameter was discussed in Section 8.6. Recall that the static scoped languages employ a method comparable to that which results from the use of FUNCTION. That is, subprograms passed as parameters execute in the referencing environment of the subprogram that sent them as actual parameters. This is called **deep binding.** Passing a LISP function in the dynamic scoped versions of LISP without using FUNCTION results in **shallow binding.** Users of dynamically scoped LISP are thus given the choice between deep and shallow binding.

13.7 A Brief Look at FP

As was stated earlier, FP is a family of functional programming languages designed by John Backus (Backus, 1978). Member languages are distinguished by the set of functions and functional forms that they provide. Our purpose in discussing FP here is modest: to introduce the simple data types and a few of the functions and functional forms of the FP languages.

Like pure LISP, FP has only very simple data structures. In the case of FP, the structures are atoms, which are like those of LISP, and sequences. Sequences are delimited by pointed brackets, as in:

    <a, b, c, d>

The notation used for function application is

    f: x

in which f is a function and x is its argument.

There are fundamental FP functions for selecting sequence elements (FIRST, LAST, TAIL), for getting the length of a sequence (LENGTH), for building a list (CONS), and for rotating a sequence left or right (ROTL and ROTR, respectively). For example:

    LAST: <a, b, c> returns c
    LENGTH: <a, b, c> returns 3

ROTL: <a, b, c> returns <b, c, a>
CONS: <a, <b, c>> returns <a, b, c>

FP includes arithmetic functions, each of which takes a sequence of two numeric atoms as arguments and returns a numeric atom. For example:

+: <3, 7> returns 10

FP also included predicate functions for the usual relational operators, and also for ATOM and NULL, as in LISP, along with some other relatively simple operations.

In addition, there are functional forms for composition and apply-to-all, the mathematical functional forms discussed in Section 13.1. Composition has the form and definition:

$$(f \circ g): x \equiv f: (g: x)$$

For example,

(FIRST ∘ ROTR): <a, b, c> = FIRST: ROTR: <a, b, c>
                                        = FIRST: <c, a, b>
                                        = c

Apply-to-all, when applied to sequences, has the form and definition:

$$\alpha f: <x_1, x_2, \ldots, x_n> = <f: x_1, f: x_2, \ldots, f: x_n>$$

For example,

α−: <<5, 2>, <6, 3>, <2, 7>> = <3, 3, −5>

Another FP functional form is construction, in which a sequence of functions is applied to a single argument. The results are placed in a sequence. The construction functional form has the following form and definition:

$$[f_1, f_2, \ldots, f_n]: x = <f_1: x, f_2: x, \ldots, f_n: x>$$

For example,

[+, −, *]: <3, 5> = <8, −2, 15>

Many other functions and functional forms have been suggested by Backus, including functional forms for controlling execution order.

Note that the FP family does not include a single complete language; rather, it is a proposal for a new style of programming language.

13.8 Applications of Functional Languages

Over the past 35 years in the history of high-level programming languages, only a few functional languages have gained widespread use. Most prominent among these is LISP. In spite of its heavy use of the assignment statement, APL is also often considered a functional language, partly because of its functional forms.

APL has been used for a wide variety of applications, ranging from a hardware description language to management information systems. Because of the great difficulty in reading a typical APL program, its most natural place in contemporary computing is in the category of throwaway programming. With its powerful collection of array operations, it is an excellent vehicle for quick but dirty solutions to problems involving many array manipulations.

LISP is a versatile and powerful language. For its first 15 years it was thought of, mostly by nonusers, as a very strange language that was very costly to use. Indeed, it was common in the 1960s and early 1970s to think of two categories of languages, one containing LISP and one with all of the other programming languages.

As described in this chapter, LISP was developed for symbolic computation and list-processing applications, which lie mainly in the AI area of computing. In AI applications, LISP and its derivative languages are still the standard languages.

Within AI, a number of areas have been developed, primarily through the use of LISP. Although other kinds of languages can be used—primarily logic programming languages—most existing expert systems, for example, were developed in LISP. LISP also dominates in the areas of knowledge representation, machine learning, natural language processing, intelligent training systems, and the modeling of speech and vision.

Outside AI, LISP has also been successful. For example, the EMACS text editor is written in LISP, as is the symbolic mathematics system, MACSYMA, which does symbolic calculus, among other things. The LISP machine is a personal computer whose entire systems software is written in LISP. LISP has also been successfully used to construct experimental systems in a variety of application areas.

A collection of other functional languages, such as HOPE (Burstall et al., 1980), ML (Gordon et al., 1979), and FQL (Buneman and Frankel, 1979) have been used for a variety of both experimental and practical applications.

13.9 Evaluation of Functional Languages

A brief discussion of the advantages—some widely accepted and some only widely conjectured—of functional programming and functional programming languages is now in order.

It is natural to compare functional programming with programming in imperative languages. Because imperative languages are based directly on the von Neumann architecture, programmers using them must deal with the management of variables and assignment of values to them. The results of this are increased efficiency of execution but laborious construction of programs. In a functional language, the programmer need not be concerned with variables, because memory cells need not be abstracted into the language. One result of this is decreased efficiency of execution. Another result, however, is a higher level of programming, which should require less labor than programming in an imperative language. Many believe that this is the case and that it is a definite advantage of functional programming.

Functional languages can have a very simple syntactic structure. The list structure of LISP is an example. The syntax of the imperative languages is much more complex. The semantics of functional languages can also be simple in comparison with that of the imperative languages.

Concurrent execution in the imperative languages is difficult to design and difficult to use. For example, consider the tasking model of Ada, in which cooperation among concurrent tasks is the responsibility of the programmer. Functional programs can be executed by first translating them into graphs. These graphs can then be executed through a graph reduction process, which can be done with a great deal of concurrency that was not specified by the programmer. The graph representation naturally exposes many opportunities for concurrent execution. Cooperation synchronization in this process is not the concern of the programmer.

In an imperative language the programmer must make a static division of the program into its concurrent parts, which are then written as tasks. This can be a complicated process. Programs in functional languages can be divided into concurrent parts dynamically by the execution system, making the process highly adaptable to the hardware on which it is running. Understanding concurrent programs in imperative languages is much more difficult.

These factors make concurrency far simpler for the programmer, placing much of the responsibility for it on the execution system, making programs easier to write and easier to read. Furthermore, although functional programs may be less efficient than imperative programs on uniprocessor machines, they may be more efficient on multiprocessor machines, which are now becoming more widely available.

SUMMARY

Mathematical functions are named or unnamed mappings that use only conditional expressions and recursion to control their evaluations. Complex functions can be built using functional forms, in which functions are used as parameters, returned values, or both.

Functional programming languages are modeled on mathematical functions. In their pure form, they do not use variables or assignment statements to produce results; rather they use functional applications, conditional expressions, and recursion for execution control, and functional forms to construct complex functions. LISP began as a purely functional language, but has since had a number of imperative language features added in order to increase its efficiency and ease of use.

The first version of LISP grew out of the need for a list-processing language for AI applications. LISP is still the most widely used language for that area.

LISP is used primarily to process symbolic data stored in lists, as opposed to numeric data stored in arrays, which is the case for most imperative languages. Therefore, LISP's primary primitives include functions for list selection and construction. LISP also includes primitives for conditional expressions and simple list predicates. Function definitions can be named or unnamed. Pure LISP's only primitive functional form is for composition, but other functional forms can and have been added by implementors and users.

The first implementation of LISP was serendipitous: The original version of EVAL was developed solely to demonstrate that a universal LISP function could be written.

Because LISP data and LISP programs have the same form, it is possible to have a program build another program. The availability of EVAL allows such programs to be executed immediately.

Although early interpretive versions of LISP used dynamic scoping, some contemporary versions such as Common LISP use static, or lexical, scoping for nonlocal references. The function FUNCTION provides the option of deep binding to replace shallow binding for functions passed as parameters.

FP is a family of pure functional languages that provide many primitive functions and functional forms.

Although LISP's primary area of application is AI, it has been successfully used for a number of different areas of problem solving.

Although there may be advantages to purely functional languages over their imperative relatives, their lower efficiency of execution on von Neumann machines has prevented them from being considered by many as replacements.

BIBLIOGRAPHIC NOTES

The first published version of LISP can be found in McCarthy (1960). A widely used version from the middle 1960s until the late 1970s is described in McCarthy et al. (1965) and Weissman (1967). The somewhat standardized contemporary version is called Common LISP, and is described in Steele (1984).

A rigorous discussion of functional programming in general can be found in Henderson (1980). A thorough discussion of the funarg problem can be found in Moses (1970). The process of implementing functional languages through graph reduction is discussed in detail in Peyton Jones (1987).

BIBLIOGRAPHY

Backus, J. (1978) "Can Programming Be Liberated from the von Neumann Style? A Functional Style and Its Algebra of Programs." *Commun. ACM*, Vol. 21, No. 8, pp. 613–641.

Buneman, O.P., and R.E. Frankel. (1979) "FQL–A Functional Query Language," *Proc. ACM SIGMOD International Conference on Management of Data*, pp. 52–57, ACM, New York.

Burstall, R.M., D.B. MacQueen, and D.T. Sannella. (1980) "HOPE: An Experimental Applicative Language." *Conf. Record of the 1980 LISP Conference*, pp. 136–143, ACM, New York.

Church, A. (1941) *Annals of Mathematics Studies. Volume 6: Calculi of Lambda Conversion.* Princeton University Press, Princeton, NJ. Reprinted by Klaus Reprint Corporation, New York, 1965.

Darlington, J. (1984) "Functional Programming." In *Distributed Computing,* ed. R.B. Chambers, D.A. Duce, and G.P. Jones. Academic Press, London.

Gordon, M.R., R. Milner, and C. Wadsworth. (1979) "Edinburgh LCF." *Lecture Notes in Computer Science,* 78, Springer-Verlag, Berlin.

Henderson, P. (1980) *Functional Programming: Application and Implementation.* Prentice-Hall, Englewood Cliffs, NJ.

McCarthy, J. (1960) "Recursive Functions of Symbolic Expressions and Their Computation by Machine, Part I." *Commun. ACM,* Vol. 3, No. 4, pp. 184–195.

McCarthy, J., P.W. Abrahams, D.J. Edwards, T.P. Hart, and M. Levin. (1965) *LISP 1.5 Programmer's Manual.* 2d ed. MIT Press, Cambridge, MA.

Moses, J. (1970) "The Function of FUNCTION in LISP." *ACM SIGSAM Bulletin,* July, pp. 13–27.

Newell, A., and H.A. Simon. (1956) "The Logic Theory Machine—A Complex Information Processing System." *IRE Transactions on Information Theory,* Vol. IT-2, No. 3, pp. 61–79.

Newell, A., and F.M. Tonge. (1960) "An Introduction to Information Processing Language V." *Commun. ACM,* Vol. 3, No. 4, pp. 205–211.

Peyton Jones, S.L. (1987) *The Implementation of Functional Programming Languages.* Prentice-Hall, Englewood Cliffs, NJ.

Steele, G.L., Jr. (1984) *Common LISP.* Digital Press, Burlington, MA.

Weissman, C. (1967) *LISP 1.5 Primer.* Dickenson Press, Belmont, CA.

PROBLEM SET

1. Write a LISP function that returns the reversal of its simple list parameter.

2. Write a LISP predicate function that tests for the structural equality of two given lists. Two lists are structurally equal if they have the same list structure, although their atoms may be different.

3. Write a LISP function that returns the union of two simple list parameters that represent sets.

4. Write a LISP function that returns the set intersection of two simple list parameters that represent sets.

5. Write a LISP function with two parameters, an atom and a list, that returns the list with all occurrences, no matter how deep, of the given atom deleted. The returned list cannot contain anything in place of the deleted atoms.

6. Read John Backus' paper on FP (Backus, 1978) and compare the features of LISP discussed in this chapter with the corresponding features of FP.

7. Find definitions of the LISP functions EVAL and APPLY, and explain their actions.

8. One of the most modern and complete programming environments for any language is the INTERLISP system for LISP, as described in "The INTERLISP Programming Environment," by Teitelmen and Masinter (*IEEE Computer*, Vol. 14, No. 4, April 1981). Read this article carefully and compare the difficulty of writing LISP programs on your system with that of using INTERLISP (assuming that you do not normally use INTERLISP).

9. Refer to a book on LISP programming and determine what arguments support the inclusion of the PROG feature in LISP.

10. A functional language could use some data structure other than the list. For example, it could use sequences of symbols. What primitives would such a language have in place of the CAR, CDR, and CONS primitives of LISP?

1) (reverse (LAMBDA (lis)
        (COND
            ((NULL list) ())
            (T (APPEND (reverse (CDR lis)) (CONS (CAR lis) ())))
        )))

2) (eqstruc (LAMBDA (list lis2)
        (COND
            ((ATOM lis1) (ATOM lis2))
            ((ATOM lis2) NIL)
            ((NULL list (NULL lis2))
            ((NULL lis) NIL)
            ((eqstruc (CAR lis1) (CAR lis2)
                (eqstruc (CDR lis1) (CDR lis2)))
            (T NIL)
        )))

3) (union (LAMBDA (lis1 lis2)
        (COND
            ((NULL lis1) lis2)
            ((MEMBER (CAR lis1) lis2) (union (CDR lis1) lis2))
            (T (union (CDR lis) (CONS (CAR lis1) lis2)))
        )))

Logic programming differs fundamentally from conventional programming in requiring us to describe the logical structure of problems rather than making us prescribe how the computer is to go about solving them.

CHRISTOPHER JOHN HOGGER

Key Concepts

- Predicate calculus
- Propositions
- Clausal form
- Resolution
- Unification
- Logic programming
- Forward versus backward chaining

```
4) (intersect (LAMBDA (list list2)
      (COND
          ((NULL list) () )
          (( MEMBER (CAR list) list2 )
              cons (car list) intersect (CDR list1 list2 ))

          (T (intersect (CDR list ) list2 )))
      )))
```

14

LOGIC PROGRAMMING LANGUAGES

Contents

Chapter 13 discusses the functional programming paradigm, which is significantly different from that typically employed by users of imperative languages. In this chapter we describe another, different programming methodology. In this case, the programming paradigm is to express programs in a form of symbolic logic and use a logical inferencing process to produce results. Programming that uses symbolic logic is often called **logic programming,** and languages based on symbolic logic are called **logic programming languages** or **declarative languages.** The example logic programming language we have chosen to describe is PROLOG, primarily because it is the most widely used among the logic languages, and is growing in popularity.

Logic programming languages are remarkably different from the imperative languages, and are even quite different from functional languages. The semantics of logic programs bears little resemblance to that of imperative language programs. These statements should lead the reader to some curiosity about the nature of logic programming and declarative languages.

The objectives of this chapter are to introduce the concepts of logic programming and declarative languages, including a brief description of a subset of the PROLOG language and its interpretive implementation. We begin with an introduction to predicate calculus, which is the basis for the most common category of logic programming languages—a category that includes PROLOG.

14.1   A Brief Introduction to Predicate Calculus

Before we can discuss logic programming, we must briefly investigate its basis, which is formal logic.

A **proposition** can be thought of as an argument, or statement, which may or may not be true, involving objects and their relationships to each other. Formal logic was developed to provide a method for describing propositions, with the goal of allowing those formally stated propositions to be checked for validity.

Symbolic logic can be used for the three basic needs of formal logic: to express propositions, to express the relationships between propositions, and to describe how new propositions can be inferred from other propositions that are assumed to be true.

There is a high degree of similarity between formal logic and mathematics. In fact, much of mathematics can be thought of in terms of logic. The fundamental axioms of number and set theory are the initial set of propositions, which are assumed to be true. Theorems are the additional propositions that can be inferred from the initial set.

The particular form of symbolic logic that has been most widely used for logic programming is called **predicate calculus.** In the following sections, we present the highlights of predicate calculus. Our goal is to lay the groundwork for a discussion of logic programming and the logic programming language PROLOG.

14.1.1 Propositions

Propositions in predicate calculus are statements of facts concerning objects or concepts. Objects are represented by simple terms, which are either constants or variables. A constant is a symbol that represents an object. A variable is a symbol that can represent different objects at different times.

The simplest propositions, which are called **atomic propositions,** consist of single compound terms. A **compound term** is a mathematical relation, written as a function expression, with a function symbol called a **functor** and an ordered list of arguments. Compound terms represent objects that depend on the set of objects that are represented by the arguments. For example, we might have

man(jake)
like(bob, redheads)

which state that jake is a man and that bob likes redheads. All of the simple terms in these propositions—man, jake, like, bob, and redheads—are constants.

Compound propositions have two or more atomic propositions, which are connected by logical connectors, or operators, in the same way compound logic expressions are constructed in imperative languages. The predicate calculus logical connectors are exactly the logical operators of ALGOL 68. The symbols and their names are:

NAME	EXAMPLE	MEANING
negation	$\neg a$	not a
conjunction	$a \cap b$	a and b
disjunction	$a \cup b$	a or b
implication	$a \supset b$	a implies b
equivalence	$a \equiv b$	a is equivalent to b

The following are examples of compound propositions:

$a \cap b \supset c$
$a \cap \neg b \supset d$

Variables can appear in propositions, but only when introduced by special symbols called quantifiers. Predicate calculus includes two quantifiers, as described below, where X is a variable and P is a proposition:

NAME	EXAMPLE	MEANING
universal	$\forall X.P$	for all X, P is true
existential	$\exists X.P$	there exists a value of X such that P is true

For example, consider the following:

$$\forall X.(woman(X) \supset human(X))$$
$$\exists X.(mother(mary,\ X) \cap male(X))$$

The first of these means that for any value of X, if X is a woman then X is a human. The second means that there exists a value of X such that mary is the mother of X and X is a male; in other words, mary has a son. The scope of the universal and existential quantifiers is the simple propositions to which they are attached. This scope can be extended using parentheses, as in the two compound propositions just described.

14.1.2 Clausal Form

One problem with the predicate calculus as we have described it thus far is that there are too many different ways of stating propositions that have the same meaning. To simplify this situation, a standard form for clauses is desirable. Clausal form, which is relatively simple, is one such standard form. Without loss of generality, all propositions can be restricted to clausal form. A proposition in clausal form has the following general syntax:

$$B_1 \cup B_2 \cup \ldots \cup B_n \subset A_1 \cap A_2 \cap \ldots \cap A_m$$

where the As and Bs are terms. This clausal form proposition is taken to mean that if all of the As are true, then at least one B is true. The primary characteristics of clausal form propositions are the following: Existential quantifiers are not required; universal quantifiers are implicit in the use of variables in atomic propositions; no operators other than conjunction and disjunction are required. Also, conjunction and disjunction need only appear in the order shown in the general clausal form: disjunction on the left side and conjunction on the right side. All predicate calculus propositions can be algorithmically converted to clausal form. A simple conversion algorithm is given by Nilsson (1971).

The right side of a clausal form proposition is called the **antecedent.** The left side is called the **consequent.** As examples of clausal form propositions, consider the following:

like(bob, mary) $\subset$ like(bob, redhead) $\cap$ redhead(mary)
redhead(carol) $\cup$ blonde(carol) $\subset$ like(bob, redhead) $\cap$
like(bob, blonde) $\cap$ like(bob, carol)

14.2 Predicate Calculus and Proving Theorems

Predicate calculus provides a method of expressing collections of propositions. One use of collections of propositions is to determine whether any interesting or useful facts can be inferred from them. This is exactly analogous to the work of mathematicians, who strive to discover new theorems that can be inferred from known axioms and theorems.

The early days of computer science (the 1950s and early 1960s) saw a great deal of interest in automating the theorem-proving process. Perhaps the most significant breakthrough in automatic theorem proving was the discovery of the resolution principle by Alan Robinson at Syracuse University (Robinson, 1965).

Resolution is an inference rule that allows inferred propositions to be computed from given propositions, thus providing a method with potential application to automatic theorem proving. Resolution was devised to apply to propositions in clausal form. The concept of resolution is the following: Suppose there are two propositions with the forms:

$$P_1 \subset P_2$$
$$Q_1 \subset Q_2$$

Their meaning is that P_2 implies P_1, and Q_2 implies Q_1. Further suppose that P_1 is identical to Q_2, so that we could rename P_1 and Q_2 as T. Then, we could rewrite the two propositions as:

$$T \subset P_2$$
$$Q_1 \subset T$$

Now, because P_2 implies T and T implies Q_1, it is logically obvious that P_2 implies Q_1, which we could write as:

$$Q_1 \subset P_2$$

This process of getting from the original two propositions to this proposition is called resolution.

As another example, consider the two propositions:

wiser(joanne, jake) $\subset$ older(joanne, jake)
older(joanne, jake) $\subset$ mother(joanne, jake)

Resolution allows the construction, from these, of the proposition:

wiser(joanne, jake) $\subset$ mother(joanne, jake)

If the propositions have multiple terms on either or both sides, the new inferred proposition contains all of the terms of both, except the one that matched. For example, if we have:

father(bob, jake) $\cup$ mother(bob, jake) $\subset$ parent(bob, jake)
grandfather(bob, fred) $\subset$ father(bob, jake) $\cap$ father(jake, fred)

resolution says that:

mother(bob, jake) $\cup$ grandfather(bob, fred) $\subset$
$\qquad\qquad$ father(jake, fred) $\cap$ parent(bob, jake)

which has all but one of the atomic propositions of both of the original propositions. The one atomic proposition that allowed the operation, father(bob, jake) in the left side of the first and in the right side of the second, is left out. In English, we would say:

if: bob is the parent of jake implies that bob is either the father or mother of jake

and: bob is the father of jake and jake is the father of fred implies that bob is the grandfather of fred

then: if jake is the father of fred and bob is the parent of jake, then either bob is jake's mother or bob is fred's grandfather

Resolution is actually more complex than these simple examples illustrate. For example, the presence of variables in propositions requires resolution to find values for those variables that allow the matching process to succeed. This process of determining useful values for variables is called **unification.** The temporary assigning of values to variables to allow unification is called **instantiation.**

It is common for the resolution process to instantiate a variable with a value, fail to complete the required matching, and then be required to backtrack and instantiate the variable with a different value. We will discuss unification more extensively in the context of PROLOG.

A critically important property of resolution is its ability to detect any inconsistency in a given set of propositions. This property allows resolution to be used to prove theorems, which can be done as follows: We can envision a theorem proof in terms of predicate calculus as a given set of pertinent propositions, with the negation of the theorem itself stated as a new proposition. The theorem is negated so that resolution can be used to prove the theorem by finding an inconsistency. This is proof by contradiction. Typically, the original propositions are called the hypotheses and the negation of the theorem is called the goal.

Theoretically, this sounds very good. However, one practical problem arises. Although resolution is a finite process if the set of propositions is finite, the time required to find an inconsistency in a large database of propositions may take a huge amount of time.

Theorem proving is the basis for logic programming. Much of what is computed can be couched in the form of a list of given facts and relationships as hypotheses, and a goal to be inferred from the hypotheses, using resolution.

When propositions are used for resolution, only a restricted kind of clausal form is required, which further simplifies the resolution process. The special kinds of propositions are called **Horn clauses,** which can be in only two forms: They have either a single atomic proposition on the left side or an empty left side. The left side of a clausal form proposition is sometimes called the head, and Horn clauses with left sides are called headed Horn clauses. Those with empty left sides are called headless Horn clauses.

14.3 An Overview of Logic Programming

Languages used for logic programming are called declarative because programs written in them consist of declarations rather than assignments and control flow statements. These declarations are actually statements in symbolic logic, which we have called propositions.

One of the essential characteristics of logic programming languages is their semantics, which is called declarative semantics. The basic concept of this semantics is that there is a simple way to determine the meaning of each statement that does not depend on how the statement might be used to solve a problem. Declarative semantics is considerably simpler than the semantics of the imperative languages. For example, the meaning of a given proposition in a logic programming language can be concisely determined from the statement itself. In an imperative language, the semantics of a simple assignment statement requires examination of local declarations, knowledge of the scoping rules of the language, and possibly even examination of programs in other files, just to determine the types of the variables in the assignment statement. Then, assuming the expression of the assignment contains variables, we must trace the execution of the program prior to the assignment statement to determine the values of those variables. The resulting action of the statement, then, depends on its run-time context. Thus, declarative semantics is often stated as one of the advantages declarative languages have over the imperative languages (Hogger, 1984, pp. 240–241).

Programming in imperative languages is primarily procedural, which means that the programmer knows *what* is to be accomplished by a program and instructs the computer on exactly *how* the computation is to be done. In other words, the computer is treated as a simple device that obeys orders. Everything that is computed must have every detail of that computation spelled out. Some people believe that this is the essence of the difficulty of programming computers.

Programming in some kinds of nonimperative languages, and in particular in logic programming languages, is nonprocedural. Programs in such languages do not state exactly *how* a result is to be computed, but rather describe the form of the result. The difference is that we assume the computer system is quite resourceful, and can somehow determine *how* the result is to be gotten. What is needed to provide this capability for logic programming languages is a concise means of supplying the computer with both the relevant information and a method of inference for computing desirable results. Predicate calculus supplies the basic form of communication to the computer, and the proof method developed first by Robinson supplies the inference technique.

An example commonly used to illustrate the difference between procedural and nonprocedural systems is the process of rearranging a list of data into some particular order, otherwise known as sorting. In a procedural language like Pascal, sorting is done by explaining, in Pascal, all the details of some sorting algorithm to a computer that has a Pascal compiler. The computer, after translating the Pascal program into machine code or some interpretive intermediate code, follows the instructions and produces the sorted list.

In a nonprocedural language, it is necessary only to describe the main characteristic of the sorted list: It is some permutation of the given list such that for each pair of adjacent elements, a given relationship holds between the two elements. This can be stated formally as follows: Suppose the list to be sorted is in an array named list, which has a subscript range 1..n. Then the concept of sorting the list into a separate array named new_list can be expressed as:

$$\text{sort(list,new\_list)} \subset \text{permute(list,new\_list)} \cap$$
$$\text{sorted(new\_list)}$$
$$\text{sorted(l)} \subset \forall \text{ j such that } 1 <= j < n, \, l(j) <= l(j+1)$$

where permute is a predicate that returns true if its second parameter array is a permutation of its first parameter array.

From this description, the nonprocedural language system could produce the sorted list. That makes nonprocedural programming sound like the mere production of concise software requirements specifications, which is a fair assessment. Unfortunately, however, it is not quite that simple. Logic programs face serious problems of machine efficiency. Furthermore, the best form of a logic language has not yet been determined, and good methods of creating programs in logic programming languages for large problems have not yet been developed.

14.4   The Origins of PROLOG

During the very early 1970s, Alain Colmerauer and Phillippe Roussel in the Artificial Intelligence Group at the University of Aix-Marseille, together with Robert Kowalski of the Department of Artificial Intelligence at the University of Edinburgh, developed the fundamental design of PROLOG, which amounts to a syntax for predicate calculus propositions and an implementation of a restricted form of resolution. The first PROLOG interpreter was developed at Marseille in 1972. The version of the language that was implemented is described in Roussel (1975). The name PROLOG is from *programming logic*.

The collaboration between the University of Aix-Marseille and the University of Edinburgh continued until the middle 1970s. Since then, research on the development and use of the language has progressed independently at those two locations, resulting in, among other things, two syntactically different dialects of PROLOG.

The development of PROLOG and other research efforts in logic programming received limited attention outside of Edinburgh and Marseille until the announcement in 1981 that the Japanese government was launching a large research project called the Fifth Generation Computing Systems (FGCS) (Fuchi, 1981; Moto-oka, 1981). One of the primary objectives of the project is to develop intelligent machines, and PROLOG was chosen as the basis for this effort. The announcement of FGCS aroused in both researchers and the governments of the United States and several European countries a sudden strong interest in artificial intelligence and logic programming. Although PROLOG changed little during its first decade, the recent resurgence of interest in it will likely eventually lead to a variety of modifications and additions.

PROLOG is a logic programming language whose syntax is a modified version of predicate calculus. Its inferencing method is a restricted form of resolution.

14.5 The Basic Elements of PROLOG

There are now a number of different dialects of PROLOG. These can be grouped into three categories: those that grew from the Marseille group, those that came from the Edinburgh group, and micro-PROLOG, a version developed for Z80-based microcomputers, which is described by Clark and McCabe (1984). The syntactic forms of these three are somewhat different. Rather than attempt to describe all three or some hybrid of them, we have chosen one particular, widely available dialect, which is the one developed at Edinburgh. This form of the language is sometimes called Edinburgh syntax. It is specifically that of the DEC System-10 implementation (Warren et al., 1979), which is also available for PDP-11 and VAX computer systems.

14.5.1 Terms

As is the case with other programming languages, PROLOG programs consist of collections of statements. There are only a few kinds of statements in PROLOG, but they can become complex. All PROLOG statements are constructed from terms.

A PROLOG **term** is a constant, a variable, or a structure. A constant is either an **atom** or an integer. Atoms are the symbolic values of PROLOG, and are similar to their counterparts in LISP. In particular, an atom is either a string of letters, digits, and underscores that begins with a lowercase letter, or a string of any printable ASCII characters delimited by apostrophes.

A variable is any string of letters, digits, and underscores that begins with an uppercase letter. Variables are not bound to types by declarations.

The binding of a value, and thus a type, to a variable is called an **instan-tiation.** This binding corresponds to variable instantiation in the resolution process. A variable that has not been assigned a value is called uninstan-tiated. Instantiations last only as long as it takes to satisfy one complete goal, which involves the proof or disproof of one proposition.

The last kind of term is called a structure. Structures represent the atomic propositions of predicate calculus, and their general form is the same:

> functor(parameter list)

where the functor is any atom. The functor is used to identify the structure. The parameter list can be any list of atoms, variables, or other structures. As we discuss at length in the following section, structures are the means of specifying facts in PROLOG. They can also be thought of as objects, in which case they allow facts to be stated in terms of several related atoms.

14.5.2   Fact Statements

We begin our discussion of PROLOG statements with those statements used to construct the hypotheses, or database of assumed information—the statements from which we can infer new information.

PROLOG has two basic statement forms; these correspond to the headless and headed Horn clauses of predicate calculus. The simplest form of head-less Horn clauses in PROLOG is a single structure that is interpreted as an unconditional assertion, or fact. Logically, facts are simply propositions that are assumed to be true.

The following examples illustrate the kinds of facts one can have in a PROLOG program. Notice that every PROLOG statement is terminated by a period.

```
female(shelley).
male(bill).
female(mary).
male(jake).
father(bill, jake).
father(bill, shelley).
mother(mary, jake).
mother(mary, shelley).
```

These simple structures state certain facts about jake, shelley, bill, and mary. The first, for example, states that shelley is a female. The last four connect their two parameters with a relationship that is named in the func-tor atom. For example, the fifth proposition can be read as: "bill is the father of jake."

The more complex form of headless Horn clause is called the **conjunctive form.** Conjunctive propositions, or simply conjunctions, contain multiple atomic propositions that are separated by logical AND operations. In PROLOG, the AND operation is implied. The structures that represent atomic propositions are separated by commas. For example, we could have:

```
female (shelley), child (shelley).
mother (mary, shelley), father (frank, shelley),
    sister (megan, shelley).
```

14.5.3 Rule Statements

The other basic form of PROLOG statement for constructing the database corresponds to headed Horn clauses. This form can be related to a known theorem in mathematics from which a conclusion can be drawn if the set of given conditions is satisfied. The right side is the antecedent, or IF part, and the left side is the consequent, or THEN part. If the antecedent of a PROLOG statement is true, then the consequent of the statement must also be true. Because they are Horn clauses, the consequent of a PROLOG statement is a single term, while the antecedent can have any number of terms, separated by implied AND operations.

The general form of the PROLOG headed Horn clause statement is:

```
structure_1 : – antecedent_expression.
```

which can be read as: "structure_1 can be concluded if the antecedent expression is true or can be made to be true by some instantiation of its variables." For example,

```
ancestor(mary, shelley) :- mother(mary, shelley).
```

states that if mary is the mother of shelley, then mary is an ancestor of shelley. Headed Horn clauses are called rules because they state rules of implication between propositions.

As is the case with clausal form propositions in predicate calculus, variables are used instead of constants in PROLOG statements to generalize their meaning. Recall that variables in clausal form provide a kind of implied universal quantifier. The following demonstrates the use of variables in PROLOG statements.

```
parent(X, Y) :- mother(X, Y).
parent(X, Y) :- father(X, Y).
grandparent(X, Z) :- parent(X, Y), parent(Y, Z).
sibling(X, Y) :- mother(M, X), mother(M, Y),
                 father(F, X), father(F, Y).
```

These statements give rules of implication among some variables, or universal objects. In this case, the universal objects are X, Y, Z, M, and F. For example, the first rule states that if there are instantiations of X and Y such that mother(X, Y) is true, then for those same instantiations of X and Y, parent(X, Y) is true.

14.5.4   Goal Statements

So far we have described the PROLOG statements for logical propositions, which are used to describe both known facts and rules that describe logical relationships among facts. These statements are the basis for the theorem-proving model. The theorem is in the form of a proposition that we want the system to either prove or disprove. In PROLOG, these propositions are called goals, or queries. The syntactic form of PROLOG goal statements is identical to that of headless Horn clauses. For example, we could have:

```
father(fred, mike).
```

to which the system will respond either yes or no. The answer yes means that the system has proved the goal was true under the given database of facts and relationships. The answer no means that either the goal was proved false, or the system was simply unable to prove or disprove it. This goal statement is the simplest kind. It is relatively easy for resolution to determine—by matching the pattern of this goal against propositions in the database—whether it is true or false. It is easy in the sense that no variables are involved, and therefore no instantiations are required.

Conjunctive propositions and propositions with variables are also legal goals. When variables are present, the system not only asserts the validity of the goal, but also identifies the instantiations of the variables that make the goal true. For example, we can ask:

```
father(X, mike).
```

to which the system will attempt, through unification, to find an instantiation of X that results in a true value for the goal. Unification in this case proceeds by matching the goal against the propositions in the database. The first proposition that has the form of the goal, with any object as its first parameter, will cause X to be instantiated with that object's value. X is then displayed as the result. If there is no proposition in the form of the goal, with the functor name father and the second parameter value mike, the system indicates that the goal cannot be satisfied.

Because, in PROLOG, goal statements and some nongoal statements have the same form (headless Horn clauses), a PROLOG implementation must have some means of distinguishing between the two. Interactive PROLOG implementations do this by simply having two modes, indicated by different interactive prompts: one for entering fact and rule statements and one for entering goals. The mode can be changed by the user at any time.

14.5.5   The Inferencing Process of PROLOG

This section examines PROLOG resolution. Efficient use of PROLOG requires that the programmer know precisely what the PROLOG system does with his or her program.

There are two opposite approaches to attempting to match a given goal with the database. The system can begin with the facts and rules of the database and attempt to find a sequence of matches that lead to the goal. This approach is called bottom-up resolution, or **forward chaining.** The alternative to forward chaining is to begin with the goal and attempt to find a sequence of matching propositions that lead to some set of original facts in the database. This approach is called top-down resolution, or **backward chaining.** In general, backward chaining works well when there is only a reasonably small set of possible answers. The forward chaining approach is better when the number of possibly correct answers is large; in this situation, backward chaining would require a very large number of matches to get to an answer. PROLOG implementations use backward chaining for their form of resolution, presumably because its designers believed backward chaining was suitable for a larger class of problems than forward chaining.

The next design question arises whenever the goal has more than one structure, as in our example above. The question then is whether the solution search is done **depth-first** or **breadth-first.** A depth-first search finds a complete path of matches for the first subgoal, or structure, before working on the others. A breadth-first search works on all subgoals of a given goal in parallel. The depth-first approach was chosen by PROLOG's designers, primarily because it can be done with fewer computer resources. The breadth-first approach is a parallel search, which can take a large amount of memory.

The last feature of PROLOG's resolution mechanism that we must discuss is backtracking. When a goal with multiple subgoals is being processed and the system fails to show the truth of one of the subgoals, the system backs up to the previous subgoal, if there is one, and attempts to find another solution to it. A new solution is found by beginning the search where the previous search for that subgoal stopped. Multiple solutions to a subgoal result from different instantiations of its variables. Resatisfaction of a subgoal is the usual backtrack technique; it can take a great deal of time and space because it may have to search all paths through a very large solution tree. The fact that the tree is not organized to minimize the search exacerbates the problem.

Let us assume that we have a set of facts and rules in a database, and that we have presented PROLOG with the compound goal:

```
male(X), parent(X, shelley).
```

This goal asks whether there is an instantiation of X such that X is a male and X is a parent of shelley. The resolution process may have to find every male in the database before it finds the one that is a parent of shelley. It definitely must find all males to prove that the goal cannot be satisfied. Note that our example goal might be processed more efficiently if the order of the two subgoals were reversed. Then, only after resolution had found a parent of shelley would it try to match that person with the male subgoal. This is more efficient if shelley has fewer parents than there are males in the database. In Section 14.7, we discuss a method of limiting the backtracking done by a PROLOG system.

The following two sections describe PROLOG examples that further illustrate the resolution process.

14.5.6 Simple Arithmetic

Recall that PROLOG has only integer numeric atoms. Therefore, only integer arithmetic is allowed. Originally, the arithmetic operators were functors, so that the sum of 7 and the variable X was formed with:

    +(7, X)

This is a somewhat primitive approach to arithmetic, even for a language in which arithmetic is considered to be outside the mainstream of use.

PROLOG now allows a more abbreviated syntax for arithmetic with the **is** operator. This operator takes an arithmetic expression as its right operand and a variable as its left operand. All variables in the expression must be already instantiated, but the left-side variable cannot be already instantiated. For example, in:

    X is Y / 17 + Z.

if Y and Z are instantiated, but X is not, then this clause will cause X to be instantiated with the value of the expression. When this happens, the clause is satisfied. If either Y or Z are not instantiated or X is instantiated, the clause is not satisfied and no instantiation of X takes place. The semantics of an **is** proposition is considerably different from that of an assignment statement in an imperative language. This difference can lead to an interesting problem. Because the **is** operator makes the clause in which it appears look like an assignment statement, a beginning PROLOG programmer may be tempted to write a statement such as:

    Sum is Sum + Number.

which is never useful in PROLOG. If Sum is not instantiated, the reference to it in the right side is undefined and the clause fails; if Sum is already instantiated, the clause fails because the left operand cannot have a current instantiation when **is** is evaluated. In either case, the instantiation of Sum to the new value will not take place.

PROLOG does not have assignment statements in the same sense as imperative languages do. They are simply not needed in most of the programming for which PROLOG was designed. The usefulness of assignment statements in imperative languages depends on the capability of the programmer to control the execution control flow of the code in which the assignment statement is embedded. Because such control is not always possible in PROLOG, such statements are far less useful.

As a simple example of the use of numeric computation in PROLOG, consider the following problem. Suppose we have the average speeds of several automobiles on a particular racetrack and the amount of time they are on the track. This basic information can be coded as facts, and the relationship between speed, time, and distance can be written as a rule, as in:

```
speed(ford, 100).
speed(chevy, 105).
speed(dodge, 95).
speed(volvo, 80).
time(ford, 20).
time(chevy, 21).
time(dodge, 24).
time(volvo, 24).
distance(X, Y) :- speed(X, Speed),
                  time(X, Time),
                  Y is Speed * Time.
```

Now, queries can request the distance traveled by a particular car. For example, the query:

```
distance(chevy, Chevy_Distance).
```

instantiates Chevy_Distance with the value 2205. The first two clauses in the right side of the distance computation statement simply instantiate the variables Speed and Time with the corresponding values of the given automobile functor. After satisfying the goal, PROLOG also displays the name Chevy_Distance and its value.

14.5.7 List Structures

So far, the only PROLOG data structure we have discussed is the atomic proposition, which looks more like a function call than a data structure. Atomic propositions, which are also called structures, are actually a form of records. The other basic data structure supported is the list, which is similar to the LISP list structure. Lists are sequences of any number of elements, where the elements can be atoms, atomic propositions, or any other terms, including other lists.

PROLOG uses a conventional sort of syntax to specify lists. The list elements are separated by commas and the entire list is delimited by square brackets, as in:

```
[apple, prune, grape, frown]
```

The notation [] is used to denote the empty list. Instead of having explicit functions for constructing and dismantling lists, PROLOG simply uses a special notation. [X | Y] denotes a list with head X and tail Y, where head and tail correspond to CAR and CDR in LISP. This is in keeping with the nonprocedural nature of the language. Rather than describing how to manipulate lists, we need only describe the characteristics of the result.

A list can be created with a simple structure, as in:

```
new_list([apple, prune, grape, frown]).
```

which states that the constant list [apple, prune, grape, frown] is a new_list, where new_list is a functor. Recall that a functor is the name of a structure, or atomic proposition. In this case, the structure is a list named new_list. This statement does not bind the list to a variable named new_list; rather, it does the kind of thing that the proposition

```
male(jake)
```

does. That is, it states that [apple, prune, grape, frown] is a new_list. Therefore, we could have a second proposition with a list argument, such as:

```
new_list([apricots, peaches, smiles])
```

In query mode, one of the lists associated with new_list can be dismantled into head and tail with:

```
new_list([New_List_Head | New_List_Tail]).
```

If new_list has been instantiated as above, this statement instantiates the user variable New_List_Head with the head of the list (in this case apple) and New_List_Tail with the tail of the list (or [prune, grape, frown]). If this were part of a compound goal and backtracking forced a new evaluation of it, New_List_Head and New_List_Tail would be reinstantiated to apricots and [peaches, smiles], respectively, because [apricots, peaches, smiles] is the next list associated with new_list.

The notation used to dismantle lists can also be used to create lists from given instantiated head and tail components, as in:

```
[Element_1 | List_2]
```

If Element_1 has been instantiated with pickle and List_2 has been instantiated with [peanut, prune, pair], the pair will create, for this one reference, the list [pickle, peanut, prune, pair].

When dealing with lists, certain basic operations are often required, such as those found in LISP. As an example of such operations in PROLOG, we examine a list append function, which is similar to that in LISP. In this example, the differences and similarities between functional and declarative languages can be seen. We need not specify how PROLOG is to construct a new list from the given lists; rather, we need only specify the characteristics of the new list in terms of the given lists.

In appearance, the PROLOG version of append is very similar to the LISP version, and recursion is used in the same way to produce the new list. In the case of PROLOG, the recursion is caused and controlled by the resolution process.

The first two parameters to the append operation in the following code are the two lists to be appended, and the third parameter is the resulting list:

```
append([], List, List).
append([Head | List_1], List_2, [Head | List_3]) :-
        append(List_1, List_2, List_3).
```

The first proposition specifies that when the empty list is appended to any other list, that other list is the result. This statement corresponds to the recursion-terminating step of the LISP append function. Note that the terminating proposition is placed before the recursion proposition. This is done because we know that PROLOG will match the two propositions in order, starting with the first.

The second proposition specifies several characteristics of the new list. It corresponds to the recursion step in the LISP function. The left-side predicate states that the first element of the new list is the same as the first element of the first given list because they are both named Head. Whenever Head is instantiated to a value, all occurrences of Head in the goal are, in effect, simultaneously instantiated to that value. The right side of the second statement specifies that the tail of the first given list (List_1) has the second given list (List_2) appended to it to form the tail (List_3) of the result list.

One way to read the second statement of append is the following: Appending the list [Head | List_1] to any list List_2 produces the list [Head | List_3], but only if the list List_3 is formed by appending List_1 to List_2. In LISP, this would be:

```
(CONS (CAR FIRST) (APPEND (CDR FIRST) SECOND))
```

In both the PROLOG and LISP versions, the resulting list is not constructed until the recursion produces the terminating condition; in this case, the first list must become empty. Then, the result list is built using the append function itself; the elements taken from the first list are added, in reverse order, to the second list. The reversing is done by the unraveling of the recursion.

PROLOG has a built-in structure named trace that displays the instantiations of values to variables at each step during the attempt to satisfy a given goal. Trace is used to understand and debug PROLOG programs. To understand trace, it is best to introduce a different model of the execution of PROLOG programs, called the **tracing model.**

The tracing model describes PROLOG execution in terms of four events: CALL, which occurs at the beginning of an attempt to satisfy a goal; EXIT, which occurs when a goal has been satisfied; REDO, which occurs when backtrack causes an attempt to resatisfy a goal; and FAIL, which occurs when a goal fails. CALL and EXIT can be related directly to the execution model of a subprogram in an imperative language, if processes like append are thought of as subprograms. The other two events are unique to logic programming systems. In the following trace example, we choose a goal that, for simplicity's sake, requires no REDO or FAIL events.

To illustrate how the append process progresses using trace, consider the following example:

```
trace.
append([bob, jo], [jake, megan], Family).
```

For the convenience of the reader, the two statements of the append operation are repeated here:

```
append([], List, List).
append([Head | List_1], List_2, [Head | List_3]) :-
            append(List_1, List_2, List_3).
```

Using the output of trace, the following CALLs, EXITs, and instantiations of variables can be determined:

EVENT	HEAD	List 1	List 2	List 3 (FAMILY)
CALL 1:		[bob, jo]	[jake, megan]	
CALL 2:	bob	[jo]	[jake, megan]	[bob | List_3]
CALL 3:	jo	[]	[jake, megan]	[jo | List_3]
EXIT 3:		[]	[jake, megan]	[jake, megan]
EXIT 2:		[jo]	[jake, megan]	[jo, jake, megan]
EXIT 1:		[bob, jo]	[jake, megan]	[bob, jo, jake, megan]

The first two CALLs, which represent subgoals, have List_1 nonempty, so they create the recursive calls from the right side of the second statement. The left side of the second statement effectively specifies the arguments for the recursive calls, or goals, thus dismantling the first list one element per step. When the first list becomes empty, in a CALL, or subgoal, the current instance of the right side of the second statement succeeds by matching the first statement. The effect of this is to return as the third parameter the value of the empty list appended to the second original parameter list. On successive EXITs, or successful matches, the elements that were removed from the first list are appended to the result list. When the EXIT from the first goal is accomplished, the process is complete, and the resulting list is displayed.

The append propositions can also be used to create other list operations, such as list reversal:

```
rev([], []).
rev([Head | Tail], List) :- rev (Tail, Reversed),
                    append(Reversed, [Head], List).
```

Once again, although the LISP and PROLOG languages are fundamentally different, similar operations can use similar approaches. In the case of reverse, both the PROLOG and LISP versions include the recursion terminating condition, along with the basic process of appending the reversal of the CDR or tail of the list to the CAR or head of the list to create the result list.

14.6 Applications of Logic Programming

In this section we briefly describe a few of the larger classes of present and potential applications of logic programming in general, and PROLOG in particular.

14.6.1 Relational Database Management Systems

Relational database management systems (RDBMS) store data in the form of tables. Queries on such databases are often stated in relational calculus, which is a form of symbolic logic. The query languages of these systems are nonprocedural in the same sense that logic programming is nonprocedural. The user does not describe how to retrieve the answer; rather, he or she only describes the characteristics of the answer. The connection between logic programming and RDBMS should be obvious. Simple tables of information can be described by PROLOG structures, and relationships between tables can be conveniently and easily described by PROLOG rules. The retrieval process is inherent in the resolution operation. The goal statements of PROLOG provide the queries for the RDBMS. Logic programming is thus a natural match to the needs of implementing a RDBMS.

One of the advantages of using logic programming to implement a RDBMS is that the relationships between fields in various database tables can be stated with the same formalism that is used to create the database tables and to state the queries. In a typical RDBMS, such relationships are often specified by special procedures, rather than in the data tables. In addition, the queries of a RDBMS are usually in another form: relational calculus. So, three different forms are involved with building and using a conventional RDBMS.

The primary disadvantage of logic programming compared with conventional RDBMS is the lower level of efficiency. Logical inferences are simply much slower than ordinary table look-up methods using imperative programming techniques. To compete in this area, it appears that logic programming must be tailored somewhat to the problem.

14.6.2 Expert Systems

Expert systems are computer systems designed to emulate human expertise in some particular domain. They consist of a database of facts, an inferencing process, some heuristics about the domain, and some friendly human interface that makes the system appear much like an expert human consultant. In addition to their initial knowledge base, which is provided by a human expert, expert systems learn from the process of being used, so their databases must be capable of growing dynamically. Also, an expert system should include the capability of interrogating the user to get additional information when it detects that such information is needed.

One of the central problems for the designer of an expert system is dealing with the inevitable inconsistencies and incompleteness of the database. Logic programming appears to be well suited for this task. For example, default inference rules can help deal with the problem of incompleteness.

PROLOG can and has been used to construct expert systems. It can easily fulfill the basic needs of expert systems, using resolution as the basis for query processing, using its ability to add facts and rules to provide the learning capability, and using its trace facility to inform the user of the "reasoning" behind a given result. Missing from PROLOG is the automatic ability of the system to query the user for additional information when it is needed.

One of the most widely known uses of logic programming in expert systems is the expert system construction system known as APES, which is described in Sergot (1983) and Hammond (1983). The APES system includes a very flexible facility for gathering information from the user during expert system construction. It also includes a second interpreter for producing explanations to its answers to queries.

APES has been successfully used to produce several expert systems, including one for the rules of a government social benefits program, and one for the British Nationality Act, which is the definitive source for rules of British citizenship.

14.6.3 Natural Language Processing

Certain kinds of natural language processing can be done with logic programming. In particular, natural language interfaces to computer software systems, such as intelligent databases, and other intelligent knowledge-based systems, can be easily done with logic programming. For describing language syntax, forms of logic programming have been found to be equivalent to context-free grammars. Proof procedures in logic programming systems have been found to be equivalent to certain parsing strategies. In fact, backward chaining resolution can be used directly to parse sentences whose structure is described by context-free grammars. It has also been discovered that some kinds of semantics of natural languages can be made clear by modeling the languages with logic programming. In particular, research in logic-based semantics networks has shown that sets of sentences in natural languages can be expressed in clausal form (Deliyanni and

Kowalski, 1979). Logic-based semantic networks are also discussed by Kowalski (1979).

14.6.4   Education

In the area of education, there have been extensive experiments in teaching children as young as 7 how to use the logic programming language micro-PROLOG (Ennals, 1980). Researchers claim a number of advantages in teaching PROLOG to young people. First, it is possible to introduce computing using this approach. It also has the side effect of teaching logic, which can result in clearer thinking and expression. This will help students in learning a variety of subjects, such as solving equations in mathematics, dealing with grammars for natural languages, and understanding the rules and order of the physical world.

The experiments in teaching logic programming to the very young have produced the interesting result that it is easier to teach logic programming to a beginner than to a programmer with a significant amount of experience in an imperative language.

14.7   Deficiencies of PROLOG

Several problems arise in using PROLOG as a logic programming language. Although it is a useful tool, it should not be considered the ultimate logic programming language.

14.7.1   Resolution Order Control

PROLOG, for reasons of efficiency, allows the user to control the ordering of pattern matching during resolution. In a pure logic programming environment, the order of attempted matches that take place during resolution could be nondeterministic, or all matches could be attempted concurrently. However, because PROLOG always matches in the same order, starting at the beginning of the database and at the left end of a given goal, the user can profoundly affect efficiency by ordering the database statements to optimize a particular application. For example, if the user has knowledge that certain rules are much more likely to succeed than the others during a particular "execution," then the program can be made more efficient by placing those rules first in the database.

In addition to allowing the user to control database and subgoal ordering, PROLOG, in another concession to efficiency, allows some explicit control of backtracking. This is done with the "cut" operator, which is specified by an exclamation point (!). The cut operator is actually a goal, not an operator. As a goal, it always succeeds immediately, but it cannot be

450 Chapter 14: Logic Programming Languages

resatisfied through backtracking. Thus, a side effect of the cut is that subgoals to its left in a compound goal also cannot be resatisfied through backtracking. For example, in the goal:

```
a, b, !, c, d.
```

if both a and b succeed, but c fails, the whole goal fails. This goal would be used if it were known that whenever c fails, the whole goal would fail. Any time used to attempt to resatisfy b would, in that case, be wasted.

The purpose of the cut, then, is to allow the user to make programs more efficient by telling the system when it should not attempt to resatisfy subgoals that will not contribute to a correct complete solution.

As an example of one use of the cut operator, consider the following. Suppose we need to be able to determine whether a given symbol is in a given list. A straightforward PROLOG description of this is:

```
member(Element, [Element | _]).
member(Element, [_ | List]) :- member(Element, List).
```

The underscore indicates an "anonymous" variable; we use it to mean that we do not care what instantiation it might get from unification. The first statement above succeeds if the Element is the head of the list, either initially or after several recursions through the second statement. The second statement succeeds if the Element is in the tail of the list.

If the list argument to member represents a set, then it can be satisfied only once. Therefore, if member is used as a subgoal in a multiple subgoal goal statement, there can be a problem. The problem is that if member succeeds, but the next subgoal fails, backtracking will attempt to resatisfy member by continuing a prior match. But because the list argument to member had only one copy of the element to begin with, member cannot possibly succeed again, which eventually causes the whole goal to fail, in spite of any additional attempts to resatisfy member. The solution to this inefficiency is to add a right side to the first statement of the member definition, with the cut operator as the sole element, as in:

```
member(Element, [Element | _]) :- !.
```

Now, backtracking will not attempt to resatisfy member, but instead will cause the entire subgoal to fail.

Use of the cut operator has been related to the use of the goto in imperative languages (Van Emden, 1980). Although it is sometimes needed, it is possible to abuse it. Indeed, it is sometimes used to make logic programs have a control flow that is inspired by imperative programming styles.

14.7.2 The Closed World Assumption

The nature of PROLOG's resolution sometimes creates misleading results. The only truths, as far as PROLOG is concerned, are those that can be proved using its database. Therefore, its knowledge of the world is highly limited. Any query about which there is insufficient information in the database to prove absolutely, is assumed to be false. PROLOG can prove that a given goal is true, but it cannot prove that a given goal is false. It simply assumes that because it cannot prove a goal true, the goal must be false.

The problem of the closed world assumption is related to the negation problem, which is discussed in the following section.

14.7.3 The Negation Problem

Another problem with PROLOG is its difficulty with negation. Consider the following database of two facts and a relationship:

```
parent(bill, jake).
parent(bill, shelley).
sibling(X, Y) :- parent(M, X), parent(M, Y).
```

Now, suppose we typed the query:

```
sibling(X, Y).
```

PROLOG will respond with:

```
X = jake
Y = jake
```

Thus, PROLOG "thinks" jake is a sibling of himself. This happens because the system first instantiates M with bill and X with jake, to make the first subgoal, parent(M, X), true. It then starts at the beginning of the database again to match the second subgoal, parent(M, Y), and arrives at the instantiations of M with bill and Y with jake. Because the two subgoals are satisfied independently, with both matchings starting at the database's beginning, we get the result shown above. To avoid this, we would need to specify that X is a sibling of Y if they have the same parents *and* that they are not equal. Unfortunately, stating that they are not equal is not straightforward in PROLOG, as we discuss below. The most exacting method would require adding a fact for every pair of atoms, stating that they were not equal. This can cause the database to become very large, for there is often far more negative information than positive information. For example, most people have 364 more unbirthdays than they have birthdays.

A simple alternative solution in our example is to state in the goal that X must not be equal to Y, as in:

```
sibling(X, Y) :- parent(M, X), parent(M, Y), not(X = Y).
```

In other cases, the solution is not so simple.

The PROLOG not operator is satisfied in this case if resolution cannot satisfy the subgoal X = Y. Therefore, if the not succeeds, it does not necessarily mean that X is not equal to Y; rather, it means that resolution cannot prove from the database that X is equal to Y. Thus, the PROLOG not operator is not equivalent to a logical NOT operator, in which NOT means that its operand is provably true. This nonequivalency can lead to a problem if we happen to have a goal of the form

```
not(not(some_goal)).
```

which would be equivalent to

```
some_goal.
```

if PROLOG's not operator were a true logical NOT operator. In some cases, however, they are not the same. For example, consider our earlier example for list membership:

```
member(Element, [Element | _]) :- !.
member(Element, [_ | List]) :- member(Element, List).
```

Suppose we want to know one of the elements of a given list. We could use the goal

```
member(X, [mary, fred, barb]).
```

which would cause X to be instantiated with mary, which would then be printed. But if we used

```
not(not(member(X, [mary, fred, barb]))).
```

the following sequence of events would take place. First, the inner goal would succeed, instantiating X to mary. Then PROLOG would attempt to satisfy the next goal:

```
not(member(X, [mary, fred, barb])).
```

but it would fail, because member succeeded. When this goal failed, X would be uninstantiated, because PROLOG always uninstantiates all variables in all goals that fail. Next, PROLOG would attempt to satisfy the outer not goal, which would succeed, because its argument had failed. Finally, the result, which is X, would be printed. But X would not be currently instantiated, so we would get an indication to that effect. Generally, uninstantiated variables are printed in the form of a string of digits that begins with an underscore. So the fact that PROLOG's·not is not equivalent to a logical NOT can be, at very least, misleading.

The fundamental reason why logical NOT cannot be an integral part of PROLOG is the form of the Horn clause:

$$A :- B_1 \cap B_2 \cap ... \cap B_n$$

If all the B propositions are true, it can be concluded that A is true. But regardless of the truth or falseness of any or all of the Bs, it cannot be concluded that A is false. From positive logic one can only conclude positive logic. Thus, the only ways around the problem go beyond the Horn clause form.

14.8 Conclusions

Many believe that PROLOG is, at this point, still a grand experiment. It has a growing number of proponents, however, as many other languages have had, and some believe it can be the solution to the software crisis, in which the imperative languages currently in use simply cannot cope with the problems that need to be solved by computers (Cuadrado and Cuadrado, 1985).

Some of the reasons as to why adherents believe that PROLOG is better than imperative languages are the following, as originally stated by Jacques Cohen (Cohen, 1985), one of PROLOG's boosters:

1. Because PROLOG is based on logic, PROLOG programs are likely to be more logically organized and written, which should lead to fewer errors and less maintenance.

2. PROLOG processing is naturally parallel, making PROLOG interpreters particularly able to take advantage of the coming multiple-processor machines.

3. Because of the conciseness of PROLOG programs, development time is decreased, making it a good tool for prototyping.

Of course, there are people who do not agree. Many computer scientists are skeptical of PROLOG's usefulness outside a few small areas of artificial intelligence.

SUMMARY

Symbolic logic provides the basis for logic programming and logic programming languages. The approach of logic programming is to use as a database a collection of facts and rules that state relationships between facts, and to use an automatic inferencing process to check the validity of new propositions, assuming the facts and rules of the database are true. This approach is the one developed for automatic theorem proving.

PROLOG is the most widely used logic programming language. The origins of logic programming lie in Robinson's development of the resolution rule for logical inference. PROLOG was developed primarily at Marseille and Edinburgh.

Logic programs are nonprocedural, which means that the characteristics of the solution are given, but not the complete process of getting the solution.

PROLOG statements are either facts, rules, or goals. Most are made up of structures, which are atomic propositions, and logic operators, although arithmetic expressions are also allowed.

Resolution is the primary activity of a PROLOG interpreter. This process, which uses backtracking extensively, involves mainly pattern matching among propositions. When variables are involved, they can be instantiated to values to provide matches. This instantiation process is called unification.

Logic programming has been used in a number of different areas, primarily in relational database systems, expert systems, and natural language processing.

BIBLIOGRAPHIC NOTES

The PROLOG language is described in several books. Edinburgh's form of the language is covered in *Programming in PROLOG* by W.F. Clocksin and C.S. Mellish. The microcomputer implementation is described in *Micro-PROLOG: Programming in Logic* by K.L. Clark and F.G. McCabe.

Introduction to Logic Programming by Christopher Hogger is an excellent book on the general area of logic programming. It is the source of the material in this chapter's section on logic programming applications.

BIBLIOGRAPHY

Clark, K.L., and F.G. McCabe. (1984) *Micro-PROLOG: Programming in Logic.* Prentice-Hall, Englewood Cliffs, NJ.

Clocksin, W.F., and C.S. Mellish. (1984) *Programming in Prolog.* 2d ed. Springer-Verlag, New York.

Cohen, J. (1985) "Describing PROLOG by Its Implementation and Computation." *Commun. ACM,* Vol. 28, No. 12, pp. 1311–1324.

Cuadrado, C.Y., and J.L. Cuadrado. (1985) "Prolog Goes to Work." *BYTE,* August 1985, pp. 151–158.

Deliyanni, A., and R.A. Kowalski. (1979) "Logic and Semantic Networks." *Commun. ACM,* Vol. 22, No. 3, pp. 184–192.

Ennals, J.R. (1980) "Logic as a Computer Language for Children." Logic Programming Research Reports. Theory of Computing Research Group, Dept. of Computing, Imperial College of Science and Technology, London.

Fuchi, K. (1981) "Aiming for Knowledge Information Processing Systems." *Proceedings of the International Conference on Fifth Generation Computing Systems,* Japan Information Processing Development Center, Tokyo. Republished (1982) by North-Holland Publishing, Amsterdam.

Hammond, P. (1983) *APES: A User Manual.* Dept. of Computing Report 82/9. Imperial College of Science and Technology, London.

Hogger, C.J. (1984) *Introduction to Logic Programming.* Academic Press, London.

Kowalski, R.A. (1979) *Logic for Problem Solving.* Artificial Intelligence Series, Vol. 7. Elsevier-North Holland, New York.

Kowalski, R.A., and D.G. Keuhner. (1971) "Linear Resolution with Selector Function." *Artificial Intelligence* 2, pp. 227–260.

Moto-oka, T. (1981) "Challenge for Knowledge Information Processing Systems." *Proceedings of the International Conference on Fifth Generation Computing Systems,* Japan Information Processing Development Center, Tokyo. Republished (1982) by North-Holland Publishing, Amsterdam.

Nilsson, N.J. (1971) *Problem Solving Methods in Artificial Intelligence.* McGraw-Hill, New York.

Robinson, J.A. (1965) "A Machine-Oriented Logic Based on the Resolution Principle." *Journal of the ACM,* Vol. 12, pp. 23–41.

Roussel, P. (1975) "PROLOG: Manuel de Reference et D'utilisation." Research Report. Artificial Intelligence Group, Univ. of Aix-Marseille, Luminy, France.

Sergot, M.J. (1983) "A Query-the-User Facility for Logic Programming." In *Integrated Interactive Computing Systems,* ed. P. Degano and E. Sandewall. North-Holland Publishing, Amsterdam.

Van Emden, M.H. (1980) "McDermott on PROLOG: A Rejoiner." *SIGART Newsletter,* No. 72, August, pp. 19–20.

Warren, D.H.D., L.M. Pereira, and F.C.N. Pereira. (1979) "User's Guide to DEC System-10 PROLOG." Occasional Paper 15. Dept. of Artificial Intelligence, Univ. of Edinburgh, Scotland.

PROBLEM SET

1. Explain the connection between automatic theorem proving and PROLOG's inferencing process.

2. Explain the difference between procedural and nonprocedural languages.

3. Describe how a multiple-processor machine could be used to implement resolution. Could PROLOG, as currently defined, use this method?

4. Explain why PROLOG systems must do backtracking.

5. Compare the concept of data typing in Ada with that of PROLOG.

6. What is the relationship between resolution and unification in PROLOG?

7. Under what circumstances is the variable that is the left operand of the **is** operator instantiated?

8. Write a PROLOG description of your family tree, in terms of just facts, going back to your grandparents and including all descendants. Be sure to include all relationships.

9. Write a set of rules for family relationships, including all relationships from grandparents through two generations. Now, add these to the facts of Problem 8 and eliminate as many of the facts as you can.

10. Write a PROLOG program that succeeds if the intersection of two given list parameters is empty.

11. Write a PROLOG program that returns a list containing the union of the elements of two given lists.

Handwritten margin notes:

3. On a single processor machine, resolution process takes place on the rule bases, one rule at a time, starting with 1st rule, and progressing toward last until a match is found. But process on each rule is independent of the process on other rules.

4. required when a goal has multiple components + those components include a common variable.

5. ADA variables are statically bound to types. PROLOG variables are bound to types only when they are bound to values. these bindings take place during execution and are temporary.

6. Resolution is the process of matching patterns in goals with those of rules. Unification is the process of temporarily assigning a value to two instances of a variable with the intention of creating a match during resolution.

The most important part of object-oriented programming is not any technical advantage it gives, but the fact that it crosses a threshold of perception.

TED KAEHLER AND DAVE PATTERSON

Key Concepts

- Object-oriented programming
- Message passing
- Message expressions
- Control structures using message passing
- Class hierarchies and inheritance
- Generic code

```
10  intersect ([ ], X, [ ]).
    intersect ([X|R], Y, [X|Z]) :- member (X, Y), !,
                      intersect (R, Y, Z).

    intersect ([X|R], Y, Z) :- intersect (R, Y, Z).


11.  union ([ ], X, X).
     union ([X|R], Y, Z) :- member (X, Y), !, union (R, Y, Z).
     union ([X|R], Y, [X|Z]) :- union (R, Y, Z)
```

15

OBJECT-ORIENTED PROGRAMMING LANGUAGES

Object-oriented programming, like functional programming and logic programming, is a programming paradigm that has grown in parallel with the development of a language, or category of languages. In this case, the language is Smalltalk. Like LISP and PROLOG, Smalltalk is quite different from the imperative languages.

The phrase "object-oriented" is rapidly becoming as overused as "structured programming" was in the 1970s. The increasing generality of use of the phrase has already led to a good deal of confusion as to its exact meaning.

For this chapter, the object-oriented concept will be assumed to be in its strictest form, which we will clearly distinguish from the weaker concept of "object-oriented," which is used for simply programming with abstract data types, as can be done in Ada and Modula-2.

Because object-oriented programming originated with the development of the Smalltalk language, and also because Smalltalk still provides the most complete support for object-oriented programming in the strict sense, we use it to illustrate the important concepts. This, in turn, requires a discussion of at least part of the syntax and semantics of Smalltalk.

One difficulty with any attempt to present Smalltalk arises in describing its programming environment. The language itself is simple and well structured, but the environment is an integral part of the Smalltalk programming process, and it is best explained either through an actual tutorial session at a Smalltalk system or through a long series of photographs of the display of a Smalltalk system.

We have chosen to focus on the language itself, and only very briefly discuss the environment. Although the environment is a large part of what programming in Smalltalk is all about, explaining it in words is very difficult and the result is of questionable value unless the reader is actually involved in using a Smalltalk system. Section 15.14 includes several photographs of a Smalltalk screen, but we do not discuss the interface beyond that. If the reader wishes to learn to use Smalltalk, we suggest consulting the excellent books by Goldberg (1984) and Goldberg and Robson (1984).

15.1 Object-Oriented Programming

The concept of **object-oriented programming** described in this section has its roots in the Smalltalk language development effort.

Object-oriented programming focuses on data structures, and then adds functionality, or processing capability, to those structures. This is a somewhat opposite approach from the traditional programming approach, which focuses on processes and their implementation in subprograms. A data structure definition and its defined processes are packaged together in some syntactic structure, in which the structural definition and process implementation are hidden from the program units that use it, which are called clients. This is the programming paradigm being called object-oriented programming and advocated as the ideal programming methodology by many contemporary computer scientists. This methodology is well served by the data abstraction facilities of Modula-2 and Ada.

Our interpretation of object-oriented programming includes data abstraction as one of its three fundamental characteristics, the other two being inheritance and dynamic type binding. Neither Ada nor Modula-2 include facilities for these two latter characteristics.

Dynamic type binding allows abstract data types to be truly generic. The generic feature of Ada is instantiated at compile time, and is therefore a static type binding. In an ideal object-oriented language, compiled code for an abstract data type can be used for different data types—which immensely expands their reusability. This broad reusability is one of the key positive features of object-oriented programming. It means that program units are never rewritten solely because the types of object upon which they operate change.

Inheritance is another characteristic of object-oriented programming. It began in a limited form in SIMULA 67, whose classes can be defined in hierarchies. Inheritance is a method of sharing code among users. In its most common use, inheritance allows all users to inherit objects from a system collection of code, which is itself a hierarchy of capabilities.

All three of these characteristics will be further discussed in the following sections.

The unit control concept of object-oriented programming is loosely modeled on the idea that programs simulate the real world. This idea grew from the origins of SIMULA 67, which was designed for simulation applications. Because much of the real world is populated by objects, a simulation of such a world must include simulated objects. In fact, a language based on the concepts of real-world simulation need only include a model of objects that can send and receive messages and react to the messages it receives.

The essence of object-oriented programming is solving problems by identifying the real-world objects of the problem and the processing required of those objects, and then creating simulations of those objects, their processes, and the required communications between the objects. Abstract data types, dynamic type binding, and inheritance are the concepts that make object-oriented problem solving not only possible, but convenient and effective.

15.2 Object-Oriented Programming Languages

In this section we examine the primary features of an object-oriented programming language. These features are precisely those needed to support the object-oriented programming paradigm.

15.2.1 Objects

An executing program in an object-oriented language consists entirely of objects: the concept of an object is truly universal. Literally everything, from items as simple as the integer constant 2, to a file-handling system, are objects. As objects, they are treated uniformly. They all have local memory, inherent processing ability, the capability for communicating with other objects, and the ability to inherit characteristics from ancestors. Objects do not have names; they are anonymous and can only be referenced by pointers. However, they can be treated as first-class entities in the sense that they can be passed as parameters and returned from other objects as the results of received messages.

A crucial part of every object is its ability to communicate with other objects through message passing. Every object can send messages to other objects and receive messages from other objects.

All objects are faithful data abstractions, meaning that the definition of their data structures and the operations on those structures are hidden from the objects that send messages to request information or processing.

15.2.2 Classes

Classes in object-oriented languages are direct descendants of the classes of SIMULA 67. As such, they are templates for categories of objects, and provide the means for creating objects. Because objects serve as data abstractions, classes must include both data structure definitions and the processing code for instances of those data structures.

To provide for inheritance, classes can be defined as descendants of other classes. Such descendant classes literally inherit the characteristics of the ancestor class (or classes).

A class must include the means of communications, so that objects of the class can interact with other objects in a system.

15.2.3 Messages

Objects communicate with other objects by sending messages. A message is used by an object to request an operation that it or another object provides. Messages do not transmit general information. The collection of kinds of messages to which an object will respond is called its interface, or message protocol. The interface of an object is fixed when the object is created.

One can think of objects as having sockets into which other objects can place messages, but only if the message fits the socket. Ada task communication is based on the same message-passing model that object-oriented languages use. Tasks have message sockets, called **accept** clauses, into which messages from other tasks may be sent. Furthermore, messages are sent to tasks to request services, exactly as if they were objects in an object-oriented language.

Messages can be parameterized with object names, thus providing flexibility in fixed messages. Replies to messages have the form of objects, and are used to return requested information or to confirm that the requested service has been completed.

Now that we have briefly described the fundamentals of object-oriented languages, we move on to the Smalltalk language to explore a concrete example of such a language.

15.3 Roots of Smalltalk

The concepts that led to the development of Smalltalk originated in the Ph.D. thesis work of Alan Kay in the late 1960s at the University of Utah (Kay, 1969). Kay had remarkable foresight in predicting the future availability of very powerful desktop computers. Recall that the first microcomputer systems were not marketed until the middle 1970s, and they were only distantly related to the machines envisioned by Kay, which were seen to execute a million or more instructions per second and contain several megabytes of memory.

Kay believed that such computers would be used by nonprogrammers, and thus would need very powerful human interfacing capabilities. The computers of the late 1960s were largely batch-oriented, and were used exclusively by professional programmers and scientists. For use by nonprogrammers, Kay determined, a computer would have to be highly interactive and use sophisticated graphics in the interface. Some of the graphics concepts came from the LOGO experience of Seymour Papert, in which graphics was used to aid children in the use of computers (Papert, 1980).

The original Kay concept was a system he called the Dynabook, which was meant to be a general information processor. It was based in part on the Flex language, which he had helped design. Flex was based primarily on SIMULA 67. Dynabook was based on the paradigm of the typical desk, on which there are typically a number of papers, some partially covered. The top sheet is often the focus of attention, with the others temporarily out of focus. The display of Dynabook would model this scene, using the concept of screen windows. The user would interact with such a display both through a keyboard and by touching the screen with his or her fingers. After the preliminary design of Dynabook earned him a Ph.D., Kay's goal became to see such a machine constructed.

Kay found his way to the Xerox Palo Alto Research Center (Xerox PARC) and presented his ideas on Dynabook. This led to his employment there and the subsequent birth of the Learning Research Group at Xerox. The first charge of the group was to design a language to support Kay's programming paradigm and implement it on the best personal computer then available. These efforts resulted in an "Interim" Dynabook, consisting of the Xerox Alto hardware and the Smalltalk-72 software. Together, they formed a research tool for further development. A number of research projects were conducted with this system, including several experiments to teach programming to children. Along with the experiments came further developments, leading to Smalltalk-74, Smalltalk-76, Smalltalk-78, and eventually Smalltalk-80, which is the version discussed in this chapter. As the language grew, so did the power of the hardware on which it resided. By 1980, both the language and the Xerox hardware nearly matched the early vision of Alan Kay.

15.4   Smalltalk Design Concepts

Because the phrase "object-oriented programming" originated with the development of the Smalltalk language, one would assume that Smalltalk would include the fundamental characteristics of an object-oriented language (briefly described in Section 15.2.), and that is the case. The Smalltalk world is populated by objects, which are instances of classes. And, of course, those objects communicate through a mechanism of message passing.

As we stated earlier in this chapter, Smalltalk's environment is quite different from that of the typical imperative language. The Smalltalk system integrates a program editor, compiler, the usual features of an operating system, and a virtual machine into a single system. The interface to this system is highly graphical, making heavy use of multiple overlaid windows and pop-up menus, and using a mouse pointing device and a high-resolution, bit-mapped monitor.

Another important aspect of the Smalltalk environment is that it is almost entirely written in Smalltalk, and it can be modified by the user to fit his or her particular needs. This implies that the source version of most of the system is available to a user, who can edit any of its classes or objects.

In summary, Smalltalk is far more than just a programming language; it is also a programming methodology and a programming environment. The remainder of this chapter contains a brief description of a subset of the Smalltalk language, along with some simple example programs.

15.5   Overview of Smalltalk

The program units of Smalltalk are objects. Objects are similar to the structures that support data abstractions in Modula-2 and Ada—modules and packages, respectively. For example, like an Ada package, an object can have local data that is not visible outside the object. An object also contains a collection of operations that is available to other objects, similar to the procedures of an Ada package. These operation definitions are called **methods.** A method specifies the reaction of the object when it receives the particular message that corresponds to that method. The connection of a message to a method is made syntactically, as we will soon show. The entire collection of methods of an object is called the **message protocol,** or **message interface,** of the object.

All computing in Smalltalk is done by the same uniform technique: sending a message to an object to invoke one of its methods. A reply to a message is an object, which returns the requested information, or simply notifies the sender that the requested processing has been completed.

From the simulation point of view, which is never far away, Smalltalk is a simulation of a collection of computers (objects) that communicate with each other (through messages). Each object is an abstraction of a computer in the sense that it stores data and provides processing capability for manipulating that data. In addition, objects can send and receive messages. In essence, those are the fundamental capabilities of computers: to store and manipulate data, and communicate.

In Smalltalk, object abstractions are **classes,** which are very similar to the classes of SIMULA 67. The common characteristics of a category of objects is captured by a class definition. Instances of the class can be created, and are then the objects of the program. Each object has its own local data and represents a different instance of its class. The only difference between two objects of the same class is the state of their local variables.

As is the case in SIMULA 67, class hierarchies can be formed in Smalltalk. Subclasses of a given class are refinements of it, inheriting the functionality and local variables of the parent class, or superclass. Subclasses can add new local memory and functionality, and modify or hide inherited functionality. Some data and functionality are inherited by all user-defined classes, because all are subclasses of the system class, Object. Object is the only class without a superclass.

At this point it is worthwhile to describe a few of the small-scale features of Smalltalk, from which we can gradually build up to designing classes, objects, and methods.

15.6 Expressions

Smalltalk programs consist primarily of objects and messages. Objects are instances of classes, which consist largely of methods that correspond to possible messages to which those instances can respond. Methods are in turn constructed from expressions. An expression describes an object, which happens to be the value of the expression.

In Smalltalk, there are four kinds of expressions: literals, variable names, message expressions, and block expressions. Literals, variables, and message expressions are discussed in the following three sections. Block expressions are described in Section 15.9.1.

15.6.1   Literals

The most common literals are numbers, strings, and keywords. Numbers are literal objects that represent numeric values. They are quite different from the numeric literals of imperative languages, which act somewhat like named constants because they are associated with memory locations that contain their associated values. In Smalltalk, numeric literals are objects that are characterized by their message protocol and by the results that are produced when messages are received. The message protocol of numeric literals, as is the case with other objects, is defined in the class definition, along with its inherited class definitions. In the case of an integer literal, the parent class is `Integer`; it provides methods for the usual arithmetic operators, among other things.

Syntactically, a string literal is a sequence of characters delimited by apostrophes. Semantically, a string literal is an object that is capable of responding to messages that access individual characters, replace substrings, and perform comparisons with other strings.

A keyword is an identifier, which may be user-defined, with a trailing colon. The use of keywords is discussed in Section 15.6.3.

15.6.2   Variables

A Smalltalk variable name is syntactically similar to those of other programming languages: a sequence of letters and/or digits that begins with a letter. Smalltalk variables come in two varieties: private, which means they are local to an object, and shared, which means they are visible outside the object in which they are "declared." Names of private variables must begin with lowercase letters. Names of shared variables must begin with uppercase letters.

All Smalltalk variables are pointers; they can only refer to objects or classes. In a sense, they are typeless because any variable can point to any object. The only shared variables we discuss are those that refer to classes.

15.6.3   Message Expressions

Messages have the form of expressions. They provide the means of communication among objects, and are the way the operations of an object are requested.

Message expressions specify a receiver object; a selector entry, or method, in that object; and possibly some parameters. Parameters are pointers to other objects. When a message is evaluated, it is sent to the specified receiver object. Methods are discussed in Sections 15.7 and 15.11.

There are three categories of messages: unary, binary, and keyword. Unary messages are the simplest kind, having just two symbols and no parameters. The first symbol of a unary message specifies a receiver object. The last symbol specifies a method of that object that is to be executed. For example,

```
firstAngle sin
```

specifies the object referred to by `firstAngle` as the receiver. The second symbol, `sin`, specifies that the `sin` method of `firstAngle` is to be executed.

Binary messages have a single parameter, an object, which is passed to the specified method of the specified receiver object. Among the most common binary messages are those for arithmetic operations—for example,

```
21 + 2
sum / kount
```

In the first, the receiver object is the number 21, to which is sent the message "+ 2". This message passes the parameter object 2 to the "+" method of the object 21. The code of that method uses the object 2 to build a new object, in this case, 23. If the system already contains the object 23, then the result is a reference to it, rather than to a new object.

In the second case, the message "/ kount" is sent to the object referred to by sum. As a result, the value of the variable kount is passed as a parameter to the "/" method of the object referred to by sum.

Keyword expressions specify one or more keywords to organize the correspondence between the actual parameters in the message and the formal parameters in the method. That is, the keywords act in concert to select the method to which the message is directed. The interspersion of keywords and parameters in messages enhances their readability. For example,

```
firstArray at: 1 put: 5
```

sends the 1 and the 5 to a particular method of the object `firstArray`. The keywords `at:` and `put:` identify the formal parameters of the method to which 1 and 5, respectively, are to be sent. The particular method to which this message is sent includes the keywords of the message, catenated together. This catenation—in this case, `at:put:`—is called a **selector.** Selectors identify the methods of an object. Methods are further discussed in Section 15.7.

Message expressions can consist of any number of any combination of the three kinds of expressions—for example,

```
total - 3 * divisor
firstArray at: index - 1 put: 77
```

To determine how these are evaluated, the precedence and associativity of expression operators must be known. Unary expressions have the highest precedence, followed by binary expressions, followed by keyword expressions. Both unary and binary expressions associate left to right. Note that this is quite different from the precedence rules commonly used in imperative languages.

The first expression above sends the 3 to the "−" method of the object, `total`. The value of the variable `divisor` is then sent to the "∗" method of the object that resulted from the first operation.

The second expression above sends the 1 to the "−" method of the object, `index`. The result of this operation, along with the 77, are then sent to the `at:put:` method of the object, `firstArray`.

Messages can be cascaded, which means that multiple messages can be sent to the same object without duplicating the receiver object's name. This is done by separating the selector-parameter groups, or messages, by semi-colons. The messages are sent sequentially, as they appear, left to right. For example,

```
ourPen home; up; goto: 500@500; down; home
```

is equivalent to:

```
ourPen home.
ourPen up.
ourPen goto: 500@500.
ourPen down.
ourPen home
```

As you will see later, this sequence would draw a line on the display, assuming that `ourPen` is an instance of the `Pen` class. An object of class `Pen` is illustrated in Section 15.14.

Notice that periods are used to separate messages that are sent to different methods and appear on adjacent lines. This is similar to the use of semicolons to separate statements in Pascal programs.

15.7 Methods

A method of a class defines the operations an instance of the class will execute when a message corresponding to the method is received. In a sense, methods are like function definitions, complete with parameters and the capability of returning values.

The general syntactic form of a method is:

message_pattern [| temporary variables |] statements

where the brackets are meta-symbols that indicate that what they enclose is optional. Because there are no type declarations, temporary variables, when present, need only be named in a list. Temporary variables exist only during execution of the method in which they are listed. There is no punctuation at the end of a method.

The message pattern corresponds to the procedure statement in a language such as Pascal. It is a prototype for messages, including the method's name if it is for unary or binary messages, or the keywords and the names of the formal parameters for keyword messages.

A value to be returned by a method is indicated by preceding the expression that describes it with an up arrow (^). In many cases, this is the last expression that appears in the method. If no return value is specified in a method, the receiver object itself is the return value.

A method for a unary message is simply the method name. An example of a unary method is:

```
currentTotal
   ^(oldTotal + newValue)
```

This method returns the value of the expression oldTotal + newValue. Binary methods are used primarily for arithmetic operations, which are predefined, so they are not discussed here.

The general form of methods for keyword messages is:

key_1: parameter_1 key_2: parameter_2 ... key_n: parameter_n

Consider the following example keyword method, which does not specify a value to be returned:

```
x: xCoord y: yCoord
   ourPen up; goto xCoord @ yCoord; down.
```

In this method, which matches the x: y: message selector, the object ourPen is sent the messages up, goto, which uses the two parameters xCoord and yCoord, and down. The message pattern is simply a list of the keyword/ formal parameter name pairs in the method.

Additional features of methods, including temporary variables, are discussed in Section 15.11.

15.8 Assignment Statements

Smalltalk has assignment statements that are similar, at least in appearance, to those of the common imperative languages. Any message expression, literal object, or variable name can be the right side of an assignment statement. The left side is a variable name, and the operator is specified with a left arrow—for example,

```
total ← 22
sum ← total
```

As might be expected, the particular object referenced by a variable is changed when that variable's name appears on the left side of an assignment. In the above example, the variable total is set to refer to the object, 22. Then the variable sum is set to refer to the same object. This operation resembles the assignment of pointer variables in an imperative language.

Recall that all methods transmit information back to the senders who sent the messages. To save that returned information, the message expression is placed on the right side of an assignment to a variable. The variable is then set to refer to the returned information—for example,

```
index ← index + 1
salesTax ←  deducts grossPay: 350.0 dependents: 4
```

In the first assignment, the message "+ 1" is sent to the object referenced by index. The variable index is set to reference the new object that results from executing the "+" method. In the second, the keyword message "grossPay: 350.0 dependents: 4" is sent to the grossPay:dependents: method of the object, deducts. The variable salesTax is set to refer to the object returned by deducts.

15.9 Blocks and Control Structures

One of the most unusual aspects of Smalltalk is that the control structures are not provided by statements in the language. Instead, they are formed with the fundamental object-oriented paradigm: message passing.

Blocks provide a way to collect expressions into groups. These groups can be used to build execution control constructs.

15.9.1 Blocks

A block is an object that contains a sequence of expressions. A block is specified in brackets, with the expressions separated by periods—for example,

```
[index ← index + 1. sum ← sum + index]
```

The expressions in a block are deferred actions because they are not executed when encountered; rather, they are executed only when the block is sent the unary message **value**. For example,

```
[sum ← sum + index] value
```

sends the message **value** to the block, causing its execution. When a block execution is completed, the value of the last expression in the block is returned.

Blocks can be assigned to variables and executed by sending the **value** message to the variable—for example,

```
addIndex ← [sum ← sum + index]
```

Then the message expression:

```
addIndex value
```

causes index to be added to sum. This message expression could also be assigned to a variable—for example,

```
addIndex ← [sum + index]
sum ← addIndex value
```

Blocks are always executed in the context of their definition, even when they are sent as parameters to a different object. Thus, they are semantically related to the pass by name parameters of ALGOL 60.

Blocks can be thought of as procedure declarations that may appear anywhere. Like procedures, blocks can have parameters. Block parameters are specified in a section at the beginning of the block that is separated from the remainder of the block by a vertical bar (|). The formal parameter specifications require a colon to be attached to the left end of each parameter. Because there are no declared types, the specifications include only the formal parameter names, which are listed without any separating punctuation. As an example of a block with parameters, consider the following:

```
[:x :y | sum ← x + 10. total ← sum * y]
```

Blocks provide a means of collecting expressions, so they are a natural way to form control structures in Smalltalk.

15.9.2 Iteration

Blocks can contain relational expressions, in which case they return one of the predefined Boolean objects, **true** or **false**. Such blocks are sometimes called conditional blocks. The two objects, **true** and **false**, have methods that provide some of the facilities for building control structures.

Logical pretest loops can be formed by using the selector whileTrue: to send the block to be controlled to a second block that contains the loop condition. This method is defined for all blocks that return Boolean objects. The whileTrue: method is defined to send **value** to the object that contains the method (either **true** or **false**), thereby causing its parameter block to be executed—for example,

```
count ← 0.
sum ← 0.
[count <= 20]
   whileTrue: [sum ← sum + count.
               count ← count + 1]
```

Although this code may have a somewhat conventional appearance, and in fact accomplishes a rather conventional operation, the process by which it does it is radically different from that used by imperative languages.

The loop control is realized as follows: The block containing the code to add count to sum and increment count, which is the code segment whose execution is to be controlled, is sent as a parameter to the whileTrue: method of the conditional block [count <= 20]. The whileTrue: method sends **value** to the block [count <= 20], thus causing that block to be evaluated. The result of this evaluation is a Boolean object, either **true** or **false**. If the result is **true**, the whileTrue: method causes the parameter sent by the whileTrue: message to be evaluated. Its parameter is the block that contains the expressions of the iteration. After they are evaluated, the process is repeated by sending the block of expressions to [count <= 20] again. The repetition stops when an evaluation of [count <= 20] produces **false** as a result object.

Another common loop control structure is simple repetition with a counter control. For this, there is a method for integers named timesRepeat:. When timesRepeat: is sent to an integer, the parameter block is executed that many times. For example:

```
xCube ← 1.
3 timesRepeat: [xCube ← xCube * x]
```

computes the cube of x in a rather lengthy fashion.

Control structures similar to ALGOL 68's **for** loops can be built with some of the methods of integers. The two most useful of these are to: do: and to: by: do:. The block that forms a loop body can have a parameter. Such a parameter takes on the internal values created by the message. The internal values are those returned by the numeric object to which the whole message is sent—for example:

```
1 to: 5 do: [sum ← sum + 10]
2 to: 10 by: 2 do: [:even | sum ← sum + even]
```

In the first line the block is executed five times. The internal values returned by the object 1 are 1, 2, 3, 4, and 5. In the second line, the block is also executed five times, but in this case the parameter, even of the block, takes on the internal values, which in this case are 2, 4, 6, 8, and 10.

15.9.3 Selection

Selection constructs also have a conventional appearance, but operate in another way. The method ifTrue: ifFalse: is included for the **true** and **false** objects. The two arguments of the ifTrue: ifFalse: message represent the then and else clauses of the selection construct. The message is sent to a Boolean expression. If the expression evaluates to **true**, then the message is sent to **true**. In this case, the ifTrue: ifFalse: method sends **value** to its first argument and ignores its second argument. If sent to **false**, the opposite takes place. For example, consider the following message:

```
total = 0
  ifTrue: [average ← 0]
  ifFalse: [average ← sum // total]
```

The Boolean expression "total = 0" causes the message "= 0" to be sent to the object total, which returns either **true** or **false**. The resulting object (either **true** or **false**) is then used as the receiver for the message, which is sent to the ifTrue:ifFalse: method. The two parameters to this method are the then and else blocks, one of which is to be executed.

The // operator is for integer division. The / operator also divides integers, but if the result is not integral, an object of class Fraction is returned. A Fraction object has two integer components—a numerator and a denominator.

Four messages can actually be sent to the **true** and **false** objects. In addition to ifTrue:ifFalse:, these are ifTrue:, ifFalse:, and ifFalse:ifTrue:.

The semantics of the control structures we have just discussed may seem rather odd, but they are really quite natural to experienced Smalltalk users. Furthermore, being able to handle control structures within this framework is a tribute to the power and flexibility of the message-passing model. It also simplifies Smalltalk by obviating the need for any structure outside the world of objects and message passing.

15.10 Classes

All Smalltalk objects are instances of classes. Classes have four parts:

1. A class name
2. The superclass name, which specifies the new class' position in the hierarchy of classes in the system
3. A declaration of the local variables that will be available to the instances of the class, which are called instance variables
4. The methods that define how instances of the class will respond to messages

Messages to an object normally cause the class to which the object belongs to be searched for a corresponding method. If the search fails, it is continued in the superclass of that class, and so forth, up to the system class, Object, which has no superclass. If no method is found anywhere in that chain, an error occurs.

Methods in a class can have the same name as a method in some superclass, which effectively hides the superclass method. If access to such a hidden method is desired, the pseudovariable **super** can be used, which specifies that the search for the method should begin in the first superclass of the class containing the method.

The private memory of an instance of a class contains its instance variables. Instance variables are not visible to other objects. Each instance variable refers to one object, called its value. The values of all of an instance's variables together represent that instance's current state.

Instance variables are either named or indexed. Named variables correspond to pointers to nonarray types in an imperative language. Indexed instance variables are not accessed by name, but rather by messages that have integers as parameters. Most indexed variables are used in a way that corresponds to arrays in imperative languages, although indexing itself is done through message passing. The integer parameter in a message to reference an indexed instance variable corresponds to the subscript in a reference to an array element in an imperative language.

Instances of classes are created by sending the message **new** to the class in an assignment, which sets the left-side variable to reference the newly created object. For example,

```
ourPen ← Pen new
```

creates an instance of the class Pen and sets the variable ourPen to reference it. This example demonstrates that messages can be sent to classes, as well as objects. The message **new** can also be sent to a class in a single expression that is not in an assignment, as in:

```
Pen new
```

but the created object is not accessible, and thus is of limited usefulness.

15.11   More about Methods

In this section we examine some features of methods that were not covered in Section 15.7.

The following method illustrates the use of temporary variables:

```
first: x second: y | temp |
   temp ← x + y.
   temp > 1000
     ifTrue: [temp ← 1000].
   ^ temp
```

This method adds the values of its two parameters together and places the sum in the temporary variable temp. If the value of temp is greater than 1000, it is set to 1000. The value of temp is the returned object.

The pseudovariable **self** is an object name that refers to the object in which it appears. Therefore, **self** is used for recursive messages, or messages to the object itself. The object name **self** is often used for error message display, as in:

```
total = 0
   ifTrue: [self error: 'Error - cannot compute average']
   ifFalse: [^ sum / total]
```

If total is equal to zero, this code sends the message "error: 'Error - cannot compute average'" to the object in which the code resides. Otherwise, it returns the value of the expression sum / total.

The message "error", like other messages, is directed to a superclass of the object to which it is sent if that object does not include a method for it. If no other ancestor class has a method for the "error" message, the system object, Object, which does include an "error" method, receives the message. Object's method for "error" prints the message parameter and terminates the program.

For a somewhat more familiar example of recursion, consider the following method, which is understood by integers. It is taken from Goldberg and Robson (1984).

```
factorial
  self = 0
    ifTrue:  [^1].
  self < 0
    ifTrue:  [self error 'Factorial not defined']
    ifFalse: [^ self * (self - 1) factorial]
```

This is a binary method for integer objects. It can be invoked by a message such as:

```
5 factorial
```

The first Boolean expression, **self** = 0, sends the parameter 0 to the "=" method of the integer to which the factorial message was sent. The message "ifTrue: [^1]" is then sent to the result of the "=" method execution. If the result is the object **true**, as it would be for the message "0 factorial", the value 1 is returned to the sender of factorial. If the result of the "=" method execution is **false**, no action is taken because the ifTrue: method in **false** is defined to do nothing.

The next Boolean expression, **self** < 0, sends the parameter 0 to the "<" method of the integer to which factorial was sent. The rest of the factorial message (the entire ifTrue: ifFalse: message) is then sent to the result of the "<" method execution. If the resulting object is **true**, the error message is sent to the object to which factorial was sent. If the result of the "<" method is **false**, then the block on the ifFalse: part of the ifTrue: ifFalse: method is executed and the result is returned to the sender of factorial.

To understand the ifFalse: message, the precedence rules of message evaluation must be known. In this expression, there are two binary expressions (those with ∗ and -) and one unary expression (factorial). Recall that unary expressions take precedence over binary expressions unless the binary expression is parenthesized. Also, all expressions have left associativity. Now, the order of evaluation is clear: First, "- 1" is sent to **self**, producing an object that is smaller by 1 than the object to which the message was sent. Then factorial is sent to this new object. The final result of this message, after all recursion, is sent with ∗ to **self**, which is the original object to which factorial was sent. The result of this message is the factorial value.

Once again, we see the similarity in recursion across widely differing language semantics.

15.12   Type Checking and Generics

Smalltalk variables are not typed; any object can be bound to any name. The only type checking that is done occurs dynamically when a message is sent to an object. If the object has a method for the message, the message is legal and the object reacts to it. If the object does not have a method that corresponds to a message, it is a run-time error. This is a significantly different concept of type checking than that of the imperative languages. So, Smalltalk type checking has the simple form of ensuring that a message matches a method.

All Smalltalk code is generic in the sense that the types of the variables are irrelevant, as long as they are consistent. For example, consider the expression:

```
a * b - c
```

Evaluation of this expression begins by sending the message "* b" to the object referenced by a. Then the message "- c" is sent to the result of the first. If a, b, and c reference any numeric type objects, this process is all predefined.

If we define a class for complex numbers to have methods for * and -, then the expression above is also legal for variables a, b, and c that refer to objects of the class complex numbers. This is, in essence, the overloading of the * and - operators.

The point of this discussion is not overloading, however. It is, rather, that as long as the objects referenced in an expression have methods for the messages of the expression, the types of the objects are irrelevant. This means that all code is generic; none is tied to a particular type. A sort method, for example, could be written for a class. Then, all new classes that needed that sort capability could simply be made subclasses of that class. This is precisely how the Smalltalk system itself is constructed—as a hierarchy of classes, where the hierarchy is designed to maximize reuse through inheritance of fundamental capabilities.

15.13   A Simple Table Handler

The example class of this section demonstrates that simple table management problems typically implemented in imperative languages can also be implemented in Smalltalk. The problem is to build a program that creates and does look-ups in a table of department names and their code numbers. Because of the lack of static typing, the resulting system could be used for any table consisting of two parallel arrays of data, where the look-ups are based on the data elements in the first array.

One of the interesting features used in the program is the dynamic binding of index range to array. The two arrays are always exactly the size of the stored data. Each addition to the table simply increases the size of the table. Note that while this may be interesting and space efficient, it is severely inefficient in execution time. Each addition causes the creation of two new arrays and a move of the contents of the old arrays to the new arrays—a very time-inefficient procedure.

One of the omissions of the program is the lack of a method for removing an entry.

Note that quoted strings in the program are comments.

```
class name                    DeptCodes
superclass                    Object
instance variable names       names
                              codes

"Class methods"
"Create an instance"
new
        ^ super new

"Instance methods"
"Number of table entries"
size
        ^ names size

"Fetch the code for a department"
at: name | index |
      index ← self indexOf: name.
      index = 0
        ifTrue: [self error: 'Error--Name not in table']
        ifFalse: [^codes at: index]

"Install a new code; create entry if necessary"
at: name put: code |index|
      index ← self indexOf: name.
      index = 0
        ifTrue: [index ← self newIndexOf: name].
      ^ codes at: index put: code

"Look-up index of a given department name"
indexOf: name
      1 to: names size do:
        [:index | (names at: index) = name ifTrue: [^index]].
      ^ 0
```

```
"Create a new entry with the given name and return index"
newIndexOf: name
    self grow.
    names at: names size put: name.
    ^ names size


"Stretch table by one element and put in new name"
grow | oldNames oldCodes|
    oldNames ← names.
    oldCodes ← codes.
    names ← Array new: names size + 1.
    codes ← Array new: codes size + 1.
    names replaceFrom: 1 to: oldNames size with: oldNames.
    codes replaceFrom: 1 to: oldNames size with: oldCodes


"Test for inclusion of a given name"
includes: name
    ^ (self indexOf: name) ~= 0


"Test for empty"
isEmpty
   ^ names isEmpty


"Create initial empty arrays"
initialize
    names ← Array new: 0.
    codes ← Array new: 0
```

Because it has not been previously discussed, we now briefly describe the action of the replaceFrom: method. The first replaceFrom: method used in the grow method operates by moving the elements of the array oldNames indexed with the range 1..size of oldNames to the array named names.

The following expressions and the computed results illustrate how an instance of DeptCodes behaves. Note that isEmpty: is a unary method inherited from Object.

EXPRESSION	RESULT
dCodes ← DeptCodes new	creates new instance
dCodes initialize	creates empty arrays
dCodes isEmpty	true
dCodes at: 'Physics' put: 100	100
dCodes at: 'Chemistry' put: 110	110
dCodes at: 'Biology' put: 120	120
dCodes isEmpty	false
dCodes size	3
dCodes at: 'Chemistry'	110
dCodes includes 'Physics'	true
dCodes includes 'Computing'	false

15.14   LOGO-Style Graphics

In this section we present an example program that illustrates the Smalltalk class that provides the kind of drawing that originated in the turtle graphics of LOGO. This class, named Pen, is a subclass of another system class, BitBlt, which we will not discuss.

An instance of Pen is very much like a ball point pen under computer control, writing on a screen rather than paper. A Pen object has three primary conditions: direction, position, and frame. The position is either up or down, where up means it does not write when moved and down means it does. Direction is measured counterclockwise in degrees, with 0 being toward the right on the screen. The frame of a Pen object is the region of the screen in which it can draw, measured in bits. When a Pen instance is outside its frame, it cannot draw.

The initial condition of an instance of Pen is that it is pointing at 270 degrees, which is straight up on the screen; it is located at the coordinates (300,400); and it is in the up position. The (300,400) position is the center of the assumed screen size, which is 600 bits wide and 800 bits high.

The current parameters of a Pen instance can be gotten from the methods direction, location, and frame. The frame method returns the upper-left corner and the lower-right corner coordinates of the area in which the pen can draw.

The frame can be set by a second frame message:

```
frame: (aPoint extent: aPoint)
```

where aPoint is a pair of bit positions separated by an "at" sign (@). The parentheses are required in order to force the desired precedence in the message expression. The first occurrence of aPoint in this message indicates the upper-left corner of the frame. The second indicates the distance the frame will extend in the x and y directions from the upper-left corner. For example, the message:

```
frame: (50@50 extent: 300@300)
```

sets the frame to have an upper-left corner at (50,50) and a lower-right corner at (350,350).

The message protocol for moving and drawing with objects of the class Pen is:

down	Sets the pen in the drawing position
up	Sets the pen in the nondrawing position
turn: degrees	Changes the direction of the pen by the number of degrees specified in the parameter
go: distance	Moves the pen in its current direction by the number of bits specified in the parameter
goto: aPoint	Moves the pen to the position specified by the parameter point. If the pen is currently down, it draws a line.

place: aPoint	Sets the pen at the position specified in the parameter. No lines are drawn.
home	Sets the pen at the center of the frame
north	Sets the direction of the pen to 270, which is straight up on the screen

The color of the lines drawn by instances of Pen has a default value of black. The shape of the pen tip defaults to 1 bit by 1 bit. Both can be changed. The pen tip size is changed by the message defaultNib: n, where n is the new tip size.

Simple geometric shapes can be easily drawn with instances of Pen. First, we need an instance:

```
|Our Pen|
OurPen ← Pen new defaultNib: 2
OurPen up; goto: 800@300; down
```

Now, a triangle can be drawn with:

```
OurPen go: 100; turn: 120; go: 100; turn: 120; go: 100
```

Figure 15.1 shows the result of executing this code. It also shows the rest of the screen at the time, which illustrates the flavor of the Smalltalk user interface.

Figure 15.1
Smalltalk screen with output of a triangle

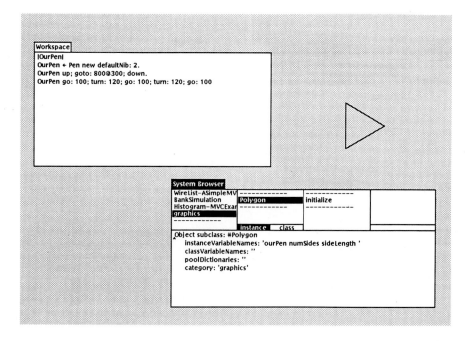

The message above can be simplified somewhat with a block, as in:

```
3 timesRepeat: [OurPen go: 100. OurPen turn: 120]
```

We can generalize this message to draw any equilateral polygon by repeating the block a number of times equal to the number of sides and turning by an amount equal to 360 divided by the number of sides—for example:

```
numSides timesRepeat: [ourPen go: 100. ourPen turn: 360 //
                       numSides]
```

Using this method, a general equilateral polygon-drawing class can be built. This example is similar to one in Goldberg and Robson (1984).

```
class name                      Polygon
superclass                      Object
instance variable names         ourPen
                                numSides
                                sideLength
"Class methods"
 "Create an instance"
 new
       ^ super new getPen

 "Instance methods"
 "Get a pen for drawing polygons"
 getPen
       ourPen ← Pen new defaultNib: 2

 "Draw a polygon"
 draw
       numSides  timesRepeat: [ourPen  go:  sideLength;
                              turn:  360  // numSides]

 "Set length of sides"
 length: len
       sideLength ← len

 "Set number of sides"
 sides: num
       numSides ← num
```

Notice that the variable ourPen in the class definition above does not begin with an uppercase letter as it did when we used it outside a class. This is because it is a local, private variable here, but had to be a global variable when it was used outside the class definition.

With this class, a sequence of polygons with various numbers of sides can be drawn, as with:

```
|MyPoly|
MyPoly ← Polygon new.
MyPoly length: 60.
3 to: 8 do: [:sides | MyPoly sides: sides. MyPoly draw]
```

This code draws what is shown in Figure 15.2.

Figure 15.2
Concentric polygons
from the object
`Polygon`

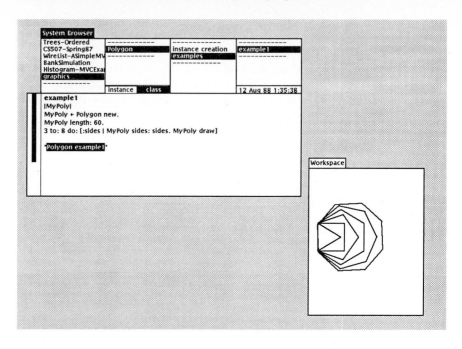

The lines in the figure can be made wider by changing the shape of the pen tip, which is done by changing the GetPen method, as in:

```
ourPen ← Pen new defaultNib: 4
```

inside the class definition. This changes the shape of the tip to 4 bits by 4 bits. The result of drawing the same polygons as above with this new tip is shown in Figure 15.3.

15.15 Applications

Smalltalk has thus far had a relatively short lifetime outside Xerox PARC. It is therefore somewhat unreasonable to expect it to have already been used in many different application areas.

Perhaps the largest application area thus far has been artificial intelligence. Another obvious application area is simulation, which is the basis for the whole concept of object-oriented programming. Smalltalk has also been used for graphics, spreadsheets, and algebraic manipulation. Finally, since the majority of the Smalltalk system is itself written in Smalltalk, it is useful for systems programming.

Figure 15.3
Concentric polygons
with nib set to 3

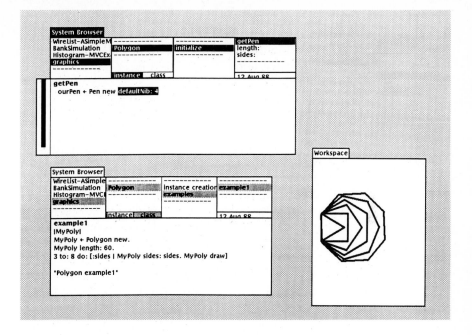

15.16 Conclusions

Smalltalk is more than a programming language; it is a vehicle for a different programming paradigm, which was created by the development of the language. Its implementation represents a radical departure from the imperative languages—in its elaborate graphical user interface; its integration of editor, compiler, and operating system; and its large hierarchy of classes that can be used, inherited to user classes, and even user-modified.

Smalltalk is really a small language, although the Smalltalk system is large. The syntax of the language is simple and very regular. It is a fine example of the power that can be provided by a small language, if that language is built around a simple but powerful concept. In the case of Smalltalk, that concept is that all programming can be based on simulation, using only objects and message passing.

It is too early to estimate the eventual impact of the Smalltalk language, although it is certainly causing a significant stir among language designers and theoreticians. Efficiency will clearly be an issue in most discussions of the practical applicability of Smalltalk. This was also the case for all of the early implementations of LISP, which were interpreted. It is also the case with PROLOG.

The Smalltalk user interface has already had an important impact on computing: It is difficult to escape the integrated use of windows, mouse pointing devices, and pop-up or pull-down menus in new software applications systems.

SUMMARY

Object-oriented programming involves three fundamental concepts: abstract data types, dynamic type binding, and inheritance. Object-oriented programming languages support the paradigm with objects, classes, and message passing.

Smalltalk developed in parallel with the concepts of object-oriented programming, beginning with the class concept of SIMULA 67.

Smalltalk programs consist primarily of objects and messages. Objects are instances of classes, which consist largely of methods that correspond to possible messages to which those instances can respond. Methods are, in turn, constructed from expressions. An expression describes an object, which happens to be the value of the expression.

Control structures in Smalltalk, like everything else, are constructed using objects and messages. While they have a somewhat conventional appearance, their semantics are very different from that of corresponding structures in the imperative languages.

BIBLIOGRAPHY

Budd, T. (1987) *A Little Smalltalk*. Addison-Wesley, Reading, MA.

Goldberg, A. (1984) *Smalltalk-80–The Interactive Programming Environment*. Addison-Wesley, Reading, MA.

Goldberg, A., and D. Robson. (1984) *Smalltalk-80–The Language and Its Implementation*. Addison-Wesley, Reading, MA.

Kaehler, T., and D. Patterson. (1986) *A Taste of Smalltalk*. W.W. Norton, New York.

Kay, A. (1969) "The Reactive Engine." Ph.D. Thesis, University of Utah, September.

Papert, S. (1980) *MindStorms: Children, Computers and Powerful Ideas*. Basic Books, New York.

Rentsch, T. (1982) "Object-Oriented Programming." *ACM SIGPLAN Notices*, Vol. 17, No. 9, pp. 51–57.

PROBLEM SET

1. What purpose does the pseudovariable **super** serve?
2. Explain what the message protocol of a Smalltalk object defines.
3. What is the relationship between Smalltalk objects and classes?

4. What are methods?
5. In essence, all Smalltalk variables are of a single type. What is that type?
6. How many parameters are there in a binary message? *pointer*
7. Explain the precedence rules of Smalltalk expressions.
8. How can one force a block to be executed? *send it the value message*
9. What purpose does the pseudovariable **self** serve? - *references object in which self appears*
10. Write the following Pascal loop structure in Smalltalk:

```
while count < 100 do
  sum := sum div (2 * count - 1);
  count := count + 1
  end
```

11. Write the following Pascal **for** loop in Smalltalk:

```
for index := 10 downto 1 do
  sum := sum + index
  end
```

12. Write the following Pascal selection construct in Smalltalk:

```
if count < 10 then
  answer := 1
else
  begin
  answer := 0;
  count := 0
  end
```

10. [count < 100]
  whileTrue: [sum ← sum / (2+ count - 1).
                count ← count + 1]

11. index ← 10.
  [index > 0]
  whileTrue: [sum ← sum + index.
                index ← index - 1]

12. [count < 10]
    ifTrue: [answer ← 1]
    ifFalse: [answer ← 0.
                count ← 0]

INDEX